Lecture Notes
in Business Information Processing 226

More information about this series at http://www.springer.com/series/7911

Valérie Monfort · Karl-Heinz Krempels (Eds.)

Web Information Systems and Technologies

10th International Conference, WEBIST 2014
Barcelona, Spain, April 3–5, 2014
Revised Selected Papers

 Springer

Editors
Valérie Monfort
University of Paris
Paris, Paris
France

Karl-Heinz Krempels
RWTH Aachen University
Aachen
Germany

ISSN 1865-1348   ISSN 1865-1356 (electronic)
Lecture Notes in Business Information Processing
ISBN 978-3-319-27029-6   ISBN 978-3-319-27030-2   (eBook)
DOI 10.1007/978-3-319-27030-2

Library of Congress Control Number: 2015955374

Springer Cham Heidelberg New York Dordrecht London

Springer International Publishing AG Switzerland is part of Springer Science+Business Media
(www.springer.com)

Preface

This book includes extended and revised versions of a set of selected papers from WEBIST 2014 (the 10th International Conference on Web Information Systems and Technologies), held in Barcelona, Spain, in 2014, organized and sponsored by the Institute for Systems and Technologies of Information, Control and Communication (INSTICC). The conference was technically sponsored by the European Research Center for Information System (ERCIS).

The purpose of the WEBIST series of conferences is to bring together researchers, engineers, and practitioners interested in technological advances and business applications of Web-based information systems. WEBIST had five main topic areas, covering different aspects of Web Information Systems, including "Internet Technology," "Web Interfaces and Applications," "Society, e-Business, e-Government," "Web Intelligence," and "Mobile Information Systems."

The conference was also complemented by one special session, namely, the Special Session on Business Apps – BA 2014 (chaired by Tim A. Majchrzak).

WEBIST 2014 received 153 paper submissions from 49 countries on all continents. A double-blind review process was enforced, with the help of 214 experts from the International Program Committee; each of them specialized in one of the main conference topic areas. After reviewing, 23 papers were selected to be published and presented as full papers and 41 additional papers, describing work-in-progress, as short papers. Furthermore, 35 papers were presented as posters. The full-paper acceptance ratio was 15 %, and the total oral paper acceptance ratio was 42 %.

The papers included in this book were selected from those with the best reviews taking also into account the quality of their presentation at the conference, assessed by session chairs. Therefore, we hope that you find these papers interesting, and we trust they may represent a helpful reference for all those who need to address any of the research aforementioned areas.

We wish to thank all those who supported and helped to organize the conference. On behalf of the conference Organizing Committee, we would like to thank the authors, whose work mostly contributed to a very successful conference and to the members of the Program Committee, whose expertise and diligence were instrumental to ensure the quality of final contributions. We also wish to thank all the members of the Organizing Committee whose work and commitment was invaluable. Last but not least, we would like to thank Springer for their collaboration in getting this book to print.

April 2015

Valérie Monfort
Karl-Heinz Krempels

Organization

Conference Chair

Valérie Monfort   Université de Paris1 Panthéon Sorbonne, France

Program Chair

Karl-Heinz Krempels   RWTH Aachen University, Germany

Organizing Committee

Marina Carvalho	INSTICC, Portugal
Helder Coelhas	INSTICC, Portugal
Bruno Encarnação	INSTICC, Portugal
Ana Guerreiro	INSTICC, Portugal
André Lista	INSTICC, Portugal
Andreia Moita	INSTICC, Portugal
Carla Mota	INSTICC, Portugal
Raquel Pedrosa	INSTICC, Portugal
Vitor Pedrosa	INSTICC, Portugal
Cláudia Pinto	INSTICC, Portugal
Susana Ribeiro	INSTICC, Portugal
Sara Santiago	INSTICC, Portugal
Fábio Santos	INSTICC, Portugal
Mara Silva	INSTICC, Portugal
José Varela	INSTICC, Portugal
Pedro Varela	INSTICC, Portugal

Program Committee

Jose Luis Herrero Agustin	University of Extremadura, Spain
Mugurel Ionut Andreica	Polytechnic University of Bucharest, Romania
Guglielmo de Angelis	CNR – IASI, Italy
Margherita Antona	Foundation for Research and Technology – Hellas (FORTH), Greece
Valeria De Antonellis	University of Brescia, Italy
Liliana Ardissono	Università di Torino, Italy
Giuliano Armano	University of Cagliari, Italy
Ismailcem Budak Arpinar	University of Georgia, USA
Elarbi Badidi	United Arab Emirates University, UAE
Andrea Ballatore	University College Dublin, Ireland

Additional Reviewers

Alberto De La Rosa Algarin	University of Connecticut, USA
Markus C. Beutel	RWTH Aachen University, Germany
Matteo Ciman	University of Padua, Italy
José Cordeiro	Polytechnic Institute of Setúbal/INSTICC, Portugal
Javier Espinosa	LAFMIA Lab, France
Golnoosh Farnadi	Ghent University, The Netherlands
Sevket Gökay	RWTH Aachen University, Germany
Beatriz Gomez	University of the Balearic Islands, Spain
Nuno Pina Gonçalves	EST-Setúbal/IPS, Portugal
Wolfgang Kluth	RWTH Aachen University, Germany
Fangfang Li	AAi, Australia
José António Sena Pereira	IPS – ESTSetúbal, Portugal
Laura Po	University of Modena and Reggio Emilia, Italy
Michael Rogger	STI, Austria
Christian Samsel	RWTH Aachen University, Germany
Alexander Semenov	University of Jyvaskyla, NRU ITMO, Finland
Xin Wang	University of Southampton, UK
Stefan Wueller	RWTH Aachen, Germany

Invited Speakers

Steven Willmott	3scale, Spain
Fabien Gandon	INRIA, France
Andreas Pfeiffer	Hubject GmbH - joint venture of BMW Group, Bosch, Daimler, EnBW, RWE & Siemens, Germany
Zakaria Maamar	Zayed University, UAE

Contents

Invited Papers

The Three 'W' of the World Wide Web Call for the Three 'M' of a Massively Multidisciplinary Methodology

Fabien Gandon$^{(\boxtimes)}$

INRIA, Sophia Antipolis, France
`fabien.gandon@inria.fr`

Abstract. This position paper defends the idea that the development of the Web to its full potential requires addressing the challenge of massive multidisciplinarity.

Keywords: Web · Multidisciplinarity

1 Introduction: Social, Political and Economic Implications of the Web

This position paper was triggered by the topic of a joint panel at the conferences CLOSER and WEBIST 2014. The topic of the panel was: "social, political and economic implications of the cloud and the Web". I focused on the Web and the position that I defended during the panel, and that I report here, is that, while implications of the Web can be identified in social, political and economic domains, the global challenge raised by the Web is the need for massive multidisciplinarity to lead it to its full potential [1] that goes beyond any individual prediction. This article starts with three sections respectively confirming the social, political and economic impacts of the Web. The Sect. 4 shows that in fact many other domains are impacted and the Sect. 5 proposes that this spreading is in fact due to several existential characteristic of the Web. The Sect. 7 concludes insisting on the importance of preserving this open nature of the Web, of assisting it and of addressing the challenge of a massive multidisciplinary approach for developing the Web.

2 On Social Implications of the Web

The Web was initially conceived as a read-write space [2, 3]. But it took the advent of wikis in 1994, with WikiWikiWeb by Ward Cunningham, to really have a read-write Web. With wikis we moved away from a rather static document-oriented Web where a page was essentially published by one user and read by several others. This change suddenly also supported social interactions on the Web by allowing several users and even lay persons in terms of Web technologies, to contribute and interact through shared Web resources leading toward what is now sometime referred to as a global conversation.

© Springer International Publishing Switzerland 2015
V. Monfort and K.-H. Krempels (Eds.): WEBIST 2014, LNBIP 226, pp. 3–15, 2015.
DOI: 10.1007/978-3-319-27030-2_1

Almost ten years before the term "Web 2.0" was coined, Wikis were adopted and then followed by blogs, forums, social networks and a wealth of social Web applications providing new means of social interaction (e.g. object-centered sociality as in Flickr with photos, YouTube with videos, etc.) and social relations (e.g. followers, groups, circles). These agile ways of supporting social linking foster self (re)organization, collaboration, and transfers between social structures.

Therefore social constructs are impacted by Web applications. In particular, the Web can make boundaries between social groups more porous (cultures, languages, institutions, etc.). It can also bridge scales, for instance bringing local initiatives to the global scene and more generally fostering "glocal" connections [4].

Social Web networks support strong ties but also foster weak ties. For some users they increase socialization time, leading even sometime to over-socialization. Companies also started to hire "community managers" and other job titles dedicated to manage their presence and image on the Web. New practices of users creating and maintaining several online identities question the very notion of identity.

The resulting interconnectivity impacts not only online activities but propagates to offline activities. Massive socialization is spreading to many objects and activities of our lives for instance:

- cars (blablacar, zilokaoto, voiturelib)
- sailing (vogavecmoi.com, co-navigation.fr, equipier.fr)
- taxi (provoiturage.fr)
- package delivery (expediezentrevous.com)
- parking, car park (monsieurparking.com)
- housing, accommodation (AirBnB, Couchsurfing)
- storage (costockage.fr)
- funding (kisskissbankbank, kickstarter)
- offices (coworking)
- food (colunching.com, cookening.com)
- sport (Unlish.com, Cleec.com, kikourou.net)
- washing machines (lamachineduvoisin.fr)
- clothes (pretachanger.fr, vestiairecollective.com)
- etc.

The Web is not only increasing the amount of social activity, it actually creates new socialization objects. So called « social » bookmarks are an example of a personal object - the bookmark - that was massively published, shared and linked by social Web applications like delicious.com.

As soon as the Web was reopened to write access, the log files of the social applications showed how powerful the Web could be in tracing and capturing very large social activities. But an important property of the Web is that it is supporting active social media *i.e.* media that not only communicate but store, process, reuse, enrich, route, manage the information far beyond plain passive communication. This active nature is both an opportunity of enrichment and a concern. For instance the implications of over-customization and its impact in terms of socialization and knowledge diffusion are raised by the filter bubble phenomenon [5] making it harder and harder for us to find different or alternative points of view.

The Web never sleeps and these evolutions are getting faster and faster, each evolution building on the network effect of the previous one. It took 89 years for the telephone to reach 150 million users, 38 years for television to reach the same number, 14 years for the cell-phones, 8 years for the internet, 5 years for Facebook and 3 years for Instagram.

Meanwhile, with recent economic events, many people realized that in flash trading some algorithms were already taking decisions at a speed of more than 500 000 times per seconds. Hybrid communities on the Web are not only bridging different scales in terms of spaces or communities, they are also bridging different time scales. The human heart beats roughly once per second. A double click on the mouse is roughly two clicks in one second. The images of a movie are typically 24 per seconds and they are already below our ability to perceive them individually. An algorithm taking 500 000 decisions per second is far beyond our direct control for any of the individual decision it takes. When such an algorithm is acting not in the stock market but in a social network with more than a billion users, if things go wrong they can go wrong very far and very fast.

Taking a step back, the Web is raising the question of the limits and rules we should master before coupling automation and human on large scales and at high speeds as we are doing right now in social media for instance. This automation and acceleration might be alienating us [6] or hurting us.

The Web both traces and changes the social activity and therefore has become the subject of sociological studies (e.g. sociology of the internet) and at the same time a sociological probe to get social data and run social studies. For any domain, the Web now provides observatories [7] (data on users, practices, products) and active inter-action media (communication, collaboration, online services). Social machines asso-ciating people and software online [8] are being created on the Web for a huge variety of topics of interests and reasons. This trend of designing and growing hybrid Web communities is requiring massive interaction design and new social theories to allow all the participants to interact with all the actors around them.

Finally, at the time of writing the Web has nearly 3 billion direct users and we could think it impacts everyone indirectly. But is that really true? More precisely is this impact as democratic and fair as it should be? It appears the answer is no, as soon as we consider the price or even the availability of an internet connection. The open fracture of the digital divide means that 60 % of the world population does not have access to the Web, its resources, its services, its wealth. And because the Web impacts many domains and activities when it does not actively contribute to reduce the divide, it ends up making it worse. In particular a digital divide on the Web will propagate in all the domains we will mention in this article. This is one of the reasons why the Web must always tend toward the largest accessibility.

3 On Political Implications of the Web

The Web and its social applications are now heavily used to run political campaigns, encourage donations, perform recruiting, etc. Web-based political campaigns are now spreading in all democratic systems.

Fig. 1. Web platform of the Obama campaign in 2008.

Among the many social interactions the Web is supporting, the e-government applications are changing the relations between a government and the citizens, the businesses and the other governments it interacts with, at all the scales of government (citizen, city, region, state, province and nation). Obama's campaigns (Fig. 1) made extensive used of data analysis and his administration is responsible for the initiative DATA.GOV pushing the publication of governmental data to allow new applications (e.g. comparators), new analysis (e.g. data journalism) and more generally to improve the access the public has to this data, including his campaign team.

Web-based government services do not only provide new democratic means, they also raise new challenges for instance to manage this enlarged democratic bandwidth between all the actors and instances of a government in general and between the citizens and their representatives in particular. For instance the social networks and online forums have opened a new way for citizen to voice their opinions and concerns and the political system is often not ready to receive and process that massive feedback.

The effects of Web applications and the weight of Web actors have political impacts in particular because Web communities can grow to sizes comparable to largest nations. At the time of writing, Facebook for instance announces more than 1 billion active users If Facebook was a country it would be the third largest country in the world and it is currently the dominant social network in many real countries (Fig. 2). When Facebook started to adapt the content of time lines by filtering what it displays based on the profiles they learned from users and their friends, this had an impact in terms of the propagation of political views [5].

Not only could the governmental processes be impacted: the political norms and rules that govern their functions could also be influenced by and modified on the Web. For instance ConstituteProject.org provides a repository to read, search, and compare constitutions from around the world in particular to assist the creation of new constitutions. And outside the political systems themselves, Web activism now refers to the use of Web technologies to campaign and bring about political changes [9]. Designing efficient and trusted Web-based ways to manage our political systems remains an open-question.

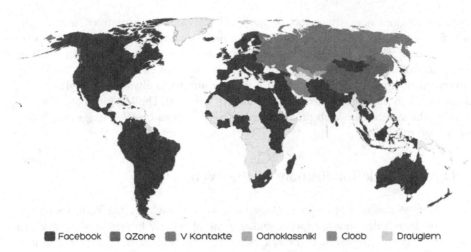

Fig. 2. World map of social networks, December 2013 by Vincenzo Cosenza and Alexa. Facebook is the dominant social network in 127 out of 137 countries analyzed and has 1,189 billion monthly active users.

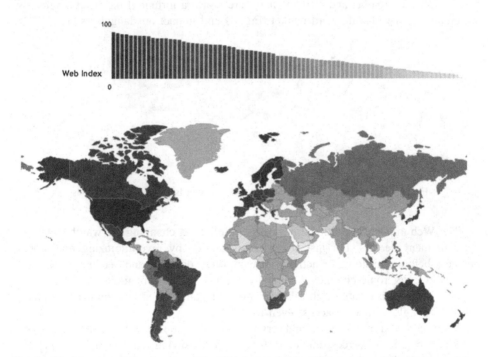

Fig. 3. World map and distribution of the Web index ranking 81 countries with a measure of the Web's contribution to development and human rights. The higher the index is, the better the situation in that country is. Scores are given by the World Wide Web foundation in the areas of: access; freedom and openness; relevant content; and empowerment.

The Web does not only impact our political activities and structures, it also calls itself for new political practices and institutions to maintain and organize this new space. In particular, a very important question today is the defense of the Web in general and of neutrality, free speech, and privacy on the Web in particular. As in any country this is a never ending fight and it will require us to always stay vigilant [10]. Again the Web can be its own support and for instance TheWebIndex.org (Fig. 3) monitors the state of the Web providing country-level data on Web usage, readiness, and human impact.

4   On Economic Implications of the Web

Because of the ability it provides to gather and share knowledge the Web has a huge impact on knowledge intensive work and in general on any human activity that can benefit from data, information and service sharing. This leads to the emergence of new giants (e.g. Google) providing services on the Web (e.g. search engine).

But new markets also appeared. For instance, initially, the URL of a page wasn't supposed to be used directly by persons surfing on the Web. It was a technical identifier essentially internal to the Web architecture. Now with the advent of the Web, domain names became a market and some domains are worth a fortune. Likewise Google ads are creating a world-wide word market (Fig. 4) and impact our languages [11, 12].

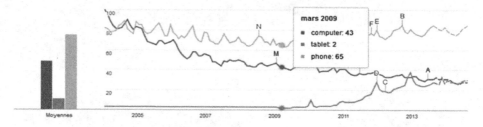

Fig. 4. Evolution of the interest and price of words in Google AdWords.

The Web impacted traditional business at their core, changing the way business is done in many sectors. For instance Amazon started by revolutionizing bookstores business before expending its activity to many other domains and becoming the most well-known electronic commerce company. And as already mentioned for the social impacts, the Web is creating "glocal links" [4] for instance, in an economic perspective, supporting a global market access even for SMEs.

With more and more content and services available on the Web the attention of the users is becoming a scarce commodity for which a growing number of Web applications compete. The approach of attention economy applies economic theory to manage attention as a resource or a currency. In 2004 the chairman of the first TV channel in France (Patrick Le Lay, TF1) declared his job was to sell "available human brain time". This could now be extended to a number of Web media competing for brain time. Of course selling a product or a service is the most obvious way of cashing attention -

thanks to advertisement for instance. But they are other ways of paying. User profiles, and private data such as tastes, hobbies, whereabouts or address books are valuable information gathered and exploited. Privacy in particular is a new currency and, more generally speaking, data is the new oil, raising concerns even at the international level as to where the data flows.

But, to put it bluntly, to more and more Web actors, available brain time also means available powerful processors. The Web has offered a perfect programming framework for crowdsourcing applications. These applications implement services, gather data and information by soliciting contributions from large groups of Web users. They rely on very different strategies. Some crowdsourcing approaches are explicit such as explicit gamification (FoldIt, GalaxyZoo), crowdfunding (e.g. KissKissBankBank, Kickstarter), surveys or votes, collaborative design or problem solving, etc. Others are implicit in the sense the user is not even aware of being used as a processor such as when the task achieved is side effect of another task (e.g. form validation and Re-Captcha for OCR) or mines the data of another activity (e.g. piggyback analysis of users' search history to tune AdWords). These approaches can be generalized to the domain of human computing where the machines outsource certain tasks to humans. Human-based computation finds on the Web an ideal platform where to recruit persons through different kinds of incentives: money as with Amazon Mechanical Turk; fun as with gamified tasks like the ESP Game; volunteerism as in Wikipedia; recognition and ego as in many Q&A forums like StakOverFlow. For instance, some companies now include their clients in the design of new products either indirectly by mining their feedback or directly and explicitly by turning them into "prosumers" who document, evaluate, suggest and design products on online platforms as Lego does with its Web platform Lego Ideas.

And again we have to be extremely vigilant here to make sure that humans don't end-up being used as just another resource.

5   On the Many Implications of the Web

The three previous sections tried to show that indeed there are important impacts of the Web in social, political and economic domains. The choice of these three domains was imposed by the topic of the joint panel at WebIST/CLOSER 2014. However the implications of the Web can in fact be found in almost all the domains of human activities. To show this, the following list mentions a number of domains of activity and interest impacted by the Web. The list in itself does not seek to be homogeneous or exhaustive. The point we are making here is that the Web has impacted not only the social, political and economic domains but virtually any domain. Consider for instance:

- Psychological implications: hypertext-based Web surfing have changed our way of reading, working and maybe memorizing and thinking; machine learning and Web mining discover very personal characteristics, profiling our inner self; online image and presence are directly transferred to our everyday lives.
- Philosophical and ethical implications: the Web offers a new space for naming, describing and linking anything and this raises new philosophical questions at the

heart of the Web architecture [13, 14]; the Web is also a platform to build social machines [8] coupling human and software on large scales thus raising ethical and moral questions; the Web architecture could support all sorts of forums and social medias and there is an important challenge to ensure the Web becomes a public space that effectively allows us to debate and philosophize.

- Educational implications: the Web changed the way we access, diffuse and assess information; pedagogical materials and methodology are adapted to the Web media in e-learning applications; traditional teaching practices are directly impacted by the availability of the Web, its resources and the interactions it supports; massive online courses also emerged on the Web as a completely different way to teach some topics.
- Scientific implications: peer-to-peer review, conference and journal processes are completely supported by Web applications now and sometime they even experiment with new approaches such as open online reviewing; data from experiences and service composition for analysis are shared and combined on the Web; runnable papers available on the Web propose a new way to support reproducibility of results.
- Medical and healthcare implications: healthcare protocols and drugs are described on the Web; patients and doctors exchange their experiences and expertize in forums; Web mining provides new indicators for epidemics.
- Statistics implications: surveys are democratized by Web applications supporting their full management; logs of Web platforms and Web usage in general provide a huge amount of data to analyze and mine.
- Legal implications: Web applications very easily cross frontiers and jurisdictions raising new problems in terms of legal status of their resources and legal actions that can be taken; terms and conditions of Web applications are not only hard to write they are also hardly read, raising the issue of creating, ensuring and conveying the legal and security context of the users.
- Linguistic implications: linguistic minorities can keep in touch through social media platform and gather linguistic resources; practices like AdWords, suggestion, auto-completion or domain names may influence the salience of words and expressions in our languages; huge corpora are now available for natural language processing leading for instance to new approaches for translation.
- Cultural implications: cultural heritage and its transmission are supported by Web applications; the cohesion of micro-culture can survive geographical and temporal distance; intermingling of communities in social medias foster the cultural exchanges;
- Artistic implications: the Web and its design is the subject of artistic creation; the Web provides new approaches to galleries and expositions; the Web provides new materials and new formats of creation; the Web supports new relations between the creators, the creation and the public.
- Media implications: our relation to classic Medias (TV, radio, newspapers) changed with the Web and the ability to influence, react, participate to the programs; the online archiving of audiovisual resources and the availability on demand of many programs revolutionized our access and use of medias; Web TVs and programs provide alternative channels for independent content creators.

- Design implications: collaboration platforms support the exchange of blue-prints, and also the co-design of products and services; coupled with other technologies like 3D printing the Web provides a social space to exchange, reproduce, adapt and reuse designs.
- Geographic implications: cartography was revolutionized by participatory approaches like OpenStreetMap.org; geolocation and navigation are impacted by Google maps and equivalent services.
- etc.

Arguably, the most important entry in the list above is "etc." in the sense that this list is by no means exhaustive. On the contrary this heterogeneous accumulation is just to show that we have in fact an open set of domains and activities impacted by the Web. This list could grow not only with additional aspects for each entry but also, and more importantly, with many other domains: mathematics, ecology, history, sexuality, dietetics, transportation, meteorology, food, religions, defense, diplomacy, sport, criminality, agriculture, etc.

Considering all the domains the Web impacts, the multidisciplinary development of the Web is both a characteristic and an issue of the Web.

6 On the Evolution of the Open Web Platform

From an architectural point this tendency of the Web to diffuse itself everywhere and in all our activities is strongly related to the very reasons that made the Web a success from the beginning. The Web became what we know today primarily because its architecture is that of a decentralized, universal, free and open platform. These characteristics are what made the Web so viral.

The Web architecture is inherently open, down to its three basic components, namely:

- open addresses (URL) or identifiers (URIs) to talk about anything on the Web;
- open languages (HTML, RDF, XML) to articulate anything on the Web;
- open protocols (HTTP, SOAP, SPARQL) to interoperate with everything on the Web.

This openness of the Web is a key reason of its adoption by many applications and through them by many domains. It is also a powerful enabler of interoperability and consequently it of cross-pollination.

A second important aspect is the change that happened in the perception of the Web itself: why do we now speak of a Web platform where before we spoke of Web pages and Web sites? We all witnessed Web pages becoming more beautiful, more interactive, more powerful, more ... application-like. Languages like HTML5, CSS3 and JavaScript are now at the heart of the Web platform. With this integration we definitively turned the page of a documentary Web for a Web of interlinked applications. Each page is a potential application or service to a user or another program. The Web still links documents but also, increasingly, data, software and objects.

The Web has become the defacto standard open platform for applications on the internet. The Web technologies cover all aspects of an application including:

- Access to material resources: geolocation, gyroscopes, cameras, NFC...
- Multimedia interactions: audio and video, graphics, animations, 3D...
- Multimodal interactions and device independence: changes in resolutions, adaptation of virtual keyboards, analysis and synthesis of voice, touch interactions, vibration, mobile Web applications...
- Communications: client-server, real-time, peer to peer, sockets...
- Security: keys, signatures, encryption, authentication...
- Automatic data processing: format interoperability, data integration, semantics of schemas...
- etc.

We went from the idea of "write once, publish everywhere" to the idea of "code once, use everywhere".

Even more important is to realize that in fact the Web never was a hypertext. It was initially perceived as a flexible and clever documentary system but the nature of the Web is now closer to a resource-oriented hyper program (Fig. 5). It is even going beyond the classical view of programming by supporting applications calling on users for some processing.

The Web also moved from URLs to identify what "exists on the Web" (Web pages, images, etc.) [15] to URIs to identify on the Web what exists in general (a person, a topic, a place, etc.) [16]. IRIs go a step further allowing these identifiers to be written in any language [17]. This change of paradigm for the Web identifier is a key enabler of the expansion of the Web turning anything we might think of into a potential subject of documents, data and services on the Web.

In parallel, references to the Web became extremely common and not necessarily technologically complex (e.g. QR codes) and the access is no longer limited to browsers on a desktop (e.g. mobile phones, TVs, cars, etc.). So, anything is now potentially subject to representations (pages, images, data, etc.) exchanged on the Web and more and more things are interacting with these representations. These parallel evolutions of the Web combine themselves in making it even more viral.

To summarize, the Web is now an open platform consisting of free technologies that allow everyone to publish and implement a new component of the Web without having to get or to waive licenses. These non-proprietary and domain-independent technologies allow an open and distributed worldwide innovation in any domain.

But we should not take these important characteristics of the Web for granted [18]. There is always a risk to loose decentralization, universality, freedom or openness with the next evolution or the next major application of the Web.

For instance, if the Web is decentralized in principle, it can be re-centralized in practice by the tools that are deployed. Continued vigilance is needed. The concentration of applications, the ensiling of data and any form of recentralization by an organization must be avoided as much as possible. The interests of an organization is not always the public interest.

Because the Web is of public interest, opening the Web is of public interest. And it is a challenge both for its technical architecture and for its governance. Beyond passive

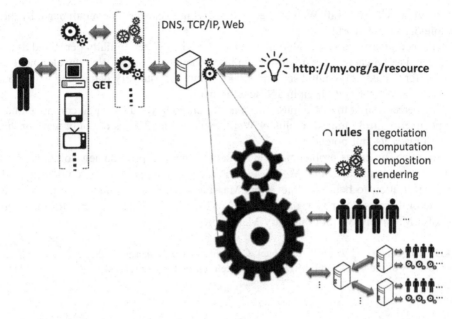

Fig. 5. Behind an HTTP GET call a whole chain reaction can now be triggered calling upon many different resources to provide an answer.

browsing, and even beyond content contribution, we must move towards a more comprehensive stakeholder participation across the Web and beyond, towards a multi-participatory governance.

Open Web is open-mindedness. By establishing a global conversation Web participates significantly to the establishment of freedom of speech. To keep the Web open is also to give a chance to preserve the global conversation it established. The Web has become a very powerful artifact of our situated cognition, our augmented intelligence. This raises the issue of the preservation of the new abilities we attained [18].

To summarize, the open Web platform calls for global developments in all aspects of our societies (economic, legal, political, etc.) and in particular to ensure an equilibrium between the sake of individuals and the sake of collectives.

7   Conclusion: MMM for WWW

If it is true to say that the Web architecture is designed through standards, its participatory nature makes the Web emerge from it as an openly co-constructed global object. This makes it one of the most complex artifacts ever produced by mankind. This complexity explains both its richness and issues. In some ways we do not know the Web, or very little. We design the architecture but the Web object that emerges and constantly evolves, needs to be studied and followed in all its developments.

And the "world-wide way" of deploying the Web everywhere and for everything implies that, as the Web is spreading in the world, the world is spreading in the Web.

The resulting world "wild" Web created and evolving every day is contaminated by the complexity of our world.

This complexity and co-evolution of what could have been initially perceived as an engineered technical artefact implies that a huge challenge for the Web development is its need for a massively multidisciplinary cooperation. By its very nature and evolution the Web calls for a multidisciplinary development.

The perception of the Web must once and for all go beyond its initial computational perspective to a truly multidisciplinary Web development. This is the only way for the Web to reach its full potential.

The Web can create problems and at the same sometime provide new solutions. The collaborative landscape the Web can be used to support new co-design and cross-fertilization to help us achieve this Massively Multidisciplinary Making. Hence the title of this position paper: the three 'W' of the World Wide Web call for the three 'M' of a Massively Multidisciplinary Methodology.

Acknowledgements. I would like to thank Catherine Faron-Zucker and Alexandre Monnin for their reviews of the article and the changes and references they suggested.

References

1. Berners-Lee, T.: Realising the full potential of the web. W3C, Based on a Talk Presented at the W3C Meeting, 3 December 1997, London (1998). http://www.w3.org/1998/02/Potential.html
2. Berners-Lee, T.: Weaving the Web - The Original Design and Ultimate Destiny of the World Wide Web, By Its Inventor. Harper, San Francisco (2000). ISBN 006251587X
3. Berners-Lee, T.: Information Management: A Proposal, CERN, March 1989, May 1990. http://www.w3.org/History/1989/proposal.html
4. Sharma, C.K.: Emerging dimensions of decentralisation debate in the age of globalisation. Indian J. Fed. Stud. **19**(1), 47–65 (2009)
5. Pariser, E.: The Filter Bubble: What the Internet is Hiding from You. Penguin Press HC, London (2011). ISBN 1594203008
6. Hartmut, R.: Alienation and Acceleration: Towards a Critical Theory of Late-Modern Temporality. Aarhus University Press, Aarhus (2010). ISBN 8787564149
7. Proceedings of the 1st International Workshop on Building Web Observatories (2013). https://sites.google.com/site/bwebobs13/
8. Shadbolt, N.R., Smith, D.A., Simperl, E., Van Kleek, M., Yang, Y., Hall, W.: Towards a classification framework for social machines. In: SOCM 2013: The Theory and Practice of Social Machines, Association for Computing Machinery, Rio de Janeiro, Brazil (2013)
9. Mauvaise, T.: Constellations: Trajectoires révolutionnaires du jeune 21e siècle, Editions de l'Eclat (2014). ISBN 2841623513
10. Carr, L., Pope, C. Halford, S.: Could the web be a temporary glitch? In: WebSci10, Raleigh, US, pp. 1–6, 26–27 April 2010
11. Kaplan, F.: Linguistic capitalism and algorithmic mediation. Representations **127**(1), 57–63 (2014)
12. Groys, B.: Google: Words beyond Grammar, dOCUMENTA (13): 100 Notizen - 100 Gedanken (2011). ISBN 978-3-7757-2895-9

13. Monnin, A.: Vers une philosophie du Web: le Web comme devenir-artefact de la philosophie (entre URIs, tags, ontologie (s) et ressources). Ph.D. Thesis, University Paris 1 (2013)
14. Halpin, H., Monnin, A.: Philosophical Engineering: Toward a Philosophy of the Web. Willey, New York (2013). ISBN 978-1-118-70018-1
15. Berners-Lee, T., Masinter, L., McCahill, M.: Uniform Resource Identifier (URI): Generic Syntax, IETF, RFC 1738 (1994). http://tools.ietf.org/html/rfc1738
16. Berners-Lee, T., Fielding, R., Masinter, L.: Uniform Resource Identifier (URI): Generic Syntax, IETF, RFC 3986 (2005). http://tools.ietf.org/html/rfc3986
17. Duerst, M., Suignard, M.: Internationalized Resource Identifiers (IRIs), IETF, RFC 3987 (2005). http://tools.ietf.org/html/rfc3987
18. Berners-Lee, T., Halpin, H.: Defend the web. Digital Enlightment Yearbook. IOS Press, Amsterdam (2012)

Enterprise 2.0: Research Challenges and Opportunities

Zakaria Maamar[1](✉), Noura Faci[2], Ejub Kajan[3], Khouloud Boukadi[4],
Sherif Sakr[5], Mohamed Boukhebouze[6], Soraya Kouadri Mostéfaoui[7],
Vanilson Burégio[8], Fadwa Yahya[4], Valérie Monfort[9], and Romain Hennion[10]

[1] Zayed University, Dubai, United Arab Emirates
zakaria.maamar@zu.ac.ae
[2] Université Lyon 1, Lyon, France
[3] State University of Novi Pazar, Novi Pazar, Serbia
[4] University of Sfax, Sfax, Tunisia
[5] University of New South Wales, Sydney, Australia
[6] CETIC, Charleroi, Belgium
[7] The Open University, Milton Keynes, UK
[8] Federal Rural University of Pernambuco, Recife, Brazil
[9] University of Paris1 Panthéon Sorbonne, Paris, France
[10] École Centrale de Paris and Global Knowledge, Paris, France

Abstract. Blending Web 2.0 technologies with enterprise information systems is setting up the stage for a new generation of information systems that will help enterprises open up new communication channels with their stakeholders. Contrary to traditional enterprises with top-down command flow and bottom-up feedback flow, the same flows in Enterprise 2.0 cross all levels and in all directions bringing people together in the development of creative and innovative ideas. The power of Web 2.0 technologies stems from their ability to capture real-world phenomena such as collaboration, competition, and partnership that can be converted into useful and structured information sources from which enterprises can draw information about markets' trends, consumers' habits, suppliers' strategies, etc. This paper discusses the research efforts that our international research group has put into the topic of Enterprise 2.0 (*aka* Social Enterprise). In particular, our research group advocates that existing practices for managing enterprise information systems need to be re-visited in a way that permits to capture social relations that arise inside and outside the enterprise, to establish guidelines and techniques to assist IT practitioners integrate social relations into their design, development, and maintenance efforts of these information systems, and last but not least to identify and tackle challenges that prevent capturing social relations.

Keywords: Business process · Social design · Social coordination · Social monitoring

This paper is based on the 1st author's invited talk at the 10th International Conference on Web Information Systems and Technologies (WEBIST'2014), April 3-5. Barcelona, Spain.

V. Monfort and K.-H. Krempels (Eds.): WEBIST 2014, LNBIP 226, pp. 16–30, 2015.
DOI: 10.1007/978-3-319-27030-2_2

1   Introduction

With the recent boom in Web 2.0 technologies (e.g., JSON and AJAX) and applications (e.g., Facebook[1] and Twitter), there is a major trend in blending social computing with other forms of computing for instance, service computing [1,2] and mobile computing [3,4]. In this paper, we look into the blending of Web 2.0 concepts and technologies with enterprise computing that results into the development of Social Business Processes (SBP)s [5,6]. In particular, SBPs capitalize on Web 2.0 technologies and applications to ensure that the social dimension of the enterprise (*aka* Enterprise 2.0 [7,8]) is not overlooked during BP design and enactment. This dimension sheds the light on the informal networks that co-exist perfectly with formal networks where relations like supervision and substitution occur [9]. Different studies have shown the value-added of weaving social computing into enterprise operations in terms of demystifying who does what, profiling customers, and even re-engineering processes [10,11]. Moreover, many enterprises recognize the need of rethinking their strategies and reevaluating their operating models, as the world is getting more "social" [12].

Despite the growing interest in enterprise 2.0 in general and SBPs in particular, several limitations continue to hinder this interest. For instance, how to equip BP engineers with the necessary methods and techniques that will assist them capture the requirements of SBPs. Enterprises are still unsure about the return-on-investment of Web 2.0 technologies [13]. A recent study by Gartner reveals that "*...many large companies are embracing internal social networks, but for the most part they're not getting much from them*" [14]. Over the last 2–3 years, our international research group has put efforts into enterprise 2.0 topic from different perspectives with focus on social design, social coordination, and social monitoring in this paper. Some of these efforts' results are reported in [6,15]. Contrary to traditional enterprises with top-down command flow and bottom-up feedback flow, the same flows in Enterprise 2.0 cross all levels and in all directions bringing people together in the development of creative and innovative ideas. In principle, the power of Web 2.0 technologies stems from their ability to capture real-world phenomena such as collaboration, competition, and partnership that can be converted into useful and structured information sources from which enterprises can draw information about markets' trends, consumers' habits, suppliers' strategies, etc.

The remainder of this paper is organized as follows. Section 2 briefly describes a case study to be used for illustration purposes. Section 3 provides an overview of three of our initiatives that look into enterprise 2.0 from the following perspectives: social design, social coordination, and social monitoring of business processes. Finally, we conclude the paper in Sect. 4.

---

[1] "*By the end of 2013, Facebook was being used by 1.23 billion users worldwide, adding 170 million in just one year*", www.theguardian.com/technology/2014/feb/04/facebook-10-years-mark-zuckerberg.

2   Illustrative Case Study

Our case study refers to the electronic-patient-folder system at Anderson Hospital that handles approximately 6000 annual inpatient admissions[2]. We leverage this system to identify first, some business processes' components (tasks, persons and machines) and second, the execution nature of some tasks. When a patient shows up at the hospital, the necessary documentation is scanned into a system known as ImageNow. Upon completion the scanned documentation is linked to the patient's MEDITECH record. An advantage of this linkage is that different stakeholders like billing staff, coders, and other authorized people have immediate, electronic access to the necessary information instead of waiting for the paper documentation to arrive. Prior to implementing the new system Anderson Hospital faced different challenges such as paper records limit access to one user at a time and paper and manual processes hamper compliance with some healthcare standards.

3   Challenges and Opportunities

Our international research group has launched several initiatives to tackle the challenges that enterprise 2.0 faces and tap into the opportunities that enterprise 2.0 offers. In the following, we discuss three of these initiatives that look into enterprise 2.0 from the following perspectives: social design, social coordination, and social monitoring of business processes.

3.1   Social-Design Research Initiative

According to Faci et al. [16], the lack of design approaches for modeling SBPs is not helping enterprises capitalize on Web 2.0 applications' capabilities such as reaching out to more customers, collecting customers' online posts, and profiling customers. A recent study of 1,160 businesses and IT professionals reveals that *"only 22 percent of organizations believed that managers are prepared to incorporate social tools and approaches into their processes. Moreover, two-thirds of respondents said they were not sure they sufficiently understood the impact these technologies would have on their organizations over the next three years"* [17].

Our initiative on BP social design sheds the light on the three components of a process as well as the relations that connect these components, i.e., task (t), person (p), and machine (m) [6]. A task is a work unit that constitutes with other tasks a business process and that a person and/or machine execute. Task execution is either manual, automatic, or mixed. Figure 1 illustrates a simple healthcare-driven BP along with some components for instance, t_1: scan documentation, m_2: ImageNow system, and p_j: cashier. To execute tasks and hence complete processes, resources are required (Sect. 3.2).

In addition to the traditional execution relation that connects persons/machines to tasks, we establish social relations between tasks, between persons, and between machines. The following are examples of social relations [6]:

---

[2] www.perceptivesoftware.com/pdfs/casestudies/psi_cs_anderson.pdf.

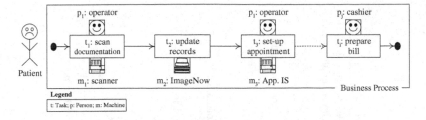

Fig. 1. Example of a business process's components.

- **Interchange**: t_i and t_j engage in an interchange relation when both produce similar output with respect to similar input submitted for processing and their requirements do not overlap (e.g., t_1: scan documentation and t_1': enter patient details manually). The non-overlap condition avoids blockage when t_i's requirements (e.g., online data entry) cannot be met due to absence of executors and thus, t_i needs to be interchanged with t_j that has different requirements (e.g., manual data entry).
- **Backup**: m_i (e.g., scanner in main reception) and m_j (e.g., three-function printer in nurse station) engage in a backup relation when both have similar capacities.
- **Delegation**: p_i and p_j engage in a delegation relation when both are already engaged in a substitution relation based on their respective capacities and p_i decides to assign a task that she will execute or is now executing to p_j due to unexpected changes in her status, e.g., call-in-sick or risk of overload (e.g., general practitioner transferring patient to emergency physician due to case severity).

Table 2 summarizes the social relations between tasks, between machines, and between persons along with their respective pre-conditions, conditions, and post-conditions. Pre-condition defines the rationale of establishing a social relation between a process's components. Condition indicates when a network built upon a social relation is used so that solutions to conflicts that prevent a business process completion are addressed (Sect. 3.2). Finally post-condition indicates when to stop using a network.

Figure 2 depicts examples of networks related to the case study that are generated at run-time. For example, a network of machines is built to specify the backup relation between m_1 (scanner) and m_2 (three-function-printer) since both machines have similar capacities. A configuration network of tasks is also constructed to express the interchange relation between t_1 (scan-documentation) and t_2 (enter-patient-details-manually). Both tasks produce similar output and their requirements do not overlap. Last and not least, a social network of persons is built to describe the peering relation between p_2 (cashier) and p_3 (financial-manager) since both persons have complementary capacities that are necessary to achieve t_5 (prepare- bill). This social network expresses also a substitution relation between p_3 (general-practitioner) and p_4 (emergency-physician) since both have the same capacity.

Table 1. Summary of social relations.

Between	Types	Pre-conditions	Conditions	Post-conditions
t_i, t_j	Coupling	t_i and t_i participated in joint business processes	Review of business process design or concern over coupling level	Business process design completion or coupling level satisfaction
	Interchange	t_i and t_j producing similar output in receipt of similar input	t_i lacking of executor who satisfies its requirements	Executor found for t_j
m_i, m_j	Backup	m_i and m_j having similar capacities	m_i unexpected failure or concern over m_i reliability	Backup/replacement machine found for m_i
	Cooperation	m_i and m_j having similar capacities	Concern over machine collective performance	collective performance level satisfaction
	Partnership	m_i and m_j having complementary capacities	Concern over machine collective performance	Collective performance level satisfaction
p_i, p_j	Substitution	p_i and p_j having similar capacities	p_i expected unavailability (e.g., annual leave and sick leave) or concern over p_i availability	Substitute found for p_i
	Delegation	p_i and p_j having similar capacities	p_j unexpected unavailability (e.g., call-in-sick, urgent tasks to complete, and risk of overload)	Delegate found for p_i
	Peering	p_i and p_j having similar or complementary capacities	Concern over peering appropriateness	Peer found for either p_i or p_j

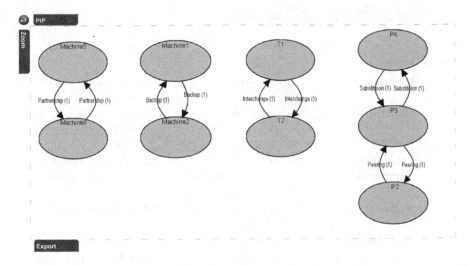

Fig. 2. Screenshot of the BP execution social analysis component. A demo video is available at https://www.youtube.com/watch?v=Py5oGPQot64.

3.2   Social-Coordination Research Initiative

According to Faci et al. [16], agility of today's enterprises should not be confined to the organizational borders of the enterprise. Other vital aspects of the enterprise need to be taken into account such as re-engineering business processes, revisiting the practices of those executing these processes, and redefining the nature of resources that are made available for these processes at run-time. Since resources (e.g., data, power, and CPU time) do not sometimes last forever and are not unlimited and/or shareable, tasks and persons/machines need to coordinate the consumption and use of these resources so that conflicts are avoided and addressed, if they occur. Besides regular conflicts in terms of data and policy incompatibilities between enterprise systems, additional conflicts exist due to time constraints and/or simultaneous access to limited and/or non-shareable resources. Coordination is the best way to address these conflicts.

Our initiative on BP social coordination includes four steps [15]: categorize resources that tasks require for their execution, define how tasks/ machines/persons of a BP bind to resources in order to achieve this execution, categorize conflicts on resources that arise between tasks, between machines, and between persons, and finally analyze the appropriateness of certain networks of tasks/persons/machines for addressing these conflicts. These networks are established during BP social design as per Sect. 3.1.

We categorize resources into (i) logical, i.e., their use/consumption does not lead into a decrease in their reliability/availability level and (ii) physical, i.e., their use/con-sumption does lead into a decrease in their reliability/availability level. This decrease requires resource replacement[3]/replenishment at a certain stage. We also define a set of properties that permit to describe a resource. These

---

[3] Replacement can be the result of degradation.

Table 2. Resource categories and examples.

Resource		Tasks	Examples of resources
Category	Property		
Logical	Unlimited (ul)	Put together medical team for surgery	Patient medical record (read mode)
	Limited (l)	Prepare on-call shifts	Doctors' weekly schedules (valid for one week only)
	Limited but renewable (lr)	Prepare interns' access rights to labs	File of interns (internship possible extension)
	Shareable (s)	Prepare patient for surgery	Patient lab results
	Non-shareable (ns)	Report on surgery outcome	Patient medical record (update mode)
Physical	Unlimited (ul)	Not applicable	Not applicable
	Limited (l)	Prepare patient for surgery	Anesthetic injection
	Limited but renewable (lr)	Carry out surgery on patient	Surgical staple cartridge
	Shareable (s)	Carry out surgery on patient	Oxygen tank
	Non-shareable (ns)	Check patient's vitals	Blood pressure tensiometer

properties are *limited* (l - when a resource use/consumption is measured or a resource ceases to exist either in compliance with its use/consumption cycle - to be introduced later - or because of constraints like temporal), *limited but renewable* (lr - when a resource use/consumption either hits a certain threshold or is subject to constraints like temporal; in either case renewal is possible), and *non-shareable* (ns - when a resource simultaneous use/consumption has to be scheduled). Unless stated a resource is by default unlimited (ul) and/or shareable (s). Table 2 suggests some examples of resources per category and property. To identify these examples we rely on the business process of Fig. 1.

Figure 3 shows a state transition diagram of a resource. The diagram is developed independently of whether the resource is logical or physical, takes into account the properties of Table 1, and permits to establish a resource's consumption cycle (cc) per property. On the one hand, the states (s_i) of a resource include not made available (neither created nor produced yet), made available (either created or produced), not consumed (waiting to be bound by a task), locked (reserved for a task in preparation for consumption), unlocked (released by a task after consumption), consumed (bound by a task for ongoing performance), withdrawn (ceased to exit after unbounding all tasks if necessary), and done (updated as per relevant property if necessary, and unbound by task). It should be noted that other states in a consumption cycle's diagram can be adopted if different properties are used without deviating from the aforementioned purpose of using this diagram. On the other hand, the transitions ($trans_j$) connecting a resource's states together include start, waiting to be bound, consumption approval, consumption update, lock, release, consumption rejection, consumption completion, renewable approval, and no-longer useful. Upon a transition satisfaction, a resource takes on a new state.

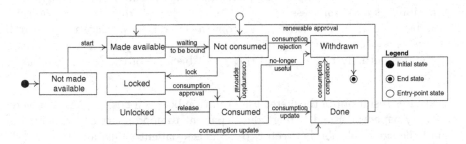

Fig. 3. State transition diagram of a resource.

We list below some sequences of states (s) and transitions ($trans$) that represent a resource's consumption cycle per property denoted as $r(cc_{\text{property}}) = s_i \overset{trans_i}{\longrightarrow} s_{i+1} \overset{trans_{i+1}}{\longrightarrow} s_{i+2} \ldots s_{j-1} \overset{trans_{j-1}}{\longrightarrow} s_j$ (subscripts in state and transition names are given for notational purposes, only).

- $r(cc_{\text{ul}})$: not made available $\overset{start}{\longrightarrow}$ made available $\overset{waiting\ to\ be\ bound}{\longrightarrow}$ not consumed $\overset{consumption\ approval}{\longrightarrow}$ consumed $\overset{no-longer\ useful}{\longrightarrow}$ withdrawn. The resource (e.g., patient medical record) remains available for additional consumption until the transition from consumed to withdrawn is satisfied (e.g., patient discharge).

- $r(cc_{\text{l}_1})$: not made available $\overset{start}{\longrightarrow}$ made available $\overset{waiting\ to\ be\ bound}{\longrightarrow}$ not consumed $\overset{consumption\ approval}{\longrightarrow}$ consumed $\overset{consumption\ update}{\longrightarrow}$ done $\overset{consumption\ completion}{\longrightarrow}$ withdrawn. The transition from done to withdrawn then end-of-state shields a resource (e.g., patient list with contagious diseases) from any new or additional tentative of consumption by tasks (e.g., submit patient list to healthcare authorities upon disease detection) after completing a consumption cycle. In done state a resource's parameters (e.g., accuracy level such as patient list obsolete) are updated and the resource is detached (or unbound) from tasks.

- $r(cc_{\text{lr}})$: not made available $\overset{start}{\longrightarrow}$ made available $\overset{waiting\ to\ be\ bound}{\longrightarrow}$ not consumed $\overset{consumption\ approval}{\longrightarrow}$ consumed $\overset{consumption\ update}{\longrightarrow}$ done $\overset{renewable\ approval}{\longrightarrow}$ made available. The transition from done to made available permits to regenerate a resource (e.g., file of interns) for another round of consumption (e.g., internship extension).

Based on resource categories and their properties and how tasks/persons/ machines bind to resources, we examine conflicts over resources between tasks, only for illustration purposes. The following notation is adopted: $t_i/m_i/p_i \rightarrow r_i$ means that a resource is made available for a task/machine/person; $r_{i,j}$ means that a resource produced by a certain task (resp. machine/person) is transferred to another similar (resp. similar/different) peer for the needs of consumption (resp. use); and, $r_{i,\{j,k,\cdots\}}$ generalizes $r_{i,j}$ but this time the resource is shared between peer$_{\{j,k,\cdots\}}$. $\mathcal{T}$-Conflict$_1$ is an example of conflicts between tasks with emphasis on resource consumption and not data (inputs and outputs) and policy incompatibilities between these tasks. $\mathcal{T}$-Conflict$_1$ arises when (i) a prerequisite relation between t_i and t_j exists, (ii) consume$(t_i, r_i) \rightarrow$ produce$(t_i, r_{i,j})$, and (iii) t_j needs $r_{i,j}$ (i.e., $t_j \nrightarrow r_j$, no r_j is made available for t_j). Potential conflicts on $r_{i,j}$ (and eventually $r_{\{i,k,\cdots\},j}$ and $r_{i,\{j,k,\cdots\}}$) because of the *limited* property of $r_{i,j}$, include:

- l: two cases result out of the prerequisite relation between $t_{\{k,\cdots\}}$ (e.g., complete necessary paperwork) and t_j (e.g., direct patient to appropriate department) on top of the same relation between t_i (e.g., check patient vitals) and t_j:
  (a) $r_{i,j}$ (e.g., report on vital levels) ceases to exist (e.g., blood sample no longer valid) before the execution of t_j begins; t_j waits for $t_{\{k,\cdots\}}$ to produce $r_{\{k,\cdots\},j}$ (e.g., insurance provider approval); (at least one) $t_{\{k,\cdots\}}$ either is still under execution (e.g., due to delay in receiving approval from insurance provider) or failed.
  (b) Only one consumption cycle of $r_{i,j}$ is permitted (per type of property) but it turns out that several consumption cycles of $r_{i,j}$ are required to complete the execution of t_j and finish the consumption of $r_{\{k,\cdots\},j}$ that $t_{\{k,\cdots\}}$ produce.

After identifying the different task conflicts on resources, we suggest solutions for these conflicts based on the networks that are established in Sect. 3.1. These solutions consider the fact that tasks are associated with transactional properties (e.g., pivot, retriable, and compensatable) that limit their re-execution in the case of failure [18]. The following examines briefly how the interchange and coupling networks of tasks are used to address $\mathcal{T}$-Conflict$_1$-Case a.

(a) $r_{i,j}$ ceases to exist before the execution of t_j begins; t_j waits for $t_{\{k,\cdots\}}$ to produce $r_{\{k,\cdots\},j}$; at least one t_k either is still under execution or failed. Current statuses of tasks and resources are: state(t_i): done; state$(r_{i,j})$: withdrawn; state(t_j): not-activated; and state(t_k): either activated (still under execution) or failed with focus on the latter state below. Because t_i now takes on done state, pivot (canceling t_i) and retriable (re-executing t_i) transactional properties are excluded from the analysis of developing solutions to address resource conflicts. This analysis is given in Table 3. The objective is to re-produce $r_{i,j}$ (or produce $r_{i',j}$ with $t_{i'}$ being obtained through the interchange network of t_i). Because of t_k failure, $r_{k',j}$ is produced using $t_{k'}$ that is obtained through the interchange network of t_k.

Table 3. Possible coordination actions for $\mathcal{T}$-Conflict$_1$/limited property/case>a.

Transactional property		Coordination actions	Network involved
t_i	t_k		
Null	Null	— re-execute t_i to re-produce $r_{i,j}$	N/A
		— re-execute t_k to produce $r_{k,j}$	
	Pivot	Deadlock	N/A
	Compensatable	Deadlock	N/A
	Retriable	— re-execute t_i to re-produce $r_{i,j}$	
		— replace t_k with $t_{k'}$ then execute $t_{k'}$ to produce $r_{k',j}$	Interchange($t_k, t_{k'}$)
Compensatable	Null	— compensate t_i; either re-execute t_i to re-produce $r_{i,j}$ or replace t_i with $t_{i'}$ then execute $t_{i'}$ to produce $r_{i',j}$	Interchange($t_i, t_{i'}$)
		— either re-execute t_k to produce $r_{k,j}$ or replace t_k with $t_{k'}$ then execute $t_{k'}$ to produce $r_{k',j}$	Interchange($t_k, t_{k'}$)
	Pivot	Deadlock	N/A
	Compensatable	— compensate t_i; either re-execute t_i to re-produce $r_{i,j}$ or replace t_i with $t_{i'}$ then execute $t_{i'}$ to produce $r_{i',j}$	Interchange($t_i, t_{i'}$)
		— replace t_k with $t_{k'}$ then execute $t_{k'}$ to produce $r_{k',j}$	Interchange($t_k, t_{k'}$)
	Retriable	— compensate t_i; either re-execute t_i to re-produce $r_{i,j}$ or replace t_i with $t_{i'}$ then execute $t_{i'}$ to produce $r_{i',j}$	Interchange($t_i, t_{i'}$)
		— re-execute t_k to produce $r_{k,j}$	

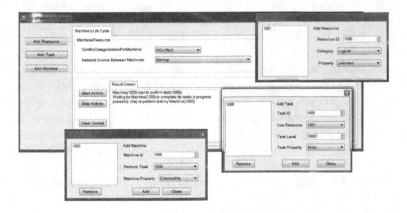

Fig. 4. System's screenshots.

Figure 4 illustrates a screenshot for an under-development proof-of-concept for a rule-based engine that focuss on implementing the strategies reported in Table 3.

3.3   Social-Monitoring Research Initiative

According to Faci et al. [16], monitoring seems to be the commonly-used technique for tracking the execution progress of BPs. Besides providing a real-time and end-to-end view of this progress, monitoring should also offer an organizational and social view over this progress in terms of who executes what, who delegates to whom, and who sends what, to whom, and when. Obstacles that hinder BP successful completion are multiple (e.g., lack of necessary machines that can execute tasks) and hence, will impact the enterprise effectiveness (e.g., delay in delivery) and efficiency (e.g., costly machine re-allocation). The difficulty of measuring intangible and ad-hoc exchanges between people when executing tasks represents a major barrier to social interaction pattern recognition like collaboration and delegation, as well as the role of these patterns in BP improvement. The way these exchanges should happen can be part of a social monitoring framework in which specialized flows connecting these messages are developed to detect anomalies.

Our initiative on BP social monitoring aims of ensuring the successful completion of BPs despite obstacles that could arise and hence, delay this completion. Absence of necessary machines to execute tasks is an example of obstacle. We develop specialized flows known as *control, communication,* and *navigation* and enact the development of these flows in conjunction with the completion of a BP. The control flow connects tasks together with respect to the BP's business logic. The communication flow connects the BP's executors (machines and/or persons) together when they execute tasks. Finally, the navigation flow connects networks of tasks, networks of machines, and networks of persons together when the BP completion runs into difficulties. These networks are established in the BP social design (Sect. 3.1). We recall that BP completion and hence, task execution requires resources that are sometimes *limited, not shareable,* and/or *not renewable* (Sect. 3.2).

BP social monitoring looks into the exchanges of messages that occur between tasks, between executors (persons/machines), and between networks during task execution and conflict resolution. These exchanges lead into developing flows that help identify who supports whom, who sent what, to whom, and when. Figure 5 illustrates the architecture of our flow-based approach for BP social monitoring. Three levels along with their respective flows constitute this architecture. The process level is linked to the control flow, the execution level is linked to the communication flow, and the network level is linked to the navigation flow.

In the following, we examine the interactions between the social, configuration, and/or support networks during a control-flow execution. These interactions establish navigation flows as per the nature of scenario that shapes the progress of this execution. We identify two scenarios: task replacement (explained hereafter) and task delay and decompose the messages supporting network interactions into vertical (v, between the control flow and networks) and horizontal (h, between networks). We associate each network with an authority component (N_{auth}, [19]).

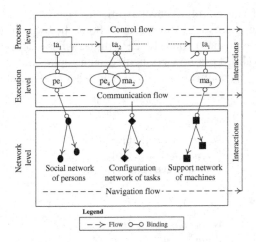

Fig. 5. Cross-flow interactions for BP social monitoring.

Assigning tasks (e.g., scan documentation and enter patient details manually) to potential executors (persons and/or machines) might turn out unsuccessful when the capacities of these executors do not satisfy the requirements of these tasks (Sect. 3.1). Using specific networks, an option consists of replacing tasks that cannot be executed with similar ones and then, looking for executors who have the capacities of satisfying the requirements of the replacement tasks. For illustration purposes, let us assume a control flow that consists of t_1, t_2, and $t_{i,i\neq3}$ and that t_1's requirements are not satisfied.

First t_1 needs to be replaced with another similar task using the interchange network. The control flow sends this network's authority ($N_{auth(interchange)}$) a v-message as shown below asking to find a replacement for t_1. t_1 now acts as an entry node in the interchange network:

v-query(
	from	:	$\mathcal{F}low^c$
	to	:	$N_{auth(interchange)}/nt_1$
	subject	:	findReplacement(t_1))

After screening the edges that connect t_1 to other tasks in the interchange network, t_3 is selected using the highest weight among all these edges as a selection criterion, for example. Prior to confirming t_3 as a replacement for t_1 the $N_{auth(interchange)}$ sends the $N_{auth(coupling)}$ a h-message asking to check for the coupling level between t_3 and those tasks, i.e., t_2, that are dependent on t_1 in the control flow. This message sending is shown below:

h-query(

from	:	$N_{auth(interchange)}/nt_1$
to	:	$N_{auth(coupling)}/nt_3$
subject	:	requestCouplingLevel(t_3, t_2))

Upon receipt of the coupling level from the $N_{auth(interchange)}$ through the $N_{auth(coupling)}$ using the h- and v-messages shown below, the control flow compares this level to a threshold that the BP engineer has set up earlier. Assuming the comparison is valid, t_3 is now confirmed as a replacement for t_1 in the control flow with t_3 being connected to t_2. Otherwise the search for another task continues.

h-reply(

from	:	$N_{auth(coupling)}/nt_3$
to	:	$N_{auth(interchange)}/nt_1$
subject	:	couplingLevel(t_3, t_2))

v-reply(

from	:	$N_{auth(interchange)}/nt_1$
to	:	$\mathcal{Flow}^c$
subject	:	couplingLevel(t_3, t_2))

After updating the control flow, the next step is to identify executors for t_3. Assuming a successful match between t_3's requirements and some executors' capacities two exclusive cases arise, which means more messages need to be exchanged. For illustration purposes we assume that executors correspond to persons (p_3 for t_3).

1. **Substitution:** if there is a concern over pe_3's availability level, the control flow sends the substitution network's authority ($N_{auth(substitution)}$) a v-message asking to find a substitute for p_3 with respect to a certain availability threshold (T_{rel}). This message along with its response are shown below with p_3' being the new executor for t_3.

   v-query(

from	:	$\mathcal{Flow}^c$
to	:	$N_{auth(substitution)}/np_3$
subject	:	findSubstitute(p_3, T_{rel}))

   v-reply(

from	:	$N_{auth(substitution)}/np_3$
to	:	$\mathcal{Flow}^c$
subject	:	substitute($p_3:p_3'$)

2. **Delegation:** if p_3 turns out unavailable unexpectedly or will become overloaded by receiving t_3 for execution, the $N_{auth(substitution)}$ sends the delegation network's authority ($N_{auth(delegation)}$) a h-message asking for identifying a delegate, e.g., p_3', who could execute the task.

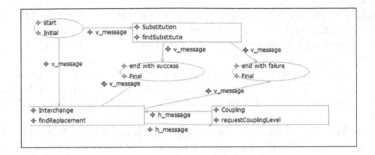

Fig. 6. Partial navigation flow for an example of business process.

The aforementioned horizontal messages constitute a navigation flow in which states and transitions correspond to nodes in networks and messages between nodes, respectively. Vertical messages trigger the establishment of navigation flows (Fig. 6).

4 Conclusion

In this paper we discussed the blend of Web 2.0 concepts and technologies with enterprise computing. This blend results into the development of Social Business Processes (SBP)s. A SBP exposes the social relations that exist between tasks, between machines, and last but not least between persons. These relations led into developing specialized networks that are used to solve conflicts over resources as well as monitoring the enterprise performance. Although we acknowledges that tasks and machines cannot "socialize" (in the strict sense) like persons do in real life, putting tasks together and machines together suggests a lot of similarities with how persons behave in their daily life. Supporting our claims that tasks and machines can to a certain extent socialize, Tan et al. state that *"... Currently, most social networks connect people or groups who expose similar interests or features. In the near future, we expect that such networks will connect **other entities, such as software components, Web-based services, data resources, and workflows.** More importantly, the interactions among people and nonhuman artifacts have significantly enhanced data scientists' productivity"* [20].

References

1. Maamar, Z., Faci, N., Boukadi, K., Sheng, Q.Z., Yao, L.: Commitments to regulate social web services operation. IEEE Trans. Serv. Comput. **7**(2), 154–167 (2014)
2. Maamar, Z., Hacid, H., Hunhs, M.N.: Why web services need social networks. IEEE Internet Comput. **15**(2), 90–94 (2011)
3. Baumer, E.P.S., Khovanskaya, V.D., Adams, P., Pollak, J.P., Voida, S., Gay, G.: Designing for engaging experiences in mobile social-health support systems. IEEE Pervasive Comput. **12**(3), 32–39 (2013)

4. Roussaki, I., Kalatzis, N., Liampotis, N., Kosmides, P., Anagnostou, M.E., Doolin, K., Jennings, E., Bouloudis, Y., Xynogalas, S.: Context-awareness in wireless and mobile computing revisited to embrace social networking. IEEE Commun. Mag. **50**, 74–81 (2012)

5. Erol, S., Granitzer, M., Happ, S., Jantunen, S., Jennings, B., Johannesson, P., Koschmider, A., Nurcan, S., Rossi, D., Schmidt, R.: Combining BPM and social software: contradiction or chance? J. Softw. Maint. Evol. Res. Pract. **22**, 449–476 (2010)

6. Kajan, E., Faci, N., Maamar, Z., Loo, A., Pljaskovic, A., Sheng, Q.Z.: The network-based business process. IEEE Internet Comput. **18**(2), 63–69 (2014)

7. Drupad, S.: Enterprise Web 2.0 Worth \$4.6 Billion in 2013 (Visited September 2008) Searchviews. www.searchviews.com/index.php/archives/2008/04/enterprise-web-20-worth-46-billion-in-2013.php. Accessed 21 April 2008

8. McAfee, A.P.: Enterprise 2.0: the dawn of emergent collaboration. MITSloan Manage. Rev. **47**(3), 21–28 (2006)

9. Grim-Yefsah, M., Rosenthal-Sabroux, C., Thion, V.: Using information of an informal network to evaluate business process robustness. In: Proceedings of the International Conference on Knowledge Management and Information Sharing (KMIS 2011), Paris, France (2011)

10. Badr, Y., Maamar, Z.: Can enterprises capitalize on their social networks? Cutter IT J. **22**(10), 10–14 (2009)

11. Cross, R., Gray, P., Cunningham, S., Showers, M., Thomas, R.J.: The collaborative organization: how to make employee networks really work. MITSloan Manage. Rev. **51**, 83–90 (2010)

12. Chandler, S.: Social BPM: Gateway to Enhanced Process Efficiency. http://www.virtusa.com/blog/2011/11/, visited September 2012 (November 2011)

13. Seshadri, S.C.: Exploring business and collaboration with web 2.0. SETLabs Briefings J. **7**(3), 3–10 (2009)

14. Gartner: How to Analyze Your Sales Processes on Efficiency versus Effectiveness. Gartner report (2012)

15. Maamar, Z., Faci, N., Kouadri Mostéfaoui, S., Kajan, E.: Network-based conflict resolution in business processes. In: Proceedings of the 10th IEEE International Conference on e-Business Engineering (ICEBE 2013), Coventry, UK (2013)

16. Faci, N., Maamar, Z., Kajan, E., Benslimane, D.: Research roadmap for the enterprise 2.0 - issues and solutions. Scientific Publications of the State University of Novi Pazar Ser. A: Appl. Math. Inf. Mech. **6**(2), 81–89 (2014)

17. Vizard, M.: IBM: business processes need to get social in 2013 (2012). http://www.itbusinessedge.com/blogs/it-unmasked/ibm-business-processes-need-to-get-social-in-2013.html

18. Little, M.: Transactions and web services. Commun. ACM **46**(10), 49–54 (2003)

19. Maamar, Z., Faci, N., Luck, M., Hachimi, S.: Specifying and implementing social web services operation using commitments. In: The Proceedings of the 27th Annual ACM Symposium on Applied Computing (SAC 2012), Riva del Garda, Trento, Italy (2012)

20. Tan, W., Blake, M.B., Saleh, I., Dustdar, S.: Social-network-sourced big data analytics. IEEE Internet Comput. **17**(5), 62–69 (2013)

Internet Technology

Multitier Debugging of Web Applications

Manuel Serrano[✉]

Inria Sophia Méditerranée, 2004 Route des Lucioles,
06902 Sophia Antipolis, France
Manuel.Serrano@inria.fr
http://www-sop.inria.fr

Abstract. Debugging Web applications is difficult because of their distributed nature and because the server-side and the client-side of the application are generally treated separately. The multitier approach, which reunifies the two ends of the application inside a unique execution environment, helps the debugging process because it lets the debugger access more runtime informations.

We have built a multitier debugger for an extension of JavaScript. Its advantage over most debuggers for the Web is that it reports the full stack trace containing all the server-side and client-side frames that have conducted to an error. Errors are reported on their actual position on the source code, wherever they occur on the server or on the client. This paper presents this debugger and sketches its implementation.

Keywords: Web debugging · Web programming · Functional programming

1 Introduction

The distributed nature of Web applications makes debugging difficult. The programming languages and tools commonly used make it even more complex. Generally the server-side and the client-side are implemented in different settings and the debugging is treated as two separated tasks: on the one hand, the debugging of the server, on the other hand, the debugging of the client. Most studies and tools focus on this latter aspect. They concentrate on the debugging of JavaScript in the browser. Although useful, this only addresses one half of the problem. Considering the debugging of Web applications as a whole raises the following difficulties:

– As the server-side and the client-side are generally implemented in different languages, debuggers for the Web do not capture the whole execution of the application. Programming the server and the client in the same language helps but is not sufficient to let the debugger expose a coherent view of the whole execution as this also demands a runtime environment that enforces consistent representations of data structures and execution traces.

© Springer International Publishing Switzerland 2015
V. Monfort and K.-H. Krempels (Eds.): WEBIST 2014, LNBIP 226, pp. 33–47, 2015.
DOI: 10.1007/978-3-319-27030-2_3

– The JavaScript tolerant semantics tends to defer errors raising. For instance, calling a function with an insufficient number of arguments may lead to filling a data structure with the unexpected undefined value which, in turn, may raise a type error when accessed. The *distance* between the error and its actual cause may be arbitrarily long, which can make the relation between the two difficult to establish, especially when an error on the server-side of the application actually raises an exception on the client-side, or *vice versa*.

– The JavaScript event loop used for the GUI and asynchronous requests splits the execution into unrelated callback procedures which get called upon event receipts. When an error occurs, the active stack trace only contains elements relative to the current callback invocation. It is oblivious of the context of the callback. Understanding the cause of the error is then uneasy.

Pursuing our research on multitier programming for the Web, we have built a multitier extension of JavaScript that eliminates most of these problems.

– When an error is raised, the full stack trace is reported. This stack trace may contain server stack frames, client stack frames, or both. We call this a *multitier stack trace*.

– When an error occurs, either on the client or on the server, its source location is reported by the debugger.

This paper presents this debugger and exposes the salient aspects of its implementation.

1.1   Debugging Web Applications

Most studies of the debugging of Web applications consider the client-side of the applications. Beside an early debugger for CGI applications by Vckovski [1], most efforts concentrate on creating JavaScript debuggers for the Web browsers. Feldman and Sharma have both developed a remote debugger for WebKit [2,3]. Mickens has developed a browser-agnostic JavaScript debugger [4]. These tools offer facilities for inspecting the JavaScript stack frame and for breakpointing. They do not address the problem of debugging Web applications globally. These studies are complementary with our effort as our debugger can use them to step inside the client side execution, provided they support the *source map* specification [5].

A study by E. Schrock [6] has identified many difficulties posed by JavaScript when debugging Web applications. *"In the early days, the [JavaScript]'s ability to handle failure silently was seen as a benefit. If an image rollover failed, it was better to preserve a seamless Web experience than to present the user with unsightly error dialogs.*

This tolerance of failure has become a central design principle of modern browsers, where errors are silently logged to a hidden error console... Now, at best, script execution failure results in an awkward experience. At worst, the application ceases to work or corrupts server-side state. Tacitly accepting script

errors is no longer appropriate, nor is a one-line number and message suffi-
cient to identify a failure in a complex AJAX application. Accordingly, the lack
of robust error messages and native stack traces has become one of the major
difficulties with AJAX development today... Ideally, we would like to be able to
obtain a complete dump of the JavaScript execution context[.]". This is exactly
what multitier debugging brings: when an error is raised, either on the client or
on the server, the full multitier execution stack that reflects the states of the
server and the client is reported.

The work presented here takes place inside a larger project that consists in
creating a multitier variant of JavaScript. This system is named Hop.js. It comprises a programming language and a runtime environment. We briefly present
the language in the following section before showing the benefits one may expect
from a multitier debugger.

1.2   The Hop.js Programming Language

Hop.js is a multitier extension of JavaScript [7]. It is the successor of the Hop
programming language [8–10] from which it reuses the main multitier constructs.
We only present here the essential aspects of Hop.js and show some examples
that should be sufficient to understand the rest of the paper.

The application server-side and client-side are both implemented within a
single Hop.js program. Client code is distinguished from server code by prefixing
it with the syntactic annotation '~'. Server-side values can be injected inside
client-side expressions using a second syntactic annotation: the '$' mark. On
the server, the client-side code is extracted, compiled on-the-fly into standard
JavaScript, and shipped to the client. This enables Hop.js clients code to be
executed by unmodified Web browsers.

Except for the unusual multitier constructs, the standard Web programming
model is used by Hop.js. A server-side Hop.js program builds an HTML tree
that creates the GUI and embeds client-side code into scripts, then ships it
to the client. A dedicated syntactic extension helps creating HTML elements,
which takes the syntactic form of tagged JavaScript object literals, where the
tags (of the shape <ident>) denote the type of the HTML elements. AJAX-like
programming is made available by service definitions, a service being a server-
side function associated with a URL. Calling a service on the client builds a
service frame whose post method triggers the actual execution of the service
on the server. Communications between clients and servers are automatically
performed by the Hop.js runtime system, with no additional user code needed,
as the runtime system handles the serialization/deserialization of values.

The Hop.js fibHtml program below consists of a server-built Web page
displaying a three-rows table whose cells enumerate positive integers. When a
cell is clicked on the browser, the corresponding Fibonacci value is computed on
the client and displayed in a popup window. Note the '~' signs used in lines 3,
6, 7, and 8 which mark client-side expressions.

```
1: service fibHtml() {
2:    return <HTML> {
3:       ~{ function fib(x) { return (x<2) ? 1 : fib(x-1)+fib(x-2); } },
4:       <TABLE> {

5:          <TR> {
6:             <TD> { onclick: ~{ alert( fib(1) ) }, "fib(1)" },
7:             <TD> { onclick: ~{ alert( fib(2) ) }, "fib(2)" },
8:             <TD> { onclick: ~{ alert( fib(3) ) }, "fib(3)" }
9:          }
10:       }
11:    }
12: }
```

Let us modify the example to illustrate some Hop.js niceties. Instead of building the rows by hand, we let Hop.js compute them. For that, an array of integers is created and the map JavaScript higher order operator is used. The expression i (line 8) of the function sent to map denotes the value of i on the server at HTML document elaboration time. That is, when the server is constructing the HTML document that it will ship in response to a user request.

```
1: service fibHtml() {
2:    return <HTML> {
3:       ~{ function fib( x ) { ... } },
4:       <TABLE> {
5:          [ 1,2,3 ].map( function( i ) {
6:             return <TR> {
7:                <TD> {
8:                   onclick: ~{ alert( fib(${i}) ) }, "fib("+ ${i} +")"
9:                } </TD>
10:             } </TR>
11:          } )
12:       } </TABLE>
13:    } </HTML>
14: }
```

Before delivery to a client, the server-side document is compiled on the server into regular HTML and JavaScript. This produces the following document[1]:

```
1: <!DOCTYPE HTML>
2: <html>
3:    <head> <meta ...>
4:       <script src='/usr/local/share/hop/hop_s.js'>
5:    </head>
6:    <script>
7:       function fib(x) {if(x<2) return 1; else ...}}
8:    </script>
9:    <table>
10:      <tr><td onclick="alert(fib(1))">fib(1)</td></tr>
11:      <tr><td onclick="alert(fib(2))">fib(2)</td></tr>
12:      <tr><td onclick="alert(fib(3))">fib(3)</td></tr>
13:    </table>
14: </html>
```

---

[1] Some generated programs have been manually modified to fit the paper layout constraints.

This program can be executed by any standard browser.

If for some reason, the programmer wants the fib calls to be evaluated on the server, three modifications are needed: *(i)* a service must be defined as the client cannot access directly server-side functions, *(ii)* the definition of the fib function must be migrated to the server, and *(iii)* a post remote call must be introduced:

```
 1: service fibHtml() {
 2:    return <HTML> {
 3:       <TABLE> {
 4:          [ 1,2,3 ].map( function( i ) {
 5:             return <TR> {
 6:                <TD> {
 7:                   onclick: ~{ fibSvc( ${i} ).post( alert ) },
 8:                   "fib("+ ${i} +")"
 9:                } </TD>
10:             } </TR>
11:          } )
12:       } </TABLE>
13:    } </HTML>
14: }
15:
16: service fibSvc( n ) {
17:    function fib( x ) { ... };
18:    return fib( n );
19: }
```

These examples illustrate the flavor of Web programming with Hop.js. Interested readers, will find many more examples on the Hop.js web site[2].

1.3   Organization of the Paper

The paper is organized as follows. Section 2 presents some debugging scenarios. Section 3 sketches the implementation of the debugger. Section 4 presents the related work.

2   Debugging Scenarios

In this section we show the error reports produced by the Hop.js *debugging* mode in typical erroneous situations. The reports are accessible on the client, *i.e.*, the Web browser, and on the server, which prints them on its console.

2.1   Client-Side Error

Let us first consider a type error that involves client-side and server-side computations. The server-side program elaborates a single-button Web page that invokes the client-side function myCallback when clicked (line 10). Note that

---

[2] http://hop.inria.fr.

this program also uses on some extensions Hop.js borrows from Nodejs. In particular, Hop.js implements the Nodejs module system of, which is extended to the client-side also. The require function imports the module. It actually returns a regular JavaScript whose property are defined, in the imported module, by the exports object. The Nodejs module system is not supported by any syntactic construct. A call to the require function is a regular expression. As such in can be used everywhere an expression is permitted by the syntax. In Hop.js the function require can also be used in client-side code, provided a first declaration is included in the HEAD of the HTML document. This is illustrated by the example below where the module client.js is imported by the client-side code (line 4 and 8).

```
1: service bug1() {
 2:    return <HTML> {
 3:       <HEAD> {
 4:          require: './client.js'
 5:       },
 6:       <BUTTON> {
 7:          id: 'myButton',
 8:          onclick: ~{ require( './client.js' ).myCallback() },
 9:          "click me to raise the error"
10:       }
11:    }
12: }
13:
14: exports.bug1Svc = service( a, b ) {
15:    return [ a, b ];
16: }
```

The function myCallback is implemented in the client.js client-side module:

```
1: ${ var server = require( './server' ); }
2:
3: function myTypeError( a ) {
4:    return a[ 0 ].name;
5: }
6:
7: exports.myCallback = function() {
8:    ${server.bug1Svc}( 11, 12 ).post( myTypeError );
9: }
```

The client-side function myCallback (line 7) calls the server service bug1Svc. When the service completes, the execution resumes on the client by invoking the function myTypeError. This function is called with the array of integers its receives from the service. This is wrong because its wants an array of objects. The integer/object type mismatch is reported as:

```
File "bug1-client.js", line 4, character 19:
#       return a[ 0 ].name;
#                  ^
*** CLIENT ERROR: http://localhost:8888/hop/bug1:
Not an object -- 11
   1. ~myTypeError, bug1-client.js:3
Service trace:
   2. ~bug1Svc.post(...), bug1-client.js:8
   3. ~myCallback, bug1-client.js:7
   4. ~button#myButton.onclick, bug1-server.js:8
```

The error report shows the position in the source file of the error and the complete stack trace. Client-side frames are prefixed with the '~' sign. (Here, all stack frames are client frames.) When the type error is raised in the client-side function myTypeError the active stack trace only contains one frame denoting the invocation of the function myTypeError. However, the report also shows the context from which myTypeError has been called. It shows that a click on the button defined line 8 of bug1-server.js module has called the client-side function myCallback which, in turn, has invoked the remote service bug1Svc.

The call trace makes explicit the whole execution flow which has conducted to the error on the client. As it also makes explicit the network traversal (frame #2) that took place before myTypeError is called, it is easier to understand which actual computation conducted to the type error.

2.2 Server-Side Error

Let us modify the definition of the previous service to introduce a server-side error:

```
16: exports.bug2Svc = service( a, b ) {
17:     return [ a.name, b.name ];
18: }
```

This is wrong as the service bug2Svc is passed an integer for the argument a while it expects an object. The new error report is as follows:

```
File "bug2-server.js", line 17, character 301:
     return [ a.name, b.name ];
#              ^
*** SERVER ERROR:bug2Svc
Not an object -- 11
   1. \@bug2Svc, bug2-server.js:17
Service trace:
   2. ~bug1Svc.post(...), bug2-client.js:8
   3. ~myCallback, bug2-client.js:7
   4. ~button#myButton.onclick, bug2-server.js:8
```

The report locates the error inside the bug2Svc service (services are prefixed with \@ to distinguish them from regular functions). The stack trace shows server-side stack frames and the client-side context that has yielded the service invocation. This time again the error is easy to follow and to understand as the complete trace before the error is exposed. The computation started with a user click on the client. The click action has been followed by a service invocation, which has raised the server-side error.

2.3   Putting Together

The Hop.js debugger keeps track of all the callbacks of the client-side program. Let the callback be associated with a service invocation as seen before, with a GUI event (mouse move, key press, ...), with a server side event (a high level facility supported by Hop built on top of websockets), or with a timer, Hop.js generates a dedicated entry in the stack trace. Callback traces can be combined without restriction. For instance, suppose a service call wrapped in an setTimeout expression as follows:

```
5: exports.myCallback = function() {
6:    setTimeout( function() {
7:        ${server.bug1Svc}( 11, 12 ).post( myTypeError );
8:    }, 1000 );
9: }
```

The new error trace shows a *service* trace preceded by a *setTimeout* trace:

```
File "bug3-server.js", line 17, character 301:
    return [ a.name, b.name ];
#              ^
*** SERVER ERROR:bug3Svc
Not an object -- 11
    1. \@bug3Svc, bug3-server.js:17
Service trace:
    2. ~bug3Svc.post(...), bug3-client.js:8
setTimeout trace:
    3. ~setTimeout( ..., 1000 );
    4. ~myCallback, bug3-client.js:7
    5. ~button#myButton.onclick, bug3-server.js:8
```

3   Implementation

The main component of the Hop.js debugger is the construction of the stack traces. It is presented in this section.

3.1   Constructing Stack Traces

Hop.js client-side programs are compiled into *natural* JavaScript programs: Hop.js functions are mapped into JavaScript functions, and Hop.js variables are mapped into JavaScript variables. HTML constructs are compiled into DOM API function calls. Hop.js services are compiled into JavaScript functions, which merely generate URLs packing the arguments of the client calls. In debug mode all Hop.js functions that spawn asynchronous evaluations (services, setTimeout, and setInterval) are replaced with instrumented versions that help elaborating the stack traces. Hence, obtaining the client-side part of the Hop.js stack frames is similar to obtaining a plain JavaScript stack frames, whose technique is well known [3,4,6]. It relies on two observations: first, JavaScript exception objects contain stack information; second, there are only four different contexts in which codes get executed:

1. the global context while loading the page;
2. event listeners (GUI or server events);
3. timeouts and intervals;
4. remote service callbacks (XmlHTTPRequest).

To obtain a stack trace, the runtime environment installs exception handlers on these four contexts, it intercepts exceptions, and extracts their stack information. Older techniques based on the two special JavaScript variables `caller` and `callee` are now impractical as JavaScript *strict mode* used by Hop.js does not support these variables.

Constructing Multitier Stack Traces. The *multitier stack trace* describes the current computation and the context in which it has been initiated. Contexts are computed as follows:

1. The context of a global top-level JavaScript evaluation is empty.
2. The context of a DOM listener specified as an attribute of an HTML node consists of a description of the node and a description of the event the listener is attached to.
3. The context of an event listener dynamically attached to a DOM event consists of a description of the DOM node plus the stack trace active at the moment the listener is attached.
4. The context of a timeout consists of the concatenation of the context and the stack trace active when the callback is registered, and a description of the timeout itself.
5. The context of a service call (`post`) consists of the concatenation of the context and the stack trace active when the remote call is spawn and a description of the called service.

Active contexts are store in the global variable `hopCurrentStack Context`. It contains an array of execution contexts. It is updated each time a new callback is registered. Of course, this approach is correct only because JavaScript execution is single-threaded and because callbacks always run up to completion, *i.e.*, they are never preempted.

Let us illustrate the construction of the multitier stack trace on two actual examples. First, let us show the compilation of an HTML button declaration as found in the examples of Sect. 2.1.

```
<BUTTON> {
   id: "myButton",
   onclick: ~{ myCallback() },
   "click me to raise the error"
}
```

The *production mode* compilation merely consists in generating the equivalent HTML+JavaScript text files:

```
<button id='myButton'
  onclick='myCallback()'>
  click me to raise the error
</button>
```

The possibility to change the compilation schema according to external configuration is a benefit of the Hop.js approach where the JavaScript code is generated on demand by an on-the-fly compiler. Switching from production mode to debugging mode and *vice versa* merely requires switching on and off a Hop.js compiler flag. In *debugging mode*, the compilation of the button is changed for:

```
 1: <button id='myButton'
 2:   onclick='
 3:     var ctx = hopCallbackHtmlContext(
 4:                  "button#myButton.onclick", "bug2-server.js", 205);
 5:     var stk = new Array(ctx);
 6:     hopCurrentStackContext = stk;
 7:     try {
 8:         myCallback()
 9:     } catch(e) {
10:         hopCallbackHandler(e, stk)
11:     }'
12:   click me to raise the error
13: </button>
```

This code constructs an HTML context that stores the source location of the button (line 4). It sets the global exception context (line 6) and it wraps the user callback (proc) into a context aware callback (line 7). This wrapped callback installs an error handler which signals potential errors in the context that was active when the callback has been installed (the variable stk line 5).

To show how contexts are accumulated, let us study the implementation of the Hop setTimeout function. It works similarly to post but it is simpler to understand as post carries its own complexity independently of stack contexts. When debugging is enabled, the client-side compiler replaces standard calls to setTimeout with an instrumented version:

```
 1: function setTimeoutDebug(proc, timeout) {
 2:    if(typeof(timeout) != "number") {
 3:       throw new Error("setTimeout: integer expected" + timeout);
 4:    } if(!("apply" in proc))
 5:       throw new Error("setTimeout: procedure expected" + proc);
 6:    try {
 7:       throw new Error("setTimeout");
 8:    } catch( e ) {
 9:       var oldctx = hopCurrentStackContext;
10:
11:       function procDbg() {
12:          hopCurrentStackContext.push(hopGetExceptionStack(e));
13:          hopCurrentStackContext.push("setTimeout trace:");
14:          var ctx = hopCurrentStackContext;
15:
16:          try {
17:             return proc.apply(this, arguments);
18:          } catch(e) {
19:             hopCallbackHandler(e, ctx);
20:          } finally {
21:             hopCurrentStackContext = oldctx;
22:          }
23:       }
24:
25:       return setTimeout(procDbg, timeout);
26:    }
27: }
```

First, initial type tests (lines 2 and 4) are executed to check the correctness of the invocation. Then, before calling the setTimeout builtin JavaScript function, an exception is raised to capture the current execution trace (the function hopGetExceptionStack). This stack trace is concatenated to the context active when the function setTimeout is called.

The proposed implementation of setTimeout breaks tail recursions. Programming patterns as:

```
function loop() {
   ...
   return setTimeout(loop, delay);
}
```

blow the memory because the contextual stack is augmented each time a new iteration of the loop is executed. Several *ad-hoc* solutions are possible to workaround this problem. The one implemented in Hop.js consists in checking the top of the contextual stack. If it is already an *after* frame, nothing is pushed on the stack. Otherwise a new frame is pushed as already described. Although simplistic, we have found this solution sufficient and convenient to debug tail-recursive programs. If needed in the future, smarter solutions will be envisioned.

Handling the context stack on the server is simpler. When a client invokes a service, it serializes the context stack and ships it along the service arguments. The server protects the execution of its service with a handler that appends the execution trace of the exception to the client-side context. This augmented context is returned to the client if a server-side error occurs.

Pretty-Printing the Stack Trace. Pretty printing stack traces requires the debugger to identify correctly Hop.js stack frames and to map the actual locations of the generated JavaScript file into the user source codes. In this process, administrative frames, *i.e.*, frames introduced automatically by the Hop.js runtime system, are stripped off from the execution stack and actual source code locations of the generated code are mapped in the user source code locations. Actual source locations are reconstructed by the Hop.js client runtime system using the extra informations produced by the Hop.js-to-JavaScript compiler. It relies on the *source map* tables [5] the compiler generates for the JavaScript steppers. These tables contain all the informations needed to map JavaScript source positions into Hop source positions. To make the source tables explicitly available from standard JavaScript code, the Hop-to-JavaScript compiler generates the extra call at the end of each generated file:

```
hopSourceMappingUrl( "bug1.js", "bug1.js.map" );
```

This merely registers that a source map table is available for the file bug1.js. When a stack frame referring bug1.js has to be translated, the table is actually downloaded from the server, and a JavaScript client library translates the JavaScript location translated into a Hop.js location.

4   Related Work

Multitier programming for the Web has been pioneered by GWT from Google, Links from the University of Edinburgh [11], and Hop. The three languages have appeared almost simultaneously in 2006. Hop.js is the successor of Hop. The two languages only differ by their core base language. Hop is based on the Scheme programming language, while Hop.js is based on JavaScript. The multitier approach is now followed by other programming languages such as Ocsigen [12], iTask3, or Opa [13].

Among the Hop.js competitors, only GWT considers the problem of debugging Web applications. GWT supports debugging of multitier applications but cannot debug JavaScript components. GWT has nothing similar to the Hop.js multitier stack.

Nodejs is a platform built on top of V8, the JavaScript runtime used by Chrome. Nodejs is used for building fast, scalable network applications, such as Web servers. Nodejs is an effective way of supporting JavaScript on both ends of the application. However a Nodejs Web application is still conceived as two separated software components and debugging is also separated.

The following example mimics the server error example of Sect. 2.2.

```
var http = require("http");
var url = require("url");

http.createServer(function(request, response) {
    var url_parts = url.parse(request.url, true);
    var query = url_parts.query;

    response.writeHead(200, {"Content-Type": "text/html"});
    response.write("<html>"+query["x"]["car"]+"</html>");
    response.end();
}).listen(8888);
```

When executed, it produces the following trace.

```
node1.js:10
                    + query["x"]["car"]
                              ^
TypeError: Cannot read property 'car' of undefined
  at Server.<anonymous> (node1.js:10:40)
  at Server.EventEmitter.emit (events.js:98:17)
  at HTTPParser.parser.onIncoming (http.js:2056:12)
  at HTTPParser.parserOnHeadersComplete (http.js:120:23)
  at Socket.socket.ondata (http.js:1946:22)
  at TCP.onread (net.js:525:27)
```

The error is correctly located in the server source file but the stack trace is oblivious of the client-side execution that has preceded the server computation. It merely reports that the error as occurred in the context of answering an HTTP request but without much details. Running Nodejs in debug mode could give access to extra informations about the nature of the HTTP request but it will still lack informations about the client state. The techniques proposed in this paper improve this situation.

Popular modern JavaScript frameworks raise the abstraction level of client-side programs by offering facilities for generating client-side programs at runtime and for communicating with the server more easily. This makes developing applications easier but as of the current versions, it also makes debugging more difficult because the code automatically generated by the runtime system shows up when an error is raised. Let us illustrates this with the Google's Angularjs framework [14]. Let us consider the tutorial available on the framework Web page which illustrates Ajax programming with the following example:

```
var catApp = angular.module('catApp', []);
catApp.controller('PhoneListCtrl', ['$scope', '$http',
    function ($scope, $http) {
        $http.get('phones.json').success( function(data) {
        $scope.phones = data; });
    $scope.orderProp = 'age'; }]);
```

Introducing a syntax error in `phones.json` produces:

```
SyntaxError: Unexpected token }
    at Object.parse (native)
    at fromJson (angular.js:1035:14)
    at $HttpProvider.defaults.defaults.transformResponse
        (angular.js:6926:18)
    at angular.js:6901:12
    at Array.forEach (native)
    at forEach (angular.js:302:11)
    at transformData (angular.js:6900:3)
    at transformResponse (angular.js:7570:17)
    at wrappedCallback (angular.js:10905:81)
    at angular.js:10991:26
```

As it can be seen, the whole execution trace is only populated with Angularjs entries which none is explicitly mentioned in the user program. Even more important, the stack trace it totally silent about the `controller`'s code and the HTTP request. The techniques presented in this paper could help presenting less obscure stack traces to the programmer.

There is a whole line of research which consists in typing JavaScript. Some focus on inferring static types of JavaScript programs [15], some such as TypeScript [16] extend the language to support type annotations. The shared objective is to enable JavaScript errors detection at compile-time. This is orthogonal to our effort as our purpose is to detect unexpected behaviors at runtime.

5   Conclusions

The lack of complete debugging information is acknowledged as a major difficulty when developing Web applications [6]. Using the Hop.js multitier setting we have solved this problem by creating a debugger which reports full stack traces. When an error is raised, the programmer is presented with the complete execution trace composed of server-side and client-side frames that have conducted to the error.

The presented debugger exposes a unified execution stack that reflects both ends of the application but it uses two separate steppers that cannot collaborate. In a further step, we will create a global stepper that will be able to traverse the network. Stepping forward seems easy to obtain because it will just require the implementation of a collaboration layer between two existing tools. Inspecting the execution stack backward is more hypothetical since it requires to save execution traces potentially infinitely.

The presented techniques rely on the multitier paradigm to expose a global and coherent view of the execution between the server and the client. They also rely on code generation to instrument the code actually executed on the browser. In Hop.js this is implemented in a single runtime environment whose main element is a custom bootstrapped web server embedding compilers for generating HTML and JavaScript on-the-fly. In addition to supporting better debugging, this approach also enables fast dynamic HTTP responses servers [17].

References

1. Vckovski, A.: wshdbg - a Debugger for CGI Applications. In: Proceedings of the 6th conference on Annual Tcl/Tk Workshop (TCLTK), pp. 89–96, Berkeley, CA, USA (1998)
2. Feldman, P.: WebKit remote debugging (2011). http://www.webkit.org/blog/1620/webkit-remote-debugging
3. Sharma, A.J.: Better web development with webkit remote debugging. In: Proceedings of the World Wide Web Conference (WWW), Lyon, France (2012)
4. Mickens, J.: Rivet: browser-agnostic remote debugging for web applications. In: Proceedings of the Usenix Annual Technical Conference (ATC), pp. 30–43, Boston, MA, USA (2012)
5. Lenz, J., Fitzgerald, N.: Source Map Revision 3 Proposal - better bidirectional mapping (2011)
6. Schrock, E.: Debugging AJAX in Production. ACM Queue **7** (2009)
7. ECMA: Ecma-262: Ecmascript language specification (2009)
8. Serrano, M., Gallesio, E., Loitsch, F.: HOP, a language for programming the web 2.0. In: Proceedings of the First Dynamic Languages Symposium (DLS), Portland, Oregon, USA (2006)
9. Boudol, G., Luo, Z., Rezk, T., Serrano, M.: Reasoning about web applications: an operational semantics for HOP. ACM Trans. Program. Lang. Syst. (TOPLAS) **34** (2012)
10. Serrano, M., Berry, G.: Multitier programming in Hop - a first step toward programming 21st-century applications. Commun. ACM **55**, 53–59 (2012)
11. Cooper, E., Lindley, S., Yallop, J.: Links: web programming without tiers. In: de Boer, F.S., Bonsangue, M.M., Graf, S., de Roever, W.-P. (eds.) FMCO 2006. LNCS, vol. 4709, pp. 266–296. Springer, Heidelberg (2007)
12. Vouillon, J., Balat, V.: From bytecode to Javascript: the Js_of_ocaml compiler. Software: Practice and Experience (2013). doi:10.1002/spe.2187
13. Binsztok, H., Koprowski, A., Swarczewskaja, I.: Opa: Up and Running. O'Reilly Media, Sebastopol (2013)
14. Google: Angularjs (2013). http://angularjs.org/
15. Jensen, S.H., Møller, A., Thiemann, P.: Type analysis for javascript. In: Palsberg, J., Su, Z. (eds.) SAS 2009. LNCS, vol. 5673, pp. 238–255. Springer, Heidelberg (2009)
16. Microsoft: TypeSscript, Language Specification, version 0.9.5 (2013)
17. Serrano, M.: Hop, a fast server for the diffuse web. In: Field, J., Vasconcelos, V.T. (eds.) COORDINATION 2009. LNCS, vol. 5521, pp. 1–26. Springer, Heidelberg (2009)

Securing a Loosely-Coupled Web-Based eLearning Ecosystem Combining Open Standards

Jean-Noël Colin$^{(\boxtimes)}$ and Hoang Minh Tien

PReCISE Research Center, University of Namur, Namur, Belgium
jean-noel.colin@unamur.be

Abstract. One of the outcomes of the EU-funded iTEC project is the design and the development of a complete eLearning ecosystem, from the design of pedagogical scenarios to their concrete implementation in a Learning Management System, through instantiation of required technical artefacts. The proposed architecture is loosely-coupled and relies on W3C widgets, mashup platforms and other autonomous components, which raise several security issues. This paper reports about the solution that has been implemented to manage user authentication and authorization in such a highly distributed environment, through the combination of various open standards. The proposed approach is based on a survey ran among european teachers about their practices in terms of user credentials usage and sharing.

Keywords: Widgets · eLearning · Authentication · oAuth · OpenId

1 Introduction

The last few years have seen the emergence of a new approach to building Web applications, in the form of mashups. Mashups are applications that reuse and combine data and services available on the web [1]. In the rest of the paper, we will follow the definition of mashup and related concepts as defined in [12]. Web mashups usually combine data and services that are available on the Internet–freely, commercially, or through other partnership agreements. In this perspective, we differentiate between the mashup platform (the system that integrates remote content) and the remote content itself, usually integrated through some standard protocol or approach like W3C Widgets[1].

The work presented in this paper is partially supported by the European Commission's FP7 programme –project iTEC: Innovative Technologies for an Engaging Classroom (Grant agreement N° 257566). The content of this paper is the sole responsibility of the authors and it does not represent the opinion of the European Commission and the Commission is not responsible for any use that might be made of information contained herein.

[1] http://www.w3.org/TR/2012/REC-widgets-20121127/#widgets-family-of-specifications.

V. Monfort and K.-H. Krempels (Eds.): WEBIST 2014, LNBIP 226, pp. 48–62, 2015.
DOI: 10.1007/978-3-319-27030-2_4

In terms of security, one of the main issues encountered when dealing with complex software web architecture is that the traditional browser security model dictates that content from different origins cannot interact with each other, while content from the same origin can interact without constraint [4]. While solutions exists (like using a proxy server or making use of `script` tags), we have to find a generic way to overcome this limitation and allow content from mixed origins to interact with each other.

A key element to this integration is the proper management of users, i.e. know who is who, and who is allowed to do what: authentication and authorisation. Users may have an account with the mashup platform or with the provider of the remote service or content; moreover, users may want to use credentials they already have with other actors on the Internet (think of the'Sign-In with your *xxx* account' button you find on many websites). Access policies may be defined centrally, while others may be specified on the remote side. This is what we call a loosely-coupled environment: independent components interacting together through identified interfaces, with little to no knowledge about remote components and policies. The challenges we face in this work are the following:

- how do we solve user authentication in such multi-layer loosely-coupled environment?
- how do we ensure proper access to mashup services and remote content, based on a decentralised policy
- how do we propagate authentication and authorisation information through the various layers of the environment?

This research takes place in the framework of the the iTEC project[2], a 4 years EU-funded project focused on the design and evaluation of the future classroom in Europe.

To solve the various issues and to ensure interoperability, we have investigated several open standards and solution, and have selected oAuth and OpenID as building blocks of our solution, in an approach similar to the one presented in [7]. We will discuss this choice further in the paper, as well as give a complete description of the solution we put in place. The rest of the paper is organised as follows: Sect. 2 presents the conclusions of a survey run with teachers to identify use of Learning Management Systems and practices regarding use and re-use of credentials. The results of the survey guided the rest of the work. Section 3 describes the overall project architecture and requirements in terms of user management and access control. Section 4 then presents the solution design and implementation. Section 5 gives some concrete examples. Finally, Sect. 6 provides some conclusions and ideas for future work.

The paper does not include a related work section, because although it relies on solid and proven components and approaches, we could find no publication relating to a similar approach of building a centrally-managed environment for authentication and authorising access to services in a loosely-coupled web environment while accepting external authenticators. This may be linked to the

---

[2] http://itec.eun.org/.

highly decoupled and distributed approach which is inherent of large European research projects.

2   Lessons from the Teachers Survey

A survey was run during the second year of the project (2012) to ask teachers about their current practices regarding the use of Learning Management Systems, the type of credentials they use, their familiarity with third parties that provide authentication services (Google, Facebook, Microsoft Hotmail, Yahoo) as well as their inclination towards re-using credentials among various websites.

We received a total of 269 responses from 17 countries. Distribution across countries is unbalanced, but since the survey is only indicative, this is not considered as a problem.

Results showed that Moodle is the most widely used LMS, but quite a long list of other systems are also in use. The LMS is installed either locally to the school, or shared among different schools, although almost half of the respondents did not really know.

More importantly, responses showed that although a majority of users have local credentials to login to their LMS, a significant number of them use external credentials, which can be provided by an education authority (school, regional or national authority) or by third parties (such as Google, Facebook, etc.)

Finally, the survey showed that the vast majority of teachers (and students) have accounts with one of the major Identity Providers on the Web (Facebook, Google, Yahoo) and that almost 70 % of them are willing to re-use those credentials to access their school services.

However, it is important to note that integration with external Identity Providers is not always an option, due to technical restrictions defined at the school level (site-blocking firewall).

Our conclusion is that if we want to add new services to existing LMS already made available to schools, we shall have to integrate them without adding an extra authentication burden on users. It means that new services will have to extend existing infrastructure and offer the possibility of re-using credentials that users may already possess. However, because some users are concerned that re-using credentials might constitute a security risk, it is important to propose a mixed approach (i.e. use both siloed and re-used credentials).

Complete results of the survey are presented in [2].

3   Project Description and Architecture

The iTEC project (*innovative Technologies for an Engaging Classroom*) is a four-year project funded by the EU; it is focused on the design of the future classroom in Europe. The project, which involves 27 partners among which 15 Ministries of Education from across Europe, brings together teachers, policymakers, pedagogical experts - representatives from each stage of the educational processes - to introduce innovative teaching practices.

The goal of iTEC is to pilot learning and teaching scenarios using integrated technology solutions in over 1,000 classrooms in 15 countries, making it by some margin the largest pan-European validation of ICT in schools yet undertaken. The scope of the project ranges from pedagogical scenario design, customisation to local technical environments, development of required technologies and school piloting. In this paper, we will focus on the technical aspects only.

3.1 Basic Concepts

The idea behind iTEC technical implementation is to pull pedagogical content and tools together into a common interface in a meaningful way, i.e. so that they can support a specific pedagogical scenario. The basic building blocks of the iTEC ecosystem (aka the iTEC Cloud) are the following:

- a *shell* is the host platform (in mashup terminology, this is the Mashup-providing platform) used to integrate the various forms of content and tools; it acts as an empty'nest' for those remote components. It is also the first user-facing component. No particular assumption is made on the shell technology, beyond the fact that it must be able to display widgets [11]. Examples of shell platforms are Learning Management Systems (LMS) like Moodle[3], mobile platform like Android[4] or Interactive Whiteboard software like Open-Sankore[5]
- a *Web application* is an autonomous piece of code that offers a set of a self-contained services. It takes care of its own rendering and embeds all necessary services to serve end-users and fulfill expected functionalities. It may include user management functionalities or rely on third-party for that purpose.
- A *widget* is an elementary piece of application or content (image, video...); it embeds some functionality that is of interest to the users and is displayed through a shell. A widget does not operate on its own, but rather, requires a widget engine or runtime to create and manage widget instances and a shell to be made available to users. Several kinds of widget engines exist, like Yahoo Konfabulator, Apple's Dashboard, Opera Widgets runtime, Apache's Wookie server. A self-contained widget is a widget that embeds all its functionalities, like a calculator widget. A WebService-backed widget is a widget that relies on other components to function. Such component may take the form of backend services reached through a REST webservices interface. This would be the case for a chat widget that stores chat messages on a separate distant datastore. Widgets may offer collaboration services, like chat or videoconferencing, access to pool of resources, geolocation functionalities or administrative functions (user management...)
- A *backend service* is a software component with no user interface, that is accessed by other components through a web service interface. In iTEC, most components are built in such a way that the user interface is implemented by a

---

[3] https://moodle.org.
[4] http://www.android.com.
[5] http://open-sankore.org.

widget while the business logic and data layer are implemented by a backend service, although in some cases, components are developed as a standalone web application, with or without access to a backend service.

iTEC's approach to assemble and deliver content and tools is through the integration of widgets in a shell; the combination of widgets is derived from a pedagogical scenario, with the aim of supporting it by providing the right tools, which may be synchronous or asynchronous collaboration and communication, calculator, simulator, geolocation or content sharing. In addition to widgets, iTEC also uses web applications for some of its services.

3.2 iTEC in Action

Starting from a pedagogical scenario, widgets are assembled in a shell's space, typically a course page in a LMS or a presentation slide in an Interactive Whiteboard notebook, in a way that they can be used by end-users, a teacher and his class for example. To support this type of usecase, iTEC designed a set of components:

- the *widget store* is the main repository for widgets. It stores widget descriptions, allowing for searching, tagging, rating and commenting about widgets. It is similar in its concept to Google's PlayStore or Apple's AppStore. It is built as a widget.
- the *Composer* is used to manage pedagogical scenarios, and assemble widgets that meet the requirements of those scenarios. For instance, a scenario may include synchronous communication, picture sharing and collaborative writing, and this would translate into a chat-, a camera- and a wiki widget. This instantiation takes into account the technical settings of the target environment, i.e. the set of technologies available in a specific school. The Composer is built as a web-application.
- the *People and Event directory* is a database of people and events that may be of interest to pedagogical actors; it can be a subject expert, or a conference or similar event. Those resources are also rated, tagged and commented. This component is built as a web-application with an integrated back-end service, thus supporting the development of widgets.
- the *Scenario Development Environment* is a recommendation engine, that can collects data from the above components, and provides recommendation to the Composer in its scenario instantiating role, by suggesting most appropriate resources to include in the setup. This component is developed as a pure back-end service since it is not meant to support any type of user interaction.

3.3 Authentication and Authorisation Challenges

From the description above, iTEC integrates a wide variety of components: shells, web applications, self-contained widgets, widget-based applications... This integration raises some questions in terms of user management and access control:

– user authentication may take place at the shell level, but also, some integrated services may require some form of authentication or at least be aware of the visiting user's identity. This implies the need for an authentication mechanism that can span the range of components and provide a consistent information about the user
– access control policies may be defined centrally, at the iTEC Cloud level, but these policies have to co-exist and be consistent with those defined at the shell level, or at the integrated services level, if any. Again, this requires an authorisation mechanism that integrates at the various levels of the architecture.

Our goal is thus to design a system that would meet the following requirements:

– allow user authentication at the shell level, and pass the information into sub-components (widgets and back-end services)
– allow access policies to be defined globally to the iTEC Cloud, based on a Role-Based Access Control [5] model, and have those policies propagated to the sub-components
– from the global access rules, provision local policies at the level of iTEC back-end services
– designed solution should support interoperability with major service providers.

4 Proposed Solution

The interoperability requirements led us to focus on open standards and protocols to build authentication and authorisation mechanisms. We performed a thorough study, and identified candidate protocols like SAMLv2[6], OpenID[7] and oAuth[8]. Due to their technological maturity, their relative simplicity, their support for web interactions, the availability of libraries and their wide adoption by main actors on the net, we selected oAuthv2 and OpenIDv2 as the basis for our solution. The fact that users are warned when an application wants to access protected data was also an element of choice.

OpenIDv2 [6] is an open and standard protocol for signing on to websites using one single set of credentials. The protocol has been developed for many years and adopted by major players on the Internet, like Google. It relies on the assumption that users have an identity defined with an Identity Provider (IdP), and want to use that identity to access various services offered by Service Providers (SP). The typical flow is a user visiting a Service Provider that requires authentication; SP prompts the user for her identity or that of her IdP. The user is then redirected to the IdP to authenticate, and if authentication succeeds, the user is sent back to the SP with the proof that successful authentication did take place. Optionally, the IdP may provide additional information about the user (this requires some protocol extensions).

---

[6] http://saml.xml.org/.
[7] http://openid.net/.
[8] http://oauth.net/2/.

oAuthv2 [8] is a protocol for managing delegation of authorisation. Its main use case is a user (the *resource owner*) needing to give access to some of its resources hosted on a server (the *resource server*) to a *client*, typically another service. To avoid forcing the user to give her credentials to the client, oAuthv2 introduces a workflow where when the user is asked by the client to give access to a resource, she is sent back to an *authorisation server* where she authenticates and is then asked to grant or deny access. Upon success, the authorisation server issues an *access token* to the client that it will use to access the resource on behalf of the user. In this way, the user's credentials are never disclosed to the client. This is the protocol that Facebook or Yahoo use for granting access to their services to remote sites, after getting the agreement of the user. oAuthv2 supports various types of 'grants', to support different profiles of this protocol and accommodate different situations:

Authorisation Code Grant. This is the most secure scenario, in which the client directs the resource owner to the authorisation server for authentication and access request; upon success, the authorisation server issues an *authorisation code* to the client, that the client then exchanges with the authorisation server for an *access token*, that is finally presented by the client to the resource server to get access to the resource. All interactions with the resource owner go through her user-agent (typically her browser). This scenario supports client authentication by the authorisation server before issuing an access token, and ensures that the access token never reaches the resource owner's user-agent, which could lead to token leakage.

Implicit Grant. This is a simplified version of the previous scenario, in which instead of being issued an authentication code by the authorisation server, the client directly receives an access token. This scenario is targeted at clients implemented in a browser, typically in javascript. In this case, the authorisation server does not authenticate the client, and the access token is exposed to the resource owner or other applications with access to its user-agent.

Resource Owner Password Credentials Grant. This scenario is built on the assumption that there exists a high degree of trust between the resource owner and the client. The resource owner provides the client with her credentials, and the client uses them to request an access token from the authorisation server. This scenario supports client authentication.

Client Credentials Grant. In this scenario, the client is acting on its own behalf, not on behalf of the user. The client authenticates directly to the authorisation server and receives an access token.

It is worthwhile noting that oAuthv2 also supports extension grants that allow to extend the token request mechanism to support different types of credentials, like SAML assertions.

Because we chose to use oAuthv2 to secure widget access to back-end services, and because widgets usually involve client-side computing and get access to the user's environment, the implicit grant is the only option of choice. However, we also successfully implemented the client credentials grant to secure access to the SDE backend service. One of the drawbacks of the implicit grant is the absence of client authentication, but this can be explained by the nature of widgets, which are running client-side, making available any sensitive information to other components running in the user's environment (user-agent). It would thus not be possible to securely store client credentials at the widget level.

To integrate those protocols into the iTEC environment, we designed the UMAC (User Management and Access Control) framework, which comprises the following components:

- the *UMAC server* is responsible for user authentication, issuance of tokens, and management of user data and privileges; it plays the role of the OpenID's Identity Provider, the oAuth's authorisation server, and implements a back-end service to access, store and manage user data and privilege information.
- the *UMAC filter* is an authorisation guard that sits in front of back-end services; the back-end service represents the oAuth's Resource Server, and the UMAC filter is in charge of validating access tokens.
- the *UMAC widgets* are a collection of widgets that allow to access and manage authentication and authorisation information in the iTEC Cloud. Those widgets allow to register a new user, to update a user's details, to create sets of users, and to assign iTEC roles.
- the *UMAC library* is a JavaScript library of tools to help the widget developer to easily integrate with the UMAC framework and not care about the various protocols' implementation.

4.1   UMAC Server

The UMAC Server serves two main purposes: authenticating users and controlling access to back-end services.

To authenticate users, UMAC Server implements the OpenID Provider specification. It handles authentication requests from iTEC relying parties, typically shells or web applications, authenticates users, and responds to relying parties; UMAC Server supports SREGv1.0 and AXv1.0 OpenID extensions to provide basic information of logged in user (username, first and last names, email address, language, timezone, country). Authentication is checked against a local database of users.

One of the requirements drawn from the survey described in Sect. 2 mandates that iTEC should allow users to login using third-party credentials, namely Google, Facebook or Yahoo. Thus the UMAC Server supports user authentication using any of those systems, by implementing an OpenID Relying Party (in the case of Google and Yahoo) and an oAuth client (in the case of Facebook).

Access control to iTEC services is handled by UMAC Server. Access requests may come from widgets or web applications, in which case the oAuthv2 scenario implemented is the implicit grant, but requests may also come from standalone applications, which are run in a more controlled environment, and for which the selected scenario is the client credentials grant. Thus UMAC Server implements the related sections of the oAuthv2 specification, and handles Authorisation Requests (for the implicit grant) and Access Token Requests (for the client credentials grant), issuing access tokens to widgets and controlled applications respectively. A token is a random string concatenated with a timestamp.

In addition to the authentication and authorisation functionalities, UMAC server is also used to store user information; this information is made accessible through a REST API, which is protected by the oAuthv2 protocol, just like any other iTEC back-end service. Basic CRUD functionalities are implemented to add, update, delete or get information about a user account. This API is accessed typically by the UMAC widgets.

Finally, UMAC server is used to manage user privileges; those privileges span all iTEC services, i.e. apply equally to shells, widgets or back-end services. Six levels of privileges are defined in a strictly hierarchical way: super-user, administrator, coordinator, teacher, student and guest. The level of privilege of a user is passed to the OpenID relying party upon authentication through SREG or AX extensions, where available, and they are checked by the token validation process between the UMAC filter and the UMAC server.

For a seamless user experience, UMAC authentication is propagated to the shell through a plugin mechanism which is dependent on the shell itself. In this way, once the user is authenticated, all shell components (typically widgets) can reuse the user information.

4.2   UMAC Filter

The UMAC filter is designed to be put in front of back-end services, and inter-acts with the UMAC server following the oAuthv2 protocol to control access to the services by ensuring that only authorised requests get served. The current implementation of the filter takes the form of a servlet filter, which makes it very easy to integrate and (de)activate and realises a separation of concerns by allowing the service developer to work independently from the access control mechanism.

In the oAuthv2 terminology, the UMAC filter acts as the protection part of the resource server. It receives requests for access in the form of REST calls (basically http requests), and for each requests, it checks that an access token is provided. If no token is present, an error is returned, and it is up to the client to obtain one. If a token is present, its validity is checked by querying the UMAC server through a secure channel, and upon success, the lifetime of the token and the userid of the token owner are returned to the filter. Based on this information, the filter then checks the local access policy that defines the rules for accessing the service. These rules are expressed using the Apache Shiro[9] system. If the rules are evaluated positively, access is granted and the request is passed to the service. Otherwise, an error is returned. For efficiency reasons, the UMAC filter caches the validated tokens for a period of time to avoid unnecessary roundtrips with the UMAC server.

---

[9] http://shiro.apache.org/.

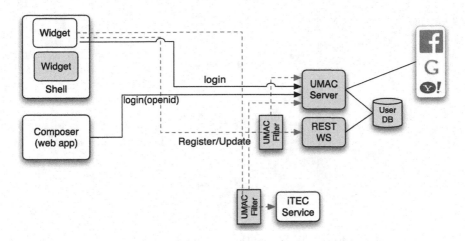

Fig. 1. UMAC components.

4.3 UMAC Library

The UMAC library is a Javascript library of functions that aims at facilitating the development of widgets and their integration with UMAC authentication service, more precisely, the oAuth authentication endpoint's service. It hides the complexity of the protocol by providing methods to manage the whole authentication process (request for token, redirect to authentication form, token transfer to requesting component and error handling).

Figure 1 presents the UMAC components (in gray) as well as the interactions with other iTEC systems. UMAC Server is used for authentication (solid lines) either from shell, widgets or web applications like the composer. This follows the OpenID protocol. Authentication may be local (using the User DB) or rely on third-party authenticators (right-most box). Regarding authorisation (dashed lines), UMAC widgets allow to register or update user information through the UMAC REST Web Service, which is protected by the UMAC filter. Similarly, any other iTEC component may access iTEC back-end services which are protected by the UMAC filter (see bottom of the diagram).

5 Example Scenarios

In this section, we provide concrete examples of the system described above.

5.1 Authenticating a User

This is the very first step to do to consume a protected service or piece of content. A user makes an authentication request directly from a widget, from a shell or from a relying web application by clicking on an URL or a button. This causes redirection to the UMAC Authentication Window (see Fig. 2), where the user

Fig. 2. UMAC authentication window.

must provide her credentials to UMAC Server or use her external authentication sources such as Yahoo, Google, Facebook to proof his identity. Upon successful authentication, an authentication response (in case of OpenID flow) or an access token (in case of oAuth flow) is generated by UMAC Server and sent back to the Relying Party or the Client respectively.

It is to be noted that even though the authentication action is triggered at the widget level, authentication information is pushed up to the container level (i.e. the Mashup Providing Platform).

5.2 User Authorisation

For fine grain and flexible authorisation, UMAC relies on both a permission-based approach and on a role-based system, in which permissions are assigned to roles rather than being assigned directly to users. Roles are then assigned to users who inherit all permissions linked to the role. At the moment, role structure is flat, i.e. we do not support hierarchical roles.

A permission is basically a tuple that expresses what action can be executed by a service on a specific data scope. Our model follows a Discretionary Access Control approach [9] where each piece of data is owned by exactly one user. Permissions are defined according to the specifications below (expressed in Augmented Backus-Naur Form [3]):

```
permission = action":"service-name *(":"data-scope)
action = (atomic-action *(","atomic-action)) /"*"
atomic-action ="create"/"read"/"update"/"delete"
service-name = 1*(DIGIT / ALPHA /"-"/"\_")
data-scope = 1*(DIGIT / ALPHA) / special-data-scope / (data-
    scope *(","data-scope))
special-data-scope ="me"/"mine"/"*"
```

The special-data-scope element can take one of three special values:

- "*me*": this data-scope represents the user currently logged in, i.e. the user who issued the access request; this is typically used for the user management to allow a user to update his own data, but others'
- "*mine*": this data-scope includes all data that is owned by the user currently logged in;
- "***": this data-scope includes all data; it does not need to be specified, e.g.: the permission `action:service-name:*` has exactly the same meaning with `action:service-name`.

The next paragraphs provide some concrete examples of expressing UMAC permissions.

The rule "any user can read and update his information and unregister his account" can be decomposed as follows:

- The actions are "*update*", "*read*" (for update and read information) and "*delete*" (for unregistering account).
- The service in used is "*users*".
- The id of the target is the identifier of the requesting user himself, which can be the real id of user as recorded in UMAC, or the special id "*me*".

The rule would then translate to: `update, read, delete:users:me`.

In UMAC this is the default permission assigned to all registered users.

Role-based rules follow a similar approach: for instance, the rule "UMAC admin Role can read and update any user information as well as grant and revoke iTEC Coordinator of Belgium role to a user" includes two different sets of permissions:

- read and update information of any user, which translates to
  `update, read:users:*` or more briefly `update, read:users`
- grant and revoke belgian coordinator role:, which translates to
  `read, delete:roles:coordinator:be` (the last `be` data scope represent the belgian record)

Permission to role assignments are stored in the UMAC server database, and are managed through the UMAC widgets; this operation can performed at run-time, which means that the role can be defined dynamically. Moreover, all modification of permission/role assignments takes effect immediately for all users to whom the role is assigned.

5.3   Securing a Webservice

As stated in Sect. 4.2, backend services are protected by the UMAC filter. Implementation of the filter takes the form of a servlet filter because most iTEC technologies use the Java language and because it is easy to integrate as a proxy in a non-Java environment. As a consequence, the protected web service provider only needs to include the declaration of the UMAC filter in the servlet mapping section of the web.xml configuration file.

In iTEC, the UMAC filter is currently deployed at the People and Event Directory (P&E Directory)[10]. With this deployment, P&E Directory developers only focus on their functional development, all authorisation rules being activated by a simple declaration in its configuration file. Authorisation rules of the filter can be defined dynamically, as shown in Sect. 5.4.

The UMAC filter is also used to protect the UMAC Backend Service (REST WS box on Fig. 1).

5.4   Central Policy Management

Permissions, roles, role-permissions assignment and user-role assignments are managed by the UMAC Server; they can be updated through the UMAC widgets or any other component that access the UMAC REST WS, provided the appropriate level of privilege is granted.

UMAC supports the `super-admin` role, a static built-in role which is assigned to the UMAC system administrator once it is installed. Since the authentication and authorisation engine is based on Apache Shiro framework [10], most of authentication authorisation information are defined in a "shiro.ini" file, including: built-in super admin accounts, default permissions granted to all authenticated user, mapping table between service names and REST service contexts which require authorisation and information for initialising authentication realms (local realm to login locally to UMAC, OpenID realm to login remotely with Yahoo, Google...).

The UMAC filter (Sect. 4.2) has a similar implementation except that there is no authentication database since it relies entirely on the authentication service of UMAC server. It only maintains an authorisation database which can also be configured through REST services. The UMAC filter administrator is defined in "shiro.ini" at filter side; it has similar function to `super-user` at UMAC server but is completely independent. This design helps the filter benefit from authentication service of UMAC server while keeping a totally independent authorisation lattice under the control of the filter administrator.

The UMAC authorisation widgets are developed to manipulate all information related to authorisation in the iTEC Cloud. The widgets also allow an authorised user to register a backend service provider and assign authorisation rules to that service provider, thus providing a central place to manage all authorisation at the iTEC components level. This allows for a more consistent and secure approach.

5.5   Implementing Widgets and Services

Integrating a new service into UMAC is a very simple process that consists of instantiating the UMAC filter in front of the new service. As stated above,

---

[10] http://itec.eun.org/web/guest/people-and-events.

the filter takes the form of a Java servlet, that intercepts all service requests, authenticates them and checks authorisation together with the central policy. A mapping between the centrally-managed iTEC roles and the service-specific roles is defined and translated into the Shire rules.

Widgets access services through the XMLHttpRequest API that allows to connect to remote sites and services. To make the integration with UMAC as easy as possible for widget developer, calls to services are wrapped through calls of the UMAC library that hide the logic of the underlying protocols. From the widget perspective, invoking a service is simply a matter of issuing a request to the service. Authentication and token issuance is handled under the control of the library.

6   Conclusions and Future Work

In this paper, we described a model and its implementation that supports centralised authentication and authorisation in a loosely-coupled multi-layered web application in the eLearning area. The model is open to third-party authenticators, following the conclusion of a survey run among potential users of the platform. Although the individual components of the approach themselves are not particularly innovative, yet state-of-the-art, we advocate that the integration approach we propose, that takes into account requirements and behaviours of end-users, and the complexity of the environment to which it applies constitute the core of the research. It could easily be transposed to other similar environments.

The whole iTEC ecosystem has been used through various cycles of piloting, involving over 2,000 classrooms across 19 European countries, and the UMAC component, although almost invisible to the vast majority of users, did work properly, securing the services from 4 main providers access through a wide variety of widgets.

In the future, we intend to work on a stronger and easier integration between shells and UMAC components, which would allow further customisation of the shell based on information received from the UMAC system. We will explore the IMS Learning Tools Interoperability specifications [11][11] as it seems to be a potential candidate for supporting tools integration.

A scope should be added to tokens, to reduce the granularity of authorisation rules and limit the potential impact of token interception, and client authentication should be added to the protocol to ensure that only authenticated clients can obtain access tokens from UMAC server.

References

1. Aghaee, S., Pautasso, C.: An evaluation of mashup tools based on support for heterogeneous mashup components. In: Harth, A., Koch, N. (eds.) ICWE 2011. LNCS, vol. 7059, pp. 1–12. Springer, Heidelberg (2012)

---

[11] http://www.imsglobal.org/toolsinteroperability2.cfm.

2. Colin, J.-N., Simon, B.: D7.2: Second generation of iTEC shells and composer. iTEC Project deliverable 7.2. University of Namur (2012)
3. Crocker, D. (ed.): Augmented BNF for Syntax Specifications: ABNF. RFC 5234 (2008). http://tools.ietf.org/html/rfc5234
4. De Keukelaere, F., Bhola, S., Steiner, M., Chari, S., and Yoshihama, S.: Smash: secure component model for cross-domain mashups on unmodified browsers. In: Proceedings of the 17th international conference on World Wide Web, pp. 535–544. ACM Press, New York (2008)
5. Ferraiolo, D.F., Sandhu, R., Gavrila, S., Kuhn, D.R., Chandramouli, R.: Proposed NIST standard for role-based access control. ACM Trans. Inf. Syst. Secur. **4**(3), 224–274 (2001)
6. OpenID Foundation: Openid authentication 2.0 (2007). http://openid.net/developers/specs/
7. Govaerts, S., et al.: Towards responsive open learning environments: the ROLE interoperability framework. In: Kloos, C.D., Gillet, D., García, R.M.C., Wild, F., Wolpers, M. (eds.) Towards Ubiquitous Learning. LNCS, vol. 6964, pp. 125–138. Springer, Heidelberg (2011)
8. Hardt, D. (ed.): The OAuth 2.0 Authorization Framework. RFC 6749 (2012). http://tools.ietf.org/html/rfc6749
9. Saltzer, J., Schroeder, M.: The protection of information in computer systems. Proc. IEEE **63**(9), 1278–1308 (1975)
10. Apache Shiro reference documentation (2013). http://shiro.apache.org/reference.html
11. Wilson, S., Sharples, P., Griffiths, D., Popat, K.: Augmenting the VLE using widget technologies. Int. J. Technol. Enhanc. Learn. **3**(1), 4–20 (2011)
12. Zibuschka, J., Herbert, M., Roßnage, H.: Towards privacy-enhancing identity management in mashup-providing platforms. In: Foresti, S., Jajodia, S. (eds.) Data and Applications Security and Privacy XXIV. LNCS, vol. 6166, pp. 273–286. Springer, Heidelberg (2010)

Permutation Based XML Compression

Tomasz Müldner[1]($\boxtimes$), Jan Krzysztof Miziołek[2], and Tyler Corbin[1]

[1] Jodrey School of Computer Science, Acadia University,
Wolfville, NS B4P 2A9, Canada
{tomasz.muldner,094568c}@acadiau.ca
[2] IBI AL, University of Warsaw, Warsaw, Poland
jkm@ibi.uw.edu.pl

Abstract. An XML document D often has a *regular* structure, i.e., it is composed of many similarly named and structured subtrees. Therefore, the entropy of a trees structuredness should be relatively low and thus the trees should be highly compressible by transforming them to an intermediate form. In general, this idea is used in permutation based XML-conscious compressors. An example of such a compressor is called XSAQCT, where the compressible form is called an *annotated tree*. While XSAQCT proved to be useful for various applications, it was never shown that it is a lossless compressor. This paper provides the formal background for the definition of an annotated tree, and a formal proof that the compression is lossless. It also shows properties of annotated trees that are useful for various applications, and discusses a measure of compressibility using this approach, followed by the experimental results showing compressibility of annotated trees.

Keywords: XML · Annotated trees · Permutation-based XML compression

1 Introduction

The eXtensible Markup Language, XML [1], is one of the most popular data formats for the storage of semi-structured data. Since XML documents are hierarchal and acyclic in nature, there have been numerous attempts to apply techniques used for general tree compression to XML, see e.g., [2–4]. A specific subset of tree-compressors designed specifically for XML (or semi-structured data in general) are called XML-conscious compressors, e.g., XQueC [5], which use the XML structure for increased efficiency. *Permutation-based* XML-conscious compressors separate the structure of an XML document (e.g., the markups and parent-child-sibling orderings) and its contents (e.g., the actual character data) during a pre-order parsing of the input. An intermediate representation of the structure is created, defining a partitioning strategy used to group the contents into a series of independent data containers, which are subsequently compressed using a general-purpose compressor (a *back-end compressor*) such as GZIP [6] or BZIP2 [7]. For example, XSAQCT [8] is a permuting, single-pass compressor.

© Springer International Publishing Switzerland 2015
V. Monfort and K.-H. Krempels (Eds.): WEBIST 2014, LNBIP 226, pp. 63–78, 2015.
DOI: 10.1007/978-3-319-27030-2_5

The compression process starts with a SAX-based parsing of the input to create a compressed intermediate representation of the XML structure, called an *annotated tree*. This tree defines how the contents are stored into data containers.

Since the annotated tree can represent the XML structure is only a fraction of space (see Fig. 12 in Sect. 4.2), the annotated tree in XSAQCT can be considered to be a light weight *index* of the XML. In addition, XSAQCT has also shown to be useful for various applications of XML, e.g., archiving XML, querying and modifying the compressed XML (and its contents), and database representations. However, no formal definition of this annotated mapping *was ever provided* nor was the proof that the mapping can be reversed. These questions are very important because without answering them, the compression process used by XSAQCT is not known to be *lossless*. This paper, based on [9], fills in these gaps. It provides a formal definition of an annotated tree and the injective mapping τ from a labelled tree to the annotated tree, as well as the discussion of the compressibility measure of using annotated trees and related experimental results. The paper provides a new characterization of annotated trees (not given in [9]) useful for algorithms that create specialized annotated trees, in which specific text values in data containers need to be analyzed; e.g., for encrypting of compressed documents. Because of space limitations, here we omit proofs of theorems and algorithms to create an annotated tree (see [9]).

Contributions. There are several novel contributions of this paper: (1) The theoretical part, i.e., the formal background for the definition of an annotated tree and a proof that the mapping from a tree to the annotated tree is injective, and therefore, the annotated tree for the labelled tree D provides a faithful representation of D; (2) An application of the annotated tree methodology with respect to XML, i.e., a formal proof that XSAQCT's compression process is lossless; (3) A compressibility measure defining the cost of using annotated trees and results of testing using an especially designed XML suite, showing high compressibility.

Organization. This paper is organized as follows. Section 2 introduces the formal background for this paper, including a definition of a tree and an annotated tree. Section 3 provides a description of trees with text elements. Section 4 provides results of testing, and finally Sect. 5 provides conclusions and describes future work.

2   Annotated Trees

2.1   Labeled Trees

Definition 1. *Let Σ be an alphabet, called the label alphabet. A **labeled tree** is an ordered tree with nodes labeled by strings from Σ^* and having arbitrary degrees (i.e., number of children).*

In what follows, by a *tree* we mean a labeled tree, and by **Trees** we denote the set of all trees. We use the letter D to denote a tree, with nodes denoted by lowercase letters x, y, u, v (with indices when needed) and by $x(a)$ we denote a node x

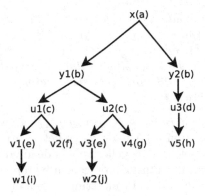

Fig. 1. Example of a tree D.

labeled with a. Let **Label**($\mathbf{x}$) denote the label of the node x, **Height**($\mathbf{D}$) denote the height of D, **Nodes**($\mathbf{D}$) denote the set of all nodes of D, and $\mathbf{D_i}$ be the tree consisting of all nodes and edges in D at levels $1, \ldots, i, where \ 1 \leq i \leq height(D)$. Example of a tree is shown in Fig. 1.

Definition 2. *A **path** in a tree is defined to be of the form* $/x_1/x_2, \ldots, /x_k$, *where x_1 is the root of D and for $1 \leq i < k, x_{i+1}$ is a child of x_i.*

We use a lower-case letter p (with indices when needed) to denote a path and **Paths**($\mathbf{D}$) to denote the set of all paths in D. For the path $p = /x_1/x_2, \ldots, /x_k$, let **Length**($\mathbf{p}$) be the number of nodes in the path p, **Last**($\mathbf{p}$) be the last element x_k, **Label**($\mathbf{p}$) $= Label(x_k)$ be the label of p, and for $Length(p) > 1$, let $\mathbf{p}{\downarrow}$ be the path p except the last element.

Definition 3. *Two paths in the tree D, $/x_1/x_2 \ldots /x_k$ and $/y_1/y_2 \ldots /y_n$ are called **similar** if $k = n$, $x_1 = y_1$ is the root of D and for $1 \leq i \leq k$, $Label(x_i) = Label(y_i)$.*

The similarity relation is an equivalence relation and we denote by $[\![\mathbf{p}]\!]$ the equivalence class of p, by **Similar**($\mathbf{D}$) the quotient set of this relation, i.e., the set of all different sets of similar paths. For $p \in Paths(D)$ let **Length**($[\![\mathbf{p}]\!]$) $= Length(p)$ be the length of the equivalence class, **Label**($[\![\mathbf{p}]\!]$) $= Label(p)$ be the label of the class (it is easy to see that both definitions of the length and the label of an equivalence class are well defined, i.e., independent of the choice of the path p from the equivalence class). Finally, for $q \in Similar(D)$ let $|\mathbf{q}|$ be the number of paths in q, and **Last**($\mathbf{q}$) be the sequence of nodes that are last elements of all paths in this class, *ordered* from left to right. Clearly, $|Last(q)| = |q|$.

In Fig. 1, $Similar(D) = \{[\![/x]\!],\ [\![/x/y_1]\!],\ [\![/x/y_1/u_1]\!],\ [\![/x/y_1/u_3]\!],\ [\![/x/y_1/u_3/v_5]\!],\ [\![/x/y_1/u_1/v_1]\!],\ [\![/x/y_1/u_1/v_2]\!],\ [\![/x/y_1/u_2/v_4]\!],\ [\![/x/y_1/u_1/v_1/w_1]\!], [\![/x/y_1/u_1/v_3/w_2]\!]\}$ and for $p = /x/y_1$, $[\![p]\!] = \{/x/y_1, /x/y_2\}$; $Length([\![p]\!]) = 2$, $Label(p) = b$, $Last([\![p]\!]) = <y_1, y_2>$, and $|[\![p]\!]| = 2$.

Definition 4. *A partial relation $\prec$ in the set $Similar(D)$ is defined as follows: $[\![p_1]\!] \prec [\![p_2]\!]$ iff $Length([\![p_1]\!]) = Length[\![p_2]\!]) > 1, [\![p_1\!\downarrow]\!] = [\![p_2\!\downarrow]\!], Label([\![p_1]\!])$ is different from $Label([\![p_2]\!])$, and there exist paths $p1 \in [\![p_1]\!]$ and $p2 \in [\![p_2]\!]$ such that the node $Last(p1)$ is the left sibling of the node $Last(p2)$. The tree D has a* **cycle** *if there exist $q_1, q_2 \in Similar(D)$ such that $q_1 \prec q_2$ and $q_2 \prec q_1$. D is* **acyclic** *if it does not have a cycle.*

For D in Fig. 1, $[\![/x/y_1/u_1/v_1]\!] \prec [\![/x/y_1/u_1/v_2]\!]$, while $[\![/x/y_1/u_1]\!]$ and $[\![/x/y_1/u_3]\!]$ are not in relation $\prec$. A node $u_0(e)$ between nodes u_1 and u_2 would create a cycle in D. The set of all acyclic trees is denoted by **Acyclic**.

When it does not lead to confusion, a tree can be represented using a *simplified notation* (used, e.g., for XML), by omitting node names, e.g., replacing $y_1(b)$ by b_1. In this notation, an equivalence class $[\![p]\!]$ will be denoted using the label $Label([\![p]\!])$, in upper case, e.g., for D from Fig. 1, using E for $[\![/x/y_1/u_1/v_1]\!]$.

Since we will show that the mapping from the set of trees to the set of g-trees is injective, we need to define the concept of "identical" or isomorphic trees, which differ only in names of the corresponding nodes. We use a similar concept for annotated trees and g-trees:

Two trees D_1 and D_2 are **isomorphic** iff they have the same height h and for each level $i, 1 \le i \le h$, the sequence of all nodes $<n_1, \ldots, n_j>$ (in left-to-right order) in D_1 at level i and the sequence of all nodes $<m_1, \ldots, m_k>$ (in left-to-right order) in D_2 at level $i, k = j$, and for $1 \le r \le k$, nodes n_r and m_r have the same degree and label.

2.2 Annotated Trees and g-Trees

A tree D can permuted to create an annotated tree with nodes represented by equivalence classes of the similarity relation. In the worst case, if for each $q \in Similar(D)$, $|q| = 1$ then the size of D would be the same as the size of the corresponding annotated tree. However, typically XML documents are regular, i.e., for majority of paths $q \in Similar(D)$, $|q| \gg 1$ and the annotated tree provides a compressed representation of D. For a single tree D, there may be *more than one annotated tree* such that *each such annotated tree can be mapped back* to D. To formalize this idea, in this section we define annotated trees and annotated g-trees. Then we define two mappings, an injective mapping from the set of trees to the set of annotated g-trees and an injective mapping from the set of annotated g-trees to set of subsets of annotated trees. Finally, we define annotated text trees and a mapping from text trees to the annotated text trees, considering only acyclic trees. By a *dag* we mean an acyclic digraph.

Definition 5. *An* **annotated tree** *is an ordered tree with nodes additionally labeled by annotations (sequences of non-negative integers). An* **annotated g-tree** *is an unordered tree A (i.e., children are not ordered) such that (1) nodes of A are dags; (2) each dag $G \in Nodes(A)$ except the root has its nodes annotated; and (3) for every node $H \in Nodes(A)$ and for every child G of H there exists exactly one node $n \in Nodes(H)$, called the* **source of G**, *and different children of H have different sources.*

Nodes in the annotated tree are denoted by upper-case letters (with indices where appropriate), e.g., $\mathbf{X(n)}[\alpha_1, \ldots, \alpha_{\mathbf{j}}]$ denotes a node X labeled with the label n and annotation $[\alpha_1, \ldots, \alpha_j]$ or in a simplified notation it is denoted as the node $N[\alpha_1, \ldots, \alpha_j]$.

The idea behind using an annotated tree to represent a document is that non-zero annotations of the node X represent consecutive occurrences of X. For the node $X[2, 0, 4, 0, 3]$ and its child $Y[1, 2, 0, 1, 0, 2, 0, 0, 1]$ there are nine such occurrences. For a child Y of X, annotations represent occurrences of $Y's$ as children of respective $X's$. Specifically, for the first two occurrences of X, i.e., the annotation 2, the first two annotations in Y represent occurrences of $Y's$ as children of these two $X's$, here the second X has two children Y, while the first X has only one such child. Similarly, the third, fourth, fifth and sixth occurrences of X are represented by the annotation 4, and they have four occurrences of $Y's$ as children of these $X's$, i.e., the fourth X has one child Y, the third and fifth X have no children Y, and the sixth X has two children Y.

For $k, 1 \leq k \leq j$, let $\mathbf{S_X(j)} = \sum_{k=1}^{j} \alpha_k$ be the sum of the first k annotations of the node $X[\alpha_1, \ldots, \alpha_j]$, $S_X(0) = 0$, and $\mathbf{S_X}$ be the sum of *all* annotation of X. By **Annotated** we denote the set of all annotated trees. Two examples of annotated trees (using a simplified notation) are shown in Figs. 2 and 3. As we will explain it later, both these trees represent the same tree D from Fig. 1.

An example of an annotated g-tree is given in Fig. 4 (the source of a node is shown using a dashed arrow). By **Annotated−G** we denote the set of all annotated g-trees and by a *chain* we mean a rooted dag such that each node except the root has the in-degree one and each node except one designated node called the sink has the out-degree one; the sink has the out-degree zero. The reason for defining g-trees is that a dag G, which is a chain, will have its nodes representing children of the source (in left-to-right order) of G. If a dag G is not a chain then G needs to be topologically sorted for our usage. For example, in Fig. 4 the topological sorting of the dag containing nodes E, F and G may produce the chain E, F, G and these three nodes can be made children of the source of this graph, i.e., the node C.

This section uses the following two standard definitions: A *subsequence* of a sequence $s = s_1, \ldots, s_m$ consists of arbitrary elements of s, and for $i, j, 1 \leq i \leq j \leq n$, a *substring* $<i, j>$ of s is a subsequence of s consisting of consecutive elements of s starting at position i and ending at position j. By $|s|$ we denote a length of the sequence s.

Now, we describe properties of an annotated tree. Consider a node $X[\alpha_1, \ldots, \alpha_n]$ and its child $Y[\beta_1, \ldots, \beta_m]$. For $\alpha_j \neq 0$ let $I(j)$ be a substring of the sequence $1, \ldots m$, called an *item* and defined as follows: $I(j) = <S_X(j-1) + 1, S_X(j)>$. Thus, if $\alpha_1 \neq 0$ then $I(1) = <1, \alpha_1>$.

Every node in an annotated tree has to satisfy the following conditions:

1. The root must have an annotation [1]
2. For any node $X[\alpha_1, \ldots, \alpha_n]$ there exists $j, 1 \leq j \leq n$ s.t. $\alpha_j \neq 0$
3. If $\alpha_{i_1}, \ldots, \alpha_{i_r}$ is a subsequence consisting of all non-zero annotations in the node $X[\alpha_1, \ldots, \alpha_n]$ and the node $Y[\beta_1, \ldots, \beta_m]$ is a child of X then items

$I(i_1), \ldots, I(i_r)$ form a disjoint partition of the sequence $1, \ldots, m$, consisting of $|I(i_1)|$ integers, followed by $|I(i_2)|$ integers,..., followed by $|I(i_r)|$ integers. Thus, the sequence $\beta_1, \ldots, \beta_m$, which annotates the child of the node X is split into a sequence of substrings $<1, I(i_1)>, <I(i_2) + 1, I(i_3)> \ldots <I(i_{r-1}) + 1, I(i_r)>$, which is the same as the sequence of substrings $<1, S_X(i_1)>,$ $<S_X(i_2) + 1, S_X(i_3)> \ldots <S_X(i_{r-1}) + 1, S_X(i_r)>$, see Fig. 5.

Corollary

1. For $\alpha_j \neq 0$, $|I(j)| = S_X(j) - (S_X(j-1) + 1) + 1 = \alpha_j$, i.e., each item $I(j)$ has α_j elements.
2. For the node $X[\alpha_1, \ldots, \alpha_n]$ and its child $Y[\beta_1, \ldots, \beta_m]$ we have:
   $m = \sum_{j=1, \alpha_j \neq 0}^{n} |I(j)| = \sum_{j=1, \alpha_j \neq 0}^{n} \alpha_j = \sum_{j=1}^{n} \alpha_j = S_X(n)$, i.e., the sum of all annotations of X is equal to the number of annotations of Y.

For example, for the node $X[2, 0, 4, 0, 3]$ and its child $Y[\underline{1, 2}, 0, \underline{1}, 0, \underline{2}, 0, 0, \underline{1}]$ (with items underlined), we have: $I(1) = <1, 2>$, $I(3) = <3, 6>$ and $I(5) = <7, 8>$, see Fig. 6.

2.3 Mapping Trees to Sets of Annotated Trees

We define the mapping $\tau : Acyclic \rightarrow Annotated-G$ in two steps; first for nodes and the tree structure, and then for annotations of nodes. Nodes in all dags are represented by equivalence classes of the similarity relation and written as $[\![p]\!](Label(p))[\alpha_1, \ldots, \alpha_j]$ or using a simplified notation $Label(p)[\alpha_1, \ldots, \alpha_j]$. If x is a node in D, which is not a root, then by $\mathbf{p_x}$ we denote a (unique) path $p \in Paths(D)$ which ends in x.

Definition 6. *Definition of mapping* $\tau : Acyclic \rightarrow Annotated-G$. *Let* $D \in Acyclic$.

– *Mapping labeled nodes and the tree structure*

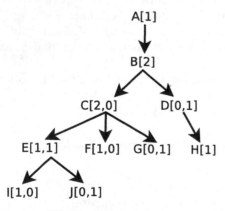

Fig. 2. Annotated tree.

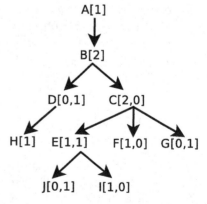

Fig. 3. Another annotated tree.

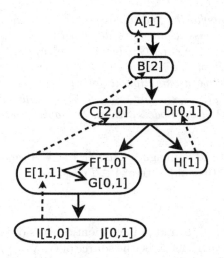

Fig. 4. Example of a g-tree.

1. *The root r of D is mapped to the root of $\tau(D)$ defined as a graph consisting of a single node $[\![/r]\!](Label(r))$.*
2. *For any level $i > 1$ of D and equivalence class $q \in Similar(D)$ of length $i-1$ let $N_{q,i}$ denote the set of nodes x in D at level i such that $[\![p_x\!\downarrow]\!] \in q$. Clearly, the sets $\{N_{q,i} : q \in Similar(D)\}$ form a disjoint coverage of the set of all nodes in D at level i. Each set $N_{q,i}$ is mapped by τ to the single graph $G \in Nodes(\tau(D))$ at the level i; $G = \{[\![p_x]\!](Label(p_x)\}$ where the source of G is the node q. For any graph $G \in Nodes(\tau(D))$ and two nodes $q_1, q_2 \in G$, there is an edge $q_1 \Longrightarrow q_2$ in G iff $q_1 \prec q_2$, (see Definition 4). Since D is assumed to have no cycles, G is acyclic. The node $H \in Nodes(\tau(D))$ is the parent of the node G if the source of G belongs to the dag $Nodes(H)$. From the definition of sets $\tau(N_{q,i})$, H is the unique parent of G.*
- *Annotations are defined by induction on the height of $\tau(D)$*
   1. *The annotation of the root is [1]*
   2. *Assume that annotations are defined up to the level i, $1 \leq i < Height(D)$ and for any equivalence class q of length i, $|Last(q)| = S_q$, i.e., the sum*

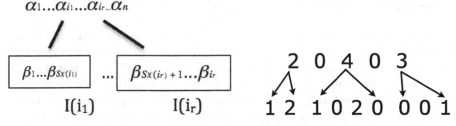

Fig. 5. Items for non-zero annotations.   **Fig. 6.** Example of items.

of all annotations for the node q is equal to the number of last elements in all paths in this class. Consider a dag G at the level $i+1$ with the source X, and a node $Y \in Nodes(G)$. Let $Y = [\![p]\!](r)[\alpha_1, \ldots, \alpha_j], X = [\![p\downarrow]\!](m)$ and $k = S_X$. First, we set the number j of annotations in Y to be k. From the inductive assumption it follows that the sequence $Last([\![p\downarrow]\!])$ has k elements $s_1, \ldots, s_k$. For $1 \le j \le k$, we define α_j to be the number of children in D of the node s_j which are labeled with r. It is easy to see that $|Last([\![p]\!])| = S_Y$.

Let **Trees**$_\tau$ denote the image $\tau(Acyclic) \subset Annotated-G$. From the Definition 6, it follows that *any* g-tree $A \in Trees_\tau$, $A = \tau(D)$ has the following properties:

1. $Height(D) = Height(A)$
2. For $1 \le i \le Height(D)$, D and A have identical sets of labels at level i
3. For a dag $G \in Nodes(A)$, let X be the source of G, $X = [\![q]\!]$ and $k = S_Y$. Then for each node $Y \in Nodes(G)$, $Y = [\![p]\!](n)[\alpha_1, \ldots, \alpha_j]$ there exists $i, 1 \le i \le k$ such that $\alpha_i > 0; j = k$, and $[\![q\downarrow]\!] = [\![p]\!]$
4. If a node q is not a source of any dag, then all nodes in the sequence $Last(q)$ are leaves in the tree D.

For the tree D from Fig. 1, the g-tree $\tau(D)$ is shown in Fig. 4. From Property 1 it follows that the height of a g-tree for the document D is the same as that of D; however typically these trees have different width and therefore represent a compressed form (see more in Sect. 4).

Theorem 1. *The mapping $\tau : Acyclic \rightarrow Trees_\tau$ is injective.*

Next, we define the mapping $\gamma : Trees_\tau \rightarrow 2^{Annotated-G}$. Let $TS(G)$ be the set of all topological sortings of a dag G, and for $G_1, \cdots, G_n$ $P(G_1, \ldots, G_n)$ be a Cartesian product $\times_{i=1}^n TS(G_i)$. If $<g_1, \ldots, g_n> \in P(G_1, \ldots, G_n)$ then each graph g_i represents a topologically sorted graph G_i.

Definition 7. *Mapping γ is defined as follows: For $T \in Trees_\tau$, let $\gamma(T) = \{\gamma_{<g_1, \ldots, g_n>}(T) : <g_1, \ldots, g_n> \in P(G_1, \ldots, G_n)\}$ where $\gamma_{<g_1, \ldots, g_n>}(T)$ is the g-tree T with all graphs $G_1, \ldots, G_n$ replaced respectively by graphs $g_1, \ldots, g_n$, and having the same arcs between dags (as well as sources) as in the tree T.*

Let **Trees**$_\gamma$ denote the image $\gamma(Trees_\tau) \subset 2^{Annotated-G}$.

Theorem 2. *The mapping $\gamma : Trees_\tau \rightarrow Trees_\gamma$ is injective.*

It is easy to see that each g-tree $T \in Trees_\gamma$ is in one-to-one correspondence with an annotated tree. Since $\tau : Acyclic \leftrightarrow Trees_\tau$ and $\gamma : Trees_\tau \leftrightarrow Trees_\gamma$, each tree D can be mapped to the set of annotated trees, denoted by **Annotated(D)** and defined by the composition of τ and γ. It is easy to see that every annotated tree from the set $Annotated(D)$ represents D. For example, both annotated trees shown in Figs. 2 and 3 belong to the set $Annotated(D)$ that uniquely represents the tree D.

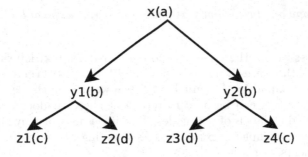

Fig. 7. Cyclic tree.

If there is a cycle in D, then we map D to an acyclic tree with the so-called dummy nodes, denoted by \$. After adding a dummy node to a cyclic document D in Fig. 7, this tree will be acyclic, see Fig. 8, and it can be mapped to the annotated tree shown in Fig. 9. We do not formally prove that the mapping from the tree with cycles to a tree with the dummy nodes is injective.

3   Text Trees and Their Compression

Since the procedure of compressing text trees is almost identical to the procedure of compressing labeled trees, in this section we provide only the description of how text nodes are dealt with.

3.1   Text Trees

Definition 8. *Let Δ be an alphabet, called the text alphabet, its elements are \0 terminated strings. A* **text tree** *is a tree with two kinds of nodes; element nodes labeled by strings from Σ^* (see Definition 1) and text nodes labeled by strings from Δ^* such that text nodes are always leaves, the root of the text tree is an*

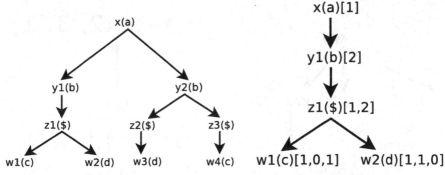

Fig. 8. Acyclic tree with dummy nodes.   **Fig. 9.** The annotated tree with dummy nodes.

element node, and any two sibling text-nodes are separated by at least one element node.

For text trees we use the same notations as for trees; text labels are denoted using letter t (with indices if needed), see Fig. 10. By **TextTrees** we denote the set of all text trees, and by **AcyclicTextTrees** we denote the set of all acyclic text trees. A text tree can be used to represent an XML document with text values represented by labels of text nodes. Text nodes may or may not be present and now we define complete text trees corresponding to the full-mixed content of XML documents, see [10].

Definition 9. *An element leaf node in the text tree is the element node that has no element child. A text tree is called **complete** if every non-leaf element node has the left and the right text sibling, and every element leaf node has exactly one text child node.*

The text tree from Fig. 10 is complete; it would not be complete if any of the text nodes were missing. Note that in XSAQCT when the input XML document D is parsed then for any missing text node, a text node labeled by an empty text (consisting of \0 only) is added. To support a unique representation of an XML document using this technique, added text nodes are removed while D is restored. In what follows, we assume that *text trees are complete.*

3.2   Compressed Representation of Text Trees

Definition 10. *For a node X in the annotated tree with m children $Y_1, \ldots, Y_m$, $m \geq 0$ let* **Number(X)** $= \sum_{j=1}^{m} S_{Y_j} + S_X$. *An **annotated text tree** is an annotated tree with nodes additionally labeled by concatenations of strings from Δ^*, called text labels, such that a text label T of a node $X(a)(T)$ is equal to the concatenation of $Number(X)$ text labels.*

Example of an annotated text tree is shown in Fig. 11. By **AcyclicAnn TextTrees** we denote the set of all acyclic annotated text trees.

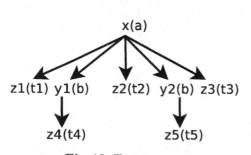

Fig. 10. Text tree.

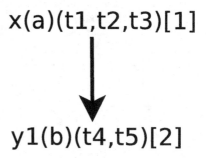

Fig. 11. The annotated text tree.

3.3   Mapping Text Elements

For every equivalence class $[\![p]\!]$, labels of text nodes that are children of element nodes (in left to right order) from the sequence $Last([\![p]\!])$ will be concatenated into a single text label of the node in the annotated tree that corresponds to this equivalence class. For example, the text tree shown in Fig. 10 will be mapped to the annotated text tree from Fig. 11, where t_1, t_2 denotes a concatenation of texts. The reason for mapping text nodes this way is that for querying of the XML documents, the query of the form $/X$ returns the concatenated texts appearing in this path.

Definition 11. *Let $D \in AcyclicTextTrees$ and let A be the image of D under τ (see Definition 6) as if there was no text nodes in D. Now, for every node $X \in A$, we will define its text label T such that the number of texts concatenated in T will be equal to $Number(X)$. Let $\tau^{-1}(X)$, as defined the proof of Theorem 1, be the sequence $x_1, \ldots, x_k$ of element nodes, where $k = S_X$ and let us consider two cases:*

1. *X is a leaf. Then for every $1 \leq i \leq k$, x_i has exactly one text child, and let T be the concatenation of labels of these k children. Clearly, $Number(X) = S_X = k$.*
2. *X is a not leaf, and it has m children, $Y_1, \ldots, Y_m$. Thus, there are $Number(X)$ text children of nodes $x_1, \ldots, x_k$, and we define T to be the concatenation of labels of these children (in left-to-right order).*

Theorem 3. *The mapping of text elements is injective.*

4   Experimental Results

4.1   Overview

Throughout this section we use the following notations: D is a tree and A belongs to the set of annotated trees $Annotated(D)$. Recall from Sect. 2.2 that this set uniquely represents D, therefore the description provided in this section does not depend on the choice of A. For any tree T (annotated or not), by $|T|$ we denote the number of nodes in T. Let the width of D at any level i be denoted by **width(D, i)**, **Ann(X)** denote the annotation list of the node $X \in Nodes(A)$ and $|\mathbf{Ann(X)}|$ denote the length of the annotated list. Finally let $X_1, X_2, \ldots, X_{N_i}$ be all nodes in A at level i (i.e., $width(A, i) = N_i$).

From the construction of an annotated tree, it follows that (see also Properties in Sect. 2.3):

1. $width(D, i) = \sum_{k=1}^{N_i} S_{X_k}$;
2. In A, for any node X and its child Y, $S_X = |Ann(Y)|$

Therefore, the larger the sum of all annotations of X, the longer the annotation list of Y. The implication of zeroes appearing in the annotations of node X is two-fold: (a) in A, they shorten the length of the annotation list; (b) in D,

Y does not appear as a child of X. If D was "completely regular" and there were no missing children, then there would be no 0s on the annotation lists. From our experiments, it follows that leaf annotation lists are usually very long, while for the leaf's ascendants, annotations they get progressively shorter. To analyze this phenomenon consider a leaf node X in A, its parent Y, and Y's parent Z (grandparent of X). Since $S_Y = |Ann(X)|$, the annotation list $Ann(X)$ must have been increased because of the structure of D, specifically Y has often appeared as a child of Z, potentially multiple times (resulting in annotations greater than 1). On the other hand, many 0's appearing in $Ann(X)$ indicates that X has "very rarely" appeared as a child of Y.

4.2   Experimental Results

The files are 1gig.xml (a randomly generated XML file, using xmlgen.xml [11]), baseball.xml [12], enwikibooks.xml and lineitem.xml from the Wratislavia corpus [13], uniprot_sprot.xml [14] and enwiki-latest.xml [15]. This suite has been chosen because XML files included there have an ability to represent specific extremes of semi-structured data. For example, enwiki-latest.xml, the current revision of English Wikipedia, while being a very large document, encompasses two extremes: the distribution of character data is very non-uniform (i.e., the majority of the data falls within one node) and that path is predominantly free-formed English. Conversely, uniprot_sprot.xml is a highly uniform XML file (i.e., the data is evenly distributed), and the file is predominantly markup. The file 1gig.xml has the property that the subtree entropy is extremely low (subtrees are quite similar); however, each subtree differs by a parent node (for example, /a/b/d/e/f vs. /a/z/d/e/f). The file lineitem.xml, has the property that it is an incredibly regular tree (few missing nodes), and in addition, has a nice mixture of text and numeric data. The file enwikibooks.xml is quite structurally similar to enwiki-latest.xml but is a fraction of its size. Finally, baseball.xml is an extremely irregular XML file.

  Characteristics of these files are shown in the first four columns of Table 1, where V(N) denotes the value $V*10^N$, Size is the size of file in Bytes, E:A denotes the number of elements and attributes, AC denotes the number of annotations, and AT denotes the number of nodes in the annotation tree. The last column of the Table 1 (denoted by C) shows the results of applying the compressibility measure derived in Eq. 2.

Persistent Representation. We will first consider the annotated tree as a persistent data structure (similar to a DOM model), ignoring the character data for the time being. A classical solution requires a struct for each node, containing the nodes label, its left child, and right sibling. If we let C be the cost of storing a single piece of information, such as a single integer annotation or a node label, then the storage cost of *a single tree node* is $3 \times C$ (and a document with D nodes is $3 \times C \times D$). To measure the cost of storing the annotated tree A compared to the cost of storing the original document D ($\frac{Cost(A)}{Cost(D)}$), we need to quantify the cost of A, which is equivalent to the cost of storing all nodes in A plus the cost

Table 1. Overview of XML test suite and results of testing.

XML File	Size	E:A	AC	AT	C
enw.latest	5.96(9)	1.84(9):1.85(8)	2.59(9)	39	0.47
UniProt	1.15(8)	9.86(5):1.44(9)	1.05(9)	217	0.36
1gig	1.17(9)	1.6(7):3.83(6)	2.05(8)	680	0.41
enw.books	1.56(8)	5.3(6):4.9(5)	6.38(5)	29	0.40
lineitem	3.22(7)	1.02(6):1	9.6(6)	19	0.31
BaseBall	6.72(5)	2.8(5):0	6.6(5)	47	0.78

of each annotation list. If we let the cost of storing an annotation list of length L to be $L \times C$, then we have

$$\frac{(3C|A|) + C(\sum_{X \in A} |Ann(X)|)}{3C|D|} \tag{1}$$

and performing a few simplifications, gives the following formula (independent of the cost C):

$$\mu_c(D) = \frac{|A| + \frac{1}{3}(\sum_{X \in A} |Ann(X)|)}{|D|}. \tag{2}$$

These results show that the annotated tree provides a well-compressed representation of the original files, even in the presence of very large files. Finally, traversal, or iterating, through the tree only requires the summation of annotation lists (something massively parallel, especially using SIMD instructions).

Archiving Representation. We now consider using the annotated tree in the context of archiving of XML (compression included). For this analysis, a series of different compressors were used: LZ77-based [16] compressors, GZIP[1] and XZ[2], BWT-based [17], BZIP2[3], Prediction by Partial Matching based PPMonster[4], and the Context-Mixing compressors ZPAQ [18][5] and PAQ8PXD_V7[6]; for the source code, or executables, to each compressor see [19]. The first general comment is that analyzing the percentage increase in compression does not take into consideration how substantial the decrease in size is. However, since the information theoretic (or Kolmogorov complexity) lower bound is generally unknown, this will still be used as the base metric of comparison.

Compressing only the XML structure and its associated annotated tree is given in Fig. 12. The annotation list of each equivalence class (similar path) has two components: (1) A single byte header that signifies if any transform (e.g.,

---

[1] gzip -9 FILE.
[2] xz -9 -e FILE.
[3] bzip2 -9 FILE.
[4] ppmonstr -m1700 -o64 FILE.
[5] zpaq add FILE.zpaq FILE -method 69 -noattributes.
[6] paq8pxd_v7 -8 FILE.

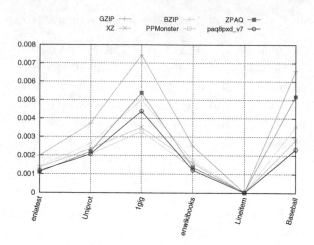

Fig. 12. Compression of annotated tree over markup density (the number of bytes to represent the XML syntax/structure).

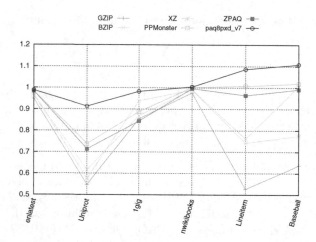

Fig. 13. Compression of annotated transform (collection of annotation lists, text containers, and skeleton tree) over compression of XML data.

a run length encoding) has been applied to the annotations; (2) A list of annotations, each encoded as a 32-bit integer. In the worst case, the annotated representation only requires one-tenth of a percent of the original markup amount (including tag names, and XML syntax data). In the best case, a very-regular (a complete tree) document, lineitem.xml, only requires one one-thousandth of a percent of the original markup amount. In either situation, both of these situations offer a very faithful representation of the XML data. This justifies the claim that the annotated tree is an incredibly lightweight index of the XML. Figure 13 plots the compression ratio of the size of the annotated tree, with character contents, over the compression ratio of the XML documents shown in Table 1. The first noticeable feature of Fig. 13 is the fact that paq8pxd and PPMonster compress the data much better as vanilla compressors than with the annotated transform for the smaller XML files. Since the files are so small, these compressors can often build a model of the entire document, allowing those compressors to compress each tag-name, and the XML markup, quite compactly. The next general trend is that the more markup-dense XML documents compress much better than the content dense XML documents, whereas the more content-dense XML documents only receive slight improvements for the larger XML documents. With respect to enlatest and enwikibooks, the majority of text is free-formed English, e.g., each <text> tag contains a substantial amount of text data (all of the content you would see on a Wikipedia page). If some nodes text data were of significant size, only the compressors that incorporate a very large scope of the data would be able to exploit the tag-to-tag redundancy (mutual information), otherwise, it would only be able to exploit the redundancy local to that tag, and the data at the boundary of two tags. From this, we can infer that the scope of compression is a necessary and sufficient factor in the performance of compression (i.e., because a larger scope allows better compression of the XML syntax and the semantic/temporal relations among subtrees). Another factor may be attributed to the fact that the lower bound of lossless compression for these documents is "close" to the obtained compression ratios.

5   Conclusions and Future Work

This paper showed that annotated trees form a faithful representation of the trees, and so the XSAQCT compression process is lossless. Besides the formal and algorithmic approaches, experiments showed that the annotated tree compressibility, without using any backend compressors is high, on average approximately 0.4. Finally, results of testing of compression of entire XML document with single instances of vanilla compressors, compression of annotated tree over markup density, and compression of annotated transform over compression of XML data were provided, showing the usefulness of the annotated tree approach.

Simple queries, such as finding all children of a given node can be efficiently evaluated using the annotated trees. Our future work will extend queries to the subset of XPath expressions known as the core XPath as defined in [20], as well as more sophisticated navigational queries, e.g. asking for the j-th level-ancestor of u.

Acknowledgements. The work of the first and third authors are partially supported by the NSERC RGPIN grant and NSERC CSG-M (Canada Graduate Scholarship-Masters) grant respectively.

References

1. XML: Extensible markup language (XML) 1.0 (Fifth edition) (2013). http://www. w3.org/tr/rec-xml/. Assessed October 2013
2. Busatto, G., Lohrey, M., Maneth, S.: Efficient memory representation of XML documents. In: Bierman, G., Koch, C. (eds.) DBPL 2005. LNCS, vol. 3774, pp. 199–216. Springer, Heidelberg (2005)
3. Ferragina, P., Luccio, F., Manzini, G., Muthukrishnan, S.: Compressing and indexing labeled trees, with applications. J. ACM **57**(1), 4:1–4:33 (2009)
4. Busatto, G., Lohrey, M., Maneth, S.: Efficient memory representation of XML document trees. Inf. Syst. **33**(4–5), 456–474 (2008)
5. Arion, A., Bonifati, A., Manolescu, I., Pugliese, A.: XQueC: a query-conscious compressed XML database. ACM Trans. Internet Technol. **7**(2), 1–32 (2007)
6. GZIP: The gzip home page (2013). http://www.gzip.org. Assessed October 2013
7. bzip2: bzip2 compression (2013). http://www.bzip.org/. Assessed October 2013
8. Müldner, T., Fry, C., Miziołek, J., Durno, S.: XSAQCT: XML queryable compressor. In: Balisage: The Markup Conference 2009, Montreal, Canada, August 2009
9. Müldner, T., Miziołek, J., Corbin, T.: Annotated trees and their applications to XML compression. In: The Tenth International Conference on Web Information Systems and Technologies, WEBIST, Barcelona, Spain, pp. 27–39 (2014)
10. Müldner, T., Corbin, T., Miziołek, J., Fry, C.: Design and implementation of an online XML compressor for large XML files. Int. J. Adv. Internet Technol. **5**(3), 115–118 (2012)
11. xmlgen: The benchmark data generator (2013). http://www.xml-benchmark.org/ generator.html. Assessed October 2013
12. Baseball.xml: baseball.xml (2013). http://rassyndrome.webs.com/cc/baseball.xml. Assessed October 2013
13. Corpus, W.: Wratislavia XML corpus (2013). http://www.ii.uni.wroc.pl/~inikep/ research/wratislavia/. Assessed October 2013
14. Consortium, T.U.: Update on activities at the Universal Protein Resource (UniProt) in 2013 (January 2013). http://dx.doi.org/10.1093/nar/gks1068. Assessed on 20 June 2013
15. enwiki dumps: enwiki-latest.xml (2013). http://dumps.wikimedia.org/enwiki/ latest/. Assessed October 2013
16. Ziv, J., Lempel, A.: A universal algorithm for sequential data compression. IEEE Trans. Inf. Theor. **23**(3), 337–343 (2006)
17. Burrows, M., Wheeler, D.: A block-sorting lossless data compression algorithm. Technical report, Digital Equipment Corporation (1994)
18. ZPAQ: Zpaq (2013). http://www.w3.org/tr/rec-xml/. Assessed October 2013
19. Mahoney, M.: Large Text Compression Benchmark (2012). http://mattmahoney. net/dc/zpaq.html. Assessed October 2013
20. Gottlob, G., Koch, C., Pichler, R.: Efficient algorithms for processing xpath queries. ACM Trans. Database Syst. **30**(2), 444–491 (2005)

Leveraging Efficient XML Interchange (EXI) for Filter-Enabled Data Dissemination in Embedded Networks

Sebastian Käbisch[✉] and Richard Kuntschke

Siemens AG, Corporate Technology, Munich, Germany
{sebastian.kaebisch,richard.kuntschke}@siemens.com

Abstract. Due to its flexibility and extensive tool support, XML is an obvious choice for a generic data exchange format. However, the verbosity and processing overhead of textual XML impedes its use in resource-restricted embedded networks. These disadvantages have been addressed by the introduction of binary representations of the XML Infoset such as W3C's Efficient XML Interchange (EXI) format. EXI can be used to significantly reduce message size and processing overhead for XML-based messaging. In this paper, we show how to leverage EXI for filter-enabled binary XML dissemination in embedded networks. The approach further reduces resource consumption by sharing common data and processing results among a set of multiple queries. Thus, through the suitable placement of pre- and post-filters on binary XML data, bandwidth on network connections and computational resources on nodes can be saved. Consequently, more data can be processed with a certain amount of available resources within an embedded network.

Keywords: Binary XML · EXI · Embedded networks · XPath · Filtering

1 Introduction

Efficient data dissemination is an important task in distributed systems where data needs to be transferred from data sources to data sinks located at different places within the system. Sharing common data and processing results among multiple data sinks helps to save network bandwidth and computational resources. While such approaches reduce resource usage in any distributed system, their usage is crucial in embedded networks (fundamental in, e.g., building or industrial automation, automotive industry, and smart grid) due to the strictly limited resources such as from microcontrollers. Using binary XML techniques such as W3C's Efficient XML Interchange (EXI) format [21] enables the dissemination of otherwise resource-intensive XML data in embedded networks. Additionally, using filter-enabled binary XML dissemination helps to further reduce resource demands.

A filter-enabled subscription mechanism in embedded networks reduces network traffic and unnecessary message processing at the client nodes. It optimizes data interaction between the service provider (data source) and the service

© Springer International Publishing Switzerland 2015
V. Monfort and K.-H. Krempels (Eds.): WEBIST 2014, LNBIP 226, pp. 79–95, 2015.
DOI: 10.1007/978-3-319-27030-2_6

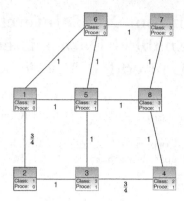

Fig. 1. Example embedded network with a service provider (node 1) and three clients (nodes 3, 4, and 7).

requester/client (data sink) in terms of data novelty and supports an efficient execution of applications in embedded networks at runtime. Consequently, more data can be processed with a certain amount of available resources within an embedded network.

An immediate evaluation at the node of service data origin prevents the dissemination of data that is outside of the scope of the corresponding service requesters. In the context of constrained embedded networks, however, a desired early evaluation at the node of service data origin sometimes cannot be realized. Two aspects support this observation: First of all, the available resources, especially when it comes to memory, are often not sufficient for installing an additional filter application. Secondly, vendors of embedded nodes do not offer the possibility of installing such filter applications.

In this paper, we introduce an approach for organizing filter-based service data dissemination in constrained embedded networks that takes into account resources such as device classes, device processing performance, and connection quality between nodes. The goal is to share relevant service data using binary XML whenever possible by using filters and sub-filters, respectively. This reduces both network traffic and computational load on nodes. Basically, this approach leads to content-based routing at the application level based on binary XML content.

1.1   Problem Statement

Consider Fig. 1 as an example embedded network that shows a simple distributed system with eight nodes and corresponding network connections. Nodes are categorized here into three classes (1 to 3) indicating their capabilities. The lower the class number, the more powerful the device. Class 1, e.g., corresponds to a consumer PC, class 2 corresponds to a hardware system with a resource complexity found in home network routers, and class 3 corresponds to constrained embedded hardware such as a microcontroller (e.g., ARM Cortex-M3[1] with 24 MHz,

---

[1] http://www.arm.com/products/processors/cortex-m/cortex-m3.php.

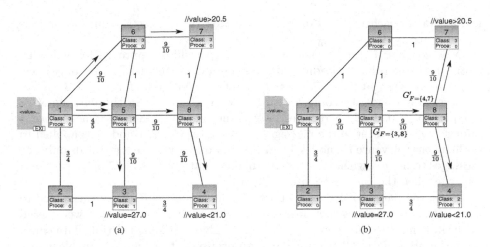

Fig. 2. (a) Naive approach for data dissemination (b) Desired pre-/post-filter approach for data dissemination purposes.

256 kB RAM, and 16 kB ROM). The boolean *proce* value indicates whether there are computational resources available at the corresponding node. A value of 0 indicates that there are no resources left for installing a potential application, while a value of 1 indicates available resources. Resources in this context may comprise memory as well as processing power. The numbers at the network connections indicate the available connection quality. Values closer to 1 indicate superior connection quality. In contrast, values closer to 0 indicate poor connection quality. Connection quality may be impacted by the technology of the underlying physical communication link, e.g., low-power wireless communication (e.g., IEEE 802.15.4 [15]) vs. Ethernet, as well as by the current system state as indicated, e.g., by the current package loss ratio, delay, and available bandwidth of the communication link. Increasing network traffic on a communication link lowers the connection quality since, e.g., increasing traffic reduces the available bandwidth.

Now, let us assume a simple data dissemination scenario. In Fig. 2(a), node 1 is the data source, sending XML-based data including a *value* information in EXI format, and nodes 3, 4, and 7 are the data sinks that are interested in the *value* information. The data sink at node 3 is only interested in data elements containing the value 27.0, node 4 is interested in data elements containing values less than 21.0, and node 7 is interested in data elements containing values greater than 20.5. Since node 1 does not have the opportunity to set up a filter mechanism (*proce* is equal to 0) to test client's relevance of a new data message, this node always sends an individual copy of the entire data message to each data sink and the nodes constituting the data sinks process the data accordingly (see Fig. 2(a)). However, this leads to relatively high bandwidth usage on the affected network connections and requires considerable computational resources at the data sink nodes, even if this message is not relevant anyway. To illustrate the impact of this naive dissemination approach in terms of connection quality, in Fig. 2(a) in each involved dissemination link the connection quality value is decremented by the value $\frac{1}{10}$.

Now consider Fig. 2(b), showing our pre-/post-filter approach for the same distributed network. All produced data is sent out by the data source only once. A pre-filter (G_F) at node 5 filters the data of relevance for nodes 3 and 8. A message for node 3 is only forwarded when the *value* in the data message is equal to 27.0. Node 8 receives only a message from node 5 when a *value* information is present in the message. A post-filter (G'_F) at node 8 is applied to evaluate the relevance for nodes 4 and 7. Consequently, node 8 forwards only the messages to node 4 when the *value* is smaller than 21.0. Node 7 only receives a message when the *value* is greater than 20.5.

Thus, compared to the naive approach, the requested data is transmitted to each data sink using less network bandwidth and less processing power overall in the system, since processing results can be shared among multiple data sinks. Also, we are able to distribute the computational load across capable nodes within the distributed system. We accept this approach even if the resources of a small number of node devices may be claimed by the filter placement. This is seen by the processablity of node 8 that is set to 0.

Such kind of mechanism can be adopted to improve the engineering process of, e.g., industry or building automation systems that consist of a multitude of diverse embedded devices with different kinds of resource capabilities. Suggestions can be made how to optimize the network traffic as well as the computational load of individual embedded devices.

1.2   Paper's Contributions and Outline

This paper presents the following contributions:

- We shortly introduce a previously developed filter mechanism based on W3C's EXI format (Sect. 2). This mechanism constitutes the basis for our further work on filter-enabled binary XML dissemination in embedded networks.
- In Sect. 3, we present our new approach for efficient filter-enabled binary XML data dissemination in embedded networks. The approach helps to reduce bandwidth usage on network connections and computational load on nodes, thus allowing larger amounts of data to be transferred and processed with a certain amount of available resources.
- Finally, we present evaluation results showing the effectiveness of our approach (Sect. 4).

2   EXI Filter Mechanism

In this section we give a short introduction about the EXI format and the basic idea, how an EXI grammar can be transformed to a filter grammar for evaluating XPath expressions.

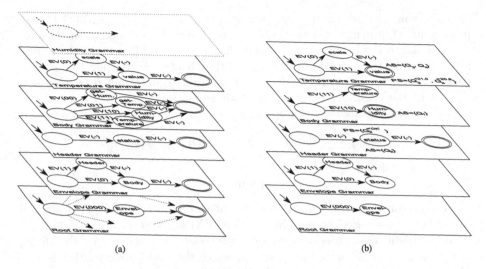

(a)   (b)

Fig. 3. (a) EXI grammar G (excerpt) for encoding and decoding purposes (b) Filter Grammar G_F with $G_F \subseteq G$ based on the queries Q_1, Q_2, Q_3, and Q_4 for evaluation purposes.

2.1 The W3C EXI Format

W3C, the inventor and standardizer of XML, faced the drawbacks of plain-text XML and created a working group called XML Binary Characterization (XBC) [11] to analyze the condition of a binary XML format that should also harmonize with the standardized plain-text XML format as well as with the XML Infoset. The outcome was the start of the W3C Efficient XML Interchange (EXI) format, which gained recommendation status at the beginning of 2011 [21].

Mainly, EXI is a grammar driven approach that is applied to bring XML-based data into a binary form and vice versa. Such a grammar is constructed based on a given XML Schema where each defined complex type is represented as a deterministic finite automaton (DFA). Figure 3(a) shows an excerpt of a sample EXI grammar (set of automaton) G that can be used for encoding and decoding. This grammar reflects an XML Schema including the SOAP framework [12] with a status information within the Header part and request/response patterns of temperature and humidity information within the Body part. Please note that the *Root* grammar is a predefined grammar that occurs in each EXI grammar representation of arbitrary XML Schemas. It contains all entry points of all root elements in a given schema. Here, we only highlight in our context the relevant root Envelope of the SOAP message framework. In general, each DFA contains one start state and one end state, which reflect the beginning and the end, respectively, of a complex type declaration. Transitions to the next state represent the sequential order of element and/or attribute declarations within a complex type. Optional definitions (e.g., *choice*, $minOccurs = 0$, etc.) are reflected by multiple transitions and assigned an event code (EV). E.g., the SOAP Envelope message framework embeds an optional Header and a mandatory Body element [12].

The equivalent EXI grammar representation, as can be seen in Fig. 3(a) (Envelope Grammar), provides two transitions from the start state: one to the Header state and one to the Body state. For signalization, a one bit event code is used and assigned to the transition (EV(1) for the Header; EV(0) for the Body). Generally, the number of bits used for m transitions is determined by $\lceil log_2 m \rceil$. EV(-) on transitions indicates, no event code is required.

An example XML message snipped such as

$$< Envelope >< Header >< status > OK < /status > ...$$

would be transformed to a

$$000\,1\,'OK'...$$

EXI (bit-)stream based on the EXI grammar shown in Fig. 3(a). This already shows, how compact EXI can be. In addition, EXI is a type aware encoder that provides efficient coding mechanisms for the most common data types (int, float, enumerations, etc.). There are use cases in which the EXI representation is said to be over 100 times smaller than XML [5]. Based on the high compression ratio and the opportunity to obtain the data content directly from the EXI stream, XML-based messaging is also feasible in the embedded domain, even if constrained devices are used [17].

2.2 EXI Filtering

EXI grammars build the bases for writing and reading binary XML data. Previous work [16] shows the functionality to create an efficient filter mechanism for binary XML data based on a number of service requesters by providing XPath expressions that address the desired service data occurrences and/or data value conditions. Two approaches which are feasible to constrained devices such as microcontrollers were presented: *BasicEXIFiltering* and *OptimizedEXIFiltering*. The *BasicEXIFiltering* operates on top of an EXI grammar and evaluates normalized XPath queries by means of binary XML. *OptimizedEXIFiltering* presents a more sophisticated approach; it maps all XPath expressions within an EXI grammar and removes all states and transitions which are not required for message evaluation. The outcome is a filter grammar denoted as G_F. Figure 3(b) shows such a constructed filter grammar G_F based on the queries

$$Q_1 = //Humidity$$
$$Q_2 = //status[text() =' OK']$$
$$Q_3 = //Temperature/value[text() < 21.0]$$
$$Q_4 = //Temperature/value[text() > 20.5]$$

applied on the data model represented by the EXI grammar G in Fig. 3(a).

Applying the previously created EXI stream

$$000\,1\,'OK'...$$

to the filter grammar G_F we would, at least, successfully find a match for the XPath expression Q_2. This is due to the remaining states and transitions in G_F

that lead via the Envelope state (reading the bits 000 from the stream) and the Header state (reading the bit 1 from the stream) to the Header status state which is dedicated as a predicate state (PS) and as an accepting state (AS). A predicate state results to a predicate evaluation. Here, we have to evaluate whether the message contains the status value 'OK' which is also the case in our example. An accepting state represents a query match of a particular query (here Q_2). This is only true, if all aforegoing relevant predicate states resulted in a positive predicate evaluation.

The next section explains how such filter grammars can be used to realize an efficient binary XML data dissemination mechanism in constrained embedded networks.

3 Dissemination Algorithm

This section presents our filter-enabled binary XML dissemination algorithm. First of all, we introduce our cost model and formalize the optimization problem (Sect. 3.1). Next, the dedicated algorithm is presented (Sect. 3.2). Finally, an example is considered for better clarification of how our algorithm works (Sect. 3.3).

3.1   Cost Model

Before we formalize our cost model we will formally define an embedded network in our context as described in Sect. 1.1 by $N_{emb} = (V, E, c, w, p)$. V describes the set of vertexes/nodes. Set E describes the set of edges/connections between two nodes. Function c with $c : V \rightarrow \mathbb{N}_{>0}$ associates the device class of a device node. The weight function w with $w : E \rightarrow \mathbb{R}_{[0,1]}$ describes the connection quality between two device nodes and p with $p : V \rightarrow \{0, 1\}$ the processing capability of a node.

A newly installed application, including a service provider node (v_s) and service subscriber clients ($C = \{v_{c_1}, ..., v_{c_n}\}$), in an embedded network N_{emb} would typically lead to additional network traffic and processing costs. To keep this overhead as small as possible, we filter the data of relevance and share this data as long as possible on a determined dissemination path that avoids constrained device class nodes and uses connections with relatively good quality. Consequently, we have two metrics which have to be considered: device class with the processability (c and p) and connection quality (w). Putting this together, we define our cost function f for a given $N_{emb}^T = (V^T, E^T, c, w, p)$ with $N_{emb}^T \subseteq N_{emb}$ that only contains the nodes and transitions (spans a tree) from v_s to all nodes in C that is used for the data dissemination:

$$f(N_{emb}^T) := \alpha \cdot \sum_{v_i \in V^T} (c(v_i) + 1 - p(v_i))$$

$$+ (1 - \alpha) \cdot \sum_{(v_i, v_j) \in E^T} \frac{1}{w(v_i, v_j)}. \tag{1}$$

The first summand formalizes the device class with the processing capability of a device node. A *hop-noise* value 1 is added to enable an influential decision when we also have only one class occurrences ($c = 1$) and each has processing capability ($p = 1$) in the network. The second summand represents the reciprocal connection quality. The $\alpha \in [0, 1]$ is a weight factor that enables us to set up a more dominant part in the cost function: the device class ($\alpha > 0.5$) or the connection quality ($\alpha < 0.5$).

Using f we are able to formalize our optimization problem to find a subgraph N_{emb}^{T} of N_{emb} for a filter-enabled service data dissemination:

$$Minimize \quad f_T \tag{2}$$

subject to

$$\sum_{v_i \in V^T} p^T(v_i) \geq 1.$$

The inequality constraint specifies the occurrence of at least one node processing capability within N_{emb}^{T} that can be used to set up a pre-filter.

Unfortunately, for any constellation in N_{emb} we are not able to find an optimized solution in polynomial time. In the next section we are going to present an heuristic approach based on greedy algorithms that approximates an optimized N_{emb}^{T} for a filter-enabled service data dissemination.

3.2   Algorithm

We are now going to describe our filter-enabled service data dissemination algorithm, the *FilterEnabledDissemination* algorithm (see Algorithm 1), for installing a new application with a service provider and a number of service requesters, which takes into account the current resources of the embedded network.

Algorithm 1. *FilterEnabledDissemination.*

Require: $N_{emb} = (V, E, c, w, p)$, a service provider v_s, set of service requesters $C = \{v_{c_1}, ..., v_{c_n}\}$, set of queries Q related to client's conditions, data model represented as XML schema XSD.

Ensure: Tree network N_{emb}^{T} with a set F of dedicated selected nodes with its filter grammars (pre- and post-filters).

1: $G_F \leftarrow FilterGrammar(G, Q)$;
2: $v_{pre} \leftarrow ClosestPreFilterNode(N_{emb}, v_s, C, G_F)$;
3: $N_{emb}^{T} \leftarrow DisseminationTree(N_{emb}, v_{pre}, C)$;
4: $F \leftarrow PostFilterPlacement(N_{emb}^{T}, Q, v_{pre}, G_F)$;
5: $extendTreeByPreRoute(V^T, E^T, V, E, v_{pre})$;
6: **return** $\{N_{emb}^{T}, F\}$

As input, the algorithm takes an embedded network N_{emb}, a dedicated service provider node v_s, a set of service requesters (the clients) C and their corresponding queries Q, and the underlying data model of the service provider described in an XML schema XSD. Its outcome is a subnetwork N^T_{emb} of N_{emb} that represents the dissemination tree/path from v_s to all clients in C and a set F that consists of the selected nodes with pre- and post-filter properties. Essentially, the processing steps of the algorithm can be divided into three parts:

1. After determining the filter grammar G_F (see Sect. 2.2) using the algorithm *FilterGrammar* in line 1, a suitable pre-filter node is searched. Doing this, the *ClosestPreFilterNode* algorithm (line 2) is called. This algorithm determines one processing node v_{pre} that is able to run the filter grammar G_F as well as that results in overall positive data dissemination. More precisely, we are not only considering the quality of the path to a processable node v_{pre} in terms of connection and device class, but also the quality from v_{pre} to all service subscribers.
2. Starting with the determined pre-filter node v_{pre} we discover an optimized dissemination tree N^T_{emb} from this v_{pre}. The *DisseminationTree* algorithm (line 3) will be called to gather such a tree. Thereby, relevant service data shall be delivered from v_{pre} to the service subscribers in a resource-optimized manner. More precisely, the data shall be routed via high quality connections, avoid very constrained embedded devices, and be shared for as long as possible if there are multi-client destinations. The latter can be fulfilled if one or more post-filters can be placed that retain the information of the final client destination nodes or the next post-filter nodes. Consequently, the *DisseminationTree* algorithm finds a dissemination tree from v_{pre} to all clients in C that takes into account the device class and connection quality metrics as well as the current processing capability of the potential post-filter placement.
3. Based on N^T_{emb}, suitable nodes are selected for the post-filter functionality to share service data as long as possible. The *PostFilterPlacement* algorithm (line 5) realizes this and provides the routing information for all filter grammars.

Before the *FilterEnabledDissemination* algorithm terminates, we extend N^T_{emb} by the involved nodes and connection that leads from v_s to v_{pre} (line 5).

For better clarification and to get an idea how our algorithm works we will consider an example in the next subsection applied on the network shown in Fig. 1.

3.3 Example

We will now consider the embedded network $N_{emb} = (V, E, c, w, p)$ which is shown in Fig. 1. Node 1 is a service provider and nodes 3, 4, and 7 are the service requesters with the following 4 query conditions as presented in Sect. 2.2:

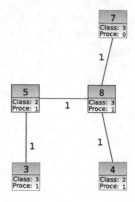

Fig. 4. Determined tree based on the *DisseminationTree* procedure from v_{pre} (node 5) to all clients in C (nodes 3, 4, and 7).

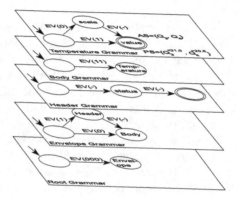

Fig. 5. Post-filter grammar.

Node 3: Q_1 and Q_2
Node 4: Q_3
Node 7: Q_4

Figure 3(b) already shows the filter grammar G_F based on this query set after applying the *FilterGrammar* procedure. Since the service requester node does not provide us with the opportunity to set up a filter mechanism for clients' subscription requests ($p(1) = 0$), we have to find an alternative node for placing a pre-filter. In order to do so, we have to identify any nodes with processing capabilities within the network that have enough resources to run G_F. The procedure *ClosestPreFilterNode* in Algorithm 1 will identify these nodes (3, 4, 5, 8) check their resource capabilities. If this results in more than one node, the node which is closest to the service provider and yields the best cost function value is selected based on test paths to clients in C using the Dijkstra algorithm [9] with our metrics. The outcome would be node 5 that is selected as pre-filter node (v_{pre}) running G_F.

The next step involves determining a data dissemination tree that spans v_{pre} and client nodes 3, 4, and 7. In order to do so, we will call the *Dissemination-Tree* procedure. This algorithm is based on the concept of the Kou-Markowsky-Berman (KMB) algorithm [18] which is a well-known heuristic for the Steiner Tree problem. Based on our metric and cost model, respectively, Fig. 4 shows the outcome of the *DisseminationTree* procedure.

The last major processing step in our dissemination algorithm involves determining suitable post-filter nodes to enable a high ratio of shared service data from service provider to service requesters. Starting with (root) node 5, the *PostFilterPlacement* procedure will first select all nodes that contain multi successor branches. Nodes 5 and 8 are candidates. Since node 5 already is a dedicated pre-filter node, we will not consider it further and instead check node 8 directly for processability of a post-filter grammar. The post-filter grammar is constructed based on the queries that can be reached from node 8. This is true for the queries Q_3 and Q_4. Figure 5 shows the post-filter as based on these queries that is constructed based on the mechanism presented in Sect. 2.2. Since node 8 is a node with processing capabilities we can successfully install the post-filter on this node.

Before the *PostFilterPlacement* algorithm is terminated, we are going to update the network's defined filters in terms of routing information. Node 5 is set up with the pre-filter G_F that is shown in Fig. 3(b) and will receive all messages from node 1. In addition, node 5 with G_F contains the associated information Q_1 and Q_2 related to node 3, Q_3 related to node 4, and query Q_4 related to node 7. Based on the post-filter to be placed on node 8, service data that matches queries Q_3 and Q_4 shall be forwarded to node 8, which then will send the data only once. Thus, G_F is updated with this information. In summary, we obtain the following routing information:

– G_F (at node 5): forwards service data to node 3 when queries Q_1 and/or Q_2 match; forwards service data to node 8 when queries Q_3 and/or Q_4 match.
– G'_F (at node 8): forwards service data to node 4 when Q_3 matches; forwards service data to node 7 when Q_4 matches

This determined data dissemination tree and the filter placement is also reflected in Fig. 2(b).

4   Evaluation

So as to organize service data dissemination of each new applied application and to estimate its influence in terms of traffic and device capacity usage of real embedded networks we wrote an embedded network simulator. The simulator provides us with the opportunity to load particular network topologies and characteristics as well as service provider and the service subscribers with their queries. Another alternative is to setup randomized embedded networks by providing different kinds of generation parameters: number of nodes, number of different kinds of device classes, and the ratio of device classes and connection quality. Based on such a network, we are able to set up new applications by selecting particular nodes, which operate a service with the provided service description, and the client nodes that subscribe service data with the predefined conditions on the service data. We can then run our dissemination algorithm for each newly installed application.

In order to evaluate the effectiveness of the approach presented in this paper, we randomly generated an embedded network that has a complexity of 50 nodes with three device classes. This network setup initially features a balanced ratio of processable and non-processable nodes. Its class ratio consists of 5 times device classes 1, 10 times device classes 2, and 35 times device classes 3. Initially, we uniformly distributed the connection quality weighting values with numbers between 0.8 and 1. We sequentially installed five different kinds of applications. In general, an application is based on a service provider and different kinds of service requesters (the clients). The distance (in terms of hop count) and client distribution to the service provider node is increased with each new installed application. We start with the first application, which has two clients; subsequently, the second has 3 clients, the third has 4 clients, there are 5 clients in the fourth application, and finally the fifth application has 6 different service requesters. For each installed application we evaluated the service data dissemination for two variants: *Filter-enabled dissemination* (abbreviated with *FD*) represents our filter-enabled dissemination approach and the separate and *direct dissemination* (abbreviated with *DD*) reflects the direct, non-filtered service data delivery (comparable with Fig. 2(a)).

Figure 6 shows the evaluation results. Figure 6(a) depicts the result for each application in terms of device class occurrences (Cl1 = Class 1 nodes, Cl2 = Class 2 nodes, and Cl3 = Class 3 nodes) in the dissemination path of our approach (FD Optimized) as compared to the simple approach, wherein each service data is delivered separately (DD Simple). In other words, we count the occurrence of the device classes in the determined dissemination path (tree) that reflects the worst case scenario when a service message is relevant for all service requesters in the network. As can be seen for all cases, our approach, as presented in this paper, results in a lower usage of class occurrences as compared to the simple service data distribution variant. This becomes especially apparent the more complex the application is. Furthermore, the occurrences also show that our determined dissemination paths always consist of the desirable, relatively small number of constrained nodes (class 3). For instance, in a worst case distribution scenario for application five, our dissemination approach uses the device class 1 sixteen times, class 2 ten times, and the most constrained device class 3 eight times. In total, 34 nodes are involved in the dissemination process. In contrast, a simple dissemination would lead to a device class ratio of class 1 thirty-five times, class 2 twenty-four times, and class 3 twenty times. In total, this involves 79 nodes. Consequently, our approach results in a better resource usage of the nodes in the embedded network since fewer total nodes are involved in the dissemination tree; the number of constrained nodes (class 3) is kept as small as possible.

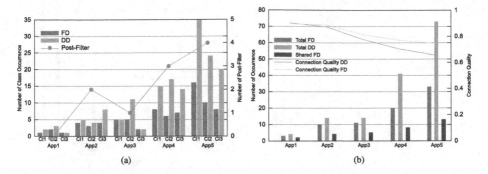

Fig. 6. Embedded network with $|V| = 50$: (a) Count of used classes (Cl1, Cl2, Cl3) in the dissemination path and number of used post-filters for each application (App1, ..., App5). (b) Number of links of the dissemination path and average value of connection quality.

Figure 6(b) shows the evaluation result in terms of the number of connection links used and average connection quality. As can be seen, the number of connections used in a dissemination process is smaller for our approach as compared to the simple variant. The figure also shows the ratio of the shared connections of the optimized variant in each application. We determined the number based on whether each connection between two nodes can reach a pre-filter or a post-filter node. If so, the number of shared connections is incremented. The presented numbers show the effectiveness of our approach, since for each application we determine a dissemination tree that consists of a high ratio of shared connections. Figure 6(b) also shows the average connection quality for each application and its dissemination based on both our approach and the simple variant. As can be observed, the simple dissemination variant loses the average connection quality faster than our approach. This is explained by the fact that the simple variant involves a lot more connection links and potentially causes more network traffic. The more applications that are installed in the network, the greater the impact on connection quality will be.

Further evaluation results shown in Fig. 7 underline our observations: The figure shows another case with a randomly created embedded network with 100 nodes, four different device classes and double the amount of service requesters compared to the case shown in Fig. 6. Figure 7(a) shows the almost equal distribution of device classes in each application even if there is a high ratio of constrained class 4 devices (60 %). Figure 7(b) shows the connection ratio and the average connection quality. Due to an increased number of service requesters, the number of used routes increases in the simple variant. Hence, the average connection quality has a higher impact than that of our optimized dissemination.

5   Related Work

Finding a suitable pre-filter node outside of the service data origin node and the position of post-filters in a dissemination tree opens the opportunity to

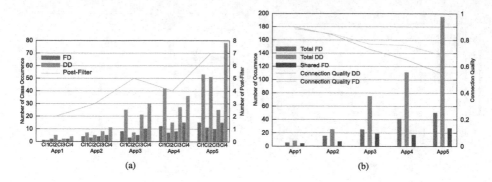

Fig. 7. Embedded network with $|V| = 100$.

share relevant service data with a number of service subscribers. This leads to a reduction of resources used within embedded networks in terms of network traffic as well as processing overhead. Similar topics are addressed by and can be found in Data Stream Management Systems (DSMSs). DSMSs complement the traditional Database Management Systems (DBMSs). Typically, a DBMS handles persistent and random accessible data and executes volatile queries. Meanwhile, in DSMSs persistent (or long-running) queries are executed over volatile and sequential data. Examples of DSMSs include *Aurora* [2], *Borealis* [1], *TelegraphCQ* [7], and *StreamGlobe* [19]. The main focus of such systems is on the efficient processing of potentially infinite data streams against a set of continuous queries. In contrast to publish/subscribe systems such as XFilter [3] or YFilter [8], continuous queries in DSMSs can be far more complex than simple filter subscriptions. Some research developed new query languages such as WindowedXQuery (WXQuery) [20] to extend query operations. In the domain of constrained embedded networks, however, we presume the presence of relatively simple data models and have found that XPath expressions are sufficient to address data interests and simple constraints by predicates. Other important work in distributed DSMSs such as StreamGlobe and Borealis revolves around network-aware stream processing and operator placement. These are issues also relevant to constrained embedded networks and, similarly, we took them into account for our approach by positioning the pre-filter and, if possible, the post-filter mechanism at the embedded nodes.

Most DSMSs, such as TelegraphCQ for example, are based on relational data. StreamGlobe, however, focuses on plain-text XML data streams as well as on XML-based query languages such as XQuery [4] or the above mentioned WXQuery. Consequently, nodes used for distributed data stream processing in systems such as StreamGlobe and Borealis generally need to be far more powerful than the microcontrollers for constrained embedded devices that we aim for in this paper. Our approach for constructing high performance filter mechanisms based on binary XML techniques enables us to bring DSMS topics to the domain of constrained embedded networks.

In our approach, filter nodes such as pre-filter or post-filter nodes decide how to best forward service messages if there are one or more matches. The destinations may include service requester nodes and/or other post-filter nodes. In the literature, this is called content-based routing or application-level routing since routing depends on the contents of data within a message. In that context, we can refer to works such as the *combined broadcast and content-based (CBCB)* routing scheme [6], the *application layer multicast algorithm (ALMA)* [10], the usage of *XML Router* [22], and *view selection for stream processing* based on XML data [14]. Below, we will concentrate on the latter since they also involve XML-based data content.

The XML Router approach [22] creates an overlay network that is implemented by multiple XML routers. An XML router is a node that receives XML packets and forwards a subset of these XML packets. The XML packets are forwarded to other routers or the final client node destinations. Thereby, the output links represent the XPath queries that describe the portion of the router's XML stream that should be sent to the host on that connection link. XML routers are comparable to our pre- and post-filter concept. However, additional strategies, such as reassembling a data packet stream from diverse senders provided by the diversity control protocol (DCP) or the usage of plain-text XML and XPath interpreters are not feasible in a resource constrained embedded environment.

The view selection for stream processing method is an interesting approach followed in [13,14]. The main concept includes selecting a set of XPath expressions which are called *views*. The service data producers evaluate the views and add the result to the data package in the form of a header. The advantage is that servers which keep a local set of queries can evaluate their workload by inspecting only the values in the header and do not need to parse the XML document. This leads to a speed-up of routing decisions. However, this is only true for cases in which the evaluation in the header is positive. Otherwise, the complete (plaintext) XML document needs to be parsed and the query needs to be evaluated in a conventional way. Again, this is an obstacle in the constrained embedded environment. In addition, one of our goals is to achieve seamless protocol usage and to work with standardized message representations to support interoperability in a heterogeneous network environment. Adding a header to a message would break this principle and necessitate an adjustment of communication protocols.

6   Conclusions and Future Work

In this paper, we presented an approach to realize efficient filter-enabled service data dissemination in constrained embedded networks based on XPath expressions given by different subscribers/clients. Finding a suitable pre-filter node in an embedded network leads to an early evaluation of relevant service messages. By using post-filters in a determined dissemination tree, we are able to avoid redundant transmissions and share the service data, especially if there is a multi-query match of different kinds of service requesters. The effectiveness in terms of device class occurrences, connection quality, and number of shared connections was demonstrated in a simulated environment based on our embedded network simulator.

Topics for future work include the dynamic update of client queries and their impact on the dissemination path as well as on the placed pre- and post filter grammar.

References

1. Abadi, D.J., Ahmad, Y., Balazinska, M., Çetintemel, U., Cherniack, M., Hwang, J.H., Lindner, W., Maskey, A., Rasin, A., Ryvkina, E., Tatbul, N., Xing, Y., Zdonik, S.B.: The design of the borealis stream processing engine. In: CIDR, pp. 277–289 (2005)
2. Abadi, D.J., Carney, D., Çetintemel, U., Cherniack, M., Convey, C., Lee, S., Stonebraker, M., Tatbul, N., Zdonik, S.B.: Aurora: a new model and architecture for data stream management. VLDB J. **12**(2), 120–139 (2003)
3. Altinel, M., Franklin, M.J.: Efficient filtering of XML documents for selective dissemination of information. In: Abbadi, A.E., Brodie, M.L., Chakravarthy, S., Dayal, U., Kamel, N., Schlageter, G., Whang, K.Y. (eds.) Proceedings of 26th International Conference on Very Large Data Bases, VLDB 2000, Cairo, Egypt, 10–14 September 2000, pp. 53–64. Morgan Kaufman, San Francisco (2000)
4. Boag, S., Chamberlin, D.D., Fernández, M.F., Florescu, D., Robie, J., Siméon, J.: XQuery 1.0: An XML query language. World Wide Web Consortium, Recommendation REC-xquery-20070123, January 2007
5. Bournez, C.: Efficient XML interchange evaluation. W3C working draft, W3C, April 2009. http://www.w3.org/TR/2009/WD-exi-evaluation-20090407
6. Carzaniga, A., Wolf, A.L.: Content-based networking: a new communication infrastructure. In: König-Ries, B., Makki, K., Makki, S.A.M., Pissinou, N., Scheuermann, P. (eds.) IMWS 2001. LNCS, vol. 2538, pp. 59–68. Springer, Heidelberg (2002). http://link.springer.de/link/service/series/0558/bibs/2538/25380059.htm; http://link.springer.de/link/service/series/0558/papers/2538/25380059.pdf
7. Chandrasekaran, S., Cooper, O., Deshpande, A., Franklin, M.J., Hellerstein, J.M., Hong, W., Krishnamurthy, S., Madden, S., Raman, V., Reiss, F., Shah, M.A.: Telegraphcq: continuous dataflow processing for an uncertain world. In: CIDR (2003)
8. Diao, Y., Franklin, M.J.: High-performance XML filtering: an overview of yfilter. IEEE Data Eng. Bull. **26**(1), 41–48 (2003)
9. Dijkstra, E.W.: A note on two problems in connexion with graphs. Numer. Math. **1**, 269–271 (1959). http://gdzdoc.sub.uni-goettingen.de/sub/digbib/loader?did= D196313
10. Ge, M., Krishnamurthy, S.V., Faloutsos, M.: Application versus network layer multicasting in ad hoc networks: the ALMA routing protocol. Ad Hoc Netw. **4**(2), 283–300 (2006). http://dx.doi.org/10.1016/j.adhoc.2004.10.002
11. Goldman, O., Lenkov, D.: XML binary characterization. World Wide Web Consortium, Note NOTE-xbc-characterization-20050331, March 2005. http://www.w3.org/TR/2005/NOTE-xbc-characterization-20050331
12. Gudgin, M., Hadley, M., Mendelsohn, N., Moreau, J.J., Frystyk Nielsen, H.: SOAP version 1.2 part 1: Messaging framework. World Wide Web Consortium, Recommendation REC-soap12-part1-20030624, June 2003

13. Gupta, A.K., Halevy, A.Y., Suciu, D.: View selection for stream processing. In: WebDB, pp. 83–88 (2002). http://www.db.ucsd.edu/webdb2002/papers/58.pdf
14. Gupta, A.K., Suciu, D., Halevy, A.Y.: The view selection problem for XML content based routing. In: PODS: 22nd ACM SIGACT-SIGMOD-SIGART Symposium on Principles of Database Systems (2003)
15. IEEE: IEEE Standard for Local and metropolitan area networks-Part 15.4: Low-Rate Wireless Personal Area Networks (LR-WPANs) (2011). http://standards. ieee.org/about/get/802/802.15.html
16. Käbisch, S., Kuntschke, R., Heuer, J., Kosch, H.: Efficient filtering of binary XML in resource restricted embedded networks. In: Proceedings of the 8th International Conference on Web Information Systems and Technologies (WEBIST 2012), pp. 174–182 (2012). http://dblp.uni-trier.de/db/conf/webist/webist2012.html
17. Käbisch, S., Peintner, D., Heuer, J., Kosch, H.: Optimized XML-based web service generation for service communication in restricted embedded environments. In: Proceedings of the 16th IEEE International Conference on Emerging Technologies and Factory Automation (2011)
18. Kou, L., Markowsky, G., Berman, L.: A fast algorithm for steiner trees. ACTAINF: Acta Informatica **15**, 141–145 (1981)
19. Kuntschke, R., Stegmaier, B., Kemper, A., Reiser, A.: Streamglobe: processing and sharing data streams in grid-based p2p infrastructures. In: Böhm, K., Jensen, C.S., Haas, L.M., Kersten, M.L., Larson, P.Å., Ooi, B.C. (eds.) VLDB, pp. 1259–1262. ACM (2005)
20. Kuntschke, R.B.: Network-aware optimization in distributed data stream management systems. Ph.D. thesis, Technische Universität München (2008). http:// mediatum2.ub.tum.de/doc/625762/document.pdf
21. Schneider, J., Kamiya, T.: Efficient XML Interchange (EXI) Format 1.0, W3C Recommendation 10 March 2011 (2011). http://www.w3.org/TR/exi
22. Snoeren, A.C., Conley, K., Gifford, D.K.: Mesh based content routing using XML. In: SOSP, pp. 160–173 (2001). http://doi.acm.org/10.1145/502034.502050

Semantic Matching-Based Selection
and QoS-Aware Classification of Web Services

Salem Chakhar[(⊠)], Alessio Ishizaka, and Ashraf Labib

Portsmouth Business School, University of Portsmouth, Portsmouth PO1 3DE, UK
{Salem.Chakhar,Alessio.Ishizaka,Ashraf.Labib}@port.ac.uk

Abstract. This paper focuses on Web services matchmaking. It distinguishes three types of matching: functional attribute-level, functional service-level, and non-functional. In this paper, a series of parameterized and highly customizable algorithms are advertised for the different types of matching. A prototype has been developed and used to test the functional attribute-based conjunctive matching using the SME2 environment and the OWLS-TC4 datasets. Results show that the algorithms behave globally well in comparison to similar existing ones.

Keywords: Web service · Service composition · Matchmaking · Quality of service · Similarity measure

1 Introduction

An important issue within web service composition is related to the selection of the most appropriate one among the different candidate web services. In this paper, we propose a semantic matchmaking framework for web service composition. Three types of matching are distinguished in this paper: functional attribute-level, functional service-level, and non-functional. In [1] we discussed functional attribute-level and functional service-level matching. This paper enhances our proposal in [1] by adding generic functional attribute-level and non-functional matching. We also briefly describe the developed prototype and compares the attribute-based conjunctive matching to the ones included in the iSEM and SPARQLent frameworks. We used the Semantic Matchmaker Evaluation Environment (SME2) [2] and the OWLS-TC4 datasets to evaluate the performances of the algorithms in respect to several parameters. Results show that our algorithms behaves globally well in comparison to iSEM and SPARQLent.

The paper is structured as follows. Section 2 sets the background. Sections 3, 4 and 5 present different matching algorithms. Section 6 presents performance analysis. Section 7 discusses related work. Section 8 concludes the paper.

2 Background

2.1 Basic Definitions

The following are some basic definitions of a service and other service-specific concepts. Several definitions are due to [3].

© Springer International Publishing Switzerland 2015
V. Monfort and K.-H. Krempels (Eds.): WEBIST 2014, LNBIP 226, pp. 96–112, 2015.
DOI: 10.1007/978-3-319-27030-2_7

Definition 1. *A service S is defined as a collection of attributes that describe the service. Let S.A denotes the set of attributes of service S and $S.A_i$ denotes each member of this set. Let S.N denotes the cardinality of this set.*

Definition 2. *The capability of a service S.C, is a subset of service attributes ($S.C \subseteq S.A$), and includes only functional ones that directly relate to its working.*

Definition 3. *The quality of a service S.Q, is a subset of service attributes ($S.Q \subseteq S.A$), and includes all attributes that relate to its QoS.*

Definition 4. *The property of a service, S.P, is a subset of service attributes ($S.P \subseteq S.A$), and includes all attributes other than those included in service capability or service quality.*

2.2 Service Matching Types and Process

The input for a Web service composition is a set of specifications describing the capabilities of the desired service. These specifications can be decomposed into two groups [1,4]: (i) functional requirements that deal with the desired functionality of the composite service, and (ii) non-functional requirements that relate to the issues like cost, performance and availability. These specifications need to be expressed in an appropriate language. In this paper, we adopt an extended version of Ontology Web Language (OWL) [5] for expressing functional requirements and the Quality of Service (QoS) for non-functional requirements.

In [1], we distinguished three types of service matching: (i) *functional attribute-level matching* that implies capability and property attributes and consider each matching attribute independently of the others; (ii) *functional service-level matching* that considers capability and property attributes but the matching operation implies attributes both independently and jointly; and (iii) *non-functional matching* which focuses on the attributes related to the QoS.

The functional matching takes as input all candidate Web services and produces a set of Web services that meet the user functional matching criteria. Hence, service types that fail to meet the user functional requirements are automatically eliminated. The non-functional matching takes as input a set of Web service instances that meet the functional requirements and classify them into different predefined and ordered quality of service classes.

2.3 Similarity Measure

A semantic match between two entities frequently involves a similarity measure that quantifies the semantic distance between the two entities participating in the match. As in [3], a similarity measure is defined as follows.

Definition 5. *The similarity measure, μ, of two service attributes is a mapping that measures the semantic distance between the conceptual annotations associated with the service attributes. Mathematically,*

$$\mu : A \times A \to \{Exact, \ Plug\text{-}in, \ Subsumption, \ Container, \ Part\text{-}of, \ Fail\}$$

where A is the set of all possible attributes.

The mapping between two conceptual annotations is called:

- **Exact** map: if the two conceptual annotations are syntactically identical,
- **Plug-in** map: if the first conceptual annotation is specialized by the second,
- **Subsumption** map: if the first conceptual annotation specializes the second,
- **Container** map: if the first conceptual annotation contains the second,
- **Part-of** map: if the first conceptual annotation is a part of the second, and
- **Fail** map: if none of the previous cases applies.

A preferential total order is established on the above mentioned similarity maps.

Definition 6. *Preference amongst similarity measures is governed by the following strict total order:*

$$Exact \succ Plug\text{-}in \succ Subsumption \succ Container \succ Part\text{-}of \succ Fail$$

where $a \succ b$ *means that a is preferred over b.*

To compute the similarity degrees, we implemented the idea proposed by [6] which starts by constructing a bipartite graph where the vertices in the left side correspond to the concepts associated with advertised services, while those in the right side correspond to the concepts associated with the requested service. The edges correspond to the semantic relationships between concepts. Then, the authors in [6] assign a weight to each edge and then apply the Hungarian algorithm [7] to identify the complete matching that minimizes the maximum weight in the graph. The final returned degree is the one corresponding to the maximum weight in the graph.

3   Functional Attribute-Level Matching

Functional matching is the process of discovering a service advertisement that *sufficiently* satisfies a service request [3]. It is based on the concept of *sufficiency*, which itself is based on the *similarity* measure defined in the previous section.

3.1   Conjunctive/Disjunctive Matching

Let S^R be the service that is requested, and S^A be the service that is advertised. A first customization of functional matching is to allow the user to specify a desired similarity measure for each attribute. A sufficient match exists between S^R and S^A in respect to a given attribute if there exists an identical attribute of S^A and the values of the attributes satisfy the desired similarity measure. A second customization of the matching process is to allow the user specifying which attributes should be utilized during the matching process, and the order in which the attributes must be considered for comparison. In order to support both customizations, we use the concept of Criteria Table, introduced by [3], that serves as a parameter to the matching process.

Definition 7. *A Criteria Table, C, is a relation consisting of two attributes, C.A and C.M. C.A describes the service attribute to be compared, and C.M gives the least preferred similarity measure for that attribute. Let $C.A_i$ and $C.M_i$ denote the service attribute value and the desired measure in the ith tuple of the relation. C.N denotes the total number of tuples in C.*

Example 1. Table 1 shows a Criteria Table example.

Table 1. An example Criteria Table.

C.A	C.M
input	Exact
output	Exact
service category	Subsumes

A sufficient functional attribute-level conjunctive match between services is defined as follows.

Definition 8. *Let S^R be the service that is requested, and S^A be the service that is advertised. Let C be a criteria table. A sufficient conjunctive match exists between S^R and S^A if for every attribute in C.A there exists an identical attribute of S^R and S^A and the values of the attributes satisfy the desired similarity measure as specified in C.M. Formally,*

$$\forall_i \exists_{j,k}(C.A_i = S^R.A_j = S^A.A_k) \wedge \mu(S^R.A_j, S^A.A_k) \succeq C.M_i$$
$$\Rightarrow SuffFuncConjMatch(S^R, S^A) \quad 1 \leq i \leq C.N. \tag{1}$$

The algorithm for functional attribute-level conjunctive matching is provided in [1]. A less restrictive definition of sufficiency consists in using a disjunctive rule on the individual matching measures.

Definition 9. *Let S^R be the service that is requested, and S^A be the service that is advertised. Let C be a criteria table. A sufficient disjunctive match exists between S^R and S^A if for at least one attribute in C.A it exists an identical attribute of S^R and S^A and the values of the attributes satisfy the desired similarity measure as specified in C.M. Formally,*

$$\exists_{i,j,k}(C.A_i = S^R.A_j = S^A.A_k) \wedge \mu(S^R.A_j, S^A.A_k) \succeq C.M_i$$
$$\Rightarrow SuffFuncDisjMatch(S^R, S^A). \tag{2}$$

The algorithm for functional attribute-level disjunctive matching is given in [1].

3.2   Generic Matching

In this section we extend the algorithms proposed in [1] to generic binary connectors by allowing the user to specify the conditional relationships between the capability and property attributes. First, we need to introduce the concept of sufficient single attribute match.

Definition 10. *Let S^R be the service that is requested, and S^A be the service that is advertised. Let C be a criteria table. A sufficient match exists between S^R and S^A in respect to attribute $S^R.A_i$ if there exists an identical attribute of S^A and the values of the attributes satisfy the desired similarity measure as specified in $C.M_i$. Formally,*

$$\exists_{j,k}(C.A_i = S^R.A_j = S^A.A_k) \wedge \mu(S^R.A_j, S^A.A_k) \succeq C.M_i)$$
$$\Rightarrow SuffSingleAttrMatch(S^R, S^A, A_i). \tag{3}$$

The single attribute matching is formalized in Algorithm 1 that follows directly from Sentence (3).

Algorithm 1. SuffSingleAttrMatching.

Input : S^R, // Requested service.
$\quad\quad\quad S^A$, // Advertised service.
$\quad\quad\quad C$, // Criteria Table.
$\quad\quad\quad i$, // Service attribute index.
Output: Boolean// success/fail.
while $(j \leq S^R.N)$ **do**
$\quad$ **if** $(S^R.A_j = C.A_i)$ **then**
$\quad\quad$ Append $S^R.A_j$ to *rAttrSet*;
$\quad$ Assign $j \longleftarrow j + 1$; ;
while $(k \leq S^A.N)$ **do**
$\quad$ **if** $(S^A.A_k = C.A_i)$ **then**
$\quad\quad$ Append $S^A.A_k$ to *aAttrSet*;
$\quad$ Assign $k \longleftarrow k + 1$;
if $(\mu(rAttrSet[i], aAttrSet[i]) \succeq C.M_i)$ **then**
$\quad$ return success;
return fail;

Let now define the sufficient functional generic match.

Definition 11. *Let S^R be the service that is requested, and S^A be the service that is advertised. Let C be the criteria table. Let T be a complex logical clause where operands are the attributes related by logical operators (e.g. or, and, not). A sufficient functional generic match between S^R and S^A holds if and only the logical clause T holds. Formally,*

$$\textbf{Parse}(T) \wedge \textbf{Evaluate}(T)$$
$$\Rightarrow SuffAttrGenericMatch(S^R, S^A). \tag{4}$$

where **Parse** *and* **Evaluate** *are functions devoted respectively to parse and evaluate the logical expression T.*

The functional generic match is formalized in Algorithm 2, which follows directly from Sentence (4).

Example 2. An example of a logical expression is "$T = A_5$ or $(A_2$ and $A_3)$". In this example, the matching holds when either (i) the matching in respect to attribute A_5 holds, or (ii) the matching in respect to attribute A_2 and the matching in respect to attribute A_3 hold jointly.

Algorithm 2. SuffAttrGenericMatch.

Input : S^R, // Requested service.
$\quad\quad\quad S^A$, // Advertised service.
$\quad\quad\quad C$, // Criteria table.
$\quad\quad\quad T$, // Logical expression.
Output: Boolean// success/fail.
if $(NOT(\textbf{Parse}(T)))$ **then**
$\quad\quad$⌊ return fail;

$T' \longleftarrow T$;
$Z \longleftarrow \emptyset$;
for $(each \quad A_l \in T')$ **do**
$\quad\quad$ **if** $(A_l \notin Z)$ **then**
$\quad\quad\quad\quad$ $t \longleftarrow$ false;
$\quad\quad\quad\quad$ $t \longleftarrow$ SuffSingleAttrMatch(S^R, S^A, A_l);
$\quad\quad\quad\quad$ replace all $A_l \in T$ by the value of t;
$\quad\quad\quad\quad$ $Z \longleftarrow Z \cup \{A_l\}$;

if $(\textbf{Evaluate}(T))$ **then**
$\quad\quad$⌊ return success;

$\quad\quad$return fail;

3.3 Computational Complexity

Let first focalize on the complexity of Algorithm 1. The complexity of the two *while* loops in Algorithm 1 is equal to $O(S^R.N) + O(S^A.N)$. Since we generally have $S^A.N \gg S^R.N$, hence the complexity of the two *while* loops is equal to $O(S^A.N)$. Then, the worst case complexity of Algorithm 1 is $O(S^A.N) + \alpha$ where α is the complexity of computing μ. The value of α depends on the approach used to infer μ. As underlined in [3], inferring μ by ontological parse of pieces of information into facts and then utilizing commercial rule-based engines which use the fast Rete [8] pattern-matching algorithm leads to $\alpha = O(|R||F||P|)$ where $|R|$ is the number of rules, $|F|$ is the number of facts, and $|P|$ is the average number of patterns in each rule. In this case, the worst case complexity of Algorithm 1 is $O(S^A.N) + O(|R||F||P|)$. Furthermore, we observe, as in [3], that the process of computing μ is the most "expensive" step of the algorithm. Hence, the complexity of Algorithm 1 is $O(S^A.N) + O(|R||F||P|) \asymp O(|R||F||P|)$.

The complexity of Algorithm 2 depends on the complexity of functions **Parse** and **Evaluate**. The complexity of these functions depends on the data structure used to represent the logical expression T (graph, truth tables, etc.). Clearly the complexity of **Evaluate** function is largely greater than the complexity of **Parse** function. Hence, the complexity of Algorithm 2 is $O(|R||F||P|) + O(\gamma)$ where $O(\gamma)$ is the complexity of **Evaluate** function.

4 Functional Service-Level Matching

The functional service-level matching allows the client to use two types of desired similarity: (i) desired similarity values associated with each attribute in the criteria table, and (ii) a global desired similarity that applies to the service as a whole. The service-level similarity measure quantifies the semantic distance between the requested service and the advertised service entities participating in the match by taking into account both attribute-level and service-level desired similarity measures.

Definition 12. *Let S^R be the service that is requested, and S^A be the service that is advertised. Let C be a criteria table. Let β be the service-level desired similarity measure. A sufficient service-level match exists between S^R and S^A if (i) for every attribute in $C.A$ there exists an identical attribute of S^R and S^A and the values of the attributes satisfy the desired similarity measure as specified in $C.M$, and (ii) the value of overall similarity measure satisfies the desired overall similarity measure β. Mathematically,*

$$[\forall i \quad (\textbf{SuffSingleAttrMatch}(S^R, S^A, A_i)) \quad 1 \leq i \leq C.N] \wedge$$
$$[\exists j_1, \cdots, j_i, \cdots, j_N \quad (\zeta(s_{1,j_1}, \cdots, s_{i,j_i}, \cdots, s_{N,j_N}) \succeq \beta)] \tag{5}$$
$$\Rightarrow \textbf{SuffFuncServiceLevelMatch}(S^R, S^A),$$

where ζ is an aggregation rule; and for $i = 1, \cdots, N$ and $j_i \in \{j_1, \cdots, j_N\}$:

$$s_{i,j_i} = \mu(S^R.A_i, S^A.A_{j_i}).$$

The parameter β may be any of the maps given in Sect. 2.3. The functional service-level matching algorithm is given in [1]. The aggregation rule ζ used in the definition above is a tool to combine the similarity measures into a single similarly measure. In [1], we defined ζ as follows:

$$\zeta : F_1 \times \cdots \times F_N \rightarrow \{\text{Exact, Plug-in, Subsumption, Container, Part-of, Fail}\}$$

where $F_j = \{$Exact, Plug-in, Subsumption, Container, Part-of, Fail$\}$ ($j = 1, \cdots, N$); and N is the number of attributes included in the criteria table.

The similarity maps and the corresponding strict total order given in Sect. 2.3 still apply here. Since the similarity measures are defined on an ordinal scale, there are only a few possible aggregation rules that can be used to combine the similarity measures [1]: Minimum, Maximum, Median, Floor and Ceil. The Floor and Ceil rules apply only when there is an even number of similarity measures (which leads to two median values).

5   QoS-Oriented Classification

The QoS-oriented matching concerns QoS attributes only and applies to service instances that verify functional requirements. The objective of QoS matching is to assign to each instance an overall QoS level. Instead of sorting services from best to worst, we propose to categorize them into an ordered set of QoS classes $\mathbf{Cl} = \{Cl_1, \cdots, Cl_p\}$, such that the higher the class, the higher the QoS level. The computing of overall QoS level for each instance requires the use of a multicriteria aggregation rule. In this paper, we will use the simple majority with veto support rule.

5.1   Classification Algorithm

Let first introduce some new concepts.

Definition 13. *A QoS Attribute Table, Q, is a relation consisting of three attributes, Q.A, Q.T and Q.S. Q.A describes the service attribute to be compared, Q.T gives the attribute type and Q.S specifies the scale type. Two types of attributes are distinguished: gain and cost. The gain attributes are those to be maximized while cost attributes are those to be minimized. The scale may be nominal, ordinal, cardinal or ratio. Let $Q.A_i$, $Q.T_i$ and $Q.S_i$ denote the service attribute value, the attribute type and the scale type of the ith tuple of the relation. Let $Q.N$ be the total number of tuples in Q.*

Example 3. Table 2 shows a QoS Attribute Table example. It specifies the parameters of four QoS attributes: response time (A_1), availability (A_2), security (A_3) and cost (A_4).

Table 2. An example QoS Attribute Table.

$Q.A$	$Q.T$	$Q.S$
A_1: Response time	cost	Cardinal
A_2: Availability	gain	Cardinal
A_3: Security	gain	Ordinal
A_4: Cost	cost	Cardinal

Definition 14. *A Boundary Matrix, B, consisting of a pairwise matrix composed of $p-1$ columns $B_1, \cdots, B_{p-1}$ and N rows corresponding to the number of QoS attributes.*

Example 4. An example of Boundary Matrix is given in Table 3. It specifies three boundaries in respect to the QoS given in Table 2. Table 3 defines four QoS classes.

Table 3. An example Boundary Matrix.

$Q.A_i$	B_1	B_2	B_3
Response time	11	9.25	8
Availability	0.2	0.3	0.51
Security	2	3	4
Cost	4	3.5	3

The attribute type and scale parameters should be used to control input data, especially the definition of boundaries.

Definition 15. *A Weight Table, W, is a relation consisting of two attributes, W.A and W.V. W.A describes the service attribute and W.V specifies the weight of this attribute. Let $W.A_i$ and $W.V_i$ denote the service attribute and the attribute weight value in the ith tuple of relation W. The weights values must sum to 1.*

Example 5. An example of Weight Table is given in Table 4.

Table 4. An example Weight Table.

W.A	W.V
Response time	0.325
Availability	0.325
Security	0.175
Cost	0.175

Definition 16. *Let $h \in \{1, \cdots, p\}$. The concordance power for the outranking of advertised service S^A over boundary B_h is computed as follows:*

$$\Phi(S^A, B_h) = \sum_{i \in L_1(S^A, h)} W.V_i, \tag{6}$$

where: $L_1(S^A, B_h) = \{i : S^A.A_i \succeq B_h.A_i \wedge Q.T_i = \text{'gain'}\} \cup \{i : S^A.A_i \preceq B_h.A_i \wedge Q.T_i = \text{'cost'}\} \cup \{i : S^A.A_i = B_h.A_i \wedge Q.S_i = \text{'nominal'}\}.$

Example 6. Let consider the service instances given in Table 5. Based on the definition above we obtain $L_1(s_8, B_1) = \{1, 3, 2, 4\}$, $L_1(s_8, B_2) = \{2, 3, 4\}$ and $L_1(s_8, B_3) = \{4\}$. This leads to: $\Phi(s_8, B_1) = 1$, $\Phi(s_8, B_2) = 0.675$ and $\Phi(s_8, B_3) = 0.175$.

Definition 17. *Let $h \in \{1, \cdots, p\}$. The discordance power for the outranking of advertised service S^A over boundary B_h is computed as follows:*

$$\Psi(S^A, B_h) = \prod_{k=1}^{k=N} Z_k(S^A.A_k, B_h.A_k), \tag{7}$$

where:

$$Z_k(S^A.A_k, B_h.A_k) = \begin{cases} \frac{1 - W.V_k}{1 - \Phi(S^A, B_h)}, & \text{if } W.A_k > \Phi(S^A, B_h) \wedge k \in L_2(S^A, B_h) \\ 1, & \text{otherwise.} \end{cases} \tag{8}$$

with $L_2(S^A, B_h) = \{i : S^A.A_i \prec B_h.A_i \wedge Q.T_i = \text{'gain'}\} \cup \{i : S^A.A_i \succ B_h.A_i \wedge Q.T_i = \text{'cost'}\} \cup \{i : S^A.A_i \neq B_h.A_i \wedge Q.S_i = \text{'nominal'}\}.$

Table 5. Web service instances.

s_i	A_1	A_2	A_3	A_4
s_8	12.82	0.34296	3	2.74
s_9	10.92	0.15	1	2.08
s_{10}	9.52	0.51	4	2.5

Example 7. Let consider the service instances given in Table 5. Based on the definition above we obtain $L_2(s_8, B_1) = \{1\}$, $L_2(s_8, B_2) = \{1\}$ and $L_2(s_8, B_3) = \{1, 2\}$. This leads to: $\Psi(s_8, B_1) = 0.818$, $\Psi(s_8, B_2) = 0.818$ and $\Psi(s_2, B_3) = 0.670$.

Definition 18. *Let $h \in \{1, \cdots, p\}$. The credibility index for the outranking of advertised service S^A over boundary B_h is computed as follows:*

$$\sigma(S^A, B_h) = \Phi(S^A, B_h) \cdot \Psi(S^A, B_h). \tag{9}$$

Example 8. Based on Examples 6 and 7, we obtain $\sigma(s_8, B_1) = 0.818$, $\sigma(s_8, B_2) = 0.552$ and $\sigma(s_8, B_3) = 0.117$.

Definition 19. *Let S^R be the service that is requested and S^A be the service that is advertised. Let $S^R.Q$ be the list of QoS attributes to be utilized for classification. Service S^A is assigned to QoS class Cl_h if for every QoS attribute of S^R there is exists an identical attribute of S^A and the value of the Credibility index is greater or equal to the credibility threshold $\lambda \in [0.5, 1]$ and $\sigma(S^A, B_h) \geq \sigma(S^A, B_{h'})$ for every $h < h'$. Formally,*

$$Argmax_h[\exists_{j,k}(Q.A_i = S^R.A_j = S^A.A_k) \wedge \sigma(S^A, B_h) \geq \lambda]$$
$$\Rightarrow QoSClassification(S^R, S^A, Cl_h). \tag{10}$$

According to this definition, a service S^A is assigned to class Cl_h if and only if: (i) there is a "sufficient" majority of attributes in favor of assigning S^A to Cl_h, and (ii) when the first condition holds, none of the minority of attributes shows an "important" opposition to the assignment of S^A to Cl_h.

Example 9. Let $\lambda = 0.65$. Based on the data and results of the previous example, we conclude that s_8 in Table 5 is assigned to QoS class level 2 since $\sigma(s_8, B_1) = 0.818 > \lambda$, and $\sigma(s_8, B_2) = 0.552 < \lambda$ and $\sigma(s_8, B_3) = 0.117 < \lambda$.

The algorithm for QoS Classification is given in Algorithm 3. This algorithm compares S^A to each of the boundaries staring from the highest one and stops once a sufficient QoS measure holds. The function `CredibilityIndex` computes the credibility index as in Eq. (9).

A more simple version of the classification algorithm consists in using the simple majority only. The algorithm based on the simple majority rule is similar to Algorithm 3. We simply need to replace the test "`CredibilityIndex`$(u, h) \geq \lambda$" by "`ConcordancePower`$(u, h) \geq \lambda$". The function `ConcordancePower` computes the Concordance Power as in Eq. (6).

5.2 Computational Complexity

Algorithm 3 runs in $O(2mp \times |U|)$ where U is the set of instances. Note that function ConcordancePower runs in $O(m)$ and function CredibilityIndex runs in $O(2m)$. The complexity of the simple version of the classification algorithm which is based only on the majority rule and which is not given here, is $O(mp \times |U|)$, where m is the number of QoS attributes and p is the number of QoS classes.

Algorithm 3. QoSClassification.

> **Input** : S^A, // Advertised service.
> λ, // Credibility threshold.
> Q, // QoS Table.
> B, // Boundary Matrix.
> W, // Weight Table.
> **Output**: **Cl** $= \{Cl_1, \cdots, Cl_p\}$// Global QoS classes.
> $p \longleftarrow$ number of QoS classes;
> $Cl_i \longleftarrow \emptyset, \forall i = 1, \cdots, p$;
> $U \longleftarrow$ instances of S^A;
> **for** $(all\ u \in U)$ **do**
> $\quad$ $h \longleftarrow p - 1$;
> $\quad$ $assigned \longleftarrow$ False;
> $\quad$ **while** $(h \geq 0 \wedge NOT(assigned))$ **do**
> $\quad\quad$ **if** $(\text{CredibilityIndex}(u, h, W) \geq \lambda)$ **then**
> $\quad\quad\quad$ $Cl_{h+1} \longleftarrow Cl_{h+1} \cup \{u\}$;
> $\quad\quad\quad$ $assigned \longleftarrow$ true;
> $\quad\quad$ $h \longleftarrow h - 1$;
> **Cl** $\longleftarrow \{Cl_1, \cdots, Cl_p\}$;
> return **Cl**;

5.3 Illustration

Let us consider the list of potential compositions given in Table 6. We assume that these compositions have meet the functional requirements of the user. Table 6 shows the evaluation of the compositions in respect to four QoS attributes (response time (A_1), availability (A_2), security (A_3), and cost (A_4) attributes) given in Table 2. The objective is to classify the compositions into different ordered categories. For the purpose of this example, we assume that the four categories defined by Table 3 and the weights given in Table 4 have been used.

The final classifications obtained by the simple majority and simple majority with veto algorithms where the credibility threshold is $\lambda = 0.65$ are given in Table 6. In this table, we can see that both simple majority and majority with veto algorithms assign instances s_3 and s_{10} to the best QoS class. We remark also that both algorithms assign instances s_5 and s_9 to the worst QoS class.

Table 6. Potential compositions and final classification for λ=0.65.

s_i	$A_1(s_i)$	$A_2(s_i)$	$A_3(s_i)$	$A_4(s_i)$	Simple Majority	Majority +Veto
s_1	9.2	0.45946	1	2.48	3	3
s_2	8.12	0.41817	1	2.68	3	3
s_3	8	0.53	4	2.78	4	4
s_4	8.19	0.46967	2	3.24	3	3
s_5	11.15	0.19	1	2.74	1	1
s_6	7.42	0.40317	2	3.38	3	3
s_7	7.72	0.36676	2	3.18	3	3
s_8	12.82	0.34296	3	2.74	3	2
s_9	10.92	0.15	1	2.08	1	1
s_{10}	9.52	0.51	4	2.5	4	4
s_{11}	10.12	0.53294	3	2.68	3	3
s_{12}	10.42	0.48356	1	2.32	2	2
s_{13}	12.52	0.2	1	3.14	2	1
s_{14}	8.42	0.48	1	2.82	3	3
s_{15}	10.32	0.48	4	2.16	3	3

Which is interesting to see in Table 6 is the role of veto effect in the assignment of instances s_8 and s_{13}. Indeed, the QoS of both instances have been decreased (from 3 to 2 for instance s_8 and from 2 to 1 for instance s_{13}) by the majority with veto algorithm. This happens because the weights of attributes which are against the assignment—of instance s_8 to QoS class 3 and instance s_{13} to QoS class 2—have been taken into account.

6 Implementation and Performance Analysis

A prototype called PMCF (Parameterized Matching-Classification Framework) has been implemented. Figure 1 provides the architecture of PMCF. The inputs are the Criteria Table, the published Web services repository, the user request and its corresponding Ontologies. The inputs are parsed by the Semantic Matchmaking Module which filters service offers that match with the Criteria Table. The result should then be passed to the Classification Module which assigns the matching services into different QoS classes. We note that Classification Module is not implemented in the current version of PMCF. We used OWLS API to parse the published Web services list and the user request. The similarity between the concepts is inferred using Jena API (see http://jena.sourceforge.net). Finally, we note that in the current version, PMCF supports only Input and Output attributes and only the functional attribute-based conjunctive matching.

We used SME2 [2] to evaluate the performance of PMCF. SME2 is an open source tool for testing different semantic matchmakers in a consistent way. SME2 uses OWLS-TC collection to provide the matchmakers with services descriptions, and to compare their answers to the relevance sets of the various queries. Different experimentations was conducted on a dell Inspiron 15 3735 Laptop with an Intel Core I5 processor (1.6 GHz) and 2 GB of memory. The test collection used is OWLS-TC4, which consists of 1083 service offers described in OWL-S 1.1 and 42 queries. The implemented plugin for the experiment required a precise interface, we could not take the Criteria Table as an input, so we assigned to it a default value (Input:Fail, Output:Fail). SME2 gives several metrics to evaluate the performance and effectiveness of a service matchmaker. The metrics that have been considered in this paper are: precision and recall, query response time and memory time. The definition of these metrics are given in [2,9]. We compared the results of our PMCF matchmaker with SPARQLent approach [10] and iSEM approach [11]. SPARQLent is a logic-based matchmaker based on the OWL-DL reasoner Pellet to provide exact and relaxed service matchmaking. iSEM is an hybrid matchmaker offering different filter matchings: logic-based, approximate reasoning based on logical concept abduction for matching Inputs and Outputs. We consider only the I-O logic-based matching for the comparison issue. We note that SPARQLent and iSEM consider preconditions and effects of Web services, which is out of the scope of our approach.

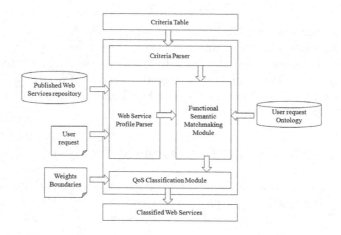

Fig. 1. Architecture of the prototype PMCF.

Figure 2a presents the recall precision of PMCF, iSEM logic-based and SPARQLent. This figure shows that PMCF recall is significantly better than both iSEM logic-based and SPARQLent. This means that our approach is able to reduce the amount of false positives.

Figure 2b compares the Query Response Time of PMCF, logic-based iSEM and SPARLent when answering the 42 queries of OWLS-TC; the first column

(Avg) gives the average response time for the three matchmakers. The experimental results show that PMCF is more faster than SPARQLent and slightly less faster than logic-based iSEM. We note that SPARQLent has especially high query response time if the query include preconditions/effects. Moreover, SPARQLent is based on an OWL DL reasoner which is an expensive processing. PMCF and iSEM have close query response time because both consider direct parent/child relations in a subsumption graph which reduce significantly the query processing. The PMCF highest query response time limit is 248 ms.

Finally, Fig. 2c shows the Memory Usage for PMCF, iSEM logic-based and SPARQLent. It is easy to see that PMCF consumes less memory than iSEM logic-based and SPARQLent. This can be explained by the fact that PMCF does not require a reasoner neither a SPARL queries in order to compute similarities between concepts.

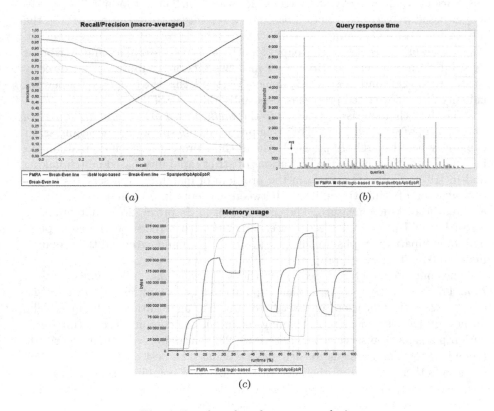

Fig. 2. Results of performance analysis.

7   Related Work

In this section we discuss some matchmaking frameworks in respect to several characteristics. The first characteristic is related to the *support of customization* which is an important issue in practice, as recognized by [3]. Most of proposed matching systems ignore this point and only a few ones take into account this aspect. In [3], for instance, the authors present a parameterized semantic matchmaking framework that enables the user to specify the matched attributes and the order in which attributes are compared. In [3], the sufficiency condition defined by the authors is very strict. This problem has been addressed in [1] and in this paper by relaxing matchmaking conditions and supporting three types of matching.

The second characteristic concerns the *type of attributes used in the matching operation*. Most of existing matchmaking frameworks [12–14] use only service capability as the criteria for the match. The authors in [3] distinguish two types of matching attributes: capability and property. In [15], the author proposes two approaches to service selection based on QoS attributes. The authors in [16] discuss various techniques of QoS based service selection. The author in [17] proposes a QoS-based web service selection based on a stochastic optimization. In [18], the authors propose a QoS-aware web service selection algorithm based on clustering. The framework presented in this paper identify three types of matching attributes by subdividing property attributes set into two sets of attributes: those directly related to the QoS and those which are not. We think that the proposed framework enhances the above cited proposals, especially the work of [3].

The third characteristic is related to the *method used to compare the requested and advertised services*. Most of existing proposals use simple syntactic and strict capability-based search. In paper [3], the authors present a semantic matchmaking framework that avoids the limitations of strict capability-based matchmaking and in [19] the authors transform the problem of matching web services to the computation of semantic similarity between concepts in domain ontology using a semantic distance measure. The proposal of [6] improve [20]'s matchmaking algorithm and propose a greedy-based algorithm that relies on the concept of matching bipartite graphs. In this paper, we adopted and extended the semantic matchmaking framework proposed by [3].

The fourth characteristic concerns the *support of the multicriteria evaluation*. There are a few proposals that explicitly support multicriteria evaluation, e.g. [21–25]. Most of them use weighted-sum like aggregation techniques. The authors in [25] use linear programming techniques to compute the optimal execution plans for web service. The author in [23] considers two evaluation criteria (time and cost) and assigns to each one a weight. The best composition of Web services is then decided on the basis of the optimum combined score and a service selection QoS broker by maximizing a utility function is provided by [24]. We note, however, that this type of methods have two main shortcomings: (i) they accept only numerical data and (ii) may lead to the compensation problem since low values may be counterbalanced by high values. The approach used in this paper accepts any type of data and resolves the compensation problem.

8   Conclusions

We presented a QoS-aware semantic matching framework. The framework supports three types of matching: functional attribute-level matching, functional service-level matching, and QoS-based matching. A series of highly customizable algorithms are advertised for each type of matching.

Several issues need to be further investigated. First, the reduction of the number of parameters required from the user by automatically generating the boundaries of QoS classes. Second, the use of the rough sets theory-based classification [26] for assigning instances to QoS classes. Third, the use of multicriteria ranking methods instead of the classification approach used in this paper.

Acknowledgements. The authors would like to thank Fatma Ezzahra Gmati (National School of Computer Sciences, University of Manouba, Tunis, Tunisia) for developing the prototype and for conducing the performance analysis. The authors would also like to thank Dr. Nadia Yacoubi-Ayadi (National School of Computer Sciences, University of Manouba, Tunis, Tunisia) who co-supervised the developing of the prototype and the performance analysis.

References

1. Chakhar, S.: Parameterized attribute and service levels semantic matchmaking framework for service composition. In: Fifth International Conference on Advances in Databases, Knowledge, and Data Applications (DBKDA 2013), Seville, Spain, pp. 159–165 (2013)
2. Klusch, M., Dudev, M., Misutka, J., Kapahnke, P., Vasileski, M.: SME^2 Version 2.2. User Manual. The German Research Center for Artificial Intelligence (DFKI), Germany (2010)
3. Doshi, P., Goodwin, R., Akkiraju, R., Roeder, S.: Parameterized semantic matchmaking for workflow composition. IBM Research Report RC23133, IBM Research Division (2004)
4. Chakhar, S.: QoS-enhanced broker for composite web service selection. In: Eighth International Conference on Signal Image Technology and Internet Based Systems (SITIS 2012), Sorrento-Naples, Italy, pp. 533–540 (2012)
5. Agarwal, V., Chafle, G., Dasgupta, K., Karnik, N., Kumar, A., Mittal, S., Srivastava, B.: Synthy: a system for end to end composition of web services. J. Web Semant. **3**, 311–339 (2005)
6. Bellur, U., Kulkarni, R.: Improved matchmaking algorithm for semantic web services based on bipartite graph matching. In: IEEE International Conference on Web Services, Salt Lake City, Utah, USA, pp. 86–93 (2007)
7. Kuhn, H.: The Hungarian method for the assignment problem. Naval Res. Logist. Q. **2**, 83–97 (1955)
8. Forgy, C.: Rete: a fast algorithm for the many patterns/many objects match problem. Artif. Intell. **19**, 17–37 (1982)
9. Küster, U., König-Ries, B.: Measures for benchmarking semantic web service matchmaking correctness. In: Aroyo, L., Antoniou, G., Hyvönen, E., ten Teije, A., Stuckenschmidt, H., Cabral, L., Tudorache, T. (eds.) ESWC 2010, Part II. LNCS, vol. 6089, pp. 45–59. Springer, Heidelberg (2010)

10. Sbodio, M., Martin, D., Moulin, C.: Discovering semantic Web services using SPARQL and intelligent agents. Web Semant.: Sci. Serv. Agent. World Wide Web **8**, 310–328 (2010)
11. Klusch, M., Kapahnke, P.: The iSEM matchmaker: a flexible approach for adaptive hybrid semantic service selection. Web Semant.: Sci. Serv. Agent. World Wide Web **15**, 1–14 (2012)
12. Ben Mokhtar, S., Kaul, A., Georgantas, N., Issarny, V.: Efficient semantic service discovery in pervasive computing environments. In: van Steen, M., Henning, M. (eds.) Middleware 2006. LNCS, vol. 4290, pp. 240–259. Springer, Heidelberg (2006)
13. Guo, R., Le, J., Xiao, X.: Capability matching of web services based on OWL-S. In: Sixteenth International Workshop on Database and Expert Systems Applications, pp. 653–657 (2005)
14. Li, L., Horrocks, I.: A software framework for matchmaking based on semantic web technology. In: 12th International World Wide Web Conference, Budapest, Hungary, pp. 331–339 (2003)
15. Ludwig, A.: Memetic algorithm for web service selection. In: Third Workshop on Biologically Inspired Algorithms for Distributed Systems, BADS 2011, pp. 1–8. ACM, New York (2011)
16. Sathya, M., Swarnamugi, M., Dhavachelvan, P., Sureshkumar, G.: Evaluation of QoS based web-service selection techniques for service composition. Int. J. Softw. Eng. **1**, 73–90 (2011)
17. Krithiga, R.: QoS-aware web service selection using SOMA. Glob. J. Comput. Sci. Tech. **12**, 46–51 (2012)
18. Xia, Y., Chen, P., Bao, L., Wang, M., Yang, J.: A QoS-aware web service selection algorithm based on clustering. In: IEEE International Conference on Web Services (ICWS), pp. 428–435 (2011)
19. Fu, P., Liu, S., Yang, H., Gu, L.: Matching algorithm of web services based on semantic distance. In: International Workshop on Information Security and Application (IWISA 2009), Qingdao, China, pp. 465–468 (2009)
20. Paolucci, M., Kawamura, T., Payne, T.R., Sycara, K.: Semantic matching of web services capabilities. In: Horrocks, I., Hendler, J. (eds.) ISWC 2002. LNCS, vol. 2342, p. 333. Springer, Heidelberg (2002)
21. Cui, L., Kumara, S., Lee, D.: Scenario analysis of web service composition based on multi-criteria mathematical goal programming. Serv. Sci. **3**, 280–303 (2011)
22. Jeong, B., Cho, H., Kulvatunyou, B., Jones, A.: A multi-criteria web services composition problem. In: IEEE International Conference on Information Reuse and Integration (IRI 2007), pp. 379–384 (2007)
23. Menascé, D.: Composing web services: a QoS view. IEEE Internet Comput. **8**, 88–90 (2004)
24. Menascé, D., Dubey, V.: Utility-based QoS brokering in service oriented architectures. In: IEEE International Conference on Web Services (ICWS 2007), pp. 422–430 (2007)
25. Zeng, L., Benatallah, B., Dumas, M., Kalagnanam, J., Sheng, Q.: Quality driven web services composition. In: 12th International Conference on World Wide Web, pp. 411–421. ACM, New York (2003)
26. Greco, S., Matarazzo, B., Słowiński, R.: Rough sets theory for multicriteria decision analysis. Eur. J. Oper. Res. **129**, 1–47 (2001)

A Social Semantic Approach to Adaptive Query Expansion

Claudio Biancalana, Fabio Gasparetti, Alessandro Micarelli,
and Giuseppe Sansonetti[✉]

Department of Engineering, Artificial Intelligence Laboratory, Roma Tre University,
Via della Vasca Navale, 79, 00146 Rome, Italy
{claudio.biancalana,gaspare,micarel,gsansone}@dia.uniroma3.it

Abstract. Classic query expansion approaches are based on the use of
two-dimensional co-occurrence matrices. In this paper, we propose the
adoption of three-dimensional matrices, where the added dimension is
represented by semantic classes (i.e., categories comprising all the terms
that share a semantic property) related to the folksonomy extracted from
social bookmarking services, such as *Delicious* and *StumbleUpon*. The
results of an in-depth experimental evaluation performed on real users
show that our approach outperforms traditional techniques, so confirming the validity and usefulness of the categorization of the user needs
and preferences in semantic classes.

Keywords: Query expansion · Social bookmarking services · Personalization

1 Introduction

Automatic query expansion (QE) techniques allow users to better characterize
their search domain by supplementing the original query with additional terms
that are somehow linked to the frequency of terms submitted by the user in
his query [3,8]. The system we present is a social semantic extension of the
traditional QE approaches, which rely on a coarse syntactic analysis for extracting co-occurrences with a view to building two-dimensional matrices [5,9]. These
matrices basically represent the distribution of co-occurring terms in a given collection of documents. For instance, if the terms *personal* and *computer* appear
together in one document, they are considered to co-occur once. The limit of
a relatively simple and easily accessible structure such as this one is the *latent
ambiguity* of the collected information. If the terms chosen by the user are polysemous (i.e., have several different meanings), the query expansion can bring
about a misinterpretation of the current user interests, thus leading to erroneous
results. So how is it therefore possible to improve this structure by focusing on
the semantic characteristics of the collected terms? To this aim, we propose the
introduction of the concept of *semantic class*. A semantic class is a category
including all the terms that share a semantic property. Our system makes use

© Springer International Publishing Switzerland 2015
V. Monfort and K.-H. Krempels (Eds.): WEBIST 2014, LNBIP 226, pp. 113–127, 2015.
DOI: 10.1007/978-3-319-27030-2_8

of three-dimensional co-occurrence matrices, where the added dimension is represented by semantic classes related to the folksonomy extracted from social bookmarking services, such as *Delicious*[1] and *StumbleUpon*[2]. Therefore each co-occurrence is associated with a specific semantic class. A comparative analysis between our results and those obtained through some state-of-the-art techniques shows that our approach is able to achieve better results. This reveals that our system can offer a stronger correlation with the actual user interests, which confirms the validity and usefulness of their categorization in semantic classes.

The rest of the paper is structured as follows. Section 2 reviews some related works, Sect. 3 describes the system architecture. The main algorithms are detailed in Sect. 4, while Sect. 5 is devoted to the presentation and discussion of the experimental findings. Finally, Sect. 6 concludes the paper and highlights some future directions.

2   Related Work

Over the last years, the literature of information retrieval systems has seen the development of several automatic query expansion (QE) approaches [7,14]. Among the various QE techniques proposed, some of them take advantage of the implicit relevance feedback through pseudo-relevance feedback [2]. All these methods follow the basic assumption: documents classified higher by an initial search contain many useful terms that can help discriminate relevant documents from irrelevant ones. Despite the large number of studies, a crucial issue is that the expansion terms identified through traditional methodologies from the pseudo-relevant documents may not be all useful [12].

Bilotti et al. [10] analyze the effects of some QE approaches on document retrieval in the context of question answering, mainly targeted to the so-called "factoid" questions, namely, fact-based, natural language questions that usually can be answered through a short noun phrase. More specifically, the authors describe a quantitative comparative analysis between two different strategies for tackling term variation: (i) employing a stemming algorithm at indexing time, or (ii) carrying out a morphological query expansion at retrieval time. The findings show that, when compared to the baseline (no stemming, nor expansion), stemming yields a lower recall, while morphological expansion results in higher recall. However, higher recall is paid at the cost of retrieving more irrelevant documents and ranking relevant documents at lower positions.

One of the failure reasons of the query expansion has been identified in the lack of relevant documents in the local collection. Consequently, some works advance the use of an external resource for query expansion in order to improve the effectiveness of query expansion, such as thesaurus [22], Wikipedia [25], browsed web pages [16], key-phrases from corpora of documents [4,6], and search engine query logs [15]. Abouenour et al. [1] point out that the adoption of a thesaurus, typically constructed through statistical techniques, poses several

---

[1] delicious.com.
[2] stumbleupon.com.

drawbacks. First of all, the construction of a thesaurus is a time-consuming task because of the great deal of data to process. Effective semantic QE techniques can also rely on ontologies instead of thesauri. Indeed, ontologies describe both semantic and concept relations, and enable semantic reasoning as well as cross-language information retrieval. The authors specifically deal with the enhancement of question answering in Arabic, a complex language for its peculiarities. They propose an approach that implements a semantic QE based on the WordNet[3] ontology in Arabic. As a result, the described QE method bears the following semantic relations: synonymy, hypernymy (supertypes), hyponymy (subtypes), and the Super Upper Merged Ontology (SUMO)[4] concept definition [23]. SUMO is a top-level ontology that defines general terms and can be used as a foundation for middle-level and more specific domain ontologies. The documents retrieved through the previous process are then re-ranked using a structure-based approach based on the Distance Density n-gram model.

More recently, several authors have focused on social annotations as external resource, largely motivated by their increasing availability through many Web-based applications. Among these, Carman et al. [13] explore how useful tag data may improve search results, but they focus primarily on data analysis rather than retrieval experiments. Zhou et al. [27] propose a query expansion framework relied on user profiles extracted from the annotations and resources bookmarked by users. The main difference with our approach is that the selection of expansion terms for a given query is not based on semantic classes, but on the assumption that they are likely to have similar weightings influenced by the documents best ranked for the original query.

3   System Architecture

In this section, we present the architecture of the system we propose (see Fig. 1), specifying the functionalities of each module and the modalities which they actively collaborate through. The modules that compose the system architecture can be described as follows.

- **Interface:** the mail purpose of this module is readdressing external requests to the specialized modules and processing the achieved results so as to show them in a more understandable form;
- **Expansion:** after the user has submitted his search query, this module is responsible of the query expansion process. To perform multiple expansions, this module has to access the user interests stored in the user model;
- **Search:** this module is in charge of the real search process, receiving (possibly expanded) queries in input and returning the corresponding results;
- **Persistence:** all the necessary information is retained in this module: login data, encountered terms (both before and after stemming), tags, co-occurrence values between terms, tag relevance, and URLs of documents visited by the

---

[3] wordnet.princeton.edu.
[4] www.ontologyportal.org.

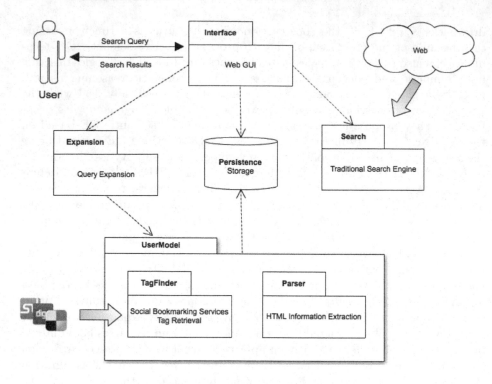

Fig. 1. The system architecture.

user; it interacts mainly with the interface (for user login and saving URLs) and the user model (for data needed for the construction and analysis of the user model);

– **UserModel:** this is the largest module in that it has to constantly update the user profile realized as a three-dimensional co-occurrence matrix. The interaction with the persistence module is the first step for achieving data (visited URLs and corresponding queries) from which to infer information for the model update. Before the necessary processing, this module makes use of two other sub-modules: Parser and TagFinder;

  • **Parser:** its main role is to filter out the unnecessary information related to the user interests collected by the system, and to provide the user model with a sorted set of terms for the three-dimensional matrix computation. It includes parsing functionalities (i.e., filtering the HTML pages visited by the user), stemming, and stopword removal;

  • **TagFinder:** it is devoted to the search of tags to be associated with the pages visited by the user. It interacts with external resources (social bookmarking services) to extract complete tags of a relevance index, in order to supply them to the user model.

Results obtained in each search session are then presented to the user so as to underline the different semantic categories of each group of them. The search of the tags associated with the pages visited by the user is performed by analyzing the information provided by main sites that offer social bookmarking services. In this case, data collection occurs directly by parsing the HTML pages containing the necessary information. In order to model the user visits, the system employes matrices based on co-occurrences at the page level: terms highly co-occurring with the issued keywords have been proven to increase precision when appended to the query [21]. The generic term t_x is in relation with all other n terms t_i (with $i = 1, \ldots, n$) according to a coefficient c_{xi} representing the co-occurrence measure between the two terms. In a classical way, we can construct the co-occurrence matrix through the Hyperspace Analogue to Language approach [11]: once a term is given, its co-occurrence is computed with n terms to its right (or its left); in particular, given a term t and considered the window f_t of n terms w_i to its right $f_t = \{w_1, \ldots, w_n\}$, we have $co\text{-}oc(t, w_i) = \frac{w_i}{i}$, $i = 1 \ldots, n$. A pair (a, b) is equal to pair (b, a), that is, the co-occurrence matrix is symmetrical. For each training document a co-occurrence matrix is generated, whose lines are then normalized to the maximum value. The matrices of the single document are then summed up, thus generating one single co-occurrence matrix representing the entire corpus. The limit of this structure lies in the latent ambiguity of collected information: in presence of polysemy of the terms adopted by the user, the result of the query expansion risks to misunderstand the interests, so leading to erroneous results. In order to overcome this problem, in our system the classical model of co-occurrence matrix has been extended. The user model consists of a three-dimensional co-occurrence matrix. Each term of the matrix is linked to an intermediate level containing the relative belonging classes, each accompanied by a relevance index. This way, each term is *contextualized* before being linked to all the other terms present in the matrix, and led to well determined semantic categories that are identified by tags.

4   Social Semantic Search

In this section, we describe in detail the two main algorithms of our approach. The former is designed for the user model creation and update (discussed in Sect. 4.1), the latter for the query expansion process (discussed in Sect. 4.2). With reference to the pseudocode shown below, we notice that the co-occurrence matrix is represented through a map of maps for encoding knowledge and connecting such knowledge to relevant information resources. Maps of maps are organized around *topics*, which represent subjects of interest; *associations*, which express relationships between the subjects; and *occurrences*, which connect the subjects to pertinent information resources.

4.1   User Model Creation and Update

The creation and update of the user model are based on the pages chosen by the user while searching. Starting with an empty model, every time the user clicks on a result after typing a search query, the system records the visited URL, together with the query originally submitted for the search. Our system performs the analysis of the visited URLs in incremental way, according to the following algorithm (see Algorithm 1, where capital deltas (Δ) denote comments):

- a temporary map M is initialized, where it is possible to store the extracted data, before updating the pre-existent model (empty at first execution). The map keys are the encountered tags, the values are the relative two-dimensional co-occurrence matrices;
- for each visited URL, the corresponding HTML page is obtained, from which the textual information is extracted through a parser, as a list of terms;
- the list of terms is filtered in order to eliminate stopwords (i.e., all those terms that are very frequent in all documents, so irrelevant to the creation of the user model);
- the list of terms undergoes a stemming process by means of the Porter's algorithm. At the same time the system retains the relations between stemmed terms and original terms;
- the co-occurrence matrix corresponding to the most relevant k_{term} keywords is evaluated. The relevance is measured by counting the occurrences within the document itself, with the exception of terms used in the query (retained by the system together with the corresponding URL), to which is assigned the maximum weight;
- tags concerning the visited URLs are obtained by accessing different sites of social bookmarking. Each extracted tag has a weight which depends on its relevance (i.e., the number of users which agree to associate that tag to the visited URL);
- the update of the temporary map M is performed by exploiting all the information derived from the co-occurrence matrix and the extracted tags in a combined fashion. For each tag_i the system updates the co-occurrence values just calculated, according to the tag relevance weight. After that, the vectors M_{tag_i,t_i} related to each term t_i are updated by inserting the new (or summing to the previous) values;
- the set $terms$ is calculated, which contains all the terms encountered during the update of the temporary map M;
- from the persistence module a subset UM_{terms} of the user model is obtained as a three-dimensional matrix of co-occurrences, corresponding only to the terms contained in $terms$;
- the matrix UM_{terms} is updated with the values of M. For each t_i belonging to $terms$, the set of keys ($tags$) is extracted from M, which points to values corresponding to t_i. For each tag_i belonging to $tags$, the vector M_{tag_i,t_i} is added to the pre-existent vector UM_{t_i,tag_i}, updating the values for the terms already present and inserting new values for the terms never encountered.

4.2   Query Expansion

The query expansion process is performed beginning from the original terms entered into the search engine by accessing the information collected in the

---

Algorithm 1. User Model Creation and Update.

---

   begin
       Δ Initialize the global co-occurrence matrix M (map of maps);
       $M \leftarrow Map([])$;
       Δ Analyze training documents;
       for $(doc, query)$ in D **do**
           Δ Parse the document (stemming and stopword removal);
           $doc = parse(doc)$;
           Δ Initialize the co-occurrence matrix of different terms; $terms \leftarrow Map([])$;
           Δ Compute the co-occurrence value of every term;
           $terms = frequency\_occurrences(doc)$;
           Δ Initialize the co-occurrence matrix of document;
           $co\_occ \leftarrow Map([])$;
           Δ Compute the co-occurrence matrix of document;
           $co\_occ = co\_occurrences(terms)$;
           Δ Get the site list of social bookmarking for tag search;
           $sites = get\_social\_bookmarking\_sites()$;
           Δ Initialize URL list tags;
           $tags \leftarrow Set([])$;
           Δ Retrieve tags by URL;
           for $i = 0$; $i < sites.size()$ & $tags.size() = 0$; $i + +$ **do**
              $tags = retrieve\_tags(url, sites[i])$;
           Δ Update the matrix M;
           $update(M, tags, terms)$;
       Δ Initialize all terms in documents;
       $all\_terms \leftarrow Set([])$;
       Δ Get unique terms set;
       $all\_terms = get\_term\_set(M)$;
       Δ Get subset of user model;
       $user\_matrix \leftarrow get\_user\_matrix(all\_terms)$;
       Δ Update user model by the intermediate matrix;
       $update(user\_matrix, M, all\_terms)$;
       Δ Store updated user model;
       $save(user\_matrix)$;

---

user model. The result is a set of expanded queries, each of them associated with one or more tags. This way, it is possible to present the user with different subgroups of results grouped in categories. Using low level boolean logic, every expansion assumes the following form:

$$(t_{11} \text{ OR } \ldots \text{OR } t_{1x}) \text{ AND } (t_{21} \text{ OR } \ldots \text{ OR } t_{2x}) \ldots$$
$$\text{AND } (t_{y1} \text{ OR } \ldots \text{ OR } t_{yx})$$

where t_{yx} represents the generic term x corresponding to the stemmed root y. The different terms coming from the same root undergo OR operation amongst them, since the result has to contain at least one of them. The algorithm of multiple expansion is the following (see Algorithm 2):

– let us suppose that the query Q is given, which consists of n terms q_i (with $i = 1, \ldots, n$). For each of them the system evaluates the corresponding stemmed term q_i', so obtaining the new query Q' as a new result;

- for each term belonging to Q', the corresponding two-dimensional vector q_i is extracted from the three-dimensional co-occurrence matrix. Each of those vectors may be viewed as a map, whose keys are the tags associated with the terms q_i' (which have a relevance factor), and the values are themselves *co-occurrence vectors* between q_i' and all the other encountered terms;
- for each encountered tag the relevance factor is recalculated, adding up the single values of each occurrence of the same tag in all two-dimensional vectors. This way, the result is a vector T in which tags are sorted according to the new relevance factor;
- amongst all tags contained in T, only the higher k_{tag} are selected and considered for the multiple expansions;
- for each selected tag t_i the vector sum_{t_i} is computed, which represents the sum of the co-occurrence values of the three-dimensional matrix, corresponding to all terms q_i' of the query Q';
- for each vector sum_{t_i}, the most relevant terms k_{qe} (corresponding to higher values) are selected. Combining the extracted terms with those of the query Q, a new query EQ' (made up of stemmed terms) is initialized;
- for each expanded query EQ', the corresponding query EQ is calculated through the substitution of stemmed terms with all the possible original terms stored into the system, exploiting the boolean logic according to the scheme previously shown;
- the query EQ and the original tag t_i are entered into the map M_{EQ}, whose keys are expanded queries and values are sets of tags. If M_{EQ} already contains an expanded query identical to the input one, the tag t_i is added to the corresponding set of tags.

5 Evaluation

In this section, we present the experimental results of the proposed approach. Specifically, we describe a comparative evaluation analysis between our social-based search engine and some state-of-the-art techniques.

5.1 Experimental Setup

In this experimental test, four different search engines have been included: Google (denoted simply as *Google* hereafter), the personalized version of Google (*PersGoogle*), a query expansion search engine based on co-occurrence data (*CoOcc*), and our system (*OurSystem*). In the first personalized version of Google back in 2004, the search engine showed a directory like category drop-down menu, where users could select the categories that matched their interests. During the search process, the search engine adapts the results according to each user needs, assigning a higher score to the resources related to what the user has seen in the past. A slider in the graphic user interface allows the user to control the level of personalization in the results. Unfortunately, no details or evaluations are

---

Algorithm 2. Multiple Query Expansion.

---

begin
  Δ Initialize the query to be expanded (a list of n terms)
  $query \leftarrow [q_1, q_2, ..., q_n]$
  Δ Stemming of query terms
  $query \leftarrow stemming(query)$
  Δ Get the subset of the user model related to the query
  $user\_matrix = get\_user\_matrix(query)$
  Δ Initialize the tag map for multiple query expansion
  $expansion\_tags \leftarrow Map([])$
  Δ Compute tags for multiple expansion
  $expansion\_tags = find\_expansion\_tags(query, user\_matrix)$
  Δ Initialize the expanded query map related to tags
  $exp\_queries \leftarrow Map([])$
  Δ Compute expanded queries for every tag
  for $(tag, ranking)$ *in expansion_tags* **do**
      Δ Compute the expanded query by choosing most relevant terms
      $exp\_query = select\_relevant\_terms(query, user\_matrix)$
      Δ Enter the result in the expanded query map
      $insert\_expanded\_query(exp\_query, tag, ranking, exp\_queries)$
  end
  return $exp\_queries$
end

---

presently available for the algorithms exploited for the re-ranking process, except the ones contained in the patent application filed in 2004 [26]. Our comparative evaluation takes into account the current version of personalized Google. It basically reorders the search results based on gathered usage data, such as previous queries, web navigation behavior and, possibly, visited sites that serve Google ads, computers with Google Applications installed, such as Desktop Search and personal information, which may be implicitly or explicitly provided by the user. Query expansion based on co-occurrences is a well-known approach that collects the correlations between pairs of terms in a given corpus. It is a straightforward approach that limits the computational complexity through the idea of associating contexts to the current user needs. The two fundamental problems of information retrieval, namely, synonymy and polysemy, are addressed during the construction of the query vector. Ambiguous words have only one lemma for all their meanings. If one meaning is mentioned in a query, the documents in which the term appears with the other meanings are also retrieved and estimated as closer to the query. In case of polysemy there will be terms associated to more than one meaning, but if the query is composed by a number of keywords, the intended meaning is more likely to be referenced. These terms and their associated terms will form a cluster, which is associated to the intended meaning and outweighs the unintended meanings. Several studies in the literature have proven the effectiveness of this approach, but have also raised some doubts on its real improvements in the performance of document retrieval systems, because of the following potential issues:

- Weighting terms that occur more frequently in the whole dataset, so favoring the more popular (see, for example, [24]);
- Expanding each single term in the query in isolation, ignoring the potential meaning of the all terms as a whole;
- Co-occurrences data extracted from small collections of documents;
- Collection of documents not including relevant concepts and information during the query expansion.

In order to minimize those issues mainly related to the documents selected for the initial dataset, the co-occurrence matrix used for expansion is built on the corpus of documents retrieved during the learning process. In this way, it is certain that enough relevant documents for the expansion are included and there are less chances to see several common terms that cover several different topics of interests.

5.2   Participants

Personalized search engines, such as the system we propose, need to collect and analyze large amount of usage data related to the current and past user interests and needs in order to provide better recommendations in comparison with traditional approaches. For this reason, we present the results of an experimental evaluation conducted on real users that have tested the effectiveness of the search engines in real scenarios. Specifically, a total of 42 people have been recruited, mostly students of Computer Science courses. All participants hold a bachelor's degree. A vast majority of males (36) outnumbers females (6). All of them are aged below 30. This choice allowed us to have people deemed comfortable with using search engines in their activities. Some of the recruited people (8 %) use search engines once a week on average, while the others use these tools at least once a day. A substantial number of people (70 %) are to be considered experts, namely, they know the basic notions of boolean matching between words and page contents, and they are familiar with some advanced search techniques (e.g., boolean operators and phrase search). Each user is asked to choose two general domains of interest with the indication that the awareness and familiarity of the topic is adequate for analyzing contents retrieved on the Web. For each of these topics, the user performs five search sessions, each one related to some specific sub-topic of the chosen domain. The prototype monitors the pages the user decides to visit in the top ten results page. There is no time limit to be observed during the evaluation. After training, the user is asked to perform and evaluate a search session related to one information need in the chosen domains. In particular, the user has 40 results made up of the three lists of ten results obtained by four engines: *Google*, *PersGoogle*, *CoOcc*, and *OurSystem*. The final lists are randomized. *Google* search engine is chosen for its popularity, high effectiveness, and the state-of-the-art of ranking algorithms in Web information retrieval. Moreover, by asking users to create a personal account, Google is able to provide personalized ranks based on the users Web history. Users with a Google account were asked to clear their Web history or otherwise create a new one. *Google* evaluation is performed by asking the users to log out from the search engine before retrieving any search result. Users express a judgment for each result with a five-point Likert-type scale of values.

5.3 Results

In order to express the performance of the retrieval we employ the Precision at 20 (P@20) and the Mean Average Precision (MAP): the former evaluates the fraction of the retrieved documents that are relevant to the user information needs, the latter is useful to average various precisions when there are sets of distinct queries to be submitted to the search engine. We do not consider the recall measure, which evaluates the proportion of relevant documents that are retrieved, as it is not computable in open corpus domains. In the Web, in fact, we cannot know the whole number of relevant documents available. For the same reason, we do not consider the F1 score (or F-measure) either, an other standard statistical parameter, which combines the precision and the recall of the test to compute the resulting score. The average number of result pages viewed by a typical user for a query is 2.35 [18], and a more recent study [17] reports that about 85.92 % of users view no more than two result pages. For these reasons, the precision is evaluated at a given cut-off rank, considering only the top 20 results returned by the system. The performance of the recommendation process was assessed by evaluating the normalized version of Discounted Cumulative Gain (nDCG) [19, 20] as well. It is a well-known measure for evaluating a graded relevance scale of documents in a search engine result set. Rather than MAP, nDCG is much more focused on the top of the ranked list. nDCG is usually truncated at a particular rank level to emphasize the importance of the documents retrieved first. To focus on the top-ranked items, we considered the DCG@n by analyzing the ranking of the top n items in the recommended list with $n \in \{1, 5, 10\}$. The measure is defined as follows:

$$nDCG@n = \frac{DCG@n}{IDCG@n} \tag{1}$$

and the Discounted Cumulative Gain (DCG) is defined as:

$$DCG@n = rel_1 + \sum_{i=2}^{n} \frac{rel_i}{\log_2 i} \tag{2}$$

Table 1. Comparison in terms of MAP, P@20, and nDCG@n measures.

	MAP	P@20	nDCG@1	nDCG@5	nDCG@10
Google	0.61	0.52	0.13	0.28	0.32
PersGoogle	0.72	0.61	0.17	0.33	0.39
CoOcc	0.65	0.67	0.44	0.51	0.68
OurSystem	0.80	0.71	0.33	0.55	0.71

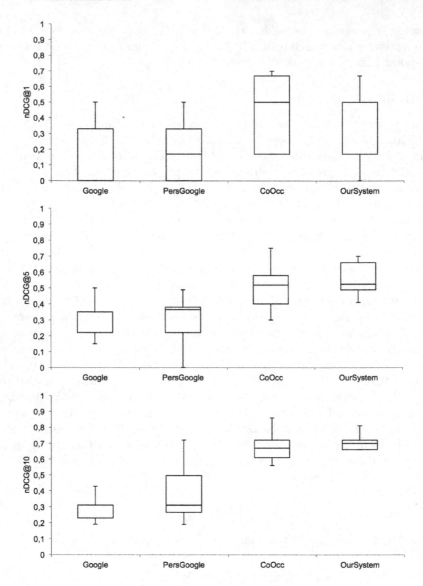

Fig. 2. Box plots of nDCG@1, nDCG@5, and nDCG@10.

where rel_i is the graded relevance of the i−th result (i.e., from $0 = non\ significant$ to $4 = very\ significant$), and the Ideal DCG ($IDCG$) for a query corresponds to the DCG measure where scores are re-sorted monotonically decreasing, that is, the maximum possible DCG value over that query. nDCG is often used to evaluate search engine algorithms and other techniques whose goal is to order a subset of items in such a way that highly relevant documents are placed on top of the list, while less important ones are moved further down. Basically, higher values of nDCG mean that the system output gets closer to the ideally ranked output.

In order to evaluate the reliability of such comparisons, all results were tested for statistical significance using *t-test*. In each case, we obtained a p-value < 0.05. Therefore, the *null hypothesis* that values are drawn from the same population (i.e., the outputs of two search engines are virtually equivalent) can be rejected. Table 1 summarizes the evaluation results. In terms of best performance, *OurSystem* wins on the ideal ranking of users, especially when the user sifts through five or more results. The worst performance is obtained by the non personalized *Google* approach. More precisely, both *CoOcc* and *OurSystem* obtain higher results. The contextual information that is included during the query expansion helps reduce ambiguity and makes the retrieval more accurate. *CoOcc* query expansion performs slightly better if the task is to recommend only one document (i.e., the more relevant), while *OurSystem* outperforms the other approaches if the task is to retrieve five or ten results in absolute terms. Figure 2 better explains the results with same medians for nDCG@1, while for nDCG@5 and nDCG@10 *OurSystem* behaves more accurately. The difference between the two approaches is also observable by the number of terms used during the expansion of the query. *OurSystem* adds 2.96 terms to the original query on average, while *CoOcc* uses 2.57 terms. Basically, *OurSystem* alters the query with more words than the co-occurrence based retrieval.

6 Conclusions

In this paper, we have proposed a novel social semantic approach for providing adaptive query expansions. Specifically, such technique introduces the definition of semantic classes (i.e., categories comprising all the terms that share a semantic property) related to the folksonomy extracted from social bookmarking services such as *Delicious* and *StumbleUpon*. The expansion process occurs analyzing multiple occurrences divided into categories related to semantic classes, which are analyzed in the folksonomy. We have presented the results of a comparative analysis on real users, which confirm the correlation with user interests and the effective coherence and utility of their categorization in semantic classes.

We intend to pursue several research thrusts in the future. Firstly, we plan to explore ways of integrating natural language processing procedures in our approach. Furthermore, we want to consider the temporal dimension for a better comprehension of the user information needs as his searches change over time. A further research challenge is to investigate alternative ways of tag categorization to be added to tag search through social bookmarking sites, for instance, those based on automatic document categorization.

References

1. Abouenour, L., Bouzouba, K., Rosso, P.: An evaluated semantic query expansion and structure-based approach for enhancing arabic question answering. Int. J. Inf. Commun. Technol. **3**(3), 37–51 (2010)

2. Baeza-Yates, R.A., Ribeiro-Neto, B.A.: Modern Information Retrieval. ACM Press / Addison-Wesley, Boston, MA, USA (1999)
3. Bai, J., Song, D., Bruza P., Nie, J.Y., Cao, G.: Query expansion using term relationships in language models for information retrieval. In: Proceedings of the 14th ACM International Conference on Information and Knowledge Management, pp. 688–695 (2005)
4. Biancalana, C., Flamini, A., Gasparetti, F., Micarelli, A., Millevolte, S., Sansonetti, G.: Enhancing traditional local search recommendations with context-awareness. In: Konstan, J.A., Conejo, R., Marzo, J.L., Oliver, N. (eds.) UMAP 2011. LNCS, vol. 6787, pp. 335–340. Springer, Heidelberg (2011)
5. Biancalana, C., Gasparetti, F., Micarelli, A., Sansonetti, G.: Enhancing query expansion through folksonomies and semantic classes. In: 2012 International Conference on Privacy, Security, Risk and Trust (PASSAT), International Conference on Social Computing (SocialCom), pp. 611–616, September 2012
6. Biancalana, C., Gasparetti, F., Micarelli, A., Sansonetti, G.: An approach to social recommendation for context-aware mobile services. ACM Trans. Intell. Syst. Technol. **4**(1), 10:1–10:31 (2013)
7. Biancalana, C., Gasparetti, F., Micarelli, A., Sansonetti, G.: Social semantic query expansion. ACM Trans. Intell. Syst. Technol. **4**(4), 60:1–60:43 (2013)
8. Biancalana, C., Lapolla, A., Micarelli, A.: Personalized web search using correlation matrix for query expansion. In: Cordeiro, J., Hammoudi, S., Filipe, J. (eds.) Web Information Systems and Technologies. LNBIP, vol. 18, pp. 186–198. Springer, Heidelberg (2009)
9. Biancalana, C., Micarelli, A.: Social tagging in query expansion: a new way for personalized web search. In: CSE (4), pp. 1060–1065 (2009)
10. Bilotti, M.W., Katz, B., Lin, J.: What works better for question answering: stemming or morphological query expansion? In: Proceedings of the Information Retrieval for Question Answering (IR4QA) Workshop at SIGIR 2004, Sheffield (2004)
11. Burgess, C., Lund, K.: Hyperspace analog to language (hal): a general model of semantic representation. In: Proceedings of the Annual Neeting of the Psychonomic Society (1995)
12. Cao, G., Nie, J.-Y., Gao, J., Robertson, S.:Selecting good expansion terms for pseudo-relevance feedback. In: Proceedings of the 31st Annual International ACM SIGIR Conference on Research and Development in Information Retrieval, SIGIR 2008, pp. 243–250, New York (2008)
13. Carman, M.J., Baillie, M., Gwadera, R., Crestani, F.: A statistical comparison of tag and query logs. In: Proceedings of the 32nd International ACM SIGIR Conference onResearch and Development in Information Retrieval, SIGIR 2009, pp. 123–130, New York (2009)
14. Carpineto, C., Romano, G.: A survey of automatic query expansion in information retrieval. ACM Comput. Surv. **44**(1), 1:1–1:50 (2012)
15. Cui, H., Wen, J.-R., Nie, J.-Y., Ma, W.-Y.: Query expansion by mining user logs. IEEE Trans. Knowl. Data Eng. **15**(4), 829–839 (2003)
16. Micarelli, A.G.F., Sansonetti, G.: Exploiting web browsing activities for user needs identification. In: Proceedings of the 2014 International Conference on Computational Science and Computational Intelligence (CSCI 2014), IEEE Computer Society, Conference Publishing Services, March 2014
17. Jansen, B.J., Spink, A., Pedersen, J.: A temporal comparison of altavista web searching: research articles. J. Am. Soc. Inf. Sci. Technol. **56**(6), 559–570 (2005)

18. Jansen, B.J., Spink, A., Saracevic, T.: Real life, real users, and real needs: a study and analysis of user queries on the web. Inf. Process. Manage. **36**(2), 207–227 (2000)
19. Järvelin, K., Kekäläinen, J.: IR evaluation methods for retrieving highly relevant documents. In: Proceedings of the 23rd Annual International ACM SIGIR Conference on Research and Development in Information Retrieval, New York, USA, pp. 41–48, (2000)
20. Järvelin, K., Kekäläinen, J.: Cumulated gain-based evaluation of IR techniques. ACM Trans. Inf. Syst. **20**(4), 422–446 (2002)
21. Kim, M.-C., Choi, K.-S.: A comparison of collocation-based similarity measures in query expansion. Inf. Process. Manage. **35**(1), 19–30 (1999)
22. Nanba, H.: Query expansion using an automatically constructed thesaurus. In: Kando, N., Evans, D.K. (eds) Proceedings of the Sixth NTCIR Workshop Meeting on Evaluation of Information Access Technologies: Information Retrieval, Question Answering, and Cross-Lingual Information Access, 2-1-2 Hitotsubashi, Chiyoda-ku, Tokyo 101–8430, Japan, pp. 414–419, May 2007
23. Niles, I., Pease, A.: Linking lexicons and ontologies: mapping wordnet to the suggested upper merged ontology. In: Proceedings of the IEEE International Conference on Information and Knowledge Engineering, Las Vegas, Nevada, USA, pp. 412–416, (2003)
24. Peat, H.J., Willett, P.: The limitations of term co-occurrence data for query expansion in document retrieval systems. J. American Soc. Inf. Sci. **42**, 378–383 (1991)
25. Xu, Y., Jones, G.J.F., Wang, B.: Query dependent pseudo-relevance feedback based on wikipedia. In: Proceedings of the 32nd International ACM SIGIR Conference on Research and Development in Information Retrieval, SIGIR 2009, pp. 59–66, New York (2009)
26. Eli Zamir, O., Korn, J.L., Fikes, A.B., Lawrence, S.R.: Us patent application #0050240580: Personalization of placed content ordering in search results, July 2004
27. Zhou, D., Lawless, S., Wade, V.: Improving search via personalized query expansion using social media. Inf. Retr. **15**(3–4), 218–242 (2012)

A Comparative Survey of Cloud Identity Management-Models

Bernd Zwattendorfer[(⊠)], Thomas Zefferer, and Klaus Stranacher

Institute for Applied Information Processing and Communications (IAIK),
Graz University of Technology, Inffeldgasse 16a, 8010 Graz, Austria
{bernd.zwattendorfer,thomas.zefferer,
klaus.stranacher}@iaik.tugraz.at

Abstract. Secure identification and authentication are essential processes for protecting access to services or applications. These processes are also crucial in new areas of application such as the cloud computing domain. Over the past years, several cloud identity management-models for managing identification and authentication in the cloud domain have emerged. In this paper, we survey existing cloud identity management-models and compare and evaluate them based on selected criteria, e.g., on practicability or privacy aspects.

Keywords: Cloud · Cloud computing · Cloud identity management-model · Identity management

1 Introduction

Secure and reliable identity management (IdM) plays a vital role in several security-sensitive areas of applications, e.g. in e-Government, e-Business, or e-Health. An identity management-system helps online applications to control access for users to protected resources or services. However, identity management is no new topic and several identity management-approaches and systems have already emerged over time. A comprehensive overview on identity management-systems is given in [1].

Due to the increasing number of cloud computing adoption and the deployment of security-sensitive cloud applications, secure identity management becomes also more and more important in the cloud domain. In addition, outsourcing identity management-systems to the cloud can bring up several benefits such as higher scalability or cost savings, since no in-house infrastructure needs to be hosted and maintained. However, the field of cloud identity management is still new and not extensively investigated yet. Therefore, the aim of this paper is to overview different cloud identity management-models, discuss advantages and disadvantages of the individual models, provide a comprehensive survey, and finally compare them based on selected criteria. The criteria for the comparison have been selected by focusing on practicability and privacy, since one of the main issues of cloud computing is the loss of data protection and privacy [2–4].

© Springer International Publishing Switzerland 2015
V. Monfort and K.-H. Krempels (Eds.): WEBIST 2014, LNBIP 226, pp. 128–144, 2015.
DOI: 10.1007/978-3-319-27030-2_9

The paper is structured as follows. Section 2 classifies existing traditional identity management-models and their implementations. Section 3 surveys existing cloud identity management-models and describes their benefits and drawbacks. These models are compared in Sect. 4 based on selected criteria. Finally, conclusions are drawn in Sect. 5.

2   Traditional Identity Management-Models

An identity management-system usually involves four entities [5]. A *service provider* (SP) provides different online services to *users*. Before being allowed to consume such services, a user has to successfully identify and authenticate. Therefore, the user usually identifies and authenticates at a so-called *identity provider* (IdP). The identity provider is then in charge of providing the users identity data and supplementary authentication results to the service provider in a secure way. Finally, a *control party*, which is usually a law or regulation enforcing body, needs to investigate identity data transactions, e.g. for data protection reasons. Hence, main purpose of such control party is auditing. Figure 1 illustrates the communication process in an identity management-system including all four entities.

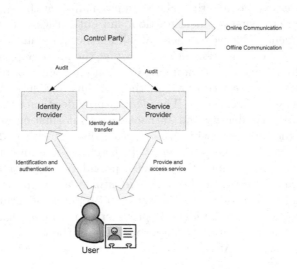

Fig. 1. Entities involved in an identity management-system.

Over time, several identity models involving these four entities and supporting similar but slightly different use cases have evolved. Some of these models have advantages in scalability, others in privacy or user control. In the following subsections we briefly describe the most important models based on the work of [6–12]. For simplicity, we skip a discussion of the control party in all subsequent models because its functionality remains the same in all models.

2.1   Isolated Model

The *isolated model* is basically the simplest traditional identity model. In this model, the service provider and identity provider merge, hence identification and authentication are directly carried out at the service provider. In addition, the functionality of the identity management-system (creating, maintaining, or deleting identities) can only be used by this specific service provider. If a user wants to access services of another service provider, she needs to register at the other service providers identity management-system again. This further means that each individual service provider has to store and maintain the identity data and credentials of the user separately. While this still may not be a huge burden for service providers, the diversity of credentials for accessing various service providers may become unmanageable for users [10]. This model can still be found by service providers on the Internet.

2.2   Central Model

The *central identity model* avoids diverse identity management-systems, where the user has to register separately. Instead, the identity management-system is outsourced by several service providers to a central identity provider. The identity provider takes over all identity-related functionality for the service provider, including credential issuance, identification and authentication, and the management of the identity lifecycle in general [5]. Furthermore, in this model users' identity data are stored in a central repository at the identity provider and service providers do not need to maintain identity data in their own repositories [6]. For authentication at a service provider, the user has to identify and authenticate at the identity provider before. The identity provider then assembles a token including all necessary identity and authentication information of the user and transmits it to the service provider[1]. [9] further distinguish the domain model for the identifier used. In the *common identifier model* one and the same identifier is used for identification at all service providers. In contrast to that, in the *meta identifier domain model* separate identifiers are used for identification at the individual service providers. However, all separate identifiers map to a common meta identifier at the identity provider to uniquely identify the user. Typical examples implementing this approach are Kerberos [13] or the Central Authentication Service (CAS)[2].

2.3   User-Centric Model

While in the central model all identity data of the user are stored in the domain of the identity provider, in the *user-centric model* all identity data are stored directly in the users domain, e.g. on a secure token such as a smart card.

---

[1] Different approaches exist; hence identity data can be either pushed to or pulled from the service provider.

[2] http://www.jasig.org/cas.

The main advantage of this model is that the user always remains the owner of her identity data and stays under their full control [8]. Identity data can only be transferred by an identity provider to a service provider if the user explicitly gives her consent to do so. Compared to the central model, this tremendously increases users' privacy. [10] discuss in detail this user-centric approach. Typical examples implementing this model are Windows CardSpace[3] or various national eID solutions such as the Austrian citizen card [14] or the German eID [15].

2.4 Federated Model

In the *federated model* identity data are not stored in a central repository but are rather stored distributed across different identity and/or service providers. No single entity is fully controlling the identity information [12]. The distributed identity data of a particular user are linked usually by the help of a common identifier[4]. All identity providers and service providers, which take part in such a federation, share a common trust relationship amongst each other. The trust relationship is usually established on organizational level whereas enforcement is carried out on technical level. This federated model particularly supports identification and authentication across different domains, which paves the way for cross-domain single sign-on [6]. Popular examples of this approach are the Security Assertion Markup Language (SAML)[5], Shibboleth[6], or WS-Federation [16].

3 Cloud Identity Management-Models

Cloud computing is currently still one of the most emerging trends in the IT sector. Many applications are already migrated to the cloud because of its benefits such as cost savings, scalability, or less maintenance efforts [17]. Due to the increasing number of cloud applications, secure identity management is equally important for cloud applications as for traditional web applications. Hence, new cloud identity management-models have already emerged, which particularly take the properties of cloud computing into account. [18–21], or [22] already describe cloud identity management-models in their publications. We take these publications as a basis to give an overview of different existing cloud identity management-models. In the following subsections we describe the individual models in more detail and explain how and where identities are stored and managed.

3.1 Identity in the Cloud-Model

The *Identity in the Cloud-Model* is similar to the *isolated identity model* described in Sect. 2.1. Again, identity provider and service provider merge also in

---

[3] http://msdn.microsoft.com/en-us/library/vstudio/ms733090%28vvs.90%29.aspx.
[4] It is not necessary that the common identifier is shared. Different identifiers mapping to the same user are also possible [6].
[5] http://saml.xml.org.
[6] http://shibboleth.net.

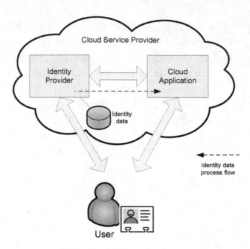

Fig. 2. Identity in the Cloud-Model.

this model. This means for the cloud case that the cloud service provider, which hosts the application, is also responsible for the identity management. Figure 2 illustrates this model.

Identity data of users, who are accessing the cloud application, are directly stored in the domain of the cloud service provider. Hence, the user has actually no control which data are processed in the cloud. Cloud service providers which already use this model for their Software as a Service (SaaS) applications are for instance Google or Salesforce.com. They offer their own user management to their customers for managing their own identities. The main advantage of this model is that organizations do not need to host and maintain their own identity management-system but can simply rely on an existing one, which will be maintained by the cloud service provider. Needless to say that costs can be decreased at an organization when applying this model. However, the use of this model also shifts responsibility in terms of security and privacy to the cloud service provider and the organization more or less looses control over the identity data stored and managed in the cloud.

3.2   Identity to the Cloud-Model

The *Identity to the Cloud-Model* is similar to the traditional *central identity model*. Also in this model, the identity provider takes over the tasks regarding identity management for the service provider. However, the main difference in this model is that the service provider and its applications are cloud-based. This further means that in this model the identity provider is not deployed in the cloud, which avoids unnecessary identity data disclosure to a cloud service provider. Figure 3 illustrates the *Identity to the Cloud-Model*.

In more detail, the complete user and identity management is still hosted by the organization e.g. in one of its data centers. Before gaining access to a

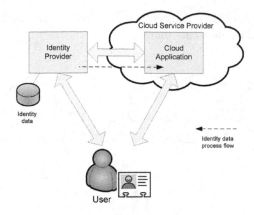

Fig. 3. Identity to the Cloud-Model.

cloud application, users have to authenticate at the identity provider first. After that, the identity provider transfers appropriate identity and authentication data to the cloud service provider through well-defined and standardized interfaces. Google or Salesforce.com, for instance, rely on SAML, OpenID[7], or OAuth[8] for these interfaces and external identity provisioning.

Appliance of this model has the advantage that an existing identity management-infrastructure of an organization can be re-used. Users are identified and authenticated at the cloud application by the use of this external identity management-system. No new user management has to be created or migrated to the cloud service provider. The organization remains under control of the identity data and provides it to the cloud service provider just on demand. However, interoperability issues may arise due to the use of external interfaces. For instance, a common agreement on the attributes transferred (e.g. format or semantic) between the identity provider and the cloud service provider must be given. In addition, the identity provider must support the interface provided by the cloud service provider.

3.3   Identity from the Cloud-Model

The *Identity from the Cloud-Model* fully features the cloud computing paradigm. In this case, both the cloud application and the identity provider are operated in the cloud. However, in contrast to the *Identity in the Cloud-Model* of Sect. 3.1 both entities are operated by distinct cloud service providers. Since identities are provided as a service from the cloud, this model is also named "Identity as a Service Model" [23]. Google or Facebook are for instance such providers, when using the authentication functionality for other services than

---

[7] http://openid.net.

[8] http://oauth.net.

their own (Google Accounts Authentication and Authorization[9] or Facebook Login[10]). Figure 4 illustrates this model.

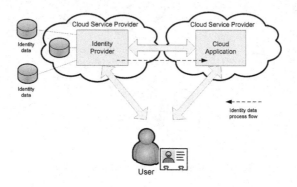

Fig. 4. Identity from the Cloud-Model.

By applying this model, an organization can benefit from the pure cloud computing advantages such as high scalability or elasticity. Besides that, compared to the previous cloud identity management-models the advantage of this model is the separation of cloud service providers. In this model, organizations can select their preferred identity provider in the cloud. This is particularly important because the organization needs to trust the identity provider, which is responsible for the organization's identity and user management. Organizations must be careful in cloud service provider selection, as e.g. legal implications such as data protection regulations might hinder the selection of a provider which stores identity data in a foreign country.

3.4   Cloud Identity Broker-Model

The *Cloud Identity Broker-Model* can be seen as an extension to the *Identity from the Cloud-Model*. In this *Cloud Identity Broker-Model*, the identity provider in the cloud acts now as an identity broker in the cloud. In other words, the cloud identity broker is some kind of hub between one or more service providers and one or more identity providers. Figure 5 illustrates this model.

The basic idea behind this model is to decouple the service provider from integrating and connecting a vast amount of identity providers. If no broker is used, a single service provider has to implement all interfaces for communication with the individual identity providers if the service provider wants to support them. By applying the broker concept, the identity broker hides the complexity of the individual identity providers from the service provider. This further means that the service provider just needs to implement one interface,

---

[9] https://developers.google.com/accounts.
[10] https://developers.facebook.com/docs/facebook-login.

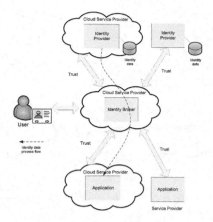

Fig. 5. Cloud Identity Broker-Model.

namely the one to the identity broker. All other interfaces are encapsulated by the identity broker and tailored or mapped to the service provider's interface. In addition, for the service provider only one strong trust relationship between the service provider and the identity broker is required. All other trust relationships with the individual identity providers are "brokered" by the identity broker. Deploying the broker in the cloud makes this model even more powerful. Due to the cloud advantages of nearly unlimited computing resources and scalability, a high number of active connections and identification/authentication processes at the broker can be easily absorbed by the cloud.

Nevertheless, still some disadvantages can be found in this model. One disadvantage is that both the user and the service provider are dependent on the functionality the cloud identity broker supports. If the identity broker does not support the desired identity provider the user wants to use for authentication, the service provider cannot provide its services to the user. Furthermore, if the broker does not support the communication interface to the service provider anymore, the service provider is cut off from any other identity provider. However, probably the main issue is that identity data runs through the cloud identity broker in plaintext. As already mentioned before, privacy issues concerning the cloud service provider might hinder adoption of this cloud-based identity management-service [2].

The *Cloud Identity Broker-Model* has already been implemented by some organizations. McAfee Cloud Single Sign On[11], the SkIDentity[12] implementation, or the Cloud ID Broker[13] of Fugen are just a few examples. Further details on this model can be found in [18, 24], or [22].

---

[11] http://www.mcafee.com/us/products/cloud-single-sign-on.aspx.
[12] http://www.skidentity.com.
[13] http://fugensolutions.com/cloud-id-broker.html.

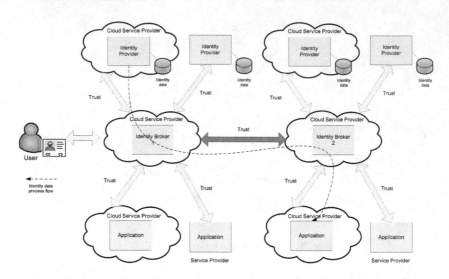

Fig. 6. Federated Cloud Identity Broker-Model.

3.5   Federated Cloud Identity Broker-Model

The *Federated Cloud Identity Broker-Model* combines the traditional *federated identity model* with the newly *Cloud Identity Broker-Model*. This combined model has been introduced by [22] and aims on eliminating the drawbacks of the central *Cloud Identity Broker-Model*. The general architecture is illustrated in Fig. 6, showing the federation of two different cloud identity brokers.

Compared to the simple *Cloud Identity Broker-Model*, in this federated model users and service providers do not need to rely on one and the same identity broker. Actually, both the user and the service provider can rely on the individual broker of their choice. This eliminates the drawback for both the user and the service provider of being dependent on the same identity broker. On the one hand, users can simply select the identity broker that supports all their desired identity providers (Identity Broker 1 in Fig. 6). On the other hand, service providers can select the broker that e.g. supports a specific communication interface (Identity Broker 2 in Fig. 6). Hence, referring to Fig. 6 the communication process flow between identity provider and service provider is brokered through the two Identity Brokers 1 and 2.

While this model eliminates some problems of the *Cloud Identity Broker-Model*, the issue of plain identity data transfer between and through cloud service providers still persists. To bypass such privacy issue, the following two models had been introduced.

3.6   BlindIdM-Model

The *BlindIdM-Model* has been introduced by [25,26][14] and can also be seen as an extension and alteration of the *Identity from the Cloud-Model*. The basic idea

---

[14] A similar approach has been introduced by [27].

is principally the same, however, this model enables identity data storage and data processing also by semi-trusted identity providers[15] in the cloud. In fact, the identity provider in the cloud can provide identity data to service providers without actually knowing the contents of these data. Hence, the identity provider provides these data in a blind manner [25]. This particularly preserves users' privacy, as only blinded data is transferred through the cloud identity provider and the cloud provider has no possibility to inspect these data.

The identity data being transferred are actually blinded by using a proxy re-encryption scheme[16] [28,29]. In more detail, during identity management setup and user registration the organization stores the users' identity data in encrypted format at the cloud identity provider. Thereby, the private key is kept confidential by the organization, hence the cloud provider is not able to decrypt the stored identity data. In addition, the organization generates a re-encryption key for the identity provider[17], which allows the re-encryption from the stored data encrypted for the cloud identity provider into other encrypted data, which however can be decrypted by the service provider. During an authentication process, the cloud identity provider then just re-encrypts the desired identity data of the user for the service provider. The practical applicability of the *BlindIdM-Model* has been shown by an implementation in connection with OpenID [30].

3.7 Privacy-Preserving Federated Cloud Identity Broker-Model

The main aim of this model is – similar to the *BlindIdM-Model* – an improved privacy-preservation for the user. Thereby, the same concept of "blinding" identity data is applied to the basic *Federated Cloud Identity Broker-Model*. Hence, this model combines the advantages of the *Federated Cloud Identity Broker-Model* with the advantages of the *BlindIdM-Model*. Furthermore, this model can again be applied when having semi-trusted cloud identity brokers. The general concept of this model has been introduced by [31].

The general concept of this model is similar to the *BlindIdM-Model* because also proxy re-encryption is used for protecting identity data from the cloud service providers. However, the main differences are that the data can also be stored encrypted at non-cloud identity providers and that the data can also be encrypted by the user and not only by an organization. In addition – which is the basic concept of this federated model – there are two re-encryption steps required, since identity data needs to flow at least through two cloud identity brokers. For instance, lets assume that the user has stored some identity data, which are encrypted for Identity Broker 1, at an identity provider. To successfully

---

[15] A semi-trusted identity provider is an identity provider that works correctly but may be interested in inspecting private data. In other words, the identity provider acts *honest but curious*.

[16] By using proxy re-encryption a semi-trusted proxy can alter a ciphertext, which has been encrypted for person A, in such a way that it can be decrypted by person B. Thereby, the proxy gains no access to the plaintext of the data.

[17] For generating a re-encryption key, the organization requires its private key and the public key of the service provider.

run such a privacy-preserving authentication process, the user additionally has to generate two re-encryption keys (One for the direction Identity Broker 1 → Identity Broker 2 and one for the direction Identity Broker 2 → service provider) and issues them to the respective entities. Finally, after successful authentication at the identity provider, identity data are transferred through the chain identity provider → Identity Broker 1 → Identity Broker 2 → service provider by applying proxy re-encryption in the last two steps (The identity data was already encrypted for Identity Broker 1 during storage at the identity provider, hence only two instead of three re-encryption steps are required). An application of this model can be found in [32], where parts of the STORK[18] framework are realized using this architecture to enhance scalability by ensuring users' privacy at the same time.

4   Comparison of Cloud Identity Management-Models

In this section we evaluate, discuss, and compare the various cloud identity management-models based on different criteria. Comparison criteria are defined in the following Subsect. 4.1 whereas the comparison itself is elaborated in Subsect. 4.2.

4.1   Comparison Criteria

The following criteria act as a basis for comparing the various cloud identity management-models. Some of the comparison criteria were selected or derived from [6,25,33]. The selected criteria target aspects of different areas (e.g. general architecture, trust, privacy, etc.). The diversity of the criteria was deliberately considered to give a comprehensive overview on the different cloud identity management-models.

Number of SPs Supported. Is the model limited to one SP or can multiple SPs be supported?
Number of IdPs Supported. Is the model limited to one IdP or can multiple IdPs be supported?
Trust Domains. Is authentication supported only within a single trust domain or also across different trust domains?
Trust Model. Is a direct trust model or a brokered trust model applied?
Trust in the Cloud IdP/Identity Broker. Must the cloud identity provider / cloud identity broker be trusted or can they be semi-trusted?
Single Sign-On (SSO). Can the model support single sign-on (SSO)?
Storage Location of Identity Data. Where are users' identity data stored?
Scalability. Is the model applicable in a large scale?
Extensibility. Is the model easily extensible, e.g. by adding new service providers?

---

[18] Secure Identity Across Borders Linked, https://www.eid-stork.eu/.

Governance Framework. Is a governance framework involving several entities required?

Cost Effectiveness. Is the model cost effective?

Confidentiality. Does the identity data stay confidential at the identity provider / identity broker?

Minimal/Selective Disclosure. Can the user select the amount of identity data to be disclosed to the identity provider/service provider?

User Control. Does the user have full control over her identity data?

Unlinkability. Is the user unlinkable to the identity provider / identity broker? In other words, are different authentication processes of the same user linkable?

Anonymity. Can the user stay anonymous with respect to the identity provider / identity broker?

4.2   Comparison

In this section we compare the individual cloud identity management-models with respect to the prior defined criteria. Table 1 shows and summarizes this comparison. For some comparisons we use qualitative arguments, for others quantitative arguments (low, medium, high), and for the rest simply boolean (e.g. yes/no for being applicable or not) arguments. The options marked in bolt indicate the respective best option (only applicable for quantitative and boolean values). The underlying principle for all comparisons (in particular for those that are related to privacy such as confidentiality, minimal/selective disclosure, etc.) is that we assume an identity provider or an identity broker deployed in the cloud acting *honest but curious* (thus being semi-trusted). In contrast to that we assume applications in the cloud and their hosting service providers as being trusted, as they anyhow require users' identity data for service provisioning.

In the following we discuss the various models based on the individual criteria.

Number of SPs Supported. Since in the *Identity in the Cloud-Model* the service provider and the identity provider are the same entity, the identity provider can only serve one service provider. All other models have no such restriction and thus can provide multiple service providers with identity data.

Number of IdPs Supported. Only those models that rely on a broker-based approach are able to deal with multiple connected identity providers. All others just include one identity provider. Dealing with multiple identity providers has the advantage that a user can simply select her preferred identity provider for an authentication process. Different identity providers can have different identity data stored or support different qualities in the authentication mechanisms. This allows users to select the identity provider satisfying best the needs for authentication at a service provider.

Trust Domains. The broker-based models support authentication across multiple trust domains, as multiple entities are involved during an authentication process. All others support authentication in single domains only.

Table 1. Comparison of the individual cloud identity management-models based on selected criteria.

Criterion / Model	Identity in the Cloud-Model	Identity to the Cloud-Model	Identity from the Cloud-Model	Cloud Identity Broker-Model	Federated Cloud Identity Broker-Model	BlindIdM-Model	Privacy-Preserving Federated Cloud Identity Broker-Model
Number of SPs supported	One	Multiple	Multiple	Multiple	Multiple	Multiple	Multiple
Number of IdPs supported	One	One	One	Multiple	Multiple	One	Multiple
Trust domains	One	One	One	Multiple	Multiple	One	Multiple
Trust model	Direct	Direct	Direct	Brokered	Brokered	Direct	Brokered
Trust in the cloud IdP/identity broker	Trusted	Trusted	Trusted	Trusted	Trusted	Semi-Trusted	Semi-Trusted
Single sign-on (SSO)	No	Yes	Yes	Yes	Yes	Yes	Yes
Storage location of identity data	Cloud identity provider	External identity provider	Cloud identity provider	Cloud identity provider and external identity provider	Cloud identity provider and external identity provider	Cloud identity provider	Cloud identity provider and external identity provider
Scalability	Medium	Low	Medium	High	High	Medium	High
Extensibility	Low	Medium	Medium	High	High	Medium	High
Governance framework	No	No	No	Yes	Yes	Yes	Yes
Cost effectiveness	Medium	Medium	Medium	High	High	Medium	High
Confidentiality	No	No	No	No	No	Yes	Yes
Minimum / Selective disclosure	No	Yes	No	Yes	Yes	No	Yes
User Control	No	Yes	No	Yes	Yes	No	Yes
Unlinkability	No	No	No	No	No	No	Yes
Anonymity	No	No	No	No	No	Yes	Yes

Trust Model. Again, all models which rely on an identity broker also feature a brokered trust model, hence the trust relationships are segmented. All other models rely on a direct or pairwise trust model, as only the service provider and the identity provider communicate with each other during an authentication process. A clear statement which model has more advantages cannot be made. Both have their benefits and drawbacks, however, details on the individual models can be found in [34].

Trust in the Cloud IdP/Identity Broker. For the two models (*BlindIdM-Model* and *Privacy-Preserving Federated Cloud Identity Broker-Model*), which rely on proxy re-encryption for securing the data during cloud transmission, it is sufficient when the identity provider/identity broker is considered semi-trusted. In all other cloud identity models the identity provider/identity broker must be trusted.

Single Sign-On (SSO). In fact, all models that can handle multiple service providers are principally applicable to support single sign-on. This means, that only the *Identity in the Cloud-Model* cannot support a simplified log-in process.

Storage Location of Identity Data. In the *Identity to the Cloud-Model* identity data are stored on a single external identity provider, which is capable of providing identity to the cloud application through a well-defined interface. In the broker-based models, identity data can be stored distributed across multiple different identity providers, being either deployed in the cloud or in a conventional data center. However, the different identity providers could also have identity data stored redundantly, i.e. the same attribute name/value-pair is stored at different providers. No identity data are actually stored at the identity broker. In the remaining cloud identity models identity data are stored directly at the cloud identity provider.

Scalability. The *Identity to the Cloud-Model* has the lowest scalability, as an external identity provider is usually not designed for dealing with high load activities. In addition, an external identity provider has not that flexibility or elasticity that an identity provider deployed in a cloud has. Hence, such cloud identity providers (*Identity in the Cloud-Model*, *Identity from the Cloud-Model*, and *BlindIdM-Model*) have higher scalability features. Although in these three models the identity provider/identity broker is deployed in the cloud, we rated the models with just medium level scalability. The reason is that with the broker-based models load can additionally be distributed to other identity providers and thus is not bundled at one single provider. Hence, the broker-based models achieve the highest scalability.

Extensibility. The *Identity in the Cloud-Model* cannot be extended because service provider and identity provider are one and the same entity. The *Identity to the Cloud-Model*, the *Identity from the Cloud-Model*, and the *BlindIdM-Model* can be extended to integrate additional service providers. Nevertheless, the broker-based models have the best extensibility as from their nature the general aim is to support multiple service providers and identity providers.

Governance Framework. The non-broker-based cloud identity models do not require an extensive governance framework as only a simple pairwise (direct) trust model applies. In the broker-based concepts a thorough governance framework is required as multiple providers have to interact. For the privacy-preserving models (*BlindIdM-Model* and *Privacy-Preserving Federated Cloud Identity Broker-Model*) the governance framework gets even more complex, as encryption keys have to be managed for the individual entities.

Cost Effectiveness. The broker-based models have the highest cost effectiveness, since the identity brokers are deployed in the cloud and additionally multiple identity providers can be connected and re-used. Due to the re-use of existing external identity providers, costs can be saved. The same arguments also hold for the *Identity to the Cloud-Model*, where an existing identity management-system through an external interface is re-used for identity data provisioning. However, this model cannot benefit from the advantages of an identity provider in the cloud deployment, which leads to medium cost effectiveness only. All other models also have medium cost effectiveness, as the identity provider is deployed in the cloud but no existing identity providers can be re-used.

Confidentiality. Only the *BlindIdM-Model* and the *Privacy-Preserving Federated Cloud Identity Broker-Model* support confidentiality with respect to the cloud service provider because the identity data transferred through the cloud service provider are encrypted. In comparison, in all other cloud identity models identity data are routed in plaintext through the cloud service provider that hosts the cloud identity provider/identity broker.

Minimum/Selective Disclosure. For evaluating this criterion we assume that minimum/selective disclosure is only possible at trusted identity providers. Hence, this feature is only supported where external (and trusted) identity providers are part of the model. These are the broker-based models as well as the *Identity to the Cloud-Model*. All other models rely on cloud identity providers only.

User Control. Again, for evaluating this criterion we assume that full user-control is only possible at trusted identity providers. Therefore, the same results as for the comparison with respect to minimum/selective disclosure apply.

Unlinkability. The user – in fact – is only unlinkable with respect to the identity broker in the *Privacy-Preserving Federated Cloud Identity Broker-Model*. The reasons are that, on the one hand, the identity broker just sees encrypted data and, on the other hand, that the encrypted data can be randomized if certain proxy re-encryption schemes such as from [29] are used. The randomization feature allows to provide the identity broker with different ciphertexts during different authentication processes although the containing plaintext data remains the same. Hence, this avoids user linkage during different authentication processes of the same user. Although the *BlindIdm-Model* supports proxy re-encryption too, the randomization feature has no effect in this case because the encrypted data are directly stored at the cloud identity provider. If the user wants to update her encrypted identity data at the cloud identity provider, she must somehow be linkable. All other models also do not support unlinkability because identity data flows through the identity provider/identity broker in plaintext.

Anonymity. The only two models that support anonymity with respect to the identity broker are the *BlindIdM-Model* and the *Privacy-Preserving Federated Cloud Identity Broker-Model*. In these two models the identity data are fully hidden from the identity broker due to encryption. Even if the user is linkable, the broker cannot reveal the user's identity. In all other models anonymity with respect to the identity provider/identity broker is not possible because identity data are processed in plaintext.

5   Conclusions

Based on the comparison and discussion of the different cloud identity management-models it can be concluded that the *Privacy-Preserving Federated Cloud Identity Broker-Model* does the best with respect to the selected criteria. It supports the main basic functions like all other cloud identity models but additionally tremendously increases users' privacy. However, application of this model is also more complex than the others. Reasons are the support of authentication across several domains of multiple identity providers and service providers and the incorporation of privacy features due to the use of proxy re-encryption. Furthermore, the use of proxy re-encryption requires a thorough key management, which implies the necessity of an appropriate governance framework. In addition, the brokered trust model might be a blocking issue for further adoption of this model as liability is shifted to the intermediary components (identity brokers). However, in general the broker-based cloud identity management-models have more advantages than the simple cloud identity management-models. Nevertheless, the use of any cloud identity management-model is advantageous compared to traditional identity management-models as they provide higher scalability and better cost effectiveness due to the cloud computing features.

References

1. Bauer, M., Meints, M., Hansen, M.: D3.1: Structured Overview on Prototypes and Concepts of Identity Management System. FIDIS (2005)
2. Pearson, S., Benameur, A.: Privacy, security and trust issues arising from cloud computing. In: IEEE CloudCom 2010, pp. 693–702 (2010)
3. Zissis, D., Lekkas, D.: Addressing cloud computing security issues. Future Gener. Comput. Syst. **28**, 583–592 (2012)
4. Sen, J.: Security and privacy issues in cloud computing. In: Martínez, A.R., Marin-Lopez, R., Pereniguez-Garcia, F. (eds.) Architectures and Protocols for Secure Information Technology Infrastructures, pp. 1–45. IGI Global (2013)
5. Bertino, E., Takahashi, K.: Identity Management: Concepts, Technologies, and Systems. Artech House, Boston (2011)
6. Cao, Y., Yang, L.: A survey of identity management technology. In: IEEE ICITIS 2010, pp. 287–293. IEEE (2010)
7. Dabrowski, M., Pacyna, P.: Generic and complete three-level identity management model. In: SECURWARE 2008, pp. 232–237. IEEE (2008)
8. Dbrowski, M., Pacyna, P.: Overview of Identity Management. Technical report (2008). www.chinacommunications.cn
9. Jøsang, A., Fabre, J., Hay, B., Dalziel, J., Pope, S.: Trust requirements in identity management. In: Proceedings of the 2005 Australasian Workshop on Grid Computing and e-Research, pp. 99–108 (2005)
10. Jøsang, A., Pope, S.: User centric identity management. In: AusCERT 2005 (2005)
11. Jøsang, A., Zomai, M.A., Suriadi, S.: Usability and privacy in identity management architectures. In: ACSW 2007, pp. 143–152 (2007)
12. Palfrey, J., Gasser, U.: CASE STUDY: Digital Identity Interoperability and eInnovation. Berkman Publication Series (2007)
13. Neuman, C., Yu, T., Hartman, S., Raeburn, K.: The Kerberos Network Authentication Service (V5). RFC 4120 (Proposed Standard) (2005)
14. Leitold, H., Hollosi, A., Posch, R.: Security architecture of the Austrian citizen card concept. In: ACSAC 2002, pp. 391–400 (2002)
15. Frommm, J., Hoepner, P.: The new German eID card. In: Fumy, W., Paeschke, M. (eds.) Handbook of eID Security, pp. 154–166. Publicis Publishing (2011)

16. Kaler, C., McIntosh, M.: Web Services Federation Language (WS-Federation) Version 1.2. OASIS Standard (2009)
17. Armbrust, M., Fox, A., Griffith, R., Joseph, A.D., Katz, R., Konwinski, A., Lee, G., Patterson, D., Rabkin, A., Stoica, I., Zaharia, M.: Above the Clouds: A Berkeley View of Cloud Computing Cloud Computing. Technical report, RAD Lab (2009)
18. Cloud Security Alliance: Security Guidance for Critical Areas of Focus in Cloud Computing V3.0. CSA (2011)
19. Cox, P.: How to Manage Identity in the Public Cloud. InformationWeek reports (2012)
20. Gopalakrishnan, A.: Cloud computing identity management. SETLabs Brief. **7**, 45–55 (2009)
21. Goulding, J.T.: Identity and Access Management for the Cloud: CA's strategy and vision. Technical Report May, CA Technologies (2010)
22. Zwattendorfer, B., Stranacher, K., Tauber, A.: Towards a federated identity as a service model. In: Egovis 2013, pp. 43–57 (2013)
23. Ates, M., Ravet, S., Ahmat, A.M., Fayolle, J.: An identity-centric internet: identity in the cloud, identity as a service and other delights. In: ARES 2011, pp. 555–560 (2011)
24. Huang, H.Y., Wang, B., Liu, X.X., Xu, J.M.: Identity federation broker for service cloud. In: ICSS 2010, pp. 115–120 (2010)
25. Nuñez, D., Agudo, I., Lopez, J.: Leveraging privacy in identity management as a service through proxy re-encryption. In: Zimmermann, W. (ed.) Proceedings of the PhD Symposium at the 2nd European Conference on Service-Oriented and Cloud Computing, pp. 42–47 (2013)
26. Nuñez, D., Agudo, I.: BlindIdM: a privacy-preserving approach for identity management as a service. Int. J. Inf. Secur. **13**, 199–215 (2014)
27. Zwattendorfer, B., Slamanig, D.: On privacy-preserving ways to porting the austrian eID system to the public cloud. In: Janczewski, L.J., Wolfe, H.B., Shenoi, S. (eds.) SEC 2013. IFIP AICT, vol. 405, pp. 300–314. Springer, Heidelberg (2013)
28. Green, M., Ateniese, G.: Identity-based proxy re-encryption. In: Katz, J., Yung, M. (eds.) ACNS 2007. LNCS, vol. 4521, pp. 288–306. Springer, Heidelberg (2007)
29. Ateniese, G., Fu, K., Green, M., Hohenberger, S.: Improved proxy re-encryption schemes with applications to secure distributed storage. ACM Trans. Inf. Syst. Secur. **9**, 1–30 (2006)
30. Nuñez, D., Agudo, I., Lopez, J.: Integrating OpenID with proxy re-encryption to enhance privacy in cloud-based identity services. In: IEEE CloudCom 2012, pp. 241–248 (2012)
31. Zwattendorfer, B.: Towards a Privacy-Preserving Federated Identity as a Service Model. PhD Thesis, Graz University of Technology (2014)
32. Zwattendorfer, B., Slamanig, D.: Privacy-preserving realization of the STORK framework in the public cloud. In: SECRYPT 2013, pp. 419–426 (2013)
33. Birrell, E., Schneider, F.: Federated identity management systems: a privacy-based characterization. IEEE Secur. Priv. **11**, 36–48 (2013)
34. Linn, J., Boeyen, S., Ellison, G., Karhuluoma, N., Macgregor, W., Madsen, P., Sengodan, S., Shinkar, S., Thompson, P.: Trust Models Guidelines. Technical report, OASIS (2004)

Scenario-Based Design and Validation of REST Web Service Compositions

Irum Rauf[(⊠)], Faezeh Siavashi, Dragos Truscan, and Ivan Porres

Department of Information Technologies, Åbo Akademi University, Turku, Finland
{irum.rauf,faezeh.siavashi,dragos.truscan,ivan.porres}@abo.fi

Abstract. We present an approach to design and validate RESTful composite web services based on user scenarios. We use the Unified Modeling Language (UML) to specify the requirements, behavior and published resources of each web service. In our approach, a service can invoke other services and exhibit complex and timed behavior while still complying with the REST architectural style. We specify user scenarios via UML Sequence Diagrams. The service specifications are transformed into UPPAAL timed automata for verification and test generation. The service requirements are propagated to the UPPAAL timed automata during the transformation. Their reachability is verified in UPPAAL and they are used for computing coverage level during test generation. We validate our approach with a case study of a holiday booking web service.

Keywords: REST · Web service composition · Model-based testing · UPPAAL · TRON

1 Introduction

REST (REpresentational State Transfer) web services are built on the principles of the REST architectural style [12] which aims at producing scalable and extensible web services. The REST interface offers a CRUD interface (create, retrieve, update and delete) to its users via a set of standard HTTP methods. In additions, REST offers stateless behavior that facilitates scalability.

Different web services published over the internet can be composed into new composite web services which fulfill new service goals using the functionality of partner web services. Automated systems, for example hotel reservation systems, are often built as stateful composite services that require a certain sequence of method invocations that must be followed in order to fulfill service goals. Creating such composite services with advanced scenarios and REST features requires rigorous development approaches that are capable of creating web services that can be trusted for their behavior.

With the rise in use of REST web services in different domains offering complex and timed scenarios, there is an increasing need for validation approaches to effectively and efficiently detect faults in the specifications and implementations of such services.

© Springer International Publishing Switzerland 2015
V. Monfort and K.-H. Krempels (Eds.): WEBIST 2014, LNBIP 226, pp. 145–160, 2015.
DOI: 10.1007/978-3-319-27030-2_10

In this article, we present a scenario-based validation and verification approach that can help the service developer in improving the quality of service specifications and implementations. The approach supports the creation of timed and stateful behavior with the confidence that the service fulfills its advertised functionality. The Web Service Composition (WSC) is specified using the Unified Modeling Language (UML) starting from the requirements of the WSC. A code skeleton of the WSC is automatically generated and manually completed by the developer. In order to perform validation and verification of the composition, the UML specifications are transformed into UPPAAL timed automata (UPTA). We use the UPPAAL tool set [23] to simulate the specifications and to verify their properties via model-checking. We also use them to automatically generate tests in order to validate the implementation.

Requirements traceability is an important component of our approach. The requirements of the composition are included in the UML specifications and then propagated to UPTA. They are used for both verifying the reachability of those model elements implementing them and for reasoning about the coverage level of the tests generated. Upon detecting failures, the traced requirements are used to trace back errors either in the models or in the implementation.

We exemplify and validate our approach with a relatively complex example of a holiday booking composite REST web service extracted from an industrial application. The example shows how stateful and timed web services offering complex scenarios and involving other web services can be constructed efficiently using our approach.

The paper is organized as follows: Sect. 2 presents our approach and the tool support is discussed in Sect. 3. The case study is presented in Sect. 4, followed by the evaluation of the approach in Sect. 5. The related work is discussed in Sect. 6 and conclusions are drawn in Sect. 7.

2 Our Approach

Our scenario-driven approach to verify and test the composite REST web service is shown in Fig. 1. We start by inferring service requirements in tabular format from specification document and the corresponding user scenarios from the specification document of the REST WSC. Each user scenario is detailed by one or several UML sequence diagrams. In addition, we build several perspectives of the WSC such as a resource, a behavioral and a domain model using UML class and state machine diagrams. This is an extension of our previous work, in which we designed behavioral interfaces for web services that were RESTful by construction [26]. We transform the service design models to UPTA, which are simulated and model-checked by reasoning the properties such as deadlock, liveness, reachability, and safety. If inconsistencies are found, the UML-based service design models are updated. These design models are used to implement the service in the Python-based Django web framework [16] using our partial code generation tool [26] which generates code skeletons with pre- and post-conditions for every service method. The skeleton is manually completed

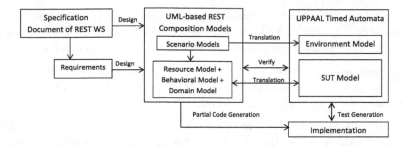

Fig. 1. Scenario-based V&V approach for REST CWS.

by the service designer. The verified UPTA specifications are used for online model-based conformance testing of the implementation.

Requirements Traceability. Service requirements are inferred from the specification document and they serve as service goals. A service should be checked for its service goals to validate that the service does what it is required to do. By addressing the service requirements at the design phase and propagating them to the verification and validation stages, we provide a mechanism by which a service implementation can be validated for its goals and the unfulfilled requirements can be traced back to the design phase to find faults in the design.

Requirements Table. Service requirements are generally domain-specific since they are inferred from the specifications. We infer functional and temporal requirements from the specification document into a table and number them. These requirements are attached to the UML state machine (SM) as *comments* on the transitions and are propagated to UPTA such that the links between requirements and the model elements are preserved. These requirements are included in all the models and traced throughout the process, i.e., at UML, UPTA and test level, respectively. The requirements are formulated as reachability properties in UPTA with the purpose of verifying them during simulation. Each requirement label is translated into a boolean variable (initialized to *False*) and attached to the corresponding edge in UPTA.

Scenario Models. The behavioral requirements are elicited as scenario models using UML sequence diagrams. These scenario models are translated to environment model in UPTA since these scenarios define different conditions under which the composite service can be invoked.

We require that our testing approach must validate that the service requirements are met by IUT, and the service works correctly in different scenarios, in order to build confidence of the developer that the system is doing what it is required to do. Thus, the coverage level of scenarios and requirements is monitored during test generation and execution. Once the test report is available, we can check which requirements have been validated and which have failed. The main strength of using both the requirements table and scenario models in our approach is that the former helps in tracing the unfulfilled requirements to the design models and locating the faults in the design of the service. On the other hand, the later helps in determining if the service works fine in different scenarios and identify under which conditions the service shows a faulty behavior.

REST Composition Models. The web service compositions that we build exhibit RESTful features such as addressability, connectivity, statelessness and uniform interface. Thus, we model several perspectives of a service composition:

Scenario Models. Some of the behavioral requirements of the service are elicited into scenario models using UML sequence diagrams. These scenario models provide details of the interaction between composite service and its partners and also insights on how a certain scenario is realized. This information facilitates the development of the composition and they are also used later on to validate the service implementation.

Resource Model. The concept of resource is central to the structure of REST web service. It represents a piece of information [28]. We represent the static structure of REST web service with resource model which is modeled with a UML class diagram. Each class defines a *resource*. The direction of the associations specify navigability (connectivity) direction between resources, while their role names give the relative URI of resources (addressability). The *collection resources* without the incoming transitions are termed as *root* such that every *resource* defined in the resource model should be reachable via the *root* and the graph formed should be connected (connectivity).

Behavioral Model. The behavioral model represents the dynamic structure of the service using UML state machines. Each state represents the service state and the transition triggers are restricted to the side-effect methods of HTTP protocol, i.e., PUT, POST and DELETE (uniform interface). The statelessness feature of the REST interface is preserved while building stateful REST web service by defining state invariants as boolean predicates over the states of different resources. The state of a resource is given by its representation retrieved by invoking a HTTP GET method on it. We are thus able to define service states as predicates over the resources without maintaining any hidden session or state information (statelessness). The state invariants in the SM are written as Object Constraint Language (OCL) expressions. OCL is commonly used to define constraints in UML models, including state invariants [5]. For modeling a service composition, the models are required to represent method invocations on the partner services. The service invocations to partner services are modeled as effects on the transitions. The composite web service requirements, inferred from the specification document, are added as UML *comments* on the transitions that satisfy them.

Domain Model. The domain model of the composite service is represented with a UML class diagram. It represents interfaces between the composite service and its partner services. The required and provided interface methods between the composite and its partner services are modeled with required and provided interfaces in the domain model, respectively.

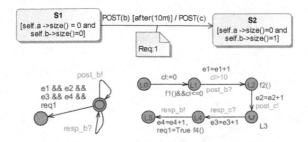

Fig. 2. Example of state model (top), corresponding environment model (bottom left), and flattened TA (bottom right).

Transformation. In order to make the models amenable for simulation and model checking we employ a set of mechanized steps for translating UML-based service specifications into UPPAAL timed automata (UPTA) [23].

The transformation from UML design models to UPTA has been discussed in [27]. It takes as input the resource model, domain model, and behavioral model and generates two artifacts in UPTA: the SUT model specifying the behavior of the service and of its partner services (a generic example is presented in Fig. 2) and an *environment model* which simulates the behavior of the service user. Two kinds of environment models are generated automatically: a canonical model which allows to simulate freely all possible behaviors of the SUT and a model used for testing different user scenarios.

The transformation of the user scenarios from sequence diagrams to UPTA environment models is applicable to Sequence Diagrams(SD) with a restricted set of elements. The following generic steps are used by the transformation:

– Each SD has may have several lifelines, which are grouped into two groups: SUT and environment. The messages exchanged between the two groups will provide the testing interface.
– For each input message to the SUT group, we define an edge to a new location in UPTA. The edge is labeled by the name of the message and it has associated a sending channel(!).
– For each output message from the SUT group, we define a new edge to a new location with a receiving channel (?).
– For SD fragments (i.e., alt, loop, opt), based on the number of conditions in the fragment, we define several edges from a location and use the conditions as guards on the edges.
– Timing constraint and duration constraint are transformed into location invariants and edge guards in UPTA.
– Tracking variables are added to each scenario trace in UPTA. If a scenario has more than one exit points (alternatives) several variables are added. A tracking variable is an updated tuple *(sd_no = false, sd_no = true)* on the first edge in the scenario trace and respectively on the last edge in the trace.
– UPTA traces stemmed from different SDs are included in one single UPTA environment.

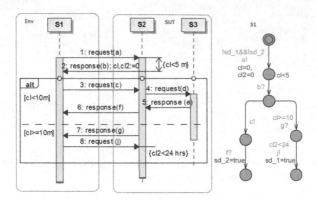

Fig. 3. Example of SD of three services (left) and the UPTA model of S1 as environment (right).

The resulting UPTA environment will have channel synchronizations matching the SUT model obtained in the first transformation.

Figure 3 shows an example of a SD with three lifelines (right) and its transformed environment model (left). Assuming *S1* as the environment, the UPTA environment model contains only emitting/receiving messages to/from *S1*. Response(b) should be received within 5 min ($cl < 5m$) and request(j) can be sent before 24 h ($cl2 < 24$ hrs).These timing constraints are modeled as location invariants and guards in UPTA. For modeling before and after a deadline ($cl < 10$ and $cl >= 10$) in sequence diagram, we used **alt**, which is transformed into two different locations with their corresponding edges (c! and g?) in UPTA. The timing constraints in **alt** are translated as location invariant and edge guard in the model.

Verification. We use the UPPAAL model-checker [23] to verify basic properties of our design models such as reachability, liveness, and safety. In addition, we check whether the service user scenarios are satisfied. This allows one to eliminate design errors that can be otherwise expensive to detect and correct at later stages of the development cycle. If problems are found, updates are manually fixed in the UML design models.

Test Generation. A skeleton of the composite service is generated automatically in the Django web development framework [16] using our partial code generation tool. The implementation is manually completed by the service developer. In order to validate that the implementation of the composite service is functioning correctly along with its partner services and if the service goals and timed constraints are being fulfilled, we generate tests from the UPTA models and execute them online (on-the-fly) against the implementation. During the test execution we monitor how different test coverage criteria are fulfilled, how the requirements are covered, and whether the user scenarios are validated.

3 Tool Support

Modeling in UML. The design models are modeled using MagicDraw [2]. Static validation of models is done via OCL using the validation engine of Magic Draw. We rely on predefined validation suites for UML contained in MagicDraw for the basic validation of the model. These validation suites contain rules that check that the designed UML model conforms to UML meta-model specifications and prevent the developer from doing basic modeling mistakes.

Code Generation. The code-skeleton of the updated service design models of REST composite web service can be generated using our tool presented in [26]. The tool generates code skeleton for design models in Django that is a high level Python web framework [16]. The generated code also has behavioral information such that *pre* and *post* conditions for each method are included and the developer just has to write the implementation of the operations.

UML→UPTA Transformation. A Python script is used to automate the transformation.

Test Generation. We generate tests using UPPAAL TRON, an extension of UPPAAL for online model-based black-box conformance testing [24]. A test adapter is used by UPPAAL TRON to expose the observable I/O communication between the test environment model and the SUT model. Our adapter implements the communication with the SUT by converting abstract test inputs into HTTP request messages and HTTP response messages into abstract test outputs. UPPAAL TRON generates tests via symbolic execution of the specifications using randomized choice of inputs. Based on the timed sequence of input actions from the simulation, the adapter preforms input actions to Implementation Under Test (IUT) and waits for the response. Output from IUT is monitored and generated as output actions for the simulation. The conformance testing is achieved by comparing outputs of IUT to the behavior of the simulation.

Test Coverage Information. In order to enable rigorous test coverage in UPPAAL TRON, a second Python script (discussed in more detail in [20]) is used to automatically add *tracking* variables (also referred to as *traps* in the UPPAAL community) for each edge of a given automaton in a UPTA model and a corresponding update of the given variable on the corresponding edge. Whenever the edge is visited during the simulation or execution, the variable is incremented, allowing thus to track which edges have been visited and how many times. This enables one to track coverage level wrt. e.g., edge coverage or edge pair coverage. This script will also be integrated in the final version of the UML→UPTA transformation script. W.r.t scenario-coverage each scenario will have its own tracking variable, changing value when the scenario is considered fulfilled (see for instance variables *Sc1* and *Sc2* in Fig. 8 (left)).

4 Case Study

Our case study is a Holiday Booking (HB) composite REST web service that is built on inspiration from the *housetrip.com* service, with the purpose of having

Table 1. Requirements of Holiday Booking CWS (excerpt).

Req	Sub-Requirements
2- Payment	2.1 - When user pays for the booking, partner service should be invoked to process the payment
	2.2 - If the partner service confirms the payment, the booking should be marked paid
	...
3- Cancel	3.1 - A paid booking can be canceled by the user
	3.2 . A canceled booking must be refunded
	...

a case study similar in complexity to real services. This service is a holiday rental online booking site, where one can search and book an apartment in the destination country.

The user of the service searches for a room in a hotel from the list of available hotels at HB before travel. He books the room (if it is available) and that booking is reserved by HB with the hotel for 24 h. The user must pay for the booking within 24 h. If the user does not pay within this time then the booking is canceled. If the booking is paid, then the HB service invokes a credit card verification service and waits for the payment confirmation. When the payment is confirmed, HB invokes the hotel service to confirm the booking of the room. If the hotel does not respond within 1 day or it does not confirm at all, the booking is canceled and the user is refunded. If the hotel service confirms, then a booking is made with the hotel. The payment is not released to the hotel until the user checks in. When the user checks in, HB releases the money to the hotel and the booking is marked by the hotel as paid. Due to space limitation, we only show some of the models in here while complete details are available at [26].

Requirements. We have inferred functional and temporal requirements from specification document for our case study. In total we specified 4 main requirements with their sub-requirements. Some of these requirements are accompanied by scenario models. For brevity, Table 1 shows only two of these requirements, *Payment* and *Cancel*. The scenario models in Figs. 4 and 5 detail how their corresponding user scenarios are fulfilled by the composite service.

Design Models. The design of HB composite REST web service is modeled with resource, behavioral and domain models. Due to space reasons only an excerpt of the state machine of HB composite service is shown (Fig. 6). Service requirements are traced to the state machine by including them (and their sub-requirements) as comments linked to transitions.

UML→UPTA Transformation. The timed automaton corresponding the HB service from Fig. 6 is given in Fig. 7. The detailed model and the specifications of the partner web services are available in [26].

Figure 8 shows the two types of environment models produced by the transformation: one modeling the user scenarios in Figs. 4 and 5, and a canonical

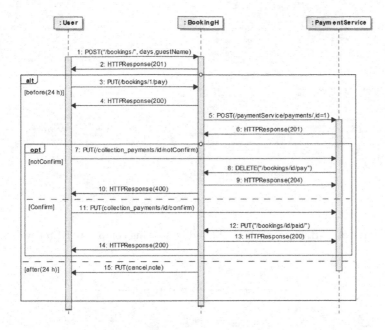

Fig. 4. Scenario model for user payment and invoking payment service.

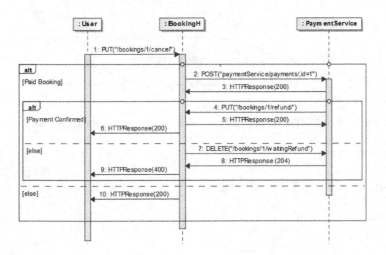

Fig. 5. Scenario model to cancel booking.

model. Each scenario has associated a tracking variable (e.g., *Sc1*) which helps in performing the verification and monitoring test coverage.

Verification. The verification properties are specialized for our case study and some of them are mentioned below.

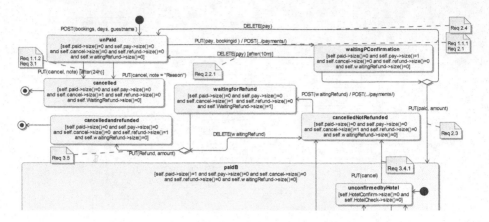

Fig. 6. Excerpt of UML state machine of holiday booking composite REST web service.

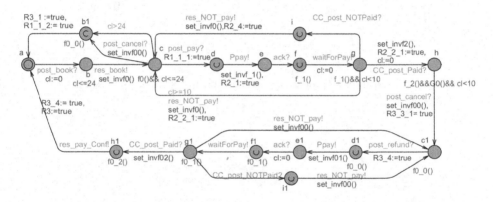

Fig. 7. Excerpt of UPTA model of holiday booking composite REST web service.

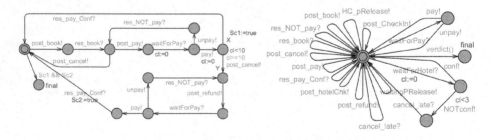

Fig. 8. Excerpt of Scenario-based environment (left) and canonical environment (right).

Deadlock Freeness. The HB Service, the hotel service and the payment service models are all deadlock free. This means that the composite service never reaches a state that cannot preform a transition (i.e., $A \square$ *not deadlock*). Note that the

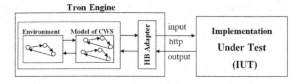

Fig. 9. UPPAAL TRON test setup.

following queries are made for complete model and only some of them can be traced in Fig. 7.

Reachability. All the locations in the HB service are reachable. This means that the model receives and sends messages to the partner services smoothly and the model is validated for its basic behavior (i.e., $E \lozenge CompService.r$), where r is the last location in the TA model and indicates that all processes for a certain booking is completed.

Safety. Some of the safety properties in our model are: (a) Payment should be released iff the user has checked in, i.e., ($E \square CompService.h2$ imply *Card Service.c2*), where $c2$ is the location after check-in and $h2$ is the location after payment release, (b) If the payment is released by the HB service then the Hotel service is paid, i.e., ($E \square CompService.h2$ imply *HotelService.p*), where p is the location in Hotel service model for hotel payment.

Liveness. Some of the liveness properties in the model are: (a) When the payment is not paid within 24 h, the booking is canceled (i.e., $CompService.c$ and $compService.cl > 24 \rightsquigarrow CompService.b1$), where c indicates waiting for the payment, cl indicates clock of the model and $b1$ indicates the booking request is going to cancel due to the delay, (b) If the Hotel Service does not confirm within 3 days then the booking is considered not confirmed (i.e., $CompService.o$ and $CompService.cl > 3 \rightsquigarrow CompService.n$), where o is the location for waiting for the hotel response and n is the location for canceling. For the scenario environment, we identified a boolean variable for each scenario. Initially, all variables are false, and at the end of each scenario the corresponding variable will be set to true. The verification rule shows that all scenarios are reachable ($E \lozenge SDEnv.Sc1$ and $SDEnv.Sc2$ and $SDEnv.Sc3$), where SDEnv indicates the environment model, and Sc1, Sc2 and Sc3 are the variables. Timing constraints in scenario environment is verified by checking if the user is waiting for the service payment confirmation more than 10 h (i.e., in location X), then she can cancel the reservation (i.e., $SDEnv.X$ and $SDEnv.cl > 10 \rightsquigarrow SDEnv.Y$), Y and X are locations.

Testing. The test setup comprises the TRON engine, the test adapter, and the IUT. The IUT is a web service composition of three web services: Holiday Booking, Hotel and Payment Services, whereas the environment model is one of the models in Fig. 8. Whenever all the tracking variables monitored by the environment models are *true*, e.g., scenario 1 and 2 are fulfilled or all edges of the SUT model are covered, the environment transitions to the final state. This approach is used as a stopping criterion for testing (Fig. 9).

Table 2. Correspondence between code coverage and edge coverage.

Run	Edge Coverage	Code Coverage
1	64 %	55 %
2	80 %	67 %
3	100 %	78 %

5   Evaluation

The UML state machines of the HB composite REST web service had 14 states and 25 transitions. These were translated into an UPTA model with 34 locations and 46 edges. Similarly, the state machines of the Payment service had 3 states and 4 transitions which were translated into an UPTA model with 5 locations and 6 edges. The Hotel service had 4 states and 5 transitions that were translated into 7 locations and 9 edges. In addition, the environment model created had 4 locations and 13 edges.

Similarly, the two user scenarios discussed in this article (Figs. 4 and 5) comprised of 15 and respectively 11 messages which were transformed into the automaton in Fig. 8-left with 13 locations and 17 edges.

One issue with using formal tools like UPPAAL for verification and test generation, is the scalability of the approach, due to the state space explosion. In contrast to offline test generation, where the entire state space has to be computed, in online test generation only the symbolic states following the current symbolic states have to computed. This reduces drastically the number of symbolic states making the test generation less prone to space explosion and thus more scalable. For instance, the number of explored symbolic states when generating, with the `verifyta` tool, traces satisfying complete edge coverage (i.e., $e_1 \& \ldots \& e_j \& \ldots \& e_m$, where e_j are tracking variables corresponding to all m edges of the HBS models) was 974. In the contrast, the maximum number of symbolic states reported by TRON during a test session achieving complete edge coverage was 12.

For benchmarking the verification process, we have used the `verifyta` command line utility of UPPAAL for verification of the specified 5 properties. We have used the `memtime` tool to measure the time and memory needed for verification. The result showed in average 2 s and 54996 KB of memory being used. Although the memory utilization depends heavily on the symbolic state space, it shows that the current size models leave room for scalability of the approach.

In order to evaluate the efficiency of our approach, we compared the specification coverage with the code coverage yielded by a given test run. Since we had access to the source code of the IUT, we used the *coverage* tool for Python [1] to report the code coverage for each test session. Table 2 lists results of several measurements.

Although many of the errors were caused by modeling mistakes, testing revealed some errors in the implementation as well. For instance, in the HB service, there was an error in sending *cancel* request and another error found in the POST header in *refund* request. Also in the Hotel service, the confirmation was sent by the wrong method, so it was rejected by Holiday Booking service. Similar errors were detected by applying Scenario-based environment model.

In order to evaluate the fault detection capabilities of our approach, we have manually created 30 mutated versions of the original HB service program code. Each mutation had one fault seeded in the code, for instance replacing POST with DELETE, removing one line of the source code, change of logical conditions, etc. The faults were always seeded in those parts of the code that is covered when achieving 100 % edge coverage of the model. We assumed that the original version of the composite web service is the correct one, as we were able to run the 100 test sessions in TRON against it. For each mutated version of the composite web service, we set the TRON to execute 100 test sessions against it. When a fault was discovered, the mutant was considered as *killed*. If the mutated statement has been covered by the test runs but no failure was detected, we mark it as *alive*. Out of the 30 mutated programs, 28 mutants were killed and 2 were alive, using the canonical test environment in Fig. 8-left. This resulted into a mutation score of 93.3 %.

6   Related Work

A large body of work on using model checking techniques for validation and verification of web service compositions has been done and overviews of works can be found in [7,29]. Mostly authors have used web service specific specification languages as starting point and converted specifications to models using model checking tools. Then, they performed simulation, verification or test generation via model-checking. Most of these works use the selected model-checking tool only for simulation and verification; only a handful generate abstract tests from the verification conditions. We can distinguish roughly two verification approaches: those that target the PROMELA language [25] which is the input language for the SPIN model-checker [17], and those that target the UPPAAL timed automata as modeling tool [4]. In the following, we will revisit those works which are most similar to ours.

Garcia [14] uses counterexamples to specify and generate test cases in model checking tool. The transitions in BPEL define the test requirements. The transitions are mapped to the model expressed in LTL properties. Fu et al. [13] provide a framework for both bottom-up and top-down approach analyzing web service compositions. In top-down, the conversation of a web service is specified as guarded automaton converted to PROMELA modeled in SPIN model-checker. The bottom-up approach translates BPEL to guarded automaton and used SPIN tool after translating guarded automaton to PROMELA. The synchronization of web service conversations are analyzed in order to verify the compatibility.

Huang et al. [18] present a work that automatically translate OWL-S specification of composite web service into a C-like specification language and PDDL. These can be processed with the BLAST model-checker which can generate positive and negative test cases of a particular formula.

These works focus on BPEL processes and OWL-S which make them dependent on specific execution languages for SOAP based services whereas our work is not dependent on implementation and supports REST architectural style. Besides, they do not support requirement traceability and is not clear how tests are generated and executed. Furthermore, the PROMELA language cannot address real-time properties, due to the limited support for time in PROMELA. Cambronero et al. verify and validate web services choreography by translating a subset of WS-CDL into a network of timed automata using UPPAAL tool [8]. They model the requirements by extending KAOS goal model. The work is supported by WST tool that provides model transformation of timed composite web services [9]. Diaz et al. also provide a translation from WS-BPEL to UPPAAL timed automata [10]. Time properties are specified in WS-BPEL and translated to UPPAAL. However, requirements are not traced explicitly, while verification and testing are not discussed.

Ibrahim and Al-Ani [19] specify safety and security non-functional properties in BPEL and later formulated into guards in the UPPAAL model. They do not consider neither real-time properties nor test generation. In [15], Nawal and Godart use UPPAAL to check compatibility of web service choreography supporting asynchronous timed communications. They distinguished between full and partial compatibility and full incompatibility of web services. Our work is somewhat similar to their work as we support time critical stateful REST webs service compositions using UPPAAL, however, in addition to verification we use UPPAAL with TRON to validate the implementation of the web services.

Zhang [30] suggest the use of the temporal logic XYZ/ADL language [31] for specifying web server compositions. They transform the specifications into a timed asynchronous communication model (TACM) which are verified in UPPAAL. In [21], uses BPEL as a reference specification and transform them to an Intermediate Format (IF) based on timed automata and then propose an algorithm to generate test cases. Similar to our approach, tests are generated via simulation in a custom tool, where the exploration is guided by test purposes. The time properties are added manually to the IF specification, while we specify them at UML level.

Biswal et al. present a test generation approach using UML activity diagram to define scenarios [6]. Arnold et al. provide a framework that supports automatic test generation from scenarios and also transforms them to test cases that can run on actual IUT [3]. Enoiu et al. presented an approach to generate test suites for PLC software using UPPAAL [11]. Larsen et al. presented an approach in which scenario-based requirements are translated to timed automata, reducing the problem of model consistency and verification effort [22]. These works provide approaches to verify and validate the service specifications by checking the properties of interest using UPPAAL. However, in our work, in addition to model checking the properties we also perform conformance testing of the service composition via online scenario-based testing with the TRON tool and we provide requirement traceability for non-deterministic systems.

7   Conclusions

We have presented a scenario-based approach to verify and validate RESTful composite web services. In our approach, a service can invoke other services and exhibit complex and timed behavior, while still complying with the REST architectural style. We showed how to model the service composition in UML, including time properties. We modeled communicating web services and explicitly define the service invocations and receiving service calls.

We use model checking approach with UPPAAL model-checker to verify and validate our design models w.r.t user scenarios. From the verified specification, we generate tests using an online model-based testing tool. The use of online model-based testing proved beneficial as our system under test exhibits non-deterministic behavior due to concurrency and real-time domain.

With the help of requirements traceability mechanism we traced requirements to UML models and, via the UML→UPTA transformation to timed automata models. Their reachability is verified in UPPAAL and they are used as test goals during test generation. Linking requirements to generated tests allowed us to quickly see which requirements have been validated and which have not. In addition, it allows us to identify from which parts of the specification/implementation the detected error has originated.

We exemplified our approach with a relatively complex case study of a holiday booking web service and we provided preliminary evaluation results.

References

1. Code coverage measurement for Python - coverage, v. 3.6 (2013). https://pypi.python.org/pypi/coverage (Retrieved: 20 August 2013)
2. Nomagic MagicDraw, August 2013. webpage at http://www.nomagic.com/products/magicdraw/
3. Arnold, D., Corriveau, J.P., Shi, W.: A scenario-driven approach to model-based testing (2010)
4. Behrmann, G., et al.: Uppaal 4.0. In: QEST 2006 Proceedings of the 3rd international conference on the Quantitative Evaluation of Systems, pp. 125–126. IEEE Computer Society, Washington, DC (2006)
5. Birgit Demuth, C.W.: Model and object verification by using Dresden OCL. In: Proceedings of the Russian-German Workshop Innovation Information Technologies: Theory and Practice, pp. 81–89 (2009)
6. Biswal, B., Nanda, P., Mohapatra, D.: A novel approach for scenario-based test case generation. In: International Conference on Information Technology, ICIT 2008, pp. 244–247, December 2008
7. Bozkurt, M., et al.: Testing web services: a survey. Department of Computer Science, Kings College London, Technical report TR-10-01 (2010)
8. Cambronero, M.E., et al.: Validation and verification of web services choreographies by using timed automata. J. Logic Algebraic Program. **80**(1), 25–49 (2011)
9. Cambronero, M., et al.: WST: a tool supporting timed composite web services model transformation. Simulation **88**(3), 349–364 (2012)
10. Diaz, G., et al.: Model checking techniques applied to the design of web services. CLEI Electron. J. 10(2) (2007)

11. Enoiu, E.P., Sundmark, D., Pettersson, P.: Model-based test suite generation for function block diagrams using the uppaal model checker. In: Proceedings of the 2013 IEEE Sixth International Conference on Software Testing, Verification and Validation Workshops, ICSTW 2013, pp. 158–167. IEEE Computer Society, Washington, DC (2013). http://dx.doi.org/10.1109/ICSTW.2013.27
12. Fielding, R.T.: Architectural styles and the design of network-based software architectures. Ph.D. thesis, University of California (2000)
13. Fu, X., et al.: Synchronizability of conversations among web services. IEEE Trans. Softw. Eng. **31**(12), 1042–1055 (2005)
14. García-Fanjul, J., et al.: Generating test cases specifications for BPEL compositions of web services using SPIN. In: International Workshop on Web Services-Modeling and Testing (WS-MaTe 2006), p. 83 (2006)
15. Guermouche, N., Godart, C.: Timed model checking based approach for web services analysis. In: IEEE International Conference on Web Services, ICWS 2009, pp. 213–221. IEEE (2009)
16. Holovaty, A., Kaplan-Moss, J.: The definitive guide to Django: web development done right. Apress (2009)
17. Holzmann, G.J.: The model checker SPIN. IEEE Trans. Softw. Eng. **23**(5), 279–295 (1997)
18. Huang, H., et al.: Automated model checking and testing for composite web services. In: Eighth IEEE International Symposium on Object-Oriented Real-Time Distributed Computing, ISORC 2005, pp. 300–307. IEEE (2005)
19. Ibrahim, N., Al Ani, I.: Beyond functional verification of web services compositions. J. Emerg. Trends Comput. Inf. Sci. **4**, 25–30 (2013). Special Issue
20. Koskinen, M., et al.: Combining model-based testing and continuous integration. In: Proceedings of the International Conference on Software Engineering Advances (ICSEA 2013). IARIA, October 2013 (to appear)
21. Lallali, M., et al.: Automatic timed test case generation for web services composition. In: IEEE Sixth European Conference on Web Services, ECOWS 2008, pp. 53–62. IEEE (2008)
22. Larsen, K., Li, S., Nielsen, B., Pusinskas, S.: Scenario-based analysis and synthesis of real-time systems using uppaal. In: Design, Automation Test in Europe Conference Exhibition (DATE), pp. 447–452, March 2010
23. Larsen, K.G., et al.: UPPAAL in a nutshell. Int. J. Softw. Tools Tech. Transf. (STTT) **1**(1), 134–152 (1997)
24. Larsen, K.G., et al.: CISS, BRICS. UPPAAL Tron user manual. Aalborg University, Aalborg (2009)
25. Part, I., Peschke, M.: Design and validation of computer protocols (2003)
26. Rauf, I.: Design and Validation of Stateful Composite RESTful Web Services. Ph.D. thesis (2014)
27. Rauf, I., et al.: An integrated approach for designing and validating rest web service compositions. In: Monfort, V., Krempels, K.H. (eds.) 10th International Conference on Web Information Systems and Technologies, vol. 1, p. 104–115. SCITEPRESS Digital Library (2014)
28. Richardson, L., Ruby, S.: RESTful web services. O'Reilly (2008)
29. Rusli, H.M., et al.: Testing web services composition: a mapping study. Commun. IBIMA **2007**, 34–48 (2011)
30. Zhang, G., Shi, H., Rong, M., Di, H.: Model checking for asynchronous web service composition based on XYZ/ADL. In: Gong, Z., Luo, X., Chen, J., Lei, J., Wang, F.L. (eds.) WISM 2011, Part II. LNCS, vol. 6988, pp. 428–435. Springer, Heidelberg (2011)
31. Zhu, X.Y., Tang, Z.S.: A temporal logic-based software architecture description language xyz/adl. J. Softw. **14**(4), 713–720 (2003)

Web Interfaces and Applications

A Client-Side Approach to Improving One-Handed Web Surfing on a Smartphone

Karsten Seipp$^{(\boxtimes)}$ and Kate Devlin

Department of Computing, Goldsmiths College, University of London,
Lewisham Way, New Cross, London SE14 6NW, UK
{k.seipp,k.devlin}@gold.ac.uk
http://www.gold.ac.uk/computing

Abstract. Our work examines the impact of natural movements on usability and efficiency of one-handed website operation on touchscreen smartphones. We present and evaluate a JavaScript framework which transforms the controls of all page elements into an interface that corresponds to the natural arcing swipe of the thumb. This can be operated via swipe and tap, without having to stretch the thumb or change the grip on the phone. The interface can be toggled on or off as required and keeps the original presentation of the website intact. Two user studies show that this choice of interface and its simplified interaction model can be applied to a diverse range of interactive elements and websites and provides a high degree of usability and efficiency.

Keywords: One-handed operation · Mobile · Web · Wheel menu · Interface adaptation · Curved interfaces · CSS3 · JavaScript · HTML

1 Introduction

The majority of smartphones sold today use modern operating systems such as Android and iOS, both of which have a powerful and largely standard-compliant browser paired with a touchscreen interface and a large screen. With the help of established adaptation techniques for websites on mobile devices [2,20] as well as responsive themes [6] employing CSS3 media queries, device-independent websites are becoming the norm. In addition, further approaches exist to adapt websites to mobile device constraints, although these are either proprietary [1], dependent on a proxy server [10] or bound to a specific browser [16,26]. For non-adapted pages, built-in actions such as pinching and tapping to zoom can improve matters. Although these approaches result in an adapted and improved display on a range of mobile devices, they do not provide an adapted interaction model for thumb-based use, which has been identified as a preferred mode of operation by many users [13]. The limited mobility and reach of the thumb represent completely different challenges to the designer regarding the layout and operation of the website; simply crafting it to ensure a correct display of the page elements does not suffice.

© Springer International Publishing Switzerland 2015
V. Monfort and K.-H. Krempels (Eds.): WEBIST 2014, LNBIP 226, pp. 163–178, 2015.
DOI: 10.1007/978-3-319-27030-2_11

While some browsers [16] offer improvements for one-handed operation as part of their interface (using simple gestures, for example), we explore whether one-handed operation can be reliably improved regardless of the browser or plugin used. We do this by improving the display and control of elements operated via direct touch, without the need for gestures. As devices and browsers become increasingly powerful, the question arises as to whether such improvements can be made directly at runtime in the browser, and how efficient and usable these improvements are in comparison to non-enhanced websites.

In this paper we present a JavaScript-based framework which we have named the One Hand Wonder (OHW). The OHW prototype provides an on-demand, thumb-optimised interface for all interactive elements on a web page, facilitating operation and navigation across a wide range of websites. It gives quick access to the most common elements and augments the interaction model of the browser and the standard HTML elements of a web page with additional one-handed UI features that can easily be toggled on and off. These augmentations are temporary and do not change the design of the website. The OHW is built using solely client-side technologies and is implemented by simply embedding the code into the the web page. Initial user testing together with informal feedback during a demo session has confirmed acceptance and learnability [18]. This paper is based on a previous publication [19], but provides more insight into the design rationale as well as a more detailed description of the various interface modules. In particular, this paper focuses on the following:

1. Detailed description of design and functionality of the framework and its modules.
2. Head-to-head comparison of the OHW's performance against normal, non-enhanced operation.
3. A performance test of the system based on its implementation into popular websites.
4. Overall discussion of the OHW as a tool for one-handed website operation on touchscreen smartphones.

2   Previous Research

When designing thumb-friendly interfaces, Wobbrock et al. [23] suggest supporting and evoking horizontal thumb movements as much as possible, as vertical movements were found to be overly challenging. On this basis they suggest a horizontal layout of interactive elements on the screen to accommodate the economic peculiarities of the thumb and improve usability. Katre [14] shows that a curved arrangement of elements on a touchscreen is perceived as comfortable and easy, as it supports a more natural circular motion of the thumb. An application of this is found in interfaces such as ArchMenu or ThumbMenu [12], where the user moves their thumb over an arch of elements placed in the bottom right corner of the screen.

Other researchers have explored the use of concentric menus such as the Wavelet menu [8] and SAM [5] to enhance thumb-based interaction, similar to the first generation Apple iPod. In the case of the Wavelet menu, research has shown that this approach with its consistent interaction model is easy to learn and efficient to use. Lü and Li [15] present Gesture Avatar where the user can highlight a GUI element on screen to gain better control of it via an enlarged avatar. While this is an innovative way of improving one-handed device operation, it requires the user to draw their interface first, depends on a proprietary application and cannot be customised by the webmaster.

In terms of general adaptation of websites for mobile devices, one approach is web page segmentation [10,11], using a proxy server to re-render the page into new logical units which are subsequently served to the device. A proprietary solution is the Read4Me browser [26] where the browser offers to optimise the page for mobile display via a proxy-server that then serves it to the user. Bandelloni et al. suggest a different system [3] where the developer creates an abstract XML-based description of the layout and a proxy server renders the information for the respective access device. In addition to these techniques, various services, themes and frameworks exist to adapt websites for mobile devices and CSS3 media queries offer a flexible approach for display adaptation.

While existing approaches are all concerned with the display of a website on mobile devices, the OHW addresses a so-far neglected aspect: the specific support of one-handed operation of the web page. By implementing the OHW into a website, improvements are made to the operation – rather than the presentation – of the site, as this remains problematic even on well-adapted sites when operating it with one hand. Most importantly, the enhancement is done at runtime and on the client, can be fully configured by the webmaster and is dependent only on the browser itself and the user (who can choose to switch the enhancements on or off at any time).

3   Development

To verify the findings of previous researchers [14,23] promoting a curved input control for thumb-based GUIs, we conducted a user study with 7 participants (3 F, mean age 31.43 years, SD 4.65), all of who declared to be frequent users of touchscreen mobile devices. Participants were asked to swipe 10 times using their right and left thumb without looking at the device. They were instructed to swipe in a way that was most natural and comfortable to them, avoiding bending and stretching of the joints. Traces of these swipes were recorded on a hidden layer and saved. Stacking the resulting images on top of each other shows the curved movement created by a horizontal swipe, supporting the findings of previous researchers and informing our design of the interface (Fig. 1). In a separate study with 27 participants (8 F, mean age 22.33 years, SD. 2.94), we explored the impact of button position on grip stability. For this we measured the gyroscope amplitude around the X, Y and Z axis when the user tries to reach an item with their thumb in 60 positions. Visualising the data shows that the least amount of movement on the Z axis is in the area highlighted by our swipe test (Fig. 1). By positioning interactive elements in this area, stretching and bending of the thumb

Fig. 1. Far left and left: Visualisation of the swipe data created by the horizontal movement of the left and right thumb. **Right and far right:** Visualisation of the Gyroscope amplitude around the Z-axis when tapping a target with left or right thumb in various locations of the screen. Darker areas present target locations that create a high amplitude (15793 Hz max.) and strong device movement when being tapped. Lighter areas represent element positions with low amplitudes (3273 Hz max.) and little movement of the device. Left images taken from [19] with permission from WEBIST.

and the resulting shifting of the phone in the user's hand is minimised, providing a more secure grip and further supporting our design decision. To develop and verify our design, we iteratively tested paper prototypes with users to transform the wheel menu metaphor into a comprehensive website interface, supporting a more natural operation and minimal strain. Building on discussions with web developers, we made the OHW as non-intrusive and supportive as possible in the form of an easily accessible, half-circle-shaped interface that can be added to a page by simply dropping the code into the website.

4   Functionality

The interface consists of three main parts:

- A *display zone* (Fig. 2, red) showing menu content or the currently active element, such as a video or a form element. When in scrolling mode or when selecting an item from the wheel menu, this zone displays the web page.
- An *interaction zone* (Fig. 2, green) on which the user swipes and taps to manipulate items in the *display zone*.
- A *Start/Back button* (Fig. 2, yellow) which is used for moving back through different states of the interface and for showing and hiding the wheel menu.

The OHW facilitates one-handed web browsing by assembling all interactive elements on request in a region easily accessible by the user's thumb and restricts the range of interactions to just two – swipe and tap. The layout of the page stays untouched and users can decide whether or not to use the interface at any time by switching it on or off (Fig. 2). Thus, the OHW is not an interface for

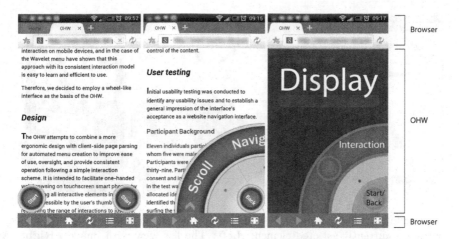

Fig. 2. Left: The OHW as it appears on start up. **Middle:** The OHW opened for right-handed use. **Right:** The three zones of the OHW. Colours were added for easier differentiation. **Red:** The *display zone*. **Green:** The *interaction zone*. **Yellow:** The *Start/Back* button. Images 1 and 2 taken from [19] with permission from WEBIST (Color figure online).

mobile optimisation, which can be achieved using the techniques outlined above. Rather, the OHW's purpose is to enhance one-handed operation of a website regardless of its degree of adaptation, without spoiling the design. It augments the interaction model, not the display. To function, the OHW requires a browser with CSS3 support together with the jQuery JavaScript library – the most popular JavaScript library to date [17] – present on the website. Other than this, there are no minimum standards required and the OHW can be implemented into pages that already include libraries such as MooTools, for example. It has been trialled on a range of Android and iOS devices with HTML4 and HTML5 mark-up in Standards and Quirks mode.

The OHW interface consists of a variety of modules whose availability depends on the content of the website and the interface's configuration. Each module is represented as a wedge and together they form a wheel-type interface, either at the right-hand or left-hand bottom corner of the screen, depending upon the user's choice (Fig. 2). Only the modules that correspond to elements found on the page are loaded, but additional modules can be added at runtime by listening to updates of the Document Object Model (DOM).

To implement the OHW, the webmaster only needs to ensure that the jQuery JavaScript library is available on the website before linking to the OHW's code using a basic <script> tag. The webmaster can optionally edit the configuration file, which is a JavaScript object, and adjust themes, selectors and custom functionality. As each and every aspect of the interface can be adjusted via CSS and HTML, the OHW can fit the look and content of a wide variety of websites. Once implemented, the code scans the website for certain tags from which to build the interface. By default these are basic HTML elements, such

Fig. 3. Far left: The standard list view. The blue *highlight zone* at the top of the screen indicates the currently selected element. **Left:** The list view with images. **Right:** A text input filed in the form overview. **Far right:** The media player view being operated by a user. Images taken from [19] with permission from WEBIST (Color figure online).

as <nav>, <video>, <audio>, <form>, <h2>, and <a>, and from these the standard names of the wedges are derived. This can easily be extended by using CSS selectors and custom wedges declared in the configuration file. The OHW contains several methods to cope with incorrect mark-up and can report any encountered problems to the webmaster.

The OHW's use is optional for the user and the interface can be hidden and brought back at any time. The interface is launched by tapping the Start button on either side of the screen to make it visible (Fig. 2). It can be spun by swiping over it to reveal all available functions. The Start button then becomes a Back button and can be used to either hide the interface completely or to go back one level. For example, if the user was standing and only had one hand free, they could tap the Start button and operate the site one-handedly with the help of the interface. As they sit down and free their other hand, they could hide the interface by tapping the Back button and continue to operate the website with both hands, without a change in the website's design.

4.1 Views

The OHW offers improved presentation and one-handed operation for all inter-active page elements. This can be achieved either by accessing them via the respective wedge in the wheel or by double-tapping them on the page. When the interface is launched, swiping and tapping actions in the *interaction zone* are used to manipulate the views in the *display zone*. A variety of views are employed by default to visualise different element types, but can be altered and combined by the webmaster to extend the OHW's functionality:

List View. This is employed whenever items are presented in a list and can hold text or images with text, depending on the content (Fig. 3). It is used for

Fig. 4. Far left: Text input via the deprecated OHW keyboard. **Left:** Text input using the system standard keyboard. **Right:** The slider input view. **Far right:** The date input view. Right and far right image taken from [19] with permission from WEBIST.

the *Headlines, Navigation, Links* and *Media* menu, as well as drop-down lists. By sliding their thumb over the *interaction zone*, the user can move the list content up or down. The circular button inside the *interaction zone* indicates the scroll position and confirms the selection within the blue *highlight zone* at the top of the screen upon tapping. Tapping on the interface (and not on the interaction button) will scroll the list view to the respective position.

Media Player. If a natively supported media element is double-tapped on the page or selected via a list view, it is played back in the media player. Swiping over the *interaction zone* controls the playback position (Fig. 3).

Form View. All elements of a form are displayed in a horizontal arrangement which the user can navigate using the semi-circular scroll pane in the *interaction zone* (Fig. 3). Tapping the interaction button will activate the current element.

Text Input. Text input uses the basic OS interface, as users preferred the standard system keyboard over an adapted semi-circular JS/CSS keyboard (Fig. 4).

Slider. An input field of the type "range" is transformed into a slider: Swiping in the *interaction zone* moves the slider head in the *display zone* (Fig. 4).

Date Selector. Activating an element of the type "datetime" will transform the content area in the form element overview into three lists which can be operated like a normal list view (Fig. 4).

On/Off Switches. Checkboxes and Radio buttons are displayed as on-off switches, operated by tapping the interaction button in the *interaction zone* (Fig. 5).

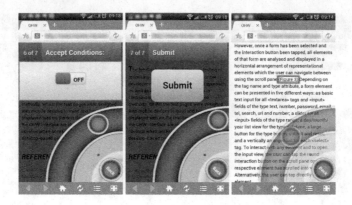

Fig. 5. Left: Checkbox and radio button view. **Middle:** Button view. **Right:** Media player view. Images taken from [19] with permission from WEBIST.

Buttons. Buttons are represented by large buttons operated via the *interaction zone* or direct tap (Fig. 5).

Scrolling. The OHW also provides scroll functionality similar to that found in the Opera Mini browser. Tapping the Scroll wedge allows the user to scroll the page by swiping their thumb over the *interaction zone*. While scrolling, interactive elements closest to the current scroll position are outlined one at a time and can be activated by tapping the interaction button of the interface without the user having to stretch their thumb to reach these distant elements (Fig. 5).

5   First User Study

After iterative paper prototyping, the interface was built and a pilot user test with 11 participants (6 F, all frequent smartphone users) was conducted to identify usability issues and to establish acceptance. Users were given a set of tasks one might perform on a page consisting of headlines, forms, videos, navigation and links, which they completed using the OHW without assistance. The page was designed to be device-independent using CSS3 media queries. All actions were recorded in video and audio, and feedback was given in a questionnaire on a five-point Likert scale. Feedback was predominantly positive and in response to the collected data we created an improved version of the interface. During a demo session at a conference [18] we presented this interface to visitors, implementing it on a range of popular websites to be experienced "hands-on". Informal feedback from users during these sessions was consistently positive, complimenting on the ease-of-use, usefulness of the approach and quality of the implementation, thus supporting the validity of our approach.

6   Second User Study

With the improved interface we conducted a second user study to determine the efficiency and speed of the OHW in comparison to the normal operation (with one hand without the OHW) of a mobile-optimised website. Altogether, 22 participants (7 F) aged 20 to 34 took part in the study, 19 of whom were final year undergraduate Computing students and the remainder were young professionals. All of them were right-handed, regular users of touchscreen mobile devices, such as phones and media players. The 19 Computing students were briefly introduced to the OHW during class and asked to do some self-directed exploring on a test page. On the day of the study, all users were given a 5-minute explanation of the usage of the OHW to ensure its operation was fully understood.

Using a within-subjects design, participants carried out the study one-handedly both with and without the use of the OHW. The study was counterbalanced by altering the mode in which the tasks were first performed. The first part of the usability study comprised 10 separate standard tasks a user might perform on a website and cover the whole spectrum of the OHW:

1. Finding a menu item in the navigation
2. Finding a video and forwarding it to a certain time
3. Finding a form and activating a checkbox
4. Finding another video and starting it
5. Finding a form and filling in a date
6. Finding a link in the body text
7. Finding a form and filling in a range value
8. Finding a headline
9. Finding a form and pressing a button
10. Scrolling and clicking on a link

The study featured a website presenting the OHW. It was coded in HTML5 and CSS3 and contained a page navigation (<nav>), headlines (<h1>, <h2>, <h3>), a form with various elements of input types ("text", "range", "datetime", "submit", "checkbox"), paragraphs of text (<p>), three video files with poster images (<video>), links (<a>), images (<img>) as well as various <div> elements for the layout. These elements are very common and can be considered as representative for many websites. CSS3 media queries and relative measures were used to make the website's presentation device-independent. To conduct the study we used a HTC Sensation XE with Android 4.03 and the Maxthon Mobile Browser.

Tasks were performed directly on the website and were preceded by an instruction screen. Each task commenced from the top of the page. The number of interactions and time needed to accomplish the task were recorded using JavaScript. Recording began when users pressed OK on the instruction screen and stopped when a task was completed. For example, recording was only stopped once the target link was clicked or a certain value was entered into a field.

While the above is well-suited for determining efficiency on discrete tasks, it is less suitable for predicting the OHW's "real-life" performance on a page containing any number of these elements, where spatial proximity could affect performance. To address this we also measured the performance in 10 additional, consecutive tasks (1c to 10c), mimicking a set of coherent actions. After each part of this use case, recording was paused to show the instructions for the next part, but the current state of the website (scroll position, opened menus etc.) remained unchanged:

1c. Navigating to a headline in the text
2c. Scrolling and clicking on a link
3c. Finding a menu item in the navigation
4c. Finding a video and forwarding it to a certain time
5c. Navigating to another headline in the text
6c. Finding a link in the body text by scrolling
7c. Finding a form and entering a word into a text field
8c. Activating a checkbox in the same form
9c. Filling in a date in the same form
10c. Pressing a button in the same form

7 Results

The data was evaluated using a Wilcoxon signed-rank test. Due to the varying, skewed results and small sample size we chose a series of non-parametric tests over the ANOVA. As tasks were not comparable in their results because of their different nature, they had to be treated as separate. Comparison of the one-handed task performance of users with the OHW against the normal, non-enhanced way draws a clear picture of the benefits the OHW offers to one-handed website operation. The effect of the OHW on efficiency can be derived from the median number of interactions required to perform a task (Table 1) as well as from the time needed to complete it (Table 2). Note: The values of the use case (shown in the tables as C) are based on the time and interactions needed to complete the whole use case, consisting of the 10 additional parts 1c to 10c, forming one large task.

7.1 Results: Number of Interactions Needed

In five out of ten tasks, the OHW allows users to complete the task with fewer interactions (Table 1). This is most visible in Tasks 1, 3 and 6 where the same task could be accomplished with only 32 %, 62 % and 47 % of the interactions required without the interface. This highlights the OHW's enhancement of tasks such as finding an item in the navigation, operating a checkbox and retrieving a link from the body text. Other tasks that took fewer interactions to perform with the OHW than without were locating a video (Task 4, 72 %) and finding a headline (Task 8, 74 %). However, the results also show areas where more interactions are required with the OHW than without. This includes finding and pressing a button (Task 9, 142 %) and lengthy scrolling to find a link (Task 10, 198 %).

Table 1. Median interactions per task and the use case (C) w/out the OHW including Z and p values as well as % of interactions (I) needed with OHW (Normal = 100 %). Table taken from [19] with permission from WEBIST.

Task	OHW	Normal	Z	p	%I OHW
1	6	19	3.49	< .001	32 %
2	14	13.5	0.63	.526	104 %
3	14	22.5	2.93	.003	62 %
4	9	12.5	2.1	.036	72 %
5	26.5	27	0.15	.884	98 %
6	7.5	16	3.9	< .001	47 %
7	12	12.5	0.06	.952	96 %
8	14	19	1.97	.049	74 %
9	13.5	9.5	2.95	.003	142 %
10	51.5	26	3.98	< .001	198 %
C	104	127	2.18	.029	82 %

7.2 Results: Amount of Time Needed

Evaluating the performance based on the actual time needed to complete a task draws an even clearer picture of the OHW's effectiveness (Table 2). Using the OHW in all tasks but one is significantly faster than performing the same tasks without the OHW. The most striking differences can be observed in Task 1 (33 % of the time needed), Task 3 (47 %), Task 4 (36 %), Task 6 (33 %) and Task 8 (46 %). However, scrolling through the document (Task 10) takes more time with the OHW (147 % of time needed).

7.3 Results of the Use Case

The results of the use case show that in a real-life application the impact of the OHW on efficiency is significant, as overall it took participants only 60 % of the time and 82 % of the interactions when using the OHW as opposed to operating the website normally (Tables 1 and 2).

7.4 Implementation into Popular Websites and General Performance

To determine the OHW's versatility and suitability for different types of websites, we implemented it on several popular websites via a proxy script that injected the OHW code into the loaded page: Wikipedia [22], BBC News [4], W3C [21], Google [9], WordPress [24] and YouTube [25], but failed to implement the OHW on Flickr [7] as our script could not successfully retrieve the site. For the implementation, the names of the wedges had to be adapted to

Table 2. Median time (T) in seconds needed per task (1 to 10) and the use case (C) w/out the OHW including Z and p values as well as % of time needed with the OHW (Normal = 100 %). Table taken from [19] with permission from WEBIST.

Task	OHW	Normal	Z	p	% T OHW
1	11.40	34.30	4.11	<.001	33 %
2	25.90	45.10	4.07	<.001	57 %
3	20.50	43.90	4.11	<.001	47 %
4	10.20	28.60	4.11	<.001	36 %
5	33.90	46.60	3.98	<.001	73 %
6	9.50	29.10	4.11	<.001	33 %
7	18.80	26.30	3.85	<.001	72 %
8	14.80	31.90	4.07	<.001	46 %
9	15.50	22.10	3.17	.002	70 %
10	65.40	44.50	3.56	<.001	147 %
C	153.20	255.10	4.11	<.001	60 %

better match the content of each page. Startup time was short (Table 3) and the interface felt very responsive on all pages. However, a performance decrease was observed on the Wikipedia implementation, where the links menu held 538 items and on the desktop version of the BBC website, where concurrent scripts and fading animations occasionally impacted the interface.

The results (Table 3) show an overall acceptable to good performance and start-up time of the OHW on an Android device and an iPhone. Whereas the time to create a view increases with the amount of elements to display on the Android device, the rendering time on the iPhone was not impacted by an increase in items. On comparatively complex websites, such as the BBC page and Wikipedia, start-up time on the iPhone is 39 % and 36 % faster than on the Android device, whereas the comparatively simple sites, such as Google.com and W3c.org, were parsed more rapidly on the Android device. The performance on the YouTube page and WordPress.com was similar on both devices.

8   Discussion

First we discuss usability and efficiency from a user perspective. Next we discuss the performance of the framework to determine the boundaries of its deployment.

8.1   Usability and Efficiency

The two user studies show that the controls for different elements can be successfully reduced to a curved interface with a consistent interaction model, completely operable within the thumb's comfort zone. In the majority of cases, using the OHW requires less interactions to complete a task and in 90 % of the

Table 3. Mean time in seconds needed by the HTC Sensation XE (S. XE) and iPhone 3GS (3GS) to create a list view (Fig. 3, right) after tapping a wedge in the wheel using each device's standard browser. For this we chose the WordPress blog [24] as a base and injected additional elements into the DOM when fetching the page using the proxy script. Second part shows mean start-up time of the system (SU) for various websites. For this we measured the start up time of the system by loading and initialising the OHW once the page had finished loading. All measurements were performed three times on each device with a cleared browser cache. Table taken from [19] with permission from WEBIST.

Task	S. XE	3GS
List view, 30 items	1.1	0.6
List view, 60 items	1.5	0.7
List view, 120 items	1.9	0.7
List view, 480 items	2.4	0.6
SU Wikipedia	1.4	0.9
SU BBC News	2.3	1.4
SU W3C	0.3	0.8
SU Google	0.3	1.0
SU WordPress	1.5	1.4
SU YouTube	0.9	0.9

examined cases, a task is completed significantly faster when using the OHW. However, the results also highlight a weak point of the OHW. When the user has to scroll a large section of the page, the performance of the OHW is significantly weaker than the normal mode of operation (147 % of time needed). It shows that scrolling with one hand is already very efficient and that the OHW's approach cannot compete with the existing solution. This has since been addressed by combining native scrolling and OHW scrolling so that the user can scroll the website as usual, but can make more precise selections by moving their thumb over the interface at the same time.

8.2 Versatility

Customisation of the OHW is easy: the webmaster can adapt the text of the wedges to reflect the website content using the supplied templates. Custom functionality is achieved by using the OHW's plugin model to accommodate a website's own set of interactions, such as the accordion-like blocks on Wikipedia [22] with custom callback functions. Thus configured, the OHW is suited to pages with categorised text and images that stretch over many screens and would otherwise need scrolling to access, as found on news websites, wikis, forums, blogs and search engines. Benefits for all types of websites include quick access and operation of forms, navigation, and control of audio or video items if supported natively by the browser.

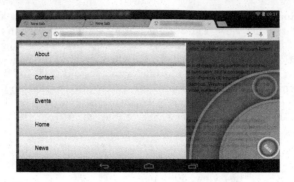

Fig. 6. The OHW on a Nexus 7 in horizontal orientation. Image taken from [19] with permission from WEBIST.

The OHW performs well on mobile-adapted pages if the content per menu is not excessive. Operation is smooth even with 120 items to be displayed and scrolled. Beyond that the list scrolling performance decreases on the HTC Sensation XE with the amount of data to be presented, whereas it stays the same on the iPhone 3GS with up to 480 list items. While this decrease is likely to only happen in rare cases on mobile websites – as observed in our Wikipedia test – it is more likely to occur on desktop-oriented pages due to the larger page load and other resource-depleting processes. Therefore the webmaster has to be considerate when implementing the OHW: a site loaded with badly coded animations that already struggles being displayed on a mobile device will not necessarily be improved by the OHW. This highlights the main problem of using an integrated client-side approach: the interface has to share the resources with the content of the website, which can directly influence performance. Luckily, this is in the hands of the webmaster implementing the OHW and thus straightforward to address. However, it also shows that the OHW is not a magical one-size-fits-all solution for making any website easier to interact with when operating the device with one hand. What it does, though, is significantly improve operation and efficiency on already mobile-adapted websites (Table 2) together with a short start-up time and high responsiveness (Table 3).

9   Conclusions

Our research shows that applying the wheel-menu metaphor as the basis for thumb-based website interaction and offering a curved input control based solely on swipe and tap for all interactive elements clearly improves one-handed website operation: it allows users to complete their goals more quickly and comfortably as they do not have to loosen their grip on the device when trying to reach elements outside the arc of their thumb. Given the demand for a simple, one-handed way to access websites on a mobile device [13], the OHW is a practical and highly effective solution from both a web developer and end-user perspective, if the technical requirements are met, and allows immediate and flexible use without prior user configuration. By dividing the display into a *display zone* and *interaction zone* (Fig. 2), interface occlusion is reduced when compared to non-enhanced interaction, but is not completely solved due to the fact that the interface is still touch-operated. However, the OHW promotes a free and inclusive way of improving user experience on the mobile web and is a promising approach for enhancing one-handed web browsing on a wide range of mobile touchscreen devices (Fig. 6). The use of standard web technologies allows it to easily adapt to new challenges and ensures its longevity and ease-of-use for the webmaster. Future work will address performance optimisations for the operation of large lists and the development of a SVG and core JavaScript implementation. We plan to evaluate the OHW's applicability as an interface for HTML5-based smartphone apps and the development of an extended plugin model to allow more advanced custom functionality.

References

1. Akmin: Build your own mobile website... in minutes (2012). http://www.mobisitegalore.com/index.html
2. Opera Software ASA: Making small devices look great (2007). http://dev.opera.com/articles/view/making-small-devices-look-great
3. Bandelloni, R., Mori, G., Paternò, F.: Dynamic generation of web migratory interfaces. In: Proceedings of the Mobile HCI 2005, pp. 83–90. ACM, New York (2005)
4. BBC: BBC news (2013). http://m.bbc.co.uk/news
5. Bonnet, D., Appert, C.: Sam: the Swiss army menu. In: Proceedings of the IHM 2011, pp. 5:1–5:4. ACM, New York (2011)
6. Envato: Signum mobile — html5 & css3 and iwebapp (2013). http://themeforest.net/item/signum-mobile-html5-css3-and-iwebapp/1614712
7. Flickr: Flickr (2013). http://m.flickr.com
8. Francone, J., Bailly, G., Lecolinet, E., Mandran, N., Nigay, L.: Wavelet menus on handheld devices: stacking metaphor for novice mode and eyes-free selection for expert mode. In: Proceedings of the AVI 2010, pp. 173–180, ACM, New York (2010)
9. Google: Google search results (2013). https://www.google.co.uk/search?q=something
10. Gupta, A., Kumar, A., Mayank, V., Tripathi, N., Tapaswi, S.: Mobile web: web manipulation for small displays using multi-level hierarchy page segmentation. In: Proceedings of the MC 2007, pp. 599–606. ACM (2007)
11. Hattori, G., Hoashi, K., Matsumoto, K., Sugaya, F.: Robust web page segmentation for mobile terminal using content-distances and page layout information. In: Proceedings of the WWW 2007, pp. 361–370. ACM (2007)
12. Huot, S., Lecolinet, E.: Archmenu et thumbmenu: contrôler son dispositif mobile "sur le pouce". In: Proceedings of the IHM 2007, pp. 107–110. ACM, New York (2007)
13. Karlson, A.K., Bederson, B.B.: Studies in one-handed mobile design: habit, desire and agility. Computer Science Dept., Uni. of Maryland, Technical report (2006)
14. Katre, D.: One-handed thumb use on smart phones by semi-literate and illiterate users in india. In: Katre, D., Orngreen, R., Yammiyavar, P., Clemmensen, T. (eds.) HWID 2009. IFIP AICT, vol. 316, pp. 189–208. Springer, Heidelberg (2010)

15. Lü, H., Li, Y.: Gesture avatar: a technique for operating mobile user interfaces using gestures. In: Proceedings of the CHI 2011, pp. 207–216. ACM (2011)
16. Mobotap: Dolphin browser (2012). http://dolphin-browser.com/
17. Pingdom: jQuery's triumphant march to success (2010). http://royal.pingdom.com/2010/03/26/jquery-triumphant-march-to-success/
18. Seipp, K., Devlin, K.: Enhancing one-handed website operation on touchscreen mobile phones. In: CHI EA 2013, pp. 3123–3126. ACM, New York (2013)
19. Seipp, K., Devlin, K.: The one hand wonder: a framework for enhancing one-handed website operation on touchscreen smartphones. In: Proceedings of the WEBIST 2014, pp. 5–13. SCITEPRESS (2014)
20. W3C: Mobile web best practices 1.0, July 2008. http://www.w3.org/TR/mobile-bp/
21. W3C: W3C (2013). http://www.w3.org
22. Wikipedia: Deusdedit of Canterbury (2013). http://en.m.wikipedia.org/wiki/Deusdedit_of_Canterbury
23. Wobbrock, J.O., Myers, B.A., Aung, H.H.: The performance of hand postures in front- and back-of-device interaction for mobile computing. Int. J. Hum. Comput. Stud. **66**(12), 857–875 (2008)
24. WordPress: Just another wordpress weblog (2013). http://en.blog.wordpress.com/
25. YouTube: Youtube mobile (2013). http://www.youtube.com/results?client=mv-google&q=sublime
26. Yu, C.-H., Miller, R.C.: Enhancing mobile browsing and reading. In: E.A. CHI 2011, pp. 1783–1788. ACM, New York (2011)

Contextinator: Addressing Information Fragmentation with a Web-Based Project Manager

Benjamin V. Hanrahan, Ankit Ahuja, and Manuel A. Pérez-Quiñones[(✉)]

Department of Computer Science, Virginia Tech, Blacksburg, VA, USA
{hanrahan.ben,ahuja.ankit}@gmail.com, perez@cs.vt.edu
http://perez.cs.vt.edu/

Abstract. The web browser has become a central workspace for knowledge workers, where they make use of cloud-based applications to access and store their information. While this solution helps reduce the difficulty of syncing information between our numerous devices, it reintroduces and proliferates faults of the desktop, particularly information fragmentation. Information fragmentation is an increasingly important issue, as cloud-based applications typically silo their data, resulting in a replication of storage and organization in the absence of a unifying structure. To probe whether knowledge workers encounter information fragmentation and in what manner, we created *Contextinator*, a tool that assists in coordinating data for web-based projects. *Contextinator* provides a method for providing the centralized, unifying structure that cloud based storage makes difficult.

Our findings contribute insight into the need for, and appropriateness of, projects as a unifying structure for the web. Our results point to two types of projects that we term 'preparatory' and 'opportunistic' based on when and for what reason users create them. We discuss the design of our system, the results of our mixed-method evaluation, and our observations about information fragmentation on the web.

Keywords: Information fragmentation · Personal information management · Tool integration · Web-based systems

1 Introduction

The web browser has emerged as a central workspace for knowledge workers. Cloud-based applications complement our diverse ecosystem of devices, as most of the data resides in a device agnostic remote storage. However, this agnostic storage comes at a cost, data on the cloud is typically accessed through one particular application or service (e.g. Dropbox for files, Gmail for email), which create silos of data that are rarely inter-operable with each other. Furthermore, these silos lack a unifying structure and proliferate information fragmentation, a problem previously identified by the Personal Information Management (PIM)

© Springer International Publishing Switzerland 2015
V. Monfort and K.-H. Krempels (Eds.): WEBIST 2014, LNBIP 226, pp. 179–194, 2015.
DOI: 10.1007/978-3-319-27030-2_12

community [13]. Without a unifying structure, or the flexibility to create one, users are prevented from creating salient structures that better reflect their real world relationship with their data.

The PIM community has documented the undesirable consequences of information fragmentation. Primarily, the consequences of information fragmentation have manifested themselves through the duplication of hierarchies between tools [5,6]. This phenomenon can be seen within cloud based applications, as it seems typical that a user has a Dropbox folder, Gmail label, and an Evernote notebook for a particular project all created separately and lacking any link between them, other than simply semantic.

As a result of this fragmentation, some 'one off' solutions have been created. However, these solutions addressing the problem are unique for each pair of tools and typically support only a few common use cases. For example, several options exist today to save attachments from email into cloud storage solutions (e.g., Dropbox). Each one of these tools closes the gap between two silos, but not all pairings have these options, and some of them go unsupported quickly.

We built *Contextinator* as a way to both study and potentially mitigate these problems. *Contextinator* is a tool that enables users to group their web sessions and cloud based artifacts into projects and was built with extensibility in mind.

In this paper, we present the related work in the areas of interest, ground our design decisions in previous research, present the results of our mixed-method evaluation, and close with implications for future systems. We not only find evidence that users need a way to group activities, but that the project metaphor is too restrictive.

2   Related Work

There are several areas of research related to this work, primarily: Information Fragmentation, Task Management, Multitasking, and Window Management. As such, we review the research for each of these areas and provide insight into how they shaped the design of *Contextinator*.

2.1   Information Fragmentation

Information fragmentation occurs when personal information becomes scattered over different devices, storage systems, or online tools and is considered a 'pervasive problem in personal information management' [13]. Typically each fragment has its own organizational structure and it is left up to the user to integrate information across their systems.

The siloing of information by applications is not a new problem unique to the cloud. Previous studies found that users used several methods to create groupings in spite of these silos. These methods include: using multiple folder hierarchies to organize related documents [12]; using a special folder (or tag) in an email client to hold related messages [8]; or using virtual spaces to more physically separate projects [9].

A drawback of offloading the organization of projects on users, is that they end up maintaining duplicate, unwieldy organizational hierarchies between tools. Boardman et al. [5,6] studied users' PIM organization strategies across different tools and identified several problems that arose. They found that data was compartmentalized between distinct tools, users had difficulty coordinating across different tools, and there were inconsistencies between equivalent functionality. To solve the second problem, Boardman et al. created a prototype to mirror folder structures between different PIM tools, which they reported users found intuitive and compelling.

Bergman et al. [4] framed the problem as project fragmentation, where information was fragmented into different collections without relation to the common activity uniting them. Their solution was to use a single hierarchy to store all files of different formats under the same folder. Similarly, Jones et al. [11] suggested the development of a common structure that could be shared and manipulated by any number of tools.

Integrating information collections in the cloud is also being pursued in the commercial and open source tool space. For example, Cloudmagic[1] creates a unified search box to access information across tools. Attachments.me[2] enables access to Dropbox files for creating attachments in Gmail. However, the majority of these tools assist users to access information, and do not enable creating structural links between them.

2.2 Task Management

An additional area of research that is highly related to our work is Task Management, as knowledge workers typically have a list of pending actions for each project. Bellotti et al. [2], in the study and development of a task manager, suggested task managers should support *informal priority lists*, to ensure near-term execution of priority actions. Furthermore, tasks within each project can help knowledge workers prioritize and maintain their attention over different projects [2,8]. Tasks can also act as good reminders when they appear *in the way* and always visible in the working space [2,3,8].

2.3 Multitasking and Interruptions

Another typical characteristics of today's knowledge workers is that they are routinely interrupted, and as a result workers are constantly multitasking and switching projects.

Czerwinski et al. [7] performed a diary study with knowledge workers to characterize how they interleave multiple tasks amidst interruptions. They found that knowledge workers switch tasks a significant number of times, with an average of 50 shifts over the week.

---

[1] https://cloudmagic.com.
[2] https://attachments.me.

González and Mark [8,15] also found that knowledge work is highly fragmented, where workers spend an average of three minutes on a task and an average of 12 min on a project before switching. They found several ways in which workers manage their information to handle constant switching, including aggregating a project's different types of information into a single artifact.

2.4   Window Management

Rooms [9] introduced the concept of virtual spaces, which is now a part of window management systems of modern operating systems. Better management of space and sessions has also been explored for the web browser. Rajamanickam et al. [17] created a task-focused web browser, where web pages were grouped into tasks. Morris et al. [16] created *SearchBar*, a tool that stored users' search query and browsing histories, to support task resumption across multiple sessions.

Multitasking Bar [20] incorporated the task concept into the browser through creating an additional bar with a tab for each project. Jhaveri and Räihä [10] created *Session Highlights* to aid cross-session task continuation. Mozilla Firefox now has the concept of *Tab Groups*, to group together similar tabs under a single label.

For web-based information systems, management of tabs and windows is a necessity. Suspending and resuming a task is problematic as it often requires either saving or reopening several independent pages from different websites.

3   Design

Based on the state of the art for the various research domains, we designed our tool with the following principles in mind:

- knowledge workers organize information into projects [8,15];
- tools like email crosscut projects [11];
- information is fragmented across different applications [4,6];
- there are structures replicated in collections [5]; and
- users need an easy way to capture and restore the state of projects [7,8,15].

A full description of the tool and the implementation details is available online [1][3]. In the following sections we outline the most prominent features of the tool.

3.1   Projects

A project in *Contextinator* is a collection of the browser tabs opened in the same window, as well as a series of tasks (todo items), bookmarks, people (emails), and a set of links to external applications. Each project has a *Project Homepage* (see Fig. 1) where project artifacts can be managed.

---

[3] MS Thesis available at http://vtechworks.lib.vt.edu/handle/10919/23120.

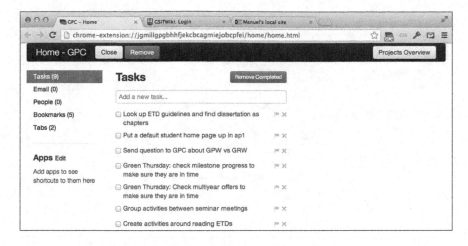

Fig. 1. Project home page.

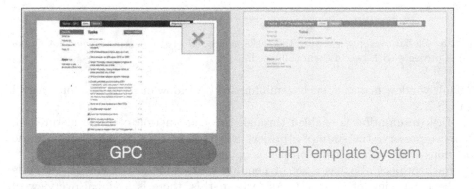

Fig. 2. The *Quick Switcher* showing two projects.

When a project is first started it begins as an empty browser window by creating the *'File > New Window'* command from Chrome. Any tabs that are added to this window, either by adding through the *'File > New Tab'* or just opened via user control (e.g. with a pop up menu using the Open Link in New Tab) are automatically captured as part of a project. A project state is saved automatically and does not require the user to provide a name.

Switching between projects is done by activating a different browser window. *Contextinator* saves the state of all windows, including all of the tabs opened and allows the user to switch between them. If a user closes a window, *Contextinator* can open it again restoring all of the tabs that were part of the project.

Users are able to see a preview of all their currently open projects and switch between them using the *Quick Switcher* page (see Fig. 2). *Quick Switcher* is similar to the approach taken in Gionarta [19]. As projects are just regular Chrome windows, users can also use any action from the operating system's

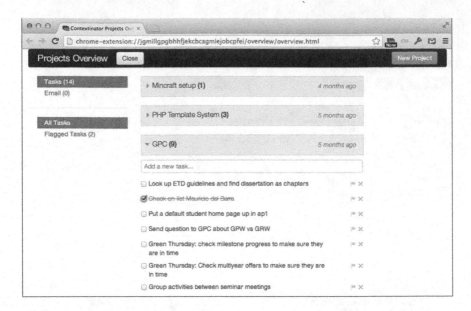

Fig. 3. Global overview showing the tasks across all projects. This screenshot shows three projects with two of them collapsed.

default window manager, such as minimizing a window or using Mission Control on OS X.

Task resumption is enabled through the combination of these features, in that we preserve the state of a project whenever it is closed and reinstate the previous state whenever the project is opened again.

Each project also has a set of pending tasks and related emails, viewable in the home view of a project. Aside from this, there is a global overview of all the user's todos and emails (see Fig. 3) organized by projects. In the global overview window, users are able to see any unread email, work with any tasks, and directly switch to a specific project homepage.

3.2   Information Views

Information views provide a way to organize related information across different tools under a single project, and is a primary method by which *Contextinator* reduces information fragmentation. These views are particularly important as users often have several accounts, spanning multiple systems, where they store different, related collections of data. As new services are frequently emerging, we found the need to have an easy way for users to incorporate new services into our tool. We accomplish this through *information views*, where each project can be related to an information view from the configured services.

Basically, an information view is comprised of a unique URL that points to an internal location in an online collection. For example, a direct link to a folder in Dropbox can be included in the appropriate project. The direct link eliminates the need for navigating to the folder within the Dropbox collection and helps to reduce the duplicate navigation associated with information fragmentation. Currently the software supports five external services, but there is no specialized code for any of these. In general, any online service that has a unique URL to an internal location can be easily incorporated into a *Contextinator* project.

Furthermore, if a user visits the application (e.g., Dropbox) directly in the web browser while having a *Contextinator* project open, they are automatically redirected to the project's *information view* eliminating redundant navigation across tools [4,5].

A special case of this approach is the information view for email, as email plays a significant role in project management [2,3,8]. In order to provide integration of email with projects in *Contextinator*, we display a filtered view of the email inbox. The filter shows only unread messages from the people that are part of the project and allows the user to quickly follow an ongoing email conversation without switching context to another program (email in this case). In addition, we also provide a direct link to particular Gmail tag or folder.

4   Method

Evaluating personal information tools and practices presents several challenges. PIM is by definition personal [14]. The strategies that users follow tend to be very personal and specific to the attributes of their own collections. Thus it is very difficult to create a series of reference tests that can be *natural* to all users. Controlled lab setting do not accurately reflect the reality of technology use in PIM settings. Several alternatives have been proposed, from using diary studies [7,18], *in-vivo* research methods where researchers observe users with their own information, as well as deploying a tool and collect data from its use, as done by Whittaker et al. [21].

To study Contextinator, we employed a method similar to Whittaker et al. [21] where they investigated email usage by deploying a program within an organization and collecting data on its use. In our work, we deployed *Contextinator* in two stages: first, we deployed the tool to a set of test users where we logged usage and later interviewed them; and second, we deployed *Contextinator* (without logging) in the Chrome Web Store where anybody could download it and install it. Several months later, we surveyed all users. This study was approved by the University IRB (#13-008). This combination of evaluation methods gives us a access to data reflecting a variety of users experiences and behaviors. We describe our research methods in stages.

4.1   First Stage: Limited Deployment

For our first stage, we recruited participants through local listservs used by computer science graduate students and faculty. We also announced the experiment in an undergraduate class where they were offered extra credit for participation. The invitation contained a URL[4] where participants could download and

---

[4] http://contextinator.cs.vt.edu.

install the tool. The website also included several videos explaining the use of the tool. Upon installing the tool, participants were required to agree to an online consent form.

During this stage of the evaluation we logged information about user interactions and recorded the majority of user actions with the tool (e.g. creating a new project, switching to a project, closing a project, creating a new task, flagging a task, marking a task as completed, creating a new bookmark, opening email, etc.). Each log item included the time stamp and relevant information about the event (e.g. the project or task name). We also conducted a semi-structured interview where we asked broad questions and followed up with specific questions about different areas of the tool (projects, tasks, information fragmentation, and tool usability).

Stage one provided us with detailed and rich data in regards to the use of the tool. At the same time, we interviewed a few heavy users to learn how they made use of the tool. Of the 30 participants that installed our tool, roughly one third of these were undergraduate students and the rest were graduate students. Of these 30 participants 15 of them used the tool a significant amount, the remaining 15 only created one or two projects named 'testing' or 'something.' As such, we decided to not use the data of the later group in our analyses. In the group of 15 active participants we identified 7 heavy users that created three or more projects. We interviewed 4 of our 30 participants, out of which 3 (U1, U2, U3) said they considered themselves to be heavy users of the tool and 1 (U4) that said they did not use the tool very much.

4.2   Second Stage: Broader Deployment

After our first evaluation we released *Contextinator* in the Chrome Web Store for free. At the time of this writing, over 3000 users have installed *Contextinator* and there are 20 comments in the Chrome Web Store for *Contextinator*. The project is also available on GitHub where it has 48 'stargazers', 9 'watchers', and has been forked 7 times.

In order to gather additional feedback and clarify findings from stage 1 of our evaluation, we also presented a survey to users of the tool. A primary purpose of this survey was to gain a deeper understanding of what users of the tool thought of the notion of 'projects'. It is worth noting that these users are not affiliated with our institution nor connected to our research group. Only those users older than 18 years old were surveyed, a restriction of our local IRB.

Stage two provided us with a much broader population and allowed us to gather information from real users of the tool. As of this writing, of the 20 comments on the Chrome Web Store, 14 are positive, 5 are negative, and 1 is neutral. Five of the messages are bug reports and 9 are requests for new features. Each of the messages with requests had more than one requested feature.

Overall, our evaluation provided a rich and varied collection of data. We have more than 3000 users that explored our tool, very rich user logs of about 7 users, interviews with 4 users, have more than 30 survey responses, and about 60 people that have either commented or followed our project in the two online repositories

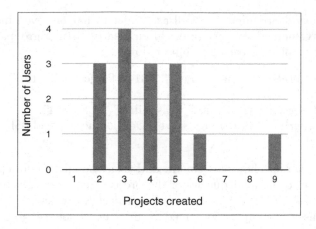

Fig. 4. Distribution of number of projects created by users in *Contextinator* (stage 1).

(Chrome Web Store and Github). The next section presents the results and our analysis of the evaluation.

5   Results

5.1   Project Appropriation

We found two interesting, and unexpected, aspects of how participants appropriated the project metaphor in our analysis. First, the scope of projects varied widely, both between and within participants' projects. Second, users thought quite differently about what a project was, again, both between and within participants' projects. These different scopes and appropriations of the project metaphor point to our naive assumption that 'projects' is the proper and complete metaphor for managing work.

Participants varied widely in how many projects they created. The number of projects created by the participants of the first stage was $\bar{x} = 4.5$, Fig. 4. Later, when we asked users in our second phase how many projects they had created, they reported an average of 8.59 projects ($\sigma = 7.13$). Of the 18 responses in our second stage, the maximum number of projects was 28, the variability in the number of projects among the users is illustrated by the high standard deviation in relation to the mean. Clearly, this points to some amount of variation in how users appropriated the project metaphor in some way.

Insight into why the number of projects differed, is the clear illustration of different scopes through the names that participants in our first phase chose for their projects. Some projects are clearly bounded as a specific task addressed, e.g. "Crypto project" and "German HW." While there are other projects that, while also bounded, provide a grouping and represent an activity that will contain multiple *projects* (at least as we envisioned them), examples include "Algorithms" or "CS 3744". There are even more broad projects that center around interests such as "Gardening," as well as, projects that are even more general, e.g. "Life" or "General." We encountered four clearly distinct groups of projects, and provide examples for each grouping below.

- *Individual Projects*: "Crypto project", "3114 Project 3", "Tax Returns" and "German HW"
- *Groups of Projects*: "Algorithms", "Usability", "CS 3744".
- *Ongoing Activities*: "Gardening", "Web Development", and "Shopping".
- *Catch All*: "Life" and "General"

Probing further into how participants and users thought about a project gives further insight into the inadequacies of the project metaphor. During our interviews the confusion over the definition of a project was clear. Not surprisingly, the most confused participant identified themselves as not using the tool much.

> When I was first using it, the title project... it made me feel like it should be like a school project or a research project [...]. It definitely threw me initially (Participant U4).

A user from the Chrome Web Store, explained that they thought of projects as *contexts* instead of projects:

> I'd rather call it context. A context can be a project I am working on, a research topic or an otherwise combined series of tabs. For example: Everything related to geocaching, travelling. Some contexts only exist for the duration of the 'project', some I keep indefinitely.

A second user from the Chrome Web Store conveyed a similar sense on their view of a project.

> A set of related tabs that I need open at the same time – this means I might have multiple Contextinator projects for different stages of the same Project.

Both of these users consider projects not as a related set of work items, but more as a contextual capture of their current goals. Those goals might be immediate or longer term. The 'projects' in these two examples, are a more expansive view of organizing information. This sentiment was echoed by a participant in our test group where they also replaced the project metaphor with their own more flexible organization.

> I have pretty broad categories. I have a General that I just throw stuff in. I have Web Development, so any time I am looking up stuff on stack overflow. I have Shopping, for different stuff I am shopping for... (Participant U2).

Another participant thought of projects more as *lists of things* to do. Yet another participant simply created projects for all his classes, enabling him to enter a context in his browser as he entered the corresponding physical context of the classroom:

The first thing I did was make a project for each class I am in. So, when i am in class, I can just open that project and have all the tabs. Esp. for Dr. XX's class, there is like Moodle, Piazza, etc. (Participant U1).

However, regardless of what projects were to the user, nearly all of our participants found the ability to capture and resume the state of a window useful. This is illustrated by an additional appropriation of projects as a "bookmark for an entire window."

I think of them as a bookmark for an entire window. In Chrome if you have a bunch of tabs open, and if I want to come back to all of them at once, bookmark it, make it a project (Participant U1).

Another participant found that projects enabled improved tab organization, and they began grouping their browser activity in a way that they had not previously.

I would have 50 tabs open in my one window. This really helps to have 10 or less in five windows. It is really nice (Participant U2).

5.2 Project Transitions

In designing our system we also imagined that our users would purposefully initiate clean transitions between projects (a context switch). However, in our analysis we found that there was a somewhat clear separation between users that *purposefully* switched projects and users that *found* themselves in a project.

In our interviews (stage one), three of the participants said that they did not use the tool to decide which project to work on, but it still made it easier to work on multiple projects at once. These participants switched projects in an emergent way, that is they found they needed to switch to or create a different project once they already had a few tabs open.

A lot of the times I would just open a bunch of new tabs, and not necessarily look for an existing project first [. . .]. So right now I am not in a project. And then I start googling something, and I have five tabs open. And then I realize, actually this should really go into the VTS project. . . (Participant U1).

We asked users from the Chrome Web store: "Why (or when) do your create a project?" The 18 responses can be grouped into two categories. The first group (10 responses) created projects before they started working on said 'project.' This group had a notion of project that was related to a goal, as if planning for work to be done ahead. The second group (8 responses), however, used projects as a way to capture work done so far but not yet completed. This group used projects as a way to suspend work to be resumed later. The goal of the project was not particularly important in the creation of the project itself.

5.3   Project Planning

In the first stage of our evaluation, 12 participants created at least one task. Overall, they created an average of 5.9 tasks ($\sigma = 9.3$). They compeleted 3.2 tasks on an average ($\sigma = 6.7$). Participants rarely used flagging. On an average, each participant flagged 0.8 tasks ($\sigma = 1.9$). Participants quick captured (added a URL or note to a task) 2.8 tasks on an average ($\sigma = 4.5$).

We saw roughly two approaches to project planning that mirrored the motivations cited by users for creating projects. The first, is a more *preparatory* approach [21], where the user creates tasks ahead of time and completes them over a longer period of time. An example of this is a user creating a new project, quickly followed by the creation of several new tasks, and in a later session marks them as completed. This approach mirrored the users that created projects before they began working on that project.

The second approach was more *opportunistic*, where a user creates new tasks as and when required, marking them as completed in the near future (usually in the same session). Here, the user does not have a specific planning phase of their session and instead plans and captures in situ. This approach mirrors the group of users that used projects to capture work that has not been completed yet.

5.4   Usage

We also asked users "Which of the following features are indispensable for your use of Contextinator?" Only one participant selected the 'Task manager', 5 selected 'Save and reopen projects' and 13 selected 'Browser tab management.' Clearly the support of managing the windows/tabs in the browser is the most used feature in our tool.

The last four questions were a likert-scale questions about their agreement or disagreement with factual statements. The results are presented below. The choices were (with score values in parenthesis): Strongly Agree (1), Agree (2), Neither Agree nor Disagree (3), Disagree (4), and Strongly Disagree (5).

"With Contextinator, I am able to work on multiple projects simultaneously." Average 2.00 (Agree) and standard deviation of 0.7.

"With Contextinator, switching projects makes me lost, so I avoid switching unless it is absolutely necessary." Average of 3.5 (close to neutral) and standard deviation of 0.9.

"With Contextinator, suspending or closing a project is easy because I don't have to worry about losing data." Average of 1.89 (Agree) and standard deviation of 1.0.

"With Contextinator, resuming a project is easy as I am able to quickly gather where I left off." Average of 1.89 (Agree) and standard deviation of 0.6.

Based on these results, it is clear that the support for grouping related items, suspending and resuming work are the most salient features of *Contextinator*.

6 Discussion

In this paper, we have presented the design and evaluation of *Contextinator*, a system built to assist people in managing their personal information stored in the cloud. The design of *Contextinator* focused on providing users support in three areas. First, it allowed users to have their project related personal information (including emails, bookmarks, todos, people in a project, etc.) in one place. Second, it provided a way to group and manage windows and tabs as a single project. Finally, the tool provided a way to capture, save, and reopen a project. While there is support for all of these features, our several rounds of evaluation only found strong evidence in favor of the third, the management of opening and closing projects.

The management of multiple tabs in a 'project' proved to be very valuable. Most users found this idea so compelling that they ranked the management of context switching within our tool the most valuable feature. Being able to organize their activity with tabs and being able to stop and resume work seems to successfully address the fragmentation that naturally occurs on the web as users access multiple websites for information. This we consider the "killer feature" of *Contextinator*.

We realize that we failed to address information fragmentation as it relates to users' social circle. Several users wanted to be able to access the context information from another computer[5]. In addition, two participants wanted to be able to share their projects with groups of people, and be able to accomplish tasks in a project together with their collaborators. Clearly the information fragmentation is not just across information silos and devices, but also across collaborators and settings of work.

Thus, we can say that we address the information fragmentation only partially. The project management features were clearly well received and might account for the broad use of the tool in the Chrome Web Store. Users liked being able to group tabs as a single unit and being able to save that group and reopened it later. The other set of features (e.g., integration of information with email, task and bookmarks) were not mentioned by users on the store, and we found little evidence that users used it.

6.1 Implications for Future Work

In this work we gained insights into other areas that might allow future researchers and developers to better address the problems we explored. We would like focus on two of them here. First is the idea of what a user considers a 'project.' The second is how 'information views' address information fragmentation.

What is a Project? First, we have provided additional insight into what users consider a 'project.' People have vastly different concepts as to what a 'project'

---

[5] This feature is now part of the tool.

is and designs of similar tools should provide for this variability. A system that seeks to improve support for knowledge work should be able to blend in with the varying scopes and purposes that users group their work into.

There is a wide variability of what users call a project. Typically the authors consider a project to be a set of related activities with a particular goal in mind. However, we found that users have a much broader definition. In some cases, users considered several 'projects' as all part of the same task at hand, thus requiring multiple active projects at once. In those cases, one or more of the projects were really collection of resources that were reused in similar tasks (e.g., having a project with reference websites for web development).

In addition, we identified two types of 'projects' based on why and when users create them. *Preparatory* projects are projects that allow users to organize their work, including creating tasks to be performed later in time. These projects are often created a priori of the work to be done. The second type of project, *opportunistic*, are projects that emerge from work that is being done. These projects might or might not have a specific goal, and instead emerge from users' work. Opportunistic projects seem to benefit from capturing the context of work for suspension and resumption of work.

Project Integration Through Information Views. The second lesson learned form our work is how well 'information views' address the problem of information fragmentation. Information fragmentation is caused by the different web-based tools in use today. This leads to wasted user effort as the user has to continuously navigate the multiple hierarchies, which can lead to difficulty in refinding information.

Our tool addressed the fragmentation problem very effectively. First, all project-related data is integrated in a single window. If a project has data stored in multiple online services (e.g., Gmail, Evernote, Dropbox), each gets a tab in the project. This eliminates the navigation across these services, as each tab will have the appropriate view for the project already set. Our tool manages the multiple tabs as part of the project, so saving and resuming work is effortless.

Second, navigating between tools is helped by redirects users either to the appropriate tab or specific location in the site. For example, a URL to Dropbox (http://dropbox.com) will be automatically redirected to the Dropbox folder for that project if one was specified. This allows for easy cross linking between services without having to copy/paste URLs to specific subfolders. So a project with an Evernote notebook can include a link to Dropbox and when clicked within the context of the project, that link will go directly to the corresponding folder for the project in Dropbox.

Third, our tool avoids specialized programming between each pair of services as it is typical today. All services are specified simply by a URL that points directly inside the collection of a service. Pairing Evernote notebooks, Dropbox folders, and Gmail labels is not only possible, but relatively easy. Cross linking, as described above makes this integration even simpler from the users perspective.

Finally, another form of information integration is to show enough information from an external source without requiring the user to visit other websites. This is the example used in the web today of 'content embedding.' Google Maps, for example, allows users and developers to embed a map view in other sites. Instead of having a link and requiring navigation to another site/tool, the information is presented in place with some minor restrictions. Our tool did this by presenting unread emails in the context of a project. This approach requires external services to provide access to their data via some API (e.g., IMAP access to email) or in some common format (e.g., XML or JSON).

Our approach to building integrated information views allowed us to address the information fragmentation that occurs on the web. A tool like *Contextinator* has the potential to create (or re-create) the context lost amid information fragmentation in today's web-based tools.

References

1. Ahuja, A.: Contextinator: Recreating the context lost amid information fragmentation on the web. Masters thesis, Department of Computer Science, Virginia Tech (2013)
2. Bellotti, V., Dalal, B., Good, N., Flynn, P., Bobrow, D.G., Ducheneaut, N.: What a to-do: studies of task management towards the design of a personal task list manager. In: Proceeding CHI 2004, pp. 735–742. ACM, New York (2004)
3. Bellotti, V., Smith, I.: Informing the design of an information management system with iterative fieldwork. In: Proceeding DIS 2000, pp. 227–237. ACM, New York (2000)
4. Bergman, O., Beyth-Marom, R., Nachmias, R.: The project fragmentation problem in personal information management. In: Proceeding CHI 2006, pp. 271–274. ACM, New York (2006)
5. Boardman, R., Spence, R., Sasse, M.A.: Too many hierarchies? the daily struggle for control of the workspace. In: Proceeding CHI 1996, pp. 406–412 (2003)
6. Boardman, R., Sasse, M.A.: "Stuff goes into the computer and doesn't come out": a cross-tool study of personal information management. In: Proceeding CHI 2004, pp. 583–590. ACM, New York (2004)
7. Czerwinski, M., Horvitz, E., Wilhite, S.: A diary study of task switching and interruptions. In: Proceeding CHI 2004, pp. 175–182. ACM (2004)
8. González, V.M., Mark, G.: "Constant, constant, multi-tasking craziness": managing multiple working spheres. In: Proceeding CHI 2004, pp. 113–120. ACM, New York (2004)
9. Henderson Jr., D.A., Card, S.: Rooms: the use of multiple virtual workspaces to reduce space contention in a window-based graphical user interface. ACM Trans. Graph. **5**(3), 211–243 (1986)
10. Jhaveri, N., Räihä, K.-J.: The advantages of a cross-session web workspace. In: Proceeding CHI EA 2005, pp. 1949–1952. ACM, New York (2005)
11. Jones, W., Anderson, K.M.: Many views, many modes, many tools ...one structure: towards a non-disruptive integration of personal information. In: Proceeding Hypertext 2011, pp. 113–122. ACM, New York (2011)
12. Jones, W., Phuwanartnurak, A.J., Gill, R., Bruce, H.: Don't take my folders away!: organizing personal information to get ghings done. In: Proceeding CHI EA 2005, pp. 1505–1508. ACM, New York (2005)

13. Karger, D.R., Jones, W.: Data unification in personal information management. Commun. ACM **49**(1), 77–82 (2006)
14. Kelly, D., Teevan, J.: Understanding what works: evaluating PIM tools. Personal Information Management, pp. 190–204. University of Washington Press, Seattle (2007)
15. Mark, G., Gonzalez, V.M., Harris, J.: No task left behind?: examining the nature of fragmented work. In: Proceeding CHI 2005, pp. 321–330. ACM, New York (2005)
16. Morris, D., Ringel Morris, M., Venolia, G.: Searchbar: a search-centric web history for task resumption and information re-finding. In: Proceeding CHI 2008, pp. 1207–1216. ACM, New York (2008)
17. Rajamanickam, M.R., MacKenzie, R., Lam, B., Su, T.: A task-focused approach to support sharing and interruption recovery in web browsers. In: Proceeding CHI EA 2010, pp. 4345–4350. ACM, New York (2010)
18. Teevan, J., Alvarado, C., Ackerman, M.S., Karger, D.R.: The perfect search engine is not enough: a study of orienteering behavior in directed search. In: Proceedings of the SIGCHI Conference on Human Factors in Computing Systems, CHI 2004, pp. 415–422. ACM, New York (2004)
19. Voida, S., Mynatt, E.D., Edwards, W.K.: Re-framing the desktop interface around the activities of knowledge work. In: Proceeding UIST 2008, pp. 211–220. ACM, New York (2008)
20. Wang, Q., Chang, H.: Multitasking bar: prototype and evaluation of introducing the task concept into a browser. In: Proceeding CHI 2010, pp. 103–112. ACM, New York (2010)
21. Whittaker, S., Matthews, T., Cerruti, J., Badenes, H., Tang, J.: Am I wasting my time organizing email?: a study of email refinding. In: Proceeding CHI 2011, pp. 3449–3458. ACM, New York (2011)

Society, e-Business and e-Government

Integrating the Technology Acceptance Model and Satisfaction to Understand Drivers of Online Travel Booking Behavior

Maria Madlberger[✉]

Webster Vienna Private University, Praterstrasse 23, 1020 Vienna, Austria
maria.madlberger@webster.ac.at

Abstract. Since the emergence of electronic commerce the tourism industry has undergone a substantial transformation. Especially travel agencies that are faced with growing online competition are increasingly dependent on achieving online sales. This study investigates antecedents of consumers' intention to book trips online on travel agencies' websites. The research draws on an integrated research model based on the technology acceptance model and customer satisfaction as introduced in the DeLone and McLean model on information system success. Two alternative models were tested: A parsimonious basic model includes information quality and system quality as object-based beliefs that influence satisfaction as an object-based attitude. The second model is extended and includes a third object-based belief, that is, service quality. Satisfaction is hypothesized to impact perceived usefulness that is a driver of perceived ease of use and online booking intention. Both models were tested with survey data from 292 consumers. The study provides several scholarly and managerial implications for the online distribution of tourism services.

Keywords: Electronic commerce · Technology acceptance model · Satisfaction · Information quality · System quality · Service quality · IS success model · Online booking intention · Travel agency · PLS analysis

1 Introduction

The tourism industry experienced substantial transformation due to electronic commerce. Especially travel agencies have been faced with e-commerce-induced disintermediation as their business can be replaced by direct online distribution of flights, hotel rooms, rental cars, organized tours, and other travel services. Worldwide, sales of traditional offline travel agencies are declining [1].

However, travel agencies can offer online service provision themselves and thus defend their position in the distribution of tourism services. Many travel agencies operate websites that offer online search and online booking tools. The emergence of online mediators such as Expedia.com demonstrates that there is a need for online platforms that offer a variety of tourism services which complement service providers' Web presences, such as airline or hotel websites. Furthermore, travel agencies frequently offer services that differ from single travel components. Especially when it

© Springer International Publishing Switzerland 2015
V. Monfort and K.-H. Krempels (Eds.): WEBIST 2014, LNBIP 226, pp. 197–211, 2015.
DOI: 10.1007/978-3-319-27030-2_13

comes to packaged tours or holiday arrangements travel agencies take the work of selecting the trip components out of the consumers' hands.

Hence, despite the increased competition by tourism service providers, online intermediaries, and even consumers who plan their trips themselves, travel agencies offer a substantial value-added. On the other hand, more and more consumers expect online booking facilities and therefore travel agencies are increasingly dependent on attracting consumers who prefer to book online. Thus travel agencies have to gain online consumers by operating websites and/or mobile applications that allow online booking of trips or single tourism services. For this purpose, deeper insights into drivers of online booking behavior are of crucial importance for travel agencies.

Although extensive research has been done on online consumer and purchasing behavior, findings on online booking behavior on travel agencies' websites are still limited. There is especially incomplete knowledge on antecedents that are based on external stimuli which can be controlled by companies when designing their websites. In order to shed light on a comprehensive model on drivers of online booking intentions, we develop a research model that integrates two seminal theories in information systems (IS) and e-commerce research: the technology acceptance model (TAM) [2, 3] and satisfaction as a key variable of the DeLone and McLean information system success model [4, 5]. In doing so, our study follows the theoretical approach developed by Wixom and Todd [6] and further extended by Xu et al. [7]. Based on the theory of reasoned action [8] we contend that online booking intention is the result of a chain of impacts that starts with external stimuli that lead to object-based beliefs (information quality and system quality) and object-based attitude (satisfaction with the website) which itself influences behavioral beliefs and behavioral attitudes or behavioral intentions [6, 7]. We propose two structural models that are tested with data collected from an online survey among 292 consumers. One model is a parsimonious model whereas the second one is a more complex extension. The partial least squares (PLS) analysis results confirm most of the proposed hypotheses of both models.

The study contributes to research by stressing the relevance, particularly of information quality, and satisfaction for booking intention on travel agencies' websites. It further demonstrates the relevance of the TAM in the online journey booking context. This research also offers important managerial implications by showing key design issues of travel agencies' websites to maximize online booking intention. The paper is organized as follows: The Sect. 2 presents the theoretical background, particularly on TAM and the role of satisfaction in the online tourism sector. The following Sect. 3 presents the research models and the hypotheses development. The subsequent Sect. 4 shows the research methodology of the survey. Section 5 presents the results which are discussed in Sect. 6. The paper proposes research and managerial implications and closes with future research directions.

2 Theoretical Background

2.1 TAM and Satisfaction in Online User Behavior

TAM is one of the most widely used theories in IS research. It is grounded in the theory of reasoned action [8] and its extension, the theory of planned behavior [9]. TAM applies these theories to the context of IS usage where perceived usefulness (PU) and perceived ease of use (PEOU) are considered main drivers of behavioral attitude, intention, and behavior. PU, the main impact factor, is defined as a person's belief that a system can enhance the task or performance [3]. The secondary factor, PEOU, is the belief that the usage of a system is free of effort [3].

In IS and e-commerce research TAM was constantly extended and further developed. An early extension is suggested by Davis [10] who considers system design features an external stimulus that precedes PU and PEOU. In e-commerce research TAM is applied and extended to predict website use and online shopping behavior in numerous studies (e.g., [11–16]). Significant modifications of TAM in the context of e-commerce and WWW usage are made by [13, 17–19] who successfully simplify TAM by eliminating behavioral attitude and confirming a direct impact of PU and PEOU on behavioral intention. Another significant contribution is made by researchers who draw on Davis' extension of TAM by external stimuli [10]. Several researchers adopt the components of the DeLone and McLean IS success model [4] or its updated version [5] including information quality, system quality, and service quality ([11, 16], see [20] for a review). Another construct of the IS success model, satisfaction, was compared with TAM [21] or successfully integrated into TAM-based research on system use [6, 7]. These studies consider object-based beliefs in the form of information quality and system quality [6] as well as service quality [7] as antecedents of object-based attitude, expressed as satisfaction with these quality dimensions which further influence PU and PEOU.

2.2 Consumer Behavior in Online Tourism

The tourism industry is characterized by a number of particularities that differentiate it from other domains, such as consumer goods. Like many services, tourism services are perishable, non-storable, differing in quality, and largely influenced by the consumers themselves. Particularly vacation trips can be highly complex products consisting of a number of single components that are difficult to assess by consumers. Since the prices of travel products are usually high in relation to the income, consumers travel rather rarely and thus are often not very experienced [22]. Travel services are further a typical experience good, that is, consumers can evaluate it only after consumption. As a result, consumers' expectations when purchasing travel services are different from expectations when purchasing physical consumer goods. For example, prior to booking, consumers need information on hotel locations, flight times, or costs of rental cars or public transportation [23]. Thus an e-commerce site that offers tourism services needs to provide necessary information that allows a sufficient assessment of the travel products prior to booking a trip.

The tourism industry is a service sector that was strongly influenced by e-commerce [24]. Especially the number of traditional offline travel agencies declined with increased competition from service providers such as airlines or hotels, but also online intermediaries like Expedia or Travelocity. Worldwide total travel sales reached estimated $962 billion in 2012, with $374 billion or 38.9 % share achieved online. In the U.S. this share is 51.5 %, in Europe 45.1 % [1].

Data from the U.S. indicate that travel agencies do not automatically suffer from the decline of offline booking. In 2011, 91 % of active travelers booked their trips online whereas the traditional offline travel agency was employed in 9 % of the cases. However, 62 % of travelers booked via online travel agencies [25]. This evidence stresses the Internet as a distribution channel is increasingly becoming a "must" for travel agencies. Whereas these figures evoke the impression that travel agencies are in a good position in the online business, these numbers also show that particularly classical travel agencies are increasingly faced with a larger and more heterogenous competition. For example, travel agencies recently have been challenged by online platforms such as Expedia.com in the domain of packaged tours [26], a very important business segment of travel agencies.

Online consumer behavior in the tourism industry was subject of several empirical studies. Particular focus is put on satisfaction and website quality [27–31]. Also research based on TAM was carried out in several empirical studies. TAM was augmented with various factors, such as trust and perceived risks [32], task ambiguity, product complexity, and consumer experience [22], or more comprehensive sets of variables like website content issues, previous visits, and accessibility [33]. Further studies analyze dimensions of website quality [34] and the impact of system security [35]. The above-mentioned studies highlight the appropriateness of TAM as well as the IS success model for explaining drivers of website use in the context of traveling and tourism.

3   Research Model and Hypotheses Development

The research models that are discussed in this study are grounded in TAM, the IS success model, and its extensions by Wixom and Todd [6] as well as Xu et al. [7]. We compare two models: One is a parsimonious model that is based on the original DeLone and McLean IS success model [4] and derived from [6, 36]. Here we consider two dimensions of website quality perception, that is, information quality and system quality. In model 1 we account for the main focus of the online booking procedure and not the full spectrum of services offered by a travel agency. The second model specifically considers the hedonic and interactive nature of e-commerce applications [7]. It is a significant extension of the first model by adding service quality of the online booking device as well as relationships between the now three object-based beliefs. It is based on Xu et al. [7] as well as the updated IS success model [5]. Figures 1 and 2 show both models:

TAM proposes that behavioral attitudes and behavior are driven by the behavioral beliefs PU and PEOU. These behavioral beliefs are themselves influenced by object-based beliefs and attitudes [6, 7]. In particular behavioral beliefs are influenced by object-based attitudes, that is, satisfaction with the system, which itself is impacted by object-based beliefs, that is, quality perceptions. This approach is different from research that suggests quality perceptions as direct antecedents of PU and PEOU [11, 16].

Among the quality perception variables, information quality denotes the perceived quality of the offered content. Information quality should assist consumers in their shopping process by facilitating the comparison of products, increasing enjoyment, and improving decision-making. In the context of e-commerce, information quality is related

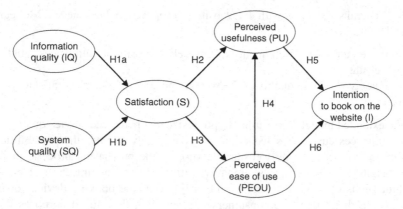

Fig. 1. Research model 1. This parsimonious model includes information quality and system quality as object-based beliefs.

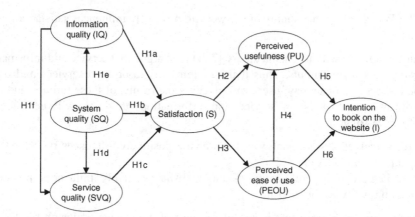

Fig. 2. Research model 2. This model extends model 1 by adding service quality as a third object-based belief as well as relationships between the object-based beliefs.

to the content of the website [11]. Characteristics that represent information quality are timeliness, completeness, and accuracy of information [5]. We thus contend that web-sites that fulfill these criteria are perceived as well-performing on information quality. System quality describes the technical performance as well as the design of the web site as an information system and thus refers to the engineering perspective [11]. Perceived system quality includes attributes such as reliability, flexibility, or availability [5, 6] as well as functionality that may influence an online shopping process [16].

There is ample e-commerce literature that demonstrates the relevance of information quality and system quality for perceptions of website quality (for example [14, 37–39]). While some studies differentiate between information and system satisfaction [6] and further introduce service satisfaction [7], we consider a more parsimonious model including general satisfaction with the website as proposed by DeLone and McLean [5]. We thus hypothesize:

H1a: Perceived information quality of the website positively influences satisfaction with the website.

H1b: Perceived system quality of the website positively influences satisfaction with the website.

In the extended model 2 we further hypothesize that perceived service quality of the website influences customer satisfaction. Service quality denotes the possibilities for customers to interact with the website and support the purchasing process. In IS literature, tangibles, responsiveness, empathy, reliability, and assurance are considered main dimensions of service quality [7, 11, 40]. As online booking devices of travel agencies are a direct interface consumers interact with, they fulfill purposes that go beyond the mere information provision and system functionality. Thus the website's service provision is perceived as a part of the company's overall service provision [7]. Therefore we contend:

H1c: Perceived service quality of the website positively influences satisfaction with the website.

Furthermore, based on schema theory [7, 41] we argue that service and information provision are system outputs. Thus if the system fails to provide services and information in an appropriate way, users will perceive the results of these failures and thus their object-based beliefs on service and information provision will be affected. Therefore we suggest:

H1d: Perceived system quality of the website positively influences perceived service quality of the website.

H1e: Perceived system quality of the website positively influences perceived information quality of the website.

Since information provision is considered part of the service provision [7, 42], we finally hypothesize:

H1f: Perceived information quality of the website positively influences perceived service quality of the website.

Satisfaction with a website is an attitude toward an object [6, 8] that can be understood as an external variable that influences behavioral beliefs, namely PU and PEOU [7]. Since PU is understood as the perceived degree to which a system increases the performance of the undertaken task [2], Wixom and Todd [6] conclude that higher information satisfaction will be positively associated with PU. Likewise, as PEOU describes the perception that using a system does not require much effort [2], satisfaction with the system is expected to impact PEOU [6]. In our more parsimonious approach, we expect that the object-based attitude satisfaction will positively influence the behavioral beliefs simultaneously. We therefore hypothesize:

H2: Satisfaction with the website positively influences perceived usefulness of the website.

H3: Satisfaction with the website positively influences perceived ease of use of the website.

The remaining variables are directly derived from the rich literature on TAM which consistently investigates and empirically confirms the impact of the behavioral beliefs PU and PEOU on behavioral attitude (for example [11, 14–16]) or, in a more parsimonious way, on behavioral intention ([13, 17–19]). In line with this literature as well as [6, 7], we hypothesize:

H4: Perceived ease of use of a website positively influences perceived usefulness of the website.

H5: Perceived usefulness of a website positively influences the intention to use the website for booking.

H6: Perceived ease of use of a website positively influences the intention to use the website for booking.

4 Research Methodology

4.1 Instrument Development

The empirical test of the research model took place by means of a quantitative consumer survey in the German-speaking area. In order to achieve comparable results, respondents were presented a website of a travel agency that was subject to evaluation based on the applied variables. The measurement of items was done on the basis of elaborated scales from IS literature [11, 15, 16, 43, 44]. All items on consumers' beliefs and behavioral intentions were related to the presented website. Where necessary, the formulation was adapted to that context (e.g., "booking on the Website"). PU was measured with items adapted from [44], PEOU items were adapted from [15, 16], the items on information, system, and service quality are based on [11, 16]. Finally, satisfaction and intention to use were adapted from [43]. Since the used items were all developed in English language, they were translated into German and back-translated by a native speaker. A pretest among eight students was made based on which a few wording modifications were done. All items were measured with a 5-point Likert scale ranging from 1 (totally disagree) to 5 (totally agree).

4.2 Sample

The research design comprised a quantitative online survey. To attract consumers interested in traveling, the survey was announced at several German-speaking online forums. 324 questionnaires were completed. 32 contained incomplete answers so that 292 questionnaires were used for further analysis. The gender distribution in the sample is 54.3 % males and 45.6 % females. The average age is 33 years; 26.2 % are younger than 25 years, 38.3 % are between 25 and 34 years, 19.5 % are between 35 and 44 years, and 16.1 % are 45 years or older. A filter question ensured that respondents travel at least once per year.

5 Results

5.1 Measurement Model

The models were tested by means of partial least squares (PLS) analysis. The used analysis software was SmartPLS [45]. The test of the measurement model includes analyzing the consistency (Cronbach's alpha), the convergent and the discriminant validity. Table 1 shows the Cronbach's alpha and average variance extracted (AVE) values of the variables.

Table 1. Reliability measures of variables.

Variable	Used in model	Number of items	Cronbach's alpha	AVE
Information quality (IQ)	1, 2	3	0.70	0.61
System quality (SQ)	1, 2	4	0.84	0.67
Service quality (SVQ)	2	4	0.79	0.61
Perceived usefulness (PU)	1, 2	4	0.69	0.51
Perceived ease of use (PEOU)	1, 2	3	0.78	0.70
Satisfaction (S)	1, 2	3	0.86	0.78
Intention to use (I)	1, 2	3	0.90	0.83

Almost all Cronbach's alpha values are higher than the recommended value of 0.7 [46]. For PU, Cronbach's alpha is 0.69 and therefore very close to the recommended value. Convergent validity is satisfactory if the AVE is higher than 0.5 [47]. This condition is met for all variables. Tables 2 and 3 display the numbers concerning discriminant validity.

Table 2. Correlation matrix model 1.

	IQ	SQ	PU	PEOU	S	I
IQ	*0.78*					
SQ	0.39	*0.82*				
PU	0.34	0.05	*0.71*			
PEOU	0.21	0.21	0.43	*0.84*		
S	0.35	0.18	0.52	0.48	*0.88*	
I	0.38	0.06	0.66	0.42	0.66	*0.91*

In Tables 2 and 3, the correlations of the variables are shown. The numbers on the diagonals in italics are the square roots of the AVE. For adequate discriminant validity, these values should exceed the interconstruct correlations. This condition is met for all constructs in both models with one exception. Further, the loadings of the individual items on the corresponding variables are well above the recommended value of 0.5 for appropriate discriminant validity. They range between 0.66 and 0.94 in model 1 and 0.54 and 0.94 in model 2. Thus overall the measurement models of both research models are highly satisfactory.

Table 3. Correlation matrix model 2.

	IQ	SQ	SVQ	PU	PEOU	S	I
IQ	0.79						
SQ	0.48	0.82					
SVQ	0.47	0.75	0.78				
PU	0.27	0.04	0.10	0.72			
PEOU	0.20	0.17	0.12	0.43	0.83		
S	0.27	0.15	0.21	0.52	0.48	0.88	
I	0.28	0.03	0.09	0.66	0.42	0.66	0.91

5.2   Hypotheses Test

The test of the structural models comprises the path coefficients, the R-square values of dependent variables as well as the p-values. The latter were obtained by bootstrapping with 100 cases and 1,000 samples. Table 4 shows the results of the PLS analysis along with the p-values of the path coefficients for model 1.

Table 4. PLS analysis results model 1.

Hypothesized impact	Path coefficient	p-value
Information quality→satisfaction (H1a)	0.333	***
System quality→satisfaction (H1b)	0.045	n.s.
Satisfaction→PU (H2)	0.409	***
Satisfaction→PEOU (H3)	0.476	***
PEOU→PU (H4)	0.235	*
PU→Intention to book (H5)	0.593	***
PEOU→Intention to book (H6)	0.163	n.s.

p-values: ***<0.001, *<0.05, n.s. not significant

As the results show, information quality shows a high positive impact on satis-faction with the travel agency website, supporting H1a. In contrast, system quality shows a path coefficient close to zero, thus H1b is rejected. The impacts of satisfaction on PU and PEOU are both strong and highly significant (0.409 and 0.476, respectively), thus supporting H2 and H3. The impact of PEOU on PU is smaller (0.235), but still significant at the five percent level. Finally, intention to book at the travel agency's website is largely influenced by PU (0.593), supporting H5. The impact of PEOU is weak (0.163) and although there is a tendency of significance (less than ten percent), H6 is rejected. The R-square values are the following: 0.12 for satisfaction, 0.31 for PU, 0.23 for PEOU, and 0.46 for booking intention.

Table 5 shows the PLS analysis results for model 2.

Only the first part of the model, that is, hypotheses 1a through 1f can show different results than model 1. Information quality still shows a positive impact on satisfaction with the travel agency website, supporting H1a. Like in model 1, the impact of system quality on satisfaction is not significant, thus H1b is rejected. The impact of service quality on satisfaction (H1c) is characterized by a path coefficient of 0.163 and is not

Table 5. PLS analysis results model 2.

Hypothesized impact	Path coefficient	p-value
Information quality→satisfaction (H1a)	0.248	*
System quality→satisfaction (H1b)	−0.090	n.s.
Service quality→satisfaction (H1c)	0.163	n.s.
System quality→service quality (H1d)	0.673	***
System quality→information quality (H1e)	0.492	***
Information quality→service quality (H1f)	0.150	*
Satisfaction→PU (H2)	0.409	***
Satisfaction→PEOU (H3)	0.476	***
PEOU→PU (H4)	0.235	*
PU→Intention to book (H5)	0.593	***
PEOU→Intention to book (H6)	0.163	n.s.

p-values: ***<0.001, *<0.05, n.s. not significant

significant. However, the impact of system quality on service quality (H1d) and information quality (H1e) is highly significant in both cases. H1d has a high path coefficient of 0.673 whereas H1e shows a path coefficient of 0.492. Lastly, H1f shows a moderate path coefficient of 0.15 which is significant at the five percent level due to a low standard error. The R-square values in model 2 are: 0.24 for information quality, 0.58 for service quality, 0.09 for satisfaction, 0.31 for PU, 0.23 for PEOU, and 0.46 for booking intention.

6   Discussion

6.1   Discussion of Results

We tested two models based on an integrated approach based on the DeLone and McLean IS success model as well as TAM. The seminal work by Wixom and Todd [6] could be confirmed in a service-oriented setting, that is, online booking at travel agencies' websites. Starting the discussion with model 1, the hypotheses tests require a differentiated view on the analyzed variables. Perceived information quality shows a positive and highly significant impact on satisfaction, thus supporting our hypothesis.

Unlike expected, perceived system quality shows no significant effect. There are several possible reasons for that. First, with increasing maturity and technical reliability of websites, the relevance of this factor may be decreasing over time. System quality is mainly caused by an advanced technical basis which can be expected to improve with growing IS sophistication of travel agencies. Second, system quality may play a minor role especially in the travel booking context where consumers may put a larger emphasis on the complex travel products and therefore on the information quality. Third, the parsimonious approach of this research that considered overall satisfaction rather than differentiation between information and system satisfaction can be a reason. The results of this study, however, are consistent with a study on Web service quality differences between online travel agencies and online service providers that identifies information content as the most important dimension of Web service quality for online travel agencies [48].

The impact of satisfaction on the TAM-based constructs PU and PEOU could clearly be confirmed. The results support the theoretical assumption that object-based attitudes (satisfaction) have an impact on behavioral beliefs (PU and PEOU). The strongest impact throughout the model is found between PU and intention to book on the website. This finding is highly consistent with previous research on TAM that identified PU as the primary impact factor on behavioral attitude and behavioral intention. The impact of PEOU on behavioral intention is not significant. This result is also consistent with previous research on TAM that shows mixed empirical evidence on the impact of PEOU [14, 49, 50]. Further, a study on website quality and behavioral beliefs on websites of different tourism companies showed that PEOU is of less importance for travel agencies' websites while it is a primary factor for online service providers [48]. Finally, as proposed in many TAM-based studies, the impact of PEOU on PU is significant, too.

The results of the extended model show that it does not provide more explanatory power than the basic parsimonious model. Service quality did not turn out to significantly impact satisfaction. The support of H1d, H1e, and H1f partly confirms the findings by Xu et al. [7], thus stressing the importance of relationships between the object-based beliefs. However, they remain without a significant impact on satisfaction. The reasons for the lacking impact of service quality on satisfaction may lie in the particularities of the tourism industry. Compared with the purchase of a product, the service component of the online purchasing process has a much smaller weight for the overall consumption experience. If a consumer purchases a physical product, a large portion of the service quality perception is related to the purchasing procedure. When booking a trip, however, the perceived service quality is likely to be dominated by the offered services during the journey. Consumers learn about these services by informing themselves about the trip on the website. Compared to that, the service quality of the booking website which was subject of the study is only a very small part of the overall service provision. Thus it can be expected that (1) consumers give the service quality of the website overall a small weight and (2) they view the evaluation of the service quality of the trip in relation to the information quality.

6.2   Research Implications

The results clearly show the relevance of two seminal theories in IS research – the IS success model and TAM – in the online tourism sector. It confirms the relevance of integrating both theories for a better understanding of online usage intention and thus supports Ajzen and Fishbein's [8] notion of an impact chain starting with external stimuli of the website that drive object-based beliefs, object-based attitudes, behavioral beliefs, and behavioral intention. It particularly shows that the chain of impacts on intention to book online starts with information quality through satisfaction, PEOU, and PU, the latter being the main direct antecedent. Hence, both satisfaction and PEOU have a mediated impact on booking intention. The study further shows that due to the particular characteristics of the travel industry service quality plays a different role than in other e-commerce settings. Thus from an academic point of view, the parsimonious model without service quality is superior to the enriched model that includes service quality.

6.3 Managerial Implications

This research also has important managerial implications. In the light of a growing dominance of online travel booking and a disintermediation threat of classical, offline travel agencies the drivers of online booking behavior at travel agencies' websites become increasingly essential. The significant role of information quality that ultimately impacts the intention to book on the agency's website stresses the importance of a careful design of the offered content on the website. Perceived information quality can be controlled by a website operator. It can be enhanced by enrichments of the website content, for example by offering multimedia contents with animations and videos, such as virtual tours or 360 degree views of hotel facilities. Travel agencies should further make use of user-generated contents by providing space for user recommendations, reviews, and numerical ratings. Consumer reviews are a core part of online traveling platforms like Expedia.com or Tripadvisor.com [51] and can further enhance the information quality of travel agency websites.

System quality does not show a significant direct impact on satisfaction, but a mediated one via information quality. Thus attention should be paid on a high degree of system availability, security, and reliability especially to ensure full access to the information. Of further importance is the key role of PU that has a much higher weight compared with PEOU. Hence a travel agency website should offer not only all necessary information and functionalities that enable online booking, but support and facilitate all transaction phases of trip booking. This includes a comprehensive after-sales service, for example by offering the provision of online feedback by customers after the trip. Since travel agencies usually provide additional information in printed catalogs and agency bureaus, they should pay large attention on avoiding outdated or inconsistent information in the different channels.

Recently, the use of mobile devices for information search and booking trips is increasing sharply along with a switch of users between devices. Today, a typical "journey" across the devices may start with information search on the smart phone or tablet and finish with the booking process via the laptop or PC [52]. Travel agencies have to account for this development and must offer a seamless and integrated information provision and booking process across these access devices without interruption. Against this background, the impact of system quality on satisfaction should be revisited.

7   Conclusions

The results of this study stress the opportunities for travel agencies to influence online purchasing behavior positively by offering information quality that satisfies users. The main contribution of this study to research lies in the investigation of drivers of usage intention at travel agencies' e-commerce sites and thus confirming Wixom and Todd's

[6] model in this context. From the managerial perspective, the study provides a theory-based framework on important website design issues that are critical for satisfaction, PU, PEOU, and usage intention which are important prerequisites of online booking behavior. Although the study was done in the context of a rather complex product, the findings can be transferred to other domains that involve experience goods or complex shopping goods, too.

Although the results largely support the assumptions particularly of research model 1, there are several limitations of this study. First, we did not differentiate between different kinds of journeys which may result in different impact strengths of the antecedents. For example, a packaged far-distance tour that takes three weeks consists of a series of service components and thus requires more information than booking a flight which can be described with few and structured pieces of information. Also differences between private and business trips may occur. Finally, socio-demographic factors and personal traits (e.g., traveling behavior or destination preferences) may have an impact on the overall proposed antecedents.

Further research should consider emerging e-commerce developments, especially the role of mobile devices and social media as well as online consumer reviews. Moreover, an analysis of different players in the online tourism sector (online service providers, electronic intermediaries etc.) should be compared with travel agencies to further increase the understanding of drivers of online travel booking.

References

1. eMarketer: online travel sales explode in Latin America. http://www.emarketer.com/Article/Online-Travel-Sales-Explode-Latin-America/1009493
2. Davis, F.D., Bagozzi, R.P., Warshaw, P.R.: User acceptance of computer technology: a comparison of two theoretical models. Manage. Sci. **35**, 982–1003 (1989)
3. Davis, F.D.: Perceived usefulness, perceived ease of use, and user acceptance of information technology. MIS Q. **13**, 319–339 (1989)
4. DeLone, W.H., McLean, E.R.: Information systems success: the quest for the dependent variable. Inf. Syst. Res. **3**, 60–95 (1992)
5. DeLone, W.H., McLean, E.R.: The DeLone and McLean model of information systems success: a ten-year update. J. Manage. Inf. Syst. **19**, 9–30 (2003)
6. Wixom, B.H., Todd, P.A.: A theoretical integration of user satisfaction and technology acceptance. Inf. Syst. Res. **16**, 85–102 (2005)
7. Xu, J.D., Benbasat, I., Cenfetelli, R.T.: Integrating service quality with system and information quality: an empirical test in the e-service context. MIS Q. **37**, 777–794 (2013)
8. Ajzen, I., Fishbein, M.: Understanding Attitudes and Predicting Social Behavior. Prentice-Hall, Englewood Cliffs (1980)
9. Ajzen, I.: Attitude structure and behavior. In: Pratkanis, A.R., Breckler, S.J., Greenwald, A.G. (eds.) Attitude Structure and Function, pp. 241–274. Lawrence Erlbaum, Hillsdale (1989)
10. Davis, F.D.: User acceptance of information technology: system characteristics, user perceptions and behavioral impacts. Int. J. Man Mach. Stud. **38**, 475–487 (1993)
11. Ahn, T., Ryu, S., Han, I.: The impact of the online and offline features on the user acceptance of internet shopping malls. Electron. Commer. Res. Appl. **3**, 405–420 (2004)

12. Ha, S., Stoel, L.: Consumer e-shopping acceptance: antecedents in a technology acceptance model. J. Bus. Res. **62**, 565–571 (2009)
13. Klopping, I.M., McKinney, E.: Extending the technology acceptance model and the task-technology fit model to consumer e-commerce. Inf. J. Technol. Learn. Perform. **22**, 35–48 (2004)
14. Lin, J.C.C., Lu, H.: Towards an understanding of the behavioural intention to use a web site. Int. J. Inf. Manage. **20**, 197–208 (2000)
15. McCloskey, D.W.: Evaluating electronic commerce acceptance with the technology acceptance model. J. Comput. Inf. Syst. **44**, 49–57 (2004)
16. Shih, H.-P.: An empirical study on predicting user acceptance of e-shopping on the web. Inf. Manage. **41**, 351–368 (2004)
17. Gefen, D., Straub, D.: The relative importance of perceived ease-of-use in IS adoption: a study of e-commerce adoption. J. Assoc. Inf. Syst. **1**, 1–21 (2000)
18. Lederer, A.L., Maupin, D.J., Sena, M.P., Zhuang, Y.: The technology acceptance model and the world wide web. Decis. Support Syst. **29**, 269–282 (2000)
19. Teo, T.S.H., Lim, V.K.G., Lai, R.Y.C.: Intrinsic and extrinsic motivation in internet usage. Omega **27**, 25–37 (1999)
20. Brown, I., Jayakody, R.: B2C e-commerce success: a test and validation of a revised conceptual model. Electron. J. Inf. Syst. Eval. **11**, 167–184 (2008)
21. Wang, Y.-S.: Assessing e-commerce systems success: a respecification and validation of the DeLone and McLean model of IS success. Inf. Syst. J. **18**, 529–557 (2008)
22. Järveläinen, J.: Online purchase intentions: an empirical testing of a multiple-theory model. J. Organ. Comput. Electron. Commer. **17**, 53–74 (2007)
23. Petre, M., Minocha, S., Roberts, D.: Usability beyond the website: an empirically-grounded e-commerce evaluation instrument for the total customer experience. Behav. Inf. Technol. **25**, 189–203 (2006)
24. Kim, M.J., Chung, N., Lee, C.K.: The effect of perceived trust on electronic commerce: shopping for online tourism products and services in South Korea. Tour. Manage. **32**, 256–265 (2011)
25. Mashable: the evolution of online travel - infographic. http://mashable.com/2012/02/21/online-travel-infographic/
26. Dooley, G.: Analysis: can travel agents compete against online tour sellers? http://www.travelagentcentral.com/home-based/tours-tour-operators/analysis-can-travel-agents-compete-against-online-tour-sellers-15638
27. Jeong, M., Oh, H., Gregoire, M.: Conceptualizing website quality and its consequences in the lodging industry. Int. J. Hosp. Manage. **22**, 161–175 (2003)
28. Law, R., Ngai, C.: Usability of travel websites: a case study of the perceptions of Hong Kong travelers. J. Hosp. Leisure Mark. **13**, 19–31 (2005)
29. Tsang, N.K.F., Lai, M.T.H., Law, R.: Measuring e-service quality for online travel agencies. J. Travel Tour. Mark. **27**, 306–323 (2010)
30. Chen, C.-F., Kao, Y.-L.: Relationships between process quality, outcome quality, satisfaction, and behavioural intentions for online travel agencies - evidence from Taiwan. Serv. Ind. J. **30**, 2081–2092 (2010)
31. Wen, I.: An empirical study of an online travel purchase intention model. J. Travel Tour. Mark. **29**, 18–39 (2012)
32. Nunkoo, R., Ramkissoon, H.: Travelers' e-purchase intent of tourism products and services. J. Hosp. Mark. Manage. **22**, 505–529 (2013)
33. Kaplanidou, K., Vogt, C.: A structural analysis of destination travel intentions as a function of web site features. J. Travel Res. **45**, 204–216 (2006)

34. Park, Y.A., Gretzel, U., Sirakaya-Turk, E.: Measuring website quality for online travel agencies. J. Travel Tour. Mark. **23**, 15–30 (2007)
35. Ryan, C., Rao, U.: Holiday users of the internet — ease of use, functionality and novelty. Int. J. Tour. Res. **10**, 329–339 (2008)
36. Seddon, P.B.: A respecification and extension of the DeLone and McLean model of IS success. Inf. Syst. Res. **8**, 240–253 (1997)
37. Aladwani, A.M., Palvia, P.C.: Developing and validating an instrument for measuring user-perceived web quality. Inf. Manage. **39**, 467–476 (2002)
38. Kim, S., Stoel, L.: Dimensional hierarchy of retail web quality. Inf. Manage. **41**, 619–633 (2002)
39. Liu, C., Arnett, K.P.: Exploring the factors associated with web success in the context of electronic commerce. Inf. Manage. **38**, 23–33 (2000)
40. Pitt, L.F., Watson, R.T., Kavan, C.B.: Service quality: a measure of information systems effectiveness. MIS Q. **19**, 173–187 (1995)
41. Louis, M.R., Sutton, R.I.: Switching cognitive gears: from habits of mind to active thinking. Hum. Relat. **44**, 55–76 (1991)
42. Cenfetelli, R.T., Benbasat, I., Al-Natour, S.: Addressing the what and how of online services: comparing service content and service quality for e-business success. Inf. Syst. Res. **19**, 161–181 (2008)
43. Devaraj, S., Fan, M., Kohli, R.: Antecedents of B2C channel satisfaction and preference: validating e-commerce metrics. Inf. Syst. Res. **13**, 316–333 (2002)
44. Shang, R.-A., Chen, Y.C., Shen, L.: Extrinsic versus intrinsic motivations for consumers to shop on-line. Inf. Manage. **42**, 401–431 (2005)
45. Ringle, C.M., Wende, S., Will, A.: Smartpls 2.0. SmartPLS, Hamburg (2005)
46. Nunnally, J.C.: Psychometric Theory. McGraw-Hill, New York (1978)
47. Fornell, C., Larcker, D.F.: Evaluating structural equation models with unobservable variables and measurement error. J. Mark. Res. **18**, 39–50 (1981)
48. Kim, W.G., Lee, H.Y.: Comparison of web service quality between online travel agencies and online travel suppliers. J. Travel Tour. Mark. **17**, 105–116 (2004)
49. Venkatesh, V.: Determinants of perceived ease of use: integrating control, intrinsic motivation, and emotion into the technology acceptance model. Inf. Syst. Res. **11**, 342–365 (2000)
50. Venkatesh, V., Davis, F.D.: A theoretical extension of the technology acceptance model: four longitudinal field studies. Manage. Sci. **46**, 186–204 (2000)
51. Park, S.-Y., Allen, J.P.: Responding to online reviews: problem solving and engagement in hotels. Cornell Hosp. Q. **54**, 64–73 (2013)
52. Marketingcharts.com: Travel research and booking seen a multi-device process. http://www.marketingcharts.com/wp/online/travel-research-and-booking-seen-a-multi-device-process-29809/

Geo-Spatial Trend Detection Through Twitter Data Feed Mining

Maarten Wijnants[✉], Adam Blazejczak, Peter Quax, and Wim Lamotte

Expertise Centre for Digital Media, Hasselt University – tUL – iMinds,
Wetenschapspark 2, 3590 Diepenbeek, Belgium
maarten.wijnants@uhasselt.be

Abstract. Present-day Social Networking Sites are steadily progressing towards becoming representative data providers. This paper proposes *TweetPos*, a versatile web-based tool that facilitates the analytical study of geographic tendencies in crowd-sourced Twitter data feeds. To accommodate the cognitive strengths of the human mind, TweetPos predominantly resorts to graphical data structures such as intensity maps and diagrams to visualize (geo-spatial) tweet metadata. The web service's asset set encompasses a hybrid tweet compilation engine that allows for the investigation of both historic and real-time tweet posting attitudes, temporal trend highlighting via an integrated animation system, and a layered visualization scheme to support tweet topic differentiation. TweetPos' data mining features and the (geo-spatial) intelligence they can amount to are comprehensively demonstrated via the discussion of two representative use cases. Courtesy of its generic design, the TweetPos service might prove valuable to an interdisciplinary customer audience including social scientists and market analysts.

Keywords: Twitter · Social networking sites · Social media · Geographic trends · Investigative tool · Data mining · TweetPos

1   Introduction

Social Networking Sites (SNSs) were conceived as a means to virtually connect users and to offer them an intuitive forum to ubiquitously contribute and disseminate information in real time. As their number of subscribers rose over time, so did the amount of content that is managed by SNSs. As a result, they nowadays host a wealth of user-generated data that is highly heterogeneous in nature.

Over the years, SNSs have also evolved functionality-wise. While many such services were purely text-based upon their inception, they nowadays typically grant users the option to attach multimedia items like pictures and video clips to their contributions. Another feature that has become nearly commonplace in the SNS landscape, is geotagging (i.e., attaching geographic coordinates as metadata to messages). It is apparent that such novel facilities embellish the core SNS content and further extend its value.

© Springer International Publishing Switzerland 2015
V. Monfort and K.-H. Krempels (Eds.): WEBIST 2014, LNBIP 226, pp. 212–227, 2015.
DOI: 10.1007/978-3-319-27030-2_14

Given their popularity and broad adoption, it is becoming evermore valid to regard SNSs as real-life, real-time and crowd-sourced sensor systems that "monitor" a varied spectrum of (physical) properties and topics (see, for example, [1]). By intelligently exploiting the data feeds that can be accumulated from SNSs, innovative and value-added services can be conceived. In addition, mining and analyzing the information that is shared by end-users through social media can lead to valuable insights and knowledge. Possible application domains include consumer behavior modeling, consumer profiling, intelligent recommendation systems, and population sentiment assessment. Extracting such kinds of intelligence from SNSs however typically requires external tools, as profound mining and analysis mechanisms by default are lacking from their feature set.

In this paper, we tend to Twitter, the authoritative microblogging platform in the western world, and we focus on investigating the data that is hosted by this SNS from a geo-spatial perspective. In particular, we introduce the web-based *TweetPos* tool, a convenient means to display and study the geographic origin of tweets, and to uncover the geographical evolution of the popularity of tweet topics. A hybrid visualization method encompassing both heatmap- and chart-based data representation allows for thorough analysis and mining with regard to the geo-spatial distribution of tweeted material over time. The TweetPos web service affords keyword-based topic selection and includes a layering system that allows for easy comparison of the geographical trends of multiple subjects. Furthermore, our tool is able to compile data sets that integrate a representative sample of tweets from the recent past with present-day tweet messages that are captured in real time, in order to grant insight in both historical and current tweet posting behavior. Finally, the accumulated data collections can be aggregated and studied on either a per-day or per-hour basis to provide some degree of analytical granularity. We argue that, combined, these features offer all necessary measures to perform significant research about the geographical sources of Twitter data. We will back this claim by presenting the results of two prototypical analyses that illustrate the versatility, effectiveness and comprehensiveness of the proposed instrument. At the same time, the provided demonstrations serve as prove of the extensive applicability of TweetPos: courtesy of its generic methodology, it may one way or another cater to the demands of a variety of human consumer profiles, including social researchers, marketeers, advertisers, analysts and journalists.

A primordial aspect of the TweetPos solution is its emphasis on providing graphical representations of the crawled Twitter data. Contrary to computers, the typical human mind does not excel at handling large quantities of raw data. On the other hand, our cognitive features make us more adept than computers at interpreting visual data structures [2] like heatmaps and charts, which are exactly the output modalities that are supported by our platform. The TweetPos tool is hence intended to offer human operators an adequate graphical workspace that allows them to readily and conveniently assess geo-spatial trends in social media contributions.

The remainder of this article is organized as follows. Section 2 presents an overview of the functional features of the TweetPos web service. Next, Sect. 3

handles the architectural design and implementation of the tool. We then evaluate our work in Sect. 4 by discussing some representative examples of investigations into the geographical evolution of recently trending Twitter themes that have been produced with the proposed tool. Section 5 briefly reviews related work on the analysis and mining of information that has been shared via social networks, and at the same time highlights our scientific contributions. Finally, we draw our conclusions and suggest potential future research directions in Sect. 6.

2   TweetPos

The TweetPos instrument is implemented as a web service that is accessible via a standard web browser. Screenshots of the tool's input widgets are bundled in Fig. 1. As these images illustrate, keywords or so-called Twitter *hashtags* are the service's essential ingress parameters. Based on the specified topic of interest, the tool will compile a corpus of tweets that deal with this subject. This corpus will encompass a representative sample of historical messages as well as a completely accurate set of current and future tweets on the topic at hand. The user is hereby granted the option to apply geographical filtering by limiting the tweet compilation to either Europe or North America, if so desired (see Fig. 1(b)). An identical filtering option is included in the input pane that controls the visualization of the accumulated data (see Fig. 1(c)). Finally, a number of standard HTML input elements allow for controlling the temporal constraints and the animation of the result set. In particular, via two HTML sliders and a checkbox, users can enforce the discrete time interval with which (the timestamps of) gathered tweets need to comply for them to be included in the output. Two fixed levels of granularity are supported for the specification of the temporal constraints, which cause TweetPos to aggregate filtered tweets per hour and per day, respectively. An animation engine that utilizes either hourly or daily increments allows for the animated, video-like presentation of the tweet data set and as such might yield valuable insights into the geo-spatial trends that are exhibited by tweet topics over time.

On the output front, the principal GUI element consists of a topographic map that scaffolds heatmap-based visualization of the geo-spatial provenances of filtered Twitter messages. Stated differently, this output component displays the intensity, from a geographic point of view, of tweets that encompass the specified input keyword. Besides a map, two additional output widgets are included in the tool. The first is a line chart that visualizes the quantitative volume of the compiled tweet archive, aggregated either on a per-hour or a per-day basis, while the second enumerates the textual contents of the collected tweets. Figure 2 illustrates the TweetPos output interface.

An important feature of TweetPos is its keyword layering functionality. The tool allows multiple keyword filters to be active simultaneously, by conceptually associating (the results of) each concurrent hashtag search with an individual layer. Figure 2(a) and (b) for instance illustrate a setup in which two queries are

(a) Topic selection.

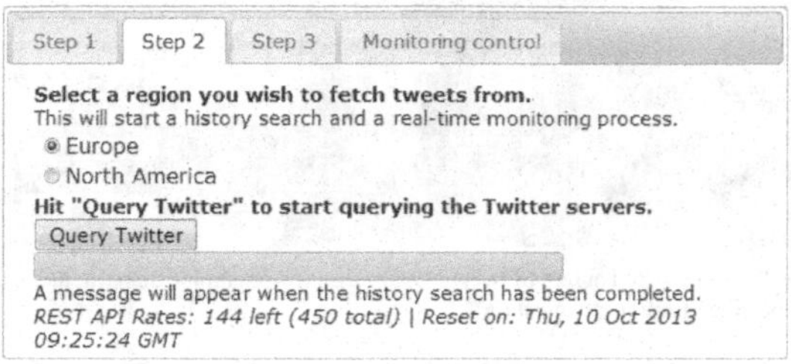

(b) Geographical filtering.

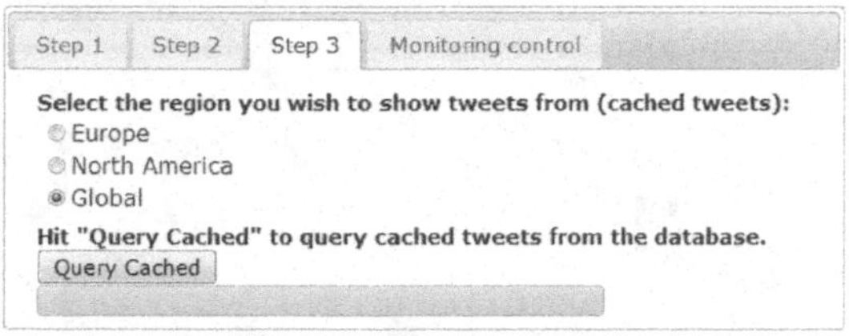

(c) Geographical constraints specification.

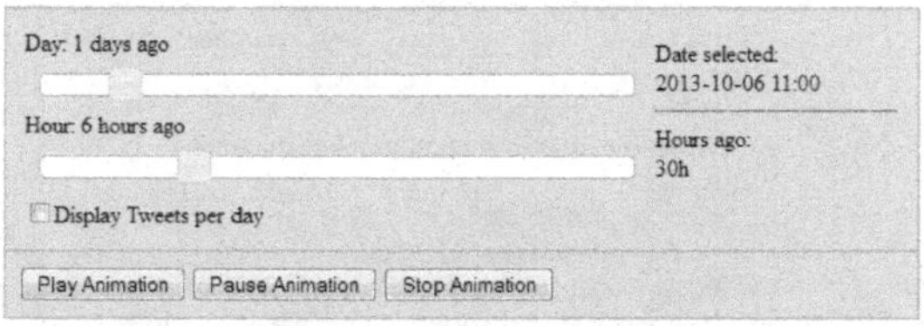

(d) Temporal constraints specification and animation control.

Fig. 1. TweetPos input GUI.

involved. Layers are rendered on top of the topographic map as uniquely colored overlays, whose visualization can be independently toggled on and off. Analogously, distinct tweet volumes are plotted in the line graph for each currently deployed keyword filter. A layer can be eliminated from the visualization process via the legend that is incorporated in the geographic map. The layering system provides a powerful means to investigate (the geo-spatial evolution of) multiple subjects concurrently, to offset them against each other, to reveal potential correlations between them, and so on.

Apart from temporal filtering parameters, the TweetPos service also supports the specification of spatial constraints. This type of constraint is deployed by clicking on the topographic map, which causes a circular area to be drawn around the selected location (see Fig. 2(a)). The map's zoom level and the stretch of the marked geographical region have been designed to be inversely proportional properties, which implies that the spatial extent of the highlighted area is controllable by zooming the map in and out. In effect, installing a spatial

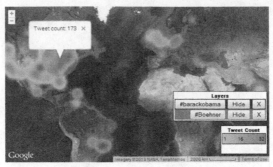

(a) Heatmap-based output of tweet locations on a topographic map (including a spatial constraint specification).

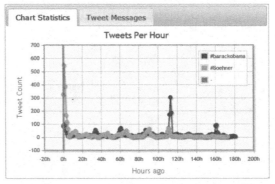

(b) Tweet volume presentation as a line diagram.

(c) Textual contents of the filtered tweets.

Fig. 2. TweetPos output GUI.

constraint under a relatively high zoom level will result in the selection of a relatively tight geographical region, while the opposite holds true when the map is heavily zoomed out.

All output components are dynamic, in the sense that their content is updated on-the-fly when the user modifies one or more input parameters. Obviously this applies to the keywords or hashtags that are searched for. In particular,

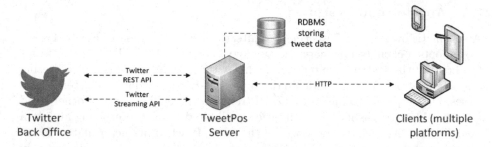

Fig. 3. High-level system architecture.

initiating a new search operation causes an additional layer to be introduced in both the 2D map and the line chart. Responding to less profound input settings however also occurs in real time. For example, exploiting the HTML sliders to modify the time constraints causes the map, the line chart as well as the list of tweet message to be updated instantaneously. The map will be adjusted to draw the geographic intensity that applied at the specified timestamp, the volume plot will be updated so that it correctly marks the currently selected time, and the textual list will only display tweet messages that satisfy the installed temporal restrictions. Analogous actions are dynamically undertaken in reaction to the definition of a spatial constraint. More precisely, the volume plot and textual message list only reckon with tweets that originated from the designated spatial area, if any. This feature allows human operators to zoom in on certain geographic regions and to perform fine-grained, localized analyses. As a final example of the dynamism of the output GUI, switching between layers via the legend in the topographic map causes the contents of the textual tweet enumeration widget to be updated so that it only displays those messages that apply to the keyword that corresponds with the currently selected layer.

3   Implementation

The TweetPos implementation is completely web-compliant. HTML and CSS are used for rendering the GUI and for handling page layout and style, while all programmatic logic is scripted in PHP and JavaScript (at server and client side, respectively).

Our motivations for realizing the TweetPos application as a web service are manifold. First of all, selecting the web as deployment platform acknowledges the pervasiveness of the Internet in modern society. At the same time, it renders the TweetPos functionality available on all environments and devices that support widespread and standardized web technologies, which maximizes the portability of our implementation. Finally, numerous utility libraries and supportive tools exist for the web, which we have gladly leveraged to expedite the development process.

3.1   Architectural Design

A schematic overview of TweetPos' architectural setup is given in Fig. 3. Tweet-Pos adopts a client/server network topology. The back-end HTTP server forms the heart of the system; it interfaces with Twitter, implements the data filtering and compilation, hosts a relational database (RDBMS) for data persistence purposes, and responds to incoming HTTP requests. The client on the other hand is very lightweight, as its responsibilities are limited to user interfacing and data visualization. As such, the server (and the RDBMS which it encapsulates) forms a level of abstraction in the TweetPos system architecture between respectively the external information source (i.e., Twitter) and the client-side presentation of the disclosed data.

3.2   Twitter Data Collection

Twitter provides multiple HTTP-based APIs to enable third-party software developers to interface with the platform and to build socially-inspired applications. The TweetPos tool exploits two of these APIs in order to harvest both historical and up-to-date (public) Twitter data. First of all, the Twitter Search API (which is embedded in the Twitter REST API as of version 1.1) is leveraged to compose a non-exhaustive yet representative sample of tweets from the past 7 days that dealt with a particular subject. The quantitative incompleteness is intrinsic to Twitter and represents a deliberate strategy in the platform's design [3]. In effect, the Search API has been designed for relevance and not completeness, which implies that it is not intended to deliver a rigorous index of past tweets. The second Twitter interface that fuels TweetPos' data collection procedure is a low-latency gateway to the global stream of tweets, called the Streaming API. This particular API allows developers to set up a long-lived HTTP connection to the Twitter back office, over which tweets from that moment on will then be streamed incrementally. In combination with extensive filtering and querying mechanisms, applications in this way obtain near-real-time and exhaustive access to exactly the type of tweets they are interested in. To facilitate the interaction with the Twitter Streaming API, the TweetPos tool integrates the 140dev Streaming API framework [4].

For the sake of comprehensiveness, we will now describe the complete set of actions and operations that constitute TweetPos' data ingestion pipeline. When a user initiates a new data collection process by transmitting a keyword-based query to the TweetPos server, the latter will spawn a total of seven PHP daemons. Each of these background processes utilize the Twitter Search API to jointly compile a pool of relevant historical tweets that were contributed during the past week (i.e., one process per day). At the same time, the back-end server manages a (PHP-based) daemon that permanently monitors the Twitter Streaming API. As an end-point is only allowed to set up a single connection to the Streaming API, this background process runs a cumulative filter to guarantee that all present and future tweets that satisfy one of the currently active queries are captured. In contrast to the Search API daemons, which have a finite execution time and are query-specific, the Streaming API process runs indefinitely and is shared by queries. A dedicated widget in the client-side GUI empowers users to stop the real-time monitoring of a particular topic (which is enforced by updating the cumulative filter of the Streaming API daemon).

3.3 Data Storage and Processing

Fetched tweets are persisted at server side in a MySQL database. To streamline the integration of the 140dev framework in the TweetPos tool, we have opted to integrally adopt its cache architecture and accompanying database schema. The caching mechanism of the 140dev framework applies a two-step approach. An aggregation step continuously filters JSON-encoded tweet data (including the actual message and all sorts of metadata) from the Twitter Streaming API and inserts the resulting data directly into a designated caching table in the back-end database. In effect, this task is fulfilled by the Streaming API daemon that was mentioned in Sect. 3.2. Simultaneously, an independent background process successively pulls single raw JSON items from this table, parses and conveniently formats the composing entities of the corresponding tweets (i.e., the textual message itself, the encapsulated hashtags and mentions, etcetera), and distributes the outcome across dedicated database tables. By isolating the aggregation from the parsing of relevant tweets, real-time and lossless data ingestion is guaranteed (the Twitter Streaming API might yield tremendous quantities of data, whose sheer volume might prohibit on-the-fly parsing and processing).

Besides leveraging the 140dev caching methodology and database schema for the Streaming API context of the TweetPos tool, we have decided to extend their application to the Twitter Search API component of our implementation. This entails that historical tweets that are harvested by the Search API daemons are just as well cached in raw JSON format and then parsed by the same process that also handles Streaming API contributions. The beneficial implications of this design are that it yields a clean software architecture, ensures uniform treatment of tweets originating from heterogeneous sources, and enables the elimination of data duplication in an integrated manner (i.e., without requiring an exogenous control loop).

Once the data collection procedure for a particular keyword-based query has been initiated, all client requests that are related to this query are handled at server side by means of pure RDBMS interactions. As an example, the execution of adequate SQL statements suffices for the server to be able to forward an up-to-date overview of Twitter data pertaining to the queried topic to the client.

3.4 Geocoding

As the TweetPos tool is chiefly concerned with the geo-spatial provenance of tweets, it is clear that geographic metadata plays a primordial role in its operation. To be more precise, geographic coordinates are needed in order to pinpoint a tweet on a topographic map. Some Twitter users include these coordinates directly in their posts (e.g., users with smartphones with built-in GPS receivers), yet the majority only inserts a descriptive representation of the involved location (e.g., in the form of a textual address), or even leave out all geographic references altogether.

TweetPos' data accumulation procedure is agnostic of the presence of geo-spatial metadata in tweets. Stated differently, tweets that lack any trace of geo-graphical metadata are not filtered out by either the Streaming API or Search API data compiler. Tweets holding exact geographic footprints are directly cached, as they can be readily localized on a map. In case the tweet only incorpo-rates a descriptive geo-spatial reference, the data processing daemon described in Sect. 3.3 will invoke the Google Geocoding API [5] to translate the descrip-tion into geographic coordinates prior to database insertion. Finally, although non-localized contributions are not exploitable in the current implementation, they are still recorded in the database "as is" for the sake of completeness (i.e., they may hold some value in future extensions of the tool).

3.5 Visualization

All visualization and GUI interaction operations are performed at client side by means of HTML and JavaScript.

Heatmap-Based Geolocation Clustering. The topographic output map has been implemented by means of the JavaScript variant of the Google Maps API [6]. Tweets are positioned on this map on the basis of the geographic location from which they were posted. Instead of marking (the location of) individual tweets on the map, a heatmap-based design has been adopted. Heatmaps are a general-purpose data visualization technique in which the intensity of data points is plotted in relative comparison to the absolute maximum value of the data set. Typically, data point intensity is indicated by means of a color coding scheme. Compared to mashups of discrete markers (which might easily clutter the map in the case of voluminous data sets), heatmaps hold the perceptual advantage that, without sacrificing much detail, they are naturally surveyable and interpretable. The Google Maps JavaScript API has built-in support for heatmap rendering.

Line Graph. While the heatmap at a glance provides users with an impression of the spatial characteristics of a particular Twitter topic, it fails to commu-nicate exact quantitative figures concerning the tweet volume. To counter this deficiency, the TweetPos tool includes a line graph visualization that discretely plots, either per hour or per day, the number of tweets that address the queried subject(s). As such, it visualizes a precise overview of the temporal evolution of the popularity of themes (expressed in tweet quantity). The line diagram is implemented via jqPlot, a plotting and charting plug-in for the jQuery JavaScript framework (http://www.jqplot.com/). The data values that compose the graph are interactive in the sense that they can be clicked to leap the date selection sliders (see Fig. 1(d)) to the corresponding timestamp.

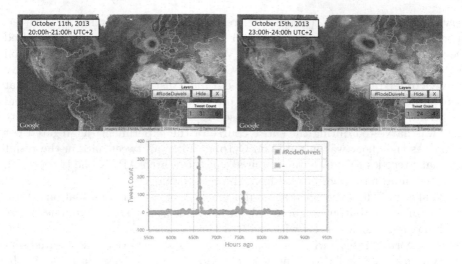

Fig. 4. Results of the 2014 FIFA World Cup qualifiers experiment.

Tweet Message Enumeration. The TweetPos tool is also able to output the textual contents of filtered tweets. This output method has been realized by means of the MegaList jQuery plug-in (http://triceam.github.io/MegaList/). Like the other output widgets, it is adaptive in the sense that it dynamically adjusts its contents to imposed spatiotemporal constraints. This widget is intended to provide users insight into the context in which the queried topic is referenced. As such, it allows for accurate, context-aware classification of tweets based on the messages they carry. For instance, a tweet about a certain incident might plead for or, conversely, against it; by inspecting the textual context, the stance of the tweet publisher becomes apparent.

4   Evaluation

This section serves to showcase the capabilities of the TweetPos instrument by presenting two representative examples of (geo-spatial) analyses of Twitter content that have been produced with it. The first test case is intended to rigorously demonstrate TweetPos' overall practicalities and to generally exemplify the data mining options which the tool scaffolds, while the second example focuses on TweetPos' layering functionality and the analytical features it entails. Space limitations force us to be brief in our discussion, and prevent us from including additional demonstrations.

4.1   2014 FIFA World Cup Qualifiers

The final two qualifier matches for the 2014 soccer World Cup were played on October 11th and 15th, 2013, respectively. We have exploited the TweetPos service to investigate the (geographic) resonance of these matches on Twitter, specifically for Belgium's national soccer team (which are nicknamed the "Red Devils" or "Rode Duivels" in Dutch). We issued a TweetPos data collection request for the `RodeDuivels` hashtag on October 13th and kept this query active until October 19th. Figure 4 shows the geographic distribution of the tweets that were gathered worldwide in the one hour interval immediately succeeding the end of the two matches, as well as a chart-based representation of the tweet quantity that was harvested during the entire course of the experiment (aggregated per hour). As the query was initiated on October 13th, all tweet data in the result set that precedes this date was acquired via the Search API, while tweets with an older timestamp were filtered from the Streaming API.

Analysis of the experimental results yields four notable observations. First and foremost, the output graph reveals two obvious peaks in tweet volume. These local maxima coincide nicely with the Red Devils' schedule of play. As such, this test case corroborates Twitter's capacity to act as a user-driven distributed sensor system that is able to identify real-world events (see also Sect. 5). As the data collection procedure was started in between the two matches, this capacity applies to both the Search API (for events from the recent past) and Streaming API (for current and future events). Secondly, tweets dealing with the match on October 11th appear to have originated practically exclusively from Belgium and its surrounding countries. In contrast, tweets about the second game exhibit a quasi worldwide distribution, yet again with a strong concentration in Western Europe. As the first set of tweets was ingested via the Twitter Search API, this outcome can likely be attributed to the operational principles of this interface (recall from Sect. 3.2 that the Search API aims for relevance, not comprehensiveness). Thirdly, although their volume is rather marginal, tweets embodying the `RodeDuivels` keyword were found to also emerge from non-Dutch speaking countries like the USA, Spain and Turkey (see the rightmost topographic map in Fig. 4). After inspecting the textual contents of these contributions (by means of the tweet mes-sage enumeration widget described in Sect. 3.5), it became clear that these types of tweets can roughly be classified into two categories:

- tweets written in Dutch by Belgian citizens (temporarily) living abroad; e.g., "Come on #RodeDuivels, I am rooting for you from my hotel room in Barcelona!" (English translation)
- retweets by the local population of English messages that include the (Dutch) `RodeDuivels` hashtag; often, the original messages were posted by Dutch natives who wanted to reach an internal audience; e.g., "Belgium versus Wales qualifier starting in 15 minutes #RodeDuivels #RedDevils #belwal #wc2014"

The fourth and final observation pertains to location-driven personalization of the tweeted contents. For example, a tweet by Toby Alderweireld (a Belgian soccer player who plays for Atletico Madrid in Spain), written in English and communicating Belgium's qualification for the 2014 FIFA World Cup, was actively retweeted by his followers in Spain and amounted to the majority of `RodeDuivels` tweets that originated from that country. A single Spanish Atletico

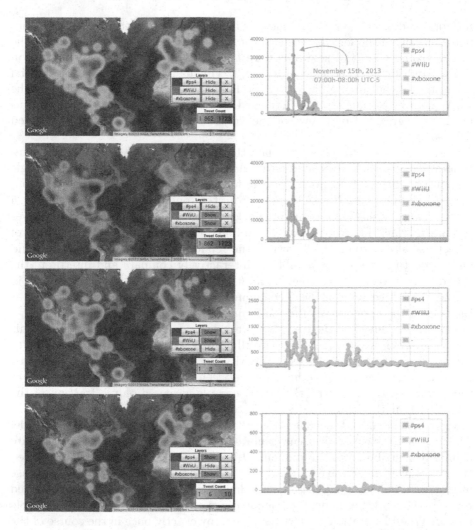

Fig. 5. Heatmap-based as well as quantitative comparison of game console popularity.

Madrid fan mentioned not only Toby Alderweireld but also his Belgian team-mate Thibaut Courtois in his tweet: "Well done to #Atleti's @thibautcourtois & @AlderweireldTob and their #RodeDuivels teammates. We'll see you in Brazil at #wc2014".

4.2 Game Console Comparison

The market of (next-gen) gaming consoles is (for the time being) dominated by Sony, Microsoft and Nintendo with their PlayStation 4, Xbox One and Wii U hardware, respectively. In this second test case, the TweetPos tool was put to use to compare the attention these three consoles receive on the Twitter network, and to uncover geographic dissimilarities between their respective popularity, if any. Therefore, between November 1st and November 16th, 2013, the ps4, xboxone and WiiU keywords were tracked with TweetPos. An impression of the resulting data set is given in Fig. 5. This figure visualizes the geo-spatial intensities of the three hashtags on the launch day of the PlayStation 4 in the USA (i.e., on November 15th between 07:00h and 08:00h UTC-5), as well as per-hour aggregated overviews of the volumetric magnitudes of the collected data sets.

These experimental results validate that TweetPos succeeds in layering multiple heatmaps, each associated with an independent query, on top of a single topographic map. The same holds true for the tweet volume plotting functionality of the line chart. Notice however from the topmost row of images in Fig. 5 that keyword visualizations might quickly conceal one another in multi-layer scenarios, which in turn is likely to impair analytical efficiency. Courtesy of TweetPos' ability to on-the-fly switch the rendering of individual layers on and off, it nonetheless remains feasible to interactively compare and interpret (the geographic provenance of) tweets in multi-query studies. In effect, the images in the bottom three rows in Fig. 5 communicate exactly the same information as the ones in the upper row, yet in an itemized fashion.

In-depth analysis of the composed data body falls beyond the scope of this article. Instead, we will point out two illustrative insights that we were able to extract from the collected tweets. Firstly, Fig. 5 at a glance reveals the existence of large quantitative differences between the three tracked keywords. In the monitored time interval, the Wii U console garnered only a fraction of the attention that the Xbox One was able to accumulate, whose Twitter coverage in turn was outclassed by that of the PlayStation 4 by an order of magnitude. The fact that the experiment encapsulated the PlayStation 4's USA release date definitely contributed to this outcome. In particular, inspection of the captured tweet messages confirmed considerable hype build-up as the PlayStation 4 release approached. For the same reason, the PlayStation 4 tweets geo-spatially tended towards the USA. Secondly, the volume diagrams show that Microsoft was able to pierce the PlayStation 4's Twitter hegemony exactly once in the course of the experiment. This achievement can be attributed to a clever marketing strategy: by retweeting a message from the official Twitter account of Xbox France, users could reveal the identity of the French Xbox One ambassador, an opportunity that was massively seized by fans. The resulting retweets primarily originated from Western Europe, and France in particular (not shown in Fig. 5).

5   Related Work

The principle of creating map mashups of the geographic sources of tweets has been considered by a number of commercialized web services. Examples include TweepsMap (http://tweepsmap.com/), Trendsmap (http://trendsmap.com/), Tweereal (http://tweereal.com/), Tweetping (http://tweetping.net/) and GlobalTweets (http://globaltweets.com/). The first maps (the home location of) the followers of a particular user's Twitter account, the second provides a real-time, localized mashup of currently trending Twitter themes, and the final three offer real-time geographic visualization of Twitter posts.

The academic literature also holds a number of articles that deal with deriving geo-spatial insights from Twitter data. Stefanidis et al. have proposed a framework to harvest and analyze ambient geographic information (i.e., not specified in terms of explicit coordinates) from tweets [7]. The iScience Maps tool targets behavioral researchers interested in exploiting Twitter for localized social media analysis purposes [8]. The global concept of applying Twitter as a distributed sensor network to identify and locate events in the physical world has been successfully explored by a number of analogous research initiatives [1,9–11]; of particular relevance is the social pixel/images/video approach by Singh et al. that allows for Twitter-powered situation detection and spatio-temporal assessments [12]. Field and O'Brien have investigated the application of cartographic principles to Twitter-powered map mashups [13]. Finally, the software architecture proposed by Oussalah et al. affords the deployment of geolocated services that are fueled by Twitter data [14].

All systems that have been cited in this section, both commercialized and academic ones, have their specific merits and feature sets. The TweetPos instrument exhibits functional overlaps with all of them. For example, the social pixel approach largely corresponds with our animated heatmap-based visualization solution. Some related tools even provide functionality that is missing in Tweet-Pos. When for instance again looking at the social pixel framework, it incorporates an automated situation detection scheme and exploits domain semantics to autonomously recommend relevant control actions in response to detected events. However, the TweetPos tool exceeds every cited initiative in terms of the variety of analytical means it integrates and the synergistic benefits that stem from this holistic design. As an example, only a minority of the related systems grants insight in both historical and current tweet posting behavior. Also, the combination of a heatmap-based representation of the geographic intensity of topics, a tweet volume diagram, and dynamic means to inspect the textual contents of tweets fosters unprecedented deep mining of (the geo-spatial evolution of) Twitter contributions. A final example of a differentiating TweetPos feature is its layering mechanism and the opportunities in terms of comparative analysis it unlocks. Only the iScience Maps tool provides similar functionality, yet its comparison options are limited to exactly two configurations; in contrast, unlimited numbers of layers can be constructed in TweetPos.

6   Conclusions and Future Work

SNSs have become prominent information channels in present-day society, as is manifested by the massive amounts of information that are shared and communicated through them. Given this quantitative overload, human operators benefit from tools that assist in transforming the constituting raw data into practical knowledge. This article has proposed *TweetPos*, a web service that provides exactly such assistive functions for the Twitter network, hereby allocating elevated attention to the geo-spatial characteristics of tweets. As the human mind is very adept at visual pattern recognition and at interpreting graphical data formats, TweetPos maximally invests in visual output modalities. The tool integrates and blends multiple complementary functions in order to yield a holistic solution for Twitter data analysis. Experimental results collected from two isolated test cases confirm this claim and prove the feasibility, effectiveness and added value of our work. In particular, it has been established that the Tweet-Pos service succeeds in streamlining the ingestion, filtering, processing, analysis and mining of tweeted information, and as such represents a valuable, highly versatile tool with cross-disciplinary application options.

Decision making logic, provisions for automated conclusion drawing and autonomous recommendation systems have deliberately been omitted from the current instantiation of the proposed tool, as we believe these tasks are more suited to human operators than to machines. As part of future research, we nonetheless plan to investigate whether the incorporation of computer-mediated aids might assist users in executing these actions more efficiently and swiftly. Potential supportive technologies include visual pattern recognition and edge detection algorithms to facilitate heatmap analysis, and linguistic processing frameworks to aid human operators in categorizing aggregated tweets on the basis of the textual message they convey. Another trajectory of future work is dynamic data delivery. In the current implementation, all tweet data pertaining to a particular query is transferred from the back-end server to the web browser in bulk. Although this design renders the TweetPos service highly responsive once all data has been downloaded, it also causes start-up delays to be high (i.e., they are directly proportional to the data set size). At the same time, network bandwidth utilization is suboptimal, as the client is likely to end up downloading data which the user will never inspect (or at least not in detail). We will therefore implement a demand-oriented transmission scheme in which relevant data is transmitted just-in-time (i.e., when it becomes needed). By doing so, we will be able to investigate the trade-off between service responsiveness and start-up delay, as well as the impact this balance has on the usage experience.

References

1. Sakaki, T., Okazaki, M., Matsuo, Y.: Earthquake shakes Twitter users: real-time event detection by social sensors. In: Proceedings of the WWW 2010, Raleigh, NC, USA, pp. 851–860 (2010)
2. Pinto, N., Majaj, N.J., Barhomi, Y., Solomon, E.A., Cox, D.D., DiCarlo, J.J.: Human versus machine: comparing visual object recognition systems on a level playing field. In: Proceedings of the Cosyne 2010, Salt Lake City, UT, USA (2010)
3. Twitter Developers: using the Twitter search API (2013). https://dev.twitter.com/docs/using-search
4. 140dev: 140dev streaming API framework (2013). http://140dev.com/free-twitter-api-source-code-library/
5. Google Developers: The Google Geocoding API (2013). https://developers.google.com/maps/documentation/geocoding/

6. Google Developers: Google Maps JavaScript API v3 (2013). https://developers. google.com/maps/documentation/javascript/
7. Stefanidis, A., Crooks, A., Radzikowski, J.: Harvesting ambient geospatial information from social media feeds. GeoJournal **78**, 319–338 (2013)
8. Reips, U.D., Garaizar, P.: Mining Twitter: a source for psychological wisdom of the crowds. Behav. Res. Methods **43**, 635–642 (2011)
9. Boettcher, A., Lee, D.: EventRadar: a real-time local event detection scheme using Twitter stream. In: Proceedings of GreenCom 2012, Besançon, France, pp. 358–367 (2012)
10. Crooks, A., Croitoru, A., Stefanidis, A., Radzikowski, J.: #Earthquake: Twitter as a distributed sensor system. Trans. GIS **17**, 124–147 (2013)
11. Takahashi, T., Abe, S., Igata, N.: Can Twitter be an alternative of real-world sensors? In: Jacko, J.A. (ed.) Human-Computer Interaction, Part III, HCII 2011. LNCS, vol. 6763, pp. 240–249. Springer, Heidelberg (2011)
12. Singh, V.K., Gao, M., Jain, R.: Situation detection and control using spatio-temporal analysis of microblogs. In: Proceedings of WWW 2010, Raleigh, NC, USA, pp. 1181–1182 (2010)
13. Field, K., O'Brien, J.: Cartoblography: experiments in using and organising the spatial context of micro-blogging. Trans. GIS **14**, 5–23 (2010)
14. Oussalah, M., Bhat, F., Challis, K., Schnier, T.: A software architecture for twitter collection, search and geolocation services. Knowl.-Based Syst. **37**, 105–120 (2013)

Web Intelligence

The GENIE System: Classifying Documents by Combining Mixed-Techniques

Angel L. Garrido[✉], Maria G. Buey, Sandra Escudero, Alvaro Peiro,
Sergio Ilarri, and Eduardo Mena

IIS Department, University of Zaragoza, Zaragoza, Spain
{garrido,mgbuey,sandra.escudero,peiro,silarri,emena}@unizar.es
http://sid.cps.unizar.es/SEMANTICWEB/GENIE/

Abstract. Today, the automatic text classification is still an open problem and its implementation in companies and organizations with large
volumes of data in text format is not a trivial matter. To achieve optimum results many parameters come into play, such as the language, the
context, the level of knowledge of the issues discussed, the format of the
documents, or the type of language that has been used in the documents
to be classified. In this paper we describe a multi-language rule-based
pipeline system, called GENIE, used for automatic document categorisation. We have used several business corpora in order to test the real
capabilities of our proposal, and we have studied the results of applying
different stages of the pipeline over the same data to test the influence
of each step in the categorization process. The results obtained by this
system are very promising, and in fact, the GENIE system is already
being used on real production environments with very good results.

Keywords: Documents categorization · Text mining · Ontologies · NLP

1 Introduction

In almost any public or private organization that manages a considerable amount
of information, activities related to text categorisation and document tagging can
be found. To do this job, large organizations have documentation departments.
However, the big amount of information in text format that organizations usually
accumulate cannot be properly processed and documented by these departments.
Besides, the manual labour of labeling carried out by these people is subject
to errors due to the subjectivity of the individuals. That is why a tool that
automates categorisation tasks would be very useful, and would help to improve
the quality of searches that are performed later over the data.

To perform these tasks, software based on statistics and the frequency of
use of words can be used, and it is also very common to use machine learning
systems. However, we think that other kinds of tools capable of dealing with
aspects related to Natural Language Processing (NLP) are also necessary to
complement and enhance the results provided by these techniques. Moreover,
to perform any task related to the processing of text documents, it is highly

V. Monfort and K.-H. Krempels (Eds.): WEBIST 2014, LNBIP 226, pp. 231–246, 2015.
DOI: 10.1007/978-3-319-27030-2_15

recommended to own the know-how of the organization, so it is highly advisable to manage ontologies and semantic tools such as reasoners to make knowledge explicit and reason over it, respectively. Furthermore, it is very common for organizations to have their own catalog of labels, known as thesaurus, so it is basic that the system is able to obtain not only keywords from the text, but also know how to relate them to the thesaurus descriptors.

Our purpose is to bring together these techniques into an architecture that enables the automatic classification of texts, with the particular feature that it exploits different semantic methods. Although there are some researches in text categorization that takes into account Spanish texts as examples, there are no tools especially focused on the Spanish language. Moreover, the proposed system has been implemented to be open to allow the possibility to add the analysis of other languages, like English, French, or Portuguese.

Other important characteristics of the architecture is that it has been proposed as a pipeline system and it has been implemented with different modules. We consider these as important features because a pipeline system gives us the chance to control the results at each phase of the process and also the structure with different modules allows us to easily upgrade its individual components. For example, geographic or lexical databases change over time, and our modular architecture easily accommodates these changes. The fact that the system is implemented in different modules is also interesting because it is ideal when performing the analysis of a text. Sometimes, we may want not to have to use all the modules that make up the architecture to achieve a desired result. For example, we may want to extract only statistical information from the words present in a text, but nothing related about their semantics. Also, it is possible that we need to change the order of the modules a text passes through depending on the type of analysis of the text we want to perform. For these reasons it is important to consider a modular architecture: it makes the system easy to use and it facilitates improving it over time.

This paper provides two main contributions: Firstly, we present a tool called GENIE, whose general architecture is valid for text categorisation tasks in any language. This system has been installed and tested in several real environments using different datasets. The set-up of our algorithm is rule-based and we use for inference the document's features as well as the linguistic content of the text and its meaning. Secondly, we experimentally quantify the influence of using linguistic and semantic tools when performing the automatic classification, working on a real case with Spanish texts previously classified by a professional documentation department.

The system has been also used for classifying and labeling documents in different scenarios such as supporting query expansion systems [1] or recommendation algorithms [2]. In both papers we used the GENIE system with very satisfactory results.

The rest of this paper is structured as follows. Section 2 explains the general architecture of the proposed categorisation system. Section 3 discusses the results of our experiments with real data. Section 4 analyzes other related works. Finally, Sect. 5 provides our conclusions and future work.

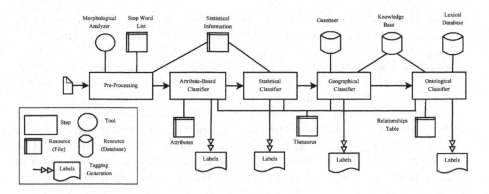

Fig. 1. General pipeline of GENIE, the proposed text categorisation system.

2 Proposed Architecture

In this section, we explain the general architecture of the proposed system as well as and the corresponding working methodology. The system relies on the existence of several resources. First, we will describe these resources, and then we will explain in detail the classification process (see Fig. 1).

2.1 Resources

Regarding resources, we have to consider both static data repositories and software tools:

– *Thesaurus.* A thesaurus is a list of words and a set of relations among them, used to classify items. We use its elements as the set of tags that must be used to categorize the set of documents. Examples of thesaurus entries are words like HEALTH, ACCIDENT, FOOTBALL, BASKETBALL, REALMADRID, CINEMA, JACK_NICHOLSON, THEATER, etc. The terms can be related. For example, FOOTBALL and BASKETBALL could depend hierarchically on SPORTS. Each document may take a variable number of terms in the thesaurus during the categorisation process.
– *Gazetteer.* It is a geographic directory containing information about places and place names [3]. In GENIE, it is used to identify geographic features.
– *Morphological Analyzer.* It is an NLP tool whose mission is the identification, analysis and description of the structure of a set of given linguistic units. This analyzer consists of a set of different analysis libraries, which can be configured and used depending on the working language, and a custom middle-ware architecture which aims to store all the different analysis results in structures that represent the desired linguistic units, such as words, sentences and texts. With this approach we can provide the same entities to the other modules that work with NLP, resulting in an architecture that can work with multiple analysis tools and languages.

- *Lexical Database.* A lexical database is a lexical resource which groups words into sets of synonyms called *synsets*, including semantic relations among them. Examples could be *WordNet* [4] and *EurowordNet* [5].
- *Stop Word List.* This is a list of frequent words that do not contain relevant semantic information. In this set we may include the following types of words: articles, conjunctions, numbers, etc.
- *Knowledge Base.* This refers to the explicit representation of knowledge related to the topics covered in the documents that have to be catalogued. As a tool for knowledge representation in a software system, we use ontologies. The idea is to represent in these ontologies the concepts that could help to label a document in a given context, and to populate the ontologies with as many instances as possible.
- *Statistical Information.* This consists of a set of files with information about the use frequency of each word, related to the attributes of the text and to the set of elements in the thesaurus. For example: the word "ONU" appears more frequently in documents of type "International" and it is related with the descriptor INTERNAT in a thesaurus used in the documentation department of a newspaper we have worked with. These frequencies allow us to estimate if a given text can be categorized with a particular element of the thesaurus.
- *Relationships Table.* This table relates items in the Gazetteer and knowledge base concepts with thesaurus elements. It may be necessary in an organization because the concepts stored in the semantic resources available may not match the labels in the thesaurus that must be considered for classification. The construction of this table could be manual or automatic, using any machine learning method.

As we will show in the experimental evaluation, the use of some resources is optional, leading to different results in terms of the expected performance of the system. This system could be used with different languages by changing the language-dependent resources, i.e. the Gazetteer, the NLP tool, the lexical database, and the stop word list.

2.2   Process Pipeline

We have used a pipeline scheme with separated stages. Each of the stages is associated with only one type of process and they communicate between themselves through different files. Although it is a pipeline system, the process can be configured so that each of the tasks can be activated or deactivated depending on whether we want the text document to go through certain phases or not. This choice has three purposes: Firstly, the early stages perform a more general classification, and later phases make more specific labeling that requires more precise resources. We have verified, through experimental evaluation, that taking advantage of a filter to select the most appropriate resources for the later stages improves the results. Secondly, separating each stage simplifies control for evaluation. We know that there are certain tasks that could be parallelized, but the aim is to analyze the results in the best possible way, rather than to provide an optimized algorithm. Finally, we have more freedom to add, delete or modify any of the stages of the pipeline if they are independent. If we would like to use a different tool in any of the stages, changing it is very easy when there is a minimum coupling between phases.

Our system works over a set of text documents, but we have to note that each of them could have a variable number of attributes (author, title, subtitle, domain, date, section, type, extension, etc.), that we will use during the categorisation process. These attributes vary according to the origin of the document: a digital library, a database, a website, etc. Numeric fields, dates, strings, or even HTML tags may be perfectly valid attributes to the system. As a very first stage, the system includes specific interfaces to convert the original documents into XML files with a specific field for plain text and others for attributes.

The tasks for the proposed automatic text categorisation system are:

1. *Preprocessing* of the text of the document, which consists of three steps:
   (a) *Lemmatization*. Through this process we obtain a new text consisting of a set of words corresponding to the lemmas (canonical forms) of the words in the initial text. This process eliminates prepositions, articles, conjunctions and other words included in the *Stop Words List*. All the word information (Part of Speech, gender, number) is stored in the corresponding structure, so it can be recovered later for future uses.
   (b) *Named Entities Recognition (NER)*. Named entities are atomic elements in a text representing, for example, names of persons, organizations or locations [6]. By using a named entity extractor, this procedure gets a list of items identified as named entities. This extractor can be paired with a statistical Named Entity Classification (NEC) in a first attempt to classify the named entity into a pre-defined group (person, place, organization) or leave it undefined so the following tasks (Geographical Classifier) can disambiguate it.
   (c) *Keywords Extraction*. Keywords are words selected from the text that are in fact key elements to consider to categorize the document. We use the lemmatized form of such words and the TF/IDF algorithm [7].
   These processes produce several results that are used in subsequent stages. The resources used in this stage are the morphological analyzer, the Stop Word List and the statistical data.
2. *Attributes-Based Classifier*. Taking advantage of the attributes of each of the documents, this ruled-based process makes a first basic and general tagging. For example, if we find the words "film review" in the "title" field the system will infer that the thesaurus descriptor CINEMA could be assigned to this document. At the same time, it establishes the values of the attributes to be used for the selection of appropriate resources in the following steps, choosing for instance an ontology about cinema for the Ontological Classifier stage.
3. *Statistical Classifier*. Using machine learning techniques [8], the document text is analyzed to try to find patterns that correspond to data in the files storing statistical information. This step is mainly useful to try to obtain labels that correspond to the general themes of the document. Trying to

deduce if a document is talking about football or basketball could be a good example.

4. *Geographical Classifier.* By using the gazetteer, named entities (NE) corresponding to geographical locations are detected. This stage is managed by a ruled-based system. Besides, it can deal with typical disambiguation problems among locations of the same name and locations whose names match other NE (e.g., people), by using the well-known techniques described in [9]: usually there is only single sense per discourse (so, an ambiguous term is likely to mean only one of its senses when it its used multiple times), and place names appearing in the same context tend to show close locations. Other important considerations that GENIE takes into account are to look at the population of the location candidates as an important aspect to disambiguate places [9] and consider the context where the text is framed to establish a list of bonuses for certain regions [10]. Other used techniques are to construct an N-term window on both sides of the entity considered to be a geographic term, as some words can contribute with a positive or negative modifier [11], or to try to find syntactic structures like "city, country" (e.g. "Madrid, Spain") [12]. Finally, using techniques explained in [13], the system uses ontologies in order to capture information about important aspects related to certain locations. For example: most important streets, monuments and outstanding buildings, neighborhoods, etc. This is useful when a text has not explicit location identified. Besides, it takes advantage too of the results of previous stages. For example, if in the previous stages we got the descriptor EUROPE we can assign higher scores to the results related to European countries and major European cities than to results related to locations in other continents. The geographical tagging unit is very useful because, empirically, near 30 % of tags in our experimental context are related to locations.

5. *Ontological Classifier.* To perform a detailed labeling, the knowledge base is queried about the named entities and keywords found in the text. If a positive response is obtained, it means that the main related concepts can be used to label the text. A great advantage is that these concepts need not appear explicitly in the text, as they may be inferred from existing ontological relations. If there is an ambiguous word, it can be disambiguated [14] by using the Lexical Database resource (for a survey on word sense disambiguation, see [15]). As soon as a concept related to the text is found, the relations stored in the *Relationships Table* are considered to obtain appropriate tags from the thesaurus. As explained before, the fact that at this phase we have a partially classified document allows us to choose the most appropriate ontologies for classification using configurable rules. For example, if we have already realised with the statistical classifier that the text speaks of the American Basketball League, we will use a specific ontology to classify the document more accurately finding out for instance the teams and the players, and we will not try to use any other resource. This particular ontology could be obtained and re-used from the Web. This ontology would probably be hand-made, or it would be adapted from other similar ontology, because this kind of resources are difficult or impossible to find for free on the Web. So,

our system is generic enough to accommodate the required and more appropriate ontologies (existing or hand-made) for the different topics covered in the texts.

The way to obtain the tags is asking about keywords and NE to the ontology by using SPARQL[1], a set of rules, and the relationship table to deduce the most suitable tags. The behaviour of the ontology is not only to be a simple *bag-of-words*, because it can contain concepts, relations and axioms, all of them very useful to inquire the implicit topics in the text.

In summary, the text categorization process that GENIE performs consists of following each of the proposed tasks that constitute the system's pipeline. This process begins with the preprocessing of the input text, which implies labours of lemmatization of the text and extraction of named entities and keywords from the text. Then it analyzes a set of attributes that are given with the text that is being analyzed in order to extract the first basic and general labels. Afterwards, it applies a statistical classification method based on machine learning techniques to obtain labels that correspond to the general themes of the document. Then it applies a geographic classifier for the purpose of identifying possible geographical references included in the text. Finally, it applies an ontological classifier in order to carry out a more detailed classification of the text, which performs an analysis of named entities and keywords obtained from the text, consults the appropriate ontology, and uses a lexical database to remove possible ambiguities.

3 Experimental Evaluation

We have performed a set of experiments to test and compare the performance of our architecture with others tools. For this purpose, we have tested in a real environment using three corpus of news previously labeled by a professional documentation department of several major Spanish Media: *Heraldo de Aragón*[2], *Diario de Navarra*[3] and *Heraldo de Soria*[4]. Each corpus had respectively 11,275, 10,200, and 4,500 news. These corpora are divided in several categories: local, national, international, sports, and culture. Every media has a different professional thesaurus used to classify documents, with more than 10,000 entries each. For classification, each document can receive any number of descriptors belonging to the thesaurus. The ideal situation would be that the automatic text categorization system could perform a work identical to the one performed by the real documentation departments.

These news are stored in several databases, in tables where different fields are used to store the different attributes explained in Sect. 2 (title, author, date, section, type, extension, etc.). For experimental evaluation, we have extracted them from the databases and we have put each text and the data of its fields in

---

[1] http://www.w3.org/TR/2006/WD-rdf-sparql-query-20061004/.
[2] http://www.heraldo.es/.
[3] http://www.diariodenavarra.es/.
[4] http://www.heraldodesoria.es/.

XML files. We have used this corpus of XML files as the input of the system, and the output is the same set of files but with an additional field: classification information. This new XML node contains the set of words (descriptors) belonging to the thesaurus used to categorize the document, i.e., this node contains the different tags that describe the XML file. As the news in the dataset considered had been previously manually annotated by the professionals working in the documentation department, we can compare the automatic categorization with that performed by humans. So, we can evaluate the number of hits, omissions and misses.

3.1   Experimental Settings

In the experiments, we have examined the following measures, commonly used in the Information Retrieval context: the *precision*, the *recall*, and the *F-Measure*. The dataset used initially in the experiments has been the Heraldo de Aragón corpus. We have used the information from this dataset to define most of the rules of the various processes associated with each of the stages of the classification system. These rules are integrated in a configuration file which contains all the information necessary to lead the process and obtain the correct result. The other two datasets (Diario de Navarra and Heraldo de Soria) have been used just to double-check if the application of those rules also produced the desired result; for comparison purposes, at the end of this section we will also present some experimental results based on them.

We have performed four experiments with the GENIE system. Each stage of the pipeline can be enabled or disabled separately. Regarding the resources and tools considered, we have used Freeling[5], as the Morphological Analyzer and Support Vector Machines (SVM) [16] to automatically classify topics in the Statistical Classifier. To obtain the frequencies we have used a different corpus of 100,000 news, in order to get a realistic frequency information. Finally, we have chosen Eurowordnet as the Lexical Database and *Geonames*[6] as the Gazetteer.

To train this Statistical Classifier we have used sets of 5,000 news for each general theme associated to one descriptor (FOOTBALL, BASKET, CINEMA, HANDBALL, and MUSIC). These sets of news are different from the datasets used in the experiments (as is obviously expected in a training phase). For each possible descriptor, we have an ontology, in this case we have designed five ontologies using OWL [17] with near a hundred concepts each one.

Next, there is an example of a piece of news:

"This weekend is the best film debut for the movie "In the Valley of Elah". The story revolves around the murder of a young man who has just returned from the Iraq war, whose parents try to clarify with the help of the police. As interpreters we have: Tommy Lee Jones, Susan Sarandon and Charlize Theron. Writer-director Paul Haggis is the author of "Crash" and writer of "Million Dollar Baby", among others."

---

[5] http://nlp.lsi.upc.edu/freeling/.
[6] http://www.geonames.org/.

In this case, the system analyzes and classifies the text with the descriptor CINEMA. Moreover, the news can be tagged with tags such as C_THERON, IRAQ, TL_JONES, etc.

3.2 Experimental Results

We have compared our classification of the 11,275 news in the first dataset with the original classification made by professionals. The results can be seen in Fig. 2. Below we analyze the experiments:

1. In the first experiment (*Basic*) we have used the process presented in Sect. 2 without the Pre-Processing step and without the Ontological Classifier. We have trained the system with SVM to classify 100 themes. In this case, as we do not use the steps of Pre-Processing and the Ontological Classifier, the system has not performed the lemmatization, the named entities recognition, the keywords extraction, and the detailed labeling of the text. For this reason, the precision and the recall are not good, as it is essential to embed semantic information and conceptual patterns in order to enhance the prediction capabilities of classification algorithms.
2. In the second one (*Semantic*), we have introduced the complete Pre-Processing stage and its associated resources, we have used the Lexical Database EuroWordNet [5] to disambiguate keywords, and we have introduced the Ontological Classifier, with five ontologies with about ten concepts and about 20 instances each. In this experiment the precision and the recall slightly improved because, as explained before, the step of Pre-Processing is important to obtain a better classification.
3. In the third one (*Sem + Geo*) we have included the Geographical Classifier but we have used only the Gazzetteer resource. Here we have improved the recall of the labeling but in exchange of a decrease in the precision. By analyzing the errors in detail, we observe that the main cause is the presence of misclassifications performed by the Geographical Classifier.
4. Finally, in the fourth experiment (*Full Mode*), we have executed all the pipeline, exploited all the resources and populated the ontologies with about one hundred instances, leading to an increase in both the precision and the recall. Ontology instances added in this experiment have been inferred from the observation of the errors obtained in previous experiments. The motivation to add them is that otherwise the text includes certain entities unknown to the system, and when they were incorporated this helped to improve the classification.

If we look at the overall results obtained in the experiment 1 and the experiment 2 in the Fig. 2, we could say that the influence of using semantic and NLP tools is apparently not so significant (about 20 %). However, it seems clear that these tools significantly improve the quality of labeling in terms of precision, recall and F-measure, reaching up to about the 80 %. Therefore, the use of semantic techniques can make a difference when deciding about the possibility to perform an automatic labeling.

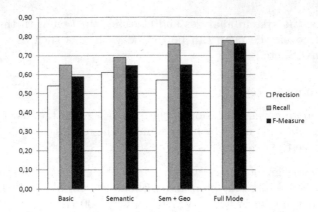

Fig. 2. Results of the four document categorisation experiments with news in the dataset 1.

After evaluating the results obtained in the reference dataset (Heraldo de Aragón), we repeated the same experiments with the two other datasets. These dataset were not considered while designing the ontologies, in order to maintain the independence of the tests. The results can be seen in Fig. 3. The results obtained with datasets different from the one used for Heraldo de Aragón, which was used to configure the rule-based system, are only slightly different (differences smaller than 10 %). In Fig. 3, it can also be seen that the trends of the results are very similar regardless of the data. This shows the generality of our approach, since the behaviour of the classification system has been reproduced with several different corpora. Experimental results have shown that with our approach, in all the experiments, the system has improved the results achieved by basic machine learning based systems.

4   Related Work

Text categorisation represents a challenging problem for the data mining and machine learning communities, due to the growing demand for automatic information retrieval systems. Systems that automatically classify text documents into predefined thematic classes, and thereby contextualize information, offer a promising approach to tackle this complexity [8].

Document classification presents difficult challenges due to the sparsity and the high dimensionality of text data, and to the complex semantics of natural language. The traditional document representation is a word-based vector where each dimension is associated with a term of a dictionary containing all the words that appear in the corpus. The value associated to a given term reflects its frequency of occurrence within the corresponding document and within the entire corpus (the *tf-idf* metric). Although this is a representation that is simple and commonly used, it has several limitations. Specifically, this technique has three main drawbacks: (1) it breaks multi-word expressions into independent features; (2) it maps synonymous words into different components; and (3) it considers

RECALL

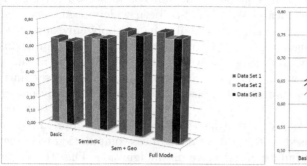 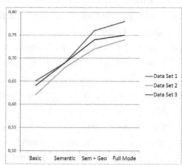

PRECISION

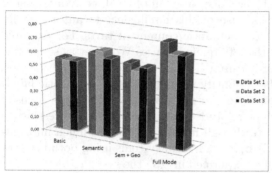 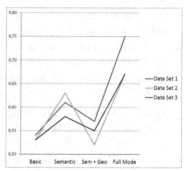

F-MEASURE

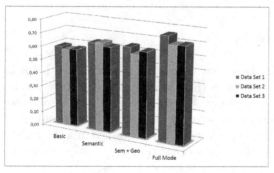 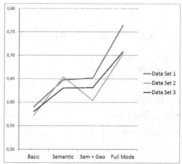

Fig. 3. Comparative results of the automatic categorisation experiments.

polysemous words as one single component. While a traditional preprocessing of documents, such as eliminating stop words, pruning rare words, stemming, and normalization, can improve the representation, its effect is also still limited. So, it is essential to embed semantic information and conceptual patterns in order to enhance the prediction capabilities of classification algorithms.

Research has been done to exploit ontologies for content-based categorisation of large corpora of documents. WordNet has been widely used, but their approaches only use synonyms and hyponyms, fail to handle polysemy, and break multi-word concepts into single terms. Our approach overcomes these limitations by incorporating background knowledge derived from ontologies. This methodology is able to keep multi-word concepts unbroken, it captures the semantic closeness to synonyms, and performs word sense disambiguation for polysemous terms.

For disambiguation tasks we have taken into account an approximation described in [18], that is based on a semantic relatedness computation to detect the set of words that could induce an effective disambiguation. That technique receives an ambiguous keyword and its context words as input and provides a list of possible senses. Other studies show how background knowledge in form of simple ontologies can improve text classification results by directly addressing these problems [19], and others make use of this intelligence to automatically generate tag suggestions based on the semantic content of texts. For example [20], which extracts keywords and their frequencies, uses WordNet as semantics and an artificial neural network for learning.

Among other related studies that quantify the quality of an automatic labeling performed by using ontologies, we could mention [21], but it was focused on a purely semantic labeling. More related to our study, it is interesting to mention the work presented in [22], although it does not include much information about the use of ontologies. Examples of hybrid systems using both types of tools include the web service classifier explained in [23], the system *NASS (News Annotation Semantic System)* described in [24,25], which is an automatic annotation tool for the Media, or *GoNTogle* [26], which is a framework for general document annotation and retrieval.

5   Conclusions and Future Work

A tool for automating categorisation tasks is very useful nowadays, as it helps to improve the quality of searches that are performed later over textual repositories like digital libraries, databases or web pages. For this reason, in this paper we have presented a pipeline architecture to help in the study of the problem of automatic text categorisation using specific vocabulary contained in a thesaurus. Our main contribution is the design of a system that combines statistics, lexical databases, NLP tools, ontologies, and geographical databases. Its stage-based architecture easily allows the use and exchange of different resources and tools. We have also performed a deep study of the impact of the semantics in a text categorisation process.

Our pipeline architecture is based on five stages: preprocessing, attribute-based classification, statistical classification, geographical classification, and ontological classification. Although the experimental part has been developed in Spanish, the tool is ready to work with any other language. Changing linguistic resources suitable for the intended language is enough to make the system work, since the process is sufficiently general to be applicable regardless of the language used. The main contribution of our work is, apart from the useful and modular pipeline architecture, the experimental study with real data of the problem of categorization of natural language documents written in Spanish. There are many studies related to such problems in English, but it is difficult to find them in Spanish. Besides, we have compared the impact of applying techniques that rely on statistics and supervised learning with the results obtained when semantic techniques are also used. There are two remarkable aspects. Firstly, enhancing the amount of knowledge available by increasing the number of instances in the ontologies leads to a substantial improvement in the results. Secondly, the use of knowledge bases helps to correct many errors from a Geographical Classifier.

Spanish vs. English language. Our research on this topic focuses on transfer projects related to the extraction of information, so for us it is very important to work with real cases. Therefore, the comparison of our work with typical benchmark data sets in English is not fundamental to us, since they are not useful to improve the performance of our system in Spanish, and we have seen that the ambient conditions (language, regional context, thematic news, etc.) have a great influence on the outcome of experiments. Many researchers have already analyzed the differences between working in NLP topics in English and in Spanish, and they have made it clear the additional difficulties of the Spanish Language [27,28], which could explain the poor performance of some software applications that work reasonably well in English. Just to mention some of these differences: in Spanish words contain much more grammatical and semantic information than the English words, the subject can be omitted in many cases, and verbs forms carry implicit conjugation, without additional words. That, coupled with the high number of meanings that the same word can have, increases the computational complexity for syntactic, semantic and morphological analyzers, which so behave differently in Spanish and English. Spanish is the third language in the world according to the number of speakers, after Mandarin and English, but in terms of studies related to NLP we have not found many scientific papers.

Impact of NLP and semantics. Our experimental evaluation suggests that the influence of NLP and semantic tools is not quantitatively as important as the classic statistical approaches, although their contribution can tip the scales when evaluating the quality of a labeling technique, since the difference in terms of precision and recall is sufficiently influential (near 20 %). So, our conclusion is that a statistical approach can be successfully complemented with semantic techniques to obtain an acceptable automatic categorisation. Our experience also proves that facing this issue in a real environment when professional results are needed, the typical machine learning approach is the best option but is not always enough. We have seen that it should be complemented with other techniques, in our case semantic and linguistic ones. Anyway, the main drawback of the semantic techniques is that the work of searching or constructing the ontologies for each set of tags of every topic, populating them, and building the relationship tables, is harder than the typical training of the machine learning approaches. So, although the results are better, the scalability could be problematic. Sometimes it can be quite costly, especially if detailed knowledge of the topic to tag is required in order to appropriately configure the system.

NLP future tasks. In some categorisation scenarios, like bigger analysis (novels, reports, etc.) or groups of documents of the same field, it can be interesting to obtain a summary of the given inputs in order to categorise them with their general terms before entering a more detailed analysis which requires the entire texts. These summaries, alongside with the previous defined tasks, can led to a more suitable detailed labeling, providing hints of which knowledge bases might be interesting to work with. In order to achieve this, we can perform syntactic analysis to simplify the sentences of the summaries, as we have seen in works like [29], and then we will use the obtained results to filter unnecessary information and select the most relevant sentences without compromising the text integrity. Although the required structures have been implemented and some approaches as [30] are being designed and tested, they are into an early stage and they require more work before trying to use it inside the categorisation pipeline.

Open tasks. As future work, we plan to increase the number of methods used in the pipeline, and to test this methodology in new contexts and languages. It is noteworthy that a piece of news is a very specific type of text, characterized by objectivity, clarity, and the use of synonyms and acronyms, the high presence of specific and descriptive adjectives, the tendency to use impersonal or passive constructions, and the use of connectors. Therefore it is not sufficient to test only with this kind of text, and to make a more complete study it is necessary to work with other types. In fact, some tests have been made with GENIE with other types of documents very different from news, such as book reviews, business reports, lyrics, blogs, etc., and the results are very promising, but it is early to assert the generality of the solution in different contexts because the studies are still in progress.

Acknowledgements. This research work has been supported by the CICYT project TIN2013-46238-C4-4-R and DGA-FSE. Thank you to Heraldo Group and Diario de Navarra.

References

1. Buey, M.G., Garrido, A.L., Escudero, S., Trillo, R., Ilarri, S., Mena, E.: SQX-Lib: developing a semantic query expansion system in a media group. In: European Conference on Information Retrieval, 780–784 (2014)
2. Garrido, A.L., Pera, M.S., Ilarri, S.: SOLE-R, a semantic and linguistic aproach for book recommendations. In: 14th IEEE International Conference on Advanced Learning Technologies - ICALT, pp. 524–528. IEEE Computer Society (2014)
3. Goodchild, M.F., Hill, L.: Introduction to digital gazetteer research. Int. J. Geogr. Inf. Sci. **22**, 1039–1044 (2008)
4. Miller, G.A.: WordNet: a lexical database for English. Commun. ACM **38**, 39–41 (1995)

5. Vossen, P.: EuroWordNet: a Multilingual Database with Lexical Semantic Networks. Kluwer Academic, Boston (1998)
6. Sekine, S., Ranchhod, E.: Named Entities: Recognition, Classification and Use. John Benjamins, Amsterdam (2009)
7. Salton, G., Buckley, C.: Term-weighting approaches in automatic text retrieval. Inf. Process. Manage. **24**, 513–523 (1988)
8. Sebastiani, F.: Machine learning in automated text categorization. ACM Comput. Surv. **34**, 1–47 (2002)
9. Amitay, E., Har'El, N., Sivan, R., Soffer, A.: Web-a-where: geotagging web content. In: 27th Annual International ACM SIGIR Conference on Research and Development in Information Retrieval, pp. 273–280. ACM (2004)
10. Quercini, G., Samet, H., Sankaranarayanan, J., Lieberman, M.D.: Determining the spatial reader scopes of news sources using local lexicons. In: Proceedings of the 18th SIGSPATIAL International Conference on Advances in Geographic Information Systems, pp. 43–52. ACM (2010)
11. Rauch, E., Bukatin, M., Baker, K.: A confidence-based framework for disambiguating geographic terms. In: HLT-NAACL 2003 Workshop on Analysis of Geographic References, vol. 1, pp. 50–54. Association for Computational Linguistics (2003)
12. Li, H., Srihari, R.K., Niu, C., Li, W.: Location normalization for information extraction. In: Proceedings of the 19th International Conference on Computational Linguistics, vol. 1, pp. 1–7. Association for Computational Linguistics (2002)
13. Garrido, A.L., Buey, M.G., Ilarri, S., Mena, E.: GEO-NASS: a semantic tagging experience from geographical data on the media. In: Catania, B., Guerrini, G., Pokorný, J. (eds.) ADBIS 2013. LNCS, vol. 8133, pp. 56–69. Springer, Heidelberg (2013)
14. Resnik, P.: Disambiguating noun groupings with respect to WordNet senses. In: Armstrong, S., Church, K., Isabelle, P., Manzi, S., Tzoukermann, E., Yarowsky, D. (eds.) Natural Language Processing Using Very Large Corpora, pp. 77–98. Springer, Berlin (1999)
15. Navigli, R.: Word sense disambiguation: a survey. ACM Comput. Surv. **41**, 10:1–10:69 (2009)
16. Joachims, T.: Text categorization with support vector machines: learning with many relevant. In: Nédellec, C., Rouveirol, C. (eds.) ECML 1998. LNCS, vol. 1398, pp. 137–142. Springer, Heidelberg (1998)
17. McGuinness, D.L., Van Harmelen, F., et al.: OWL web ontology language overview. W3C recommendation, 10 February 2004
18. Trillo, R., Gracia, J., Espinoza, M., Mena, E.: Discovering the semantics of user keywords. J. Univers. Comput. Sci. **13**, 1908–1935 (2007)
19. Bloehdorn, S., Hotho, A.: Boosting for text classification with semantic features. In: Mobasher, B., Nasraoui, O., Liu, B., Masand, B. (eds.) WebKDD 2004. LNCS (LNAI), vol. 3932, pp. 149–166. Springer, Heidelberg (2006)
20. Lee, S.O.K., Chun, A.H.W.: Automatic tag recommendation for the web 2.0 blogosphere using collaborative tagging and hybrid and semantic structures. In: Sixth Conference on WSEAS International Conference on Applied Computer Science (ACOS 2007), vol. 7, pp. 88–93. World Scientific and Engineering Academy and Society (WSEAS) (2007)
21. Maynard, D., Peters, W., Li, Y.: Metrics for evaluation of ontology-based information extraction. In: Workshop on Evaluation of Ontologies for the Web (EON) at the International World Wide Web Conference (WWW 2006) (2006)
22. Scharkow, M.: Thematic content analysis using supervised machine learning: an empirical evaluation using German online news. Qual. Quant. **47**, 761–773 (2013)

23. Bruno, M., Canfora, G., Di Penta, M., Scognamiglio, R.: An approach to support web service classification and annotation. In: 2005 IEEE International Conference on e-Technology, e-Commerce and e-Service (EEE 2005), pp. 138–143. IEEE (2005)
24. Garrido, A.L., Gomez, O., Ilarri, S., Mena, E.: NASS: news annotation semantic system. In: 23rd IEEE International Conference on Tools with Artificial Intelligence (ICTAI 2011), pp. 904–905. IEEE Computer Society, Boca Raton, Florida (USA) (2011)
25. Garrido, A.L., Gómez, O., Ilarri, S., Mena, E.: An experience developing a semantic annotation system in a media group. In: Bouma, G., Ittoo, A., Métais, E., Wortmann, H. (eds.) NLDB 2012. LNCS, vol. 7337, pp. 333–338. Springer, Heidelberg (2012)
26. Bikakis, N., Giannopoulos, G., Dalamagas, T., Sellis, T.: Integrating keywords and semantics on document annotation and search. In: Meersman, R., Dillon, T., Herrero, P. (eds.) OTM 2010. LNCS, vol. 6427, pp. 921–938. Springer, Heidelberg (2010)
27. Carrasco, R., Gelbukh, A.: Evaluation of TnT tagger for Spanish. In: Proceedings of ENC, Fourth Mexican International Conference on Computer Science, pp. 18–25. IEEE (2003)
28. Aguado de Cea, G., Puch, J., Ramos, J.: Tagging Spanish texts: the problem of 'se'. In: Sixth International Conference on Language Resources and Evaluation (LREC 2008), pp. 2321–2324 (2008)
29. Silveira, S.B., Branco, A.: Extracting multi-document summaries with a double clustering approach. In: Bouma, G., Ittoo, A., Métais, E., Wortmann, H. (eds.) NLDB 2012. LNCS, vol. 7337, pp. 70–81. Springer, Heidelberg (2012)
30. Garrido, A.L., Buey, M.G., Escudero, S., Ilarri, S., Mena, E., Silveira, S.B.: TMgen: a topic map generator from text documents. In: 25th IEEE International Conference on Tools with Artificial Intelligence (ICTAI 2013), pp. 735–740. IEEE Computer Society, Washington DC (USA) (2013)

Comparing LDA and LSA Topic Models for Content-Based Movie Recommendation Systems

Sonia Bergamaschi and Laura Po[✉]

Department of Engineering "Enzo Ferrari", University of Modena
and Reggio Emilia, 41125 Modena, Italy
{sonia.bergamaschi,laura.po}@unimore.it
http://www.dbgroup.unimo.it

Abstract. We propose a plot-based recommendation system, which is based upon an evaluation of similarity between the plot of a video that was watched by a user and a large amount of plots stored in a movie database. Our system is independent from the number of user ratings, thus it is able to propose famous and beloved movies as well as old or unheard movies/programs that are still strongly related to the content of the video the user has watched. The system implements and compares the two Topic Models, Latent Semantic Allocation (LSA) and Latent Dirichlet Allocation (LDA), on a movie database of two hundred thousand plots that has been constructed by integrating different movie databases in a local NoSQL (MongoDB) DBMS. The topic models behaviour has been examined on the basis of standard metrics and user evaluations, performance assessments with 30 users to compare our tool with a commercial system have been conducted.

Keywords: Movie recommendation · LDA · LSA · Recommendation systems

1 Introduction

A recommendation system helps users to make choices without sufficient personal experience of all the possible alternatives [1]. These system are the basis of the targeted advertisements that account for most commercial sites revenues. They are commonly used on several fields, for suggesting entertainment items like books, music, videos and also for finding people on dating sites. Recommendation systems have become relatively successful at suggesting content, however their performance greatly suffers when little information about the user's preferences is given. These situations are not rare; they usually occur when the users are new to a system, the first time a system is launched on the market (no previous users have been logged), for new items (where we do not have any history on preferences yet) and when, because of user desire for privacy, the system does

© Springer International Publishing Switzerland 2015
V. Monfort and K.-H. Krempels (Eds.): WEBIST 2014, LNBIP 226, pp. 247–263, 2015.
DOI: 10.1007/978-3-319-27030-2_16

not record their preferences [2]. In such cases, making suggestions entirely based on the content that is being recommended can be a good solution.

In recent years, some events catalized the attention on movie recommendation systems: on 2009 and 2013 Netflix announced two developer contests for improving their predictions promising conspicuous prizes; on 2010 and 2011 two editions of the International Challenges on Context-Aware Movie Recommendation[1] took place.

The focus of our paper is to provide an automatic movie recommendation system that does not need any a priori information about users, i.e. a *completely non-intrusive system*. The paper compares two specific techniques (LDA and LSA) that have been implemented in our content-based recommendation system. Although topic models are not new in the area of recommendation systems, their use has not been deeper analyzed in a specific domain, such as the movie domain. Our intention is to show how these well-known techniques can be applied in this domain and how they perform.

The context where our system works is that of video-on-demand (VOD). Generally speaking, this is the case when a user is looking for an item without being registered on the site in which he is looking for (searching a book on Amazoon, a movie on IMDb etc.). We assumed that the only information we have about the user is his first choice, i.e. the movie he has selected/ he is watching. We do not have an history about his past selections nor a profile about his general interests. When watching a VOD movie, users explicitly request to buy and to pay for that movie, then what our system attempt to do is proposing a list of similar movies assuming that the chosen film has been appreciated by the user (the system assumes the user liked the movie if his play time is more then 3/4 of the movie play time). Here, we also assume that we have no knowledge about the preferences of a user; namely, about who is watching the film, and also profile about other users who have previously accessed the system.

There are dozens of movie recommendation engines on the web. Some require little or no input before they give you movie titles, while others want to find out exactly what your interests are. However all of these systems rely on ratings directly or indirectly expressed by the users of the system (some examples are *Netflix, Rotten Tomatoes, Movielens, IMDb, Jinni*).

Our movie recommendation system permits, given a movie, to supply the user with a list of those movies that are most similar to the target one. The way the system detects the list of similar movies is based upon an evaluation of similarity among the plot of the target movie and a large amount of plots stored in a movie database. This paper is an extended version of our previous work [3] and its main additions are the extended description of LSA and LDA models and an in-depth comparison of the use of LSA in contrast with LDA.

The paper is structured as follows. Section 2 describes the structure of the local movie database. Section 3 describes hoe the system performs the similarity computations among movie plots by using the LDA and LSA Topic Models. The experimental results of this study are presented in Sect. 4: we show the

---

[1] http://2011.camrachallenge.com/.

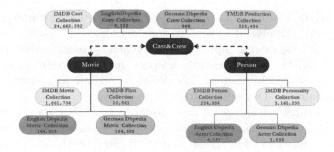

Fig. 1. The local MongoDB database.

computational costs of building the LSA and LDA matrices, and the results of off-line tests performed on three recommendation systems (LSA, LDA and a commercial approach). Section 5 presents some related work. Conclusion and future work are depicted in Sect. 6.

2   The Movie Database

The principal aim of a local repository of movies is to supply an extensive and reliable representation of multimedia that can be queried in a reasonable time. The local database of our system has been defined, as in [4], by importing data from external repositories. In particular, we selected the Internet Movie Database (IMDb)[2], DBpedia[3] and the Open Movie Database (TMDb)[4]. Since local database needs to easily import data from different sources and perform queries on a huge amount of data (thousands of movies) in a short time, we chose MongoDB[5], a non relational and schema-free database. MongoDB features allow to create databases with flexible and simple structure without decreasing the time performance when they are queried.

Information about movies can be classified in either information that are related to multimedia or information that are about people that participated in the production of multimedia. This led to the creation of three main databases, each storing collections from the 4 sources (as shown in Fig. 1). As MongoDB do not enforce document structure, this flexibility allows an easy adaptation to integrate different/new datasets into the system. A single collection can store documents with different fields. Thus there cannot really be a description of a collection, like the description of a table in the relational databases. An example of how these documents are organized within the database is shown in [3].

3   Plot Similarity Computation

The similarity of two media items depends on their features likeness. Hence, for each feature, a specific metric is defined in order to compute a similarity

---

[2] http://www.imdb.com/.

[3] http://dbpedia.org/.

[4] http://www.themoviedb.org/.

[5] http://www.mongodb.org/.

score. Most of the metrics that are adopted are calculated through only few simple operations. However, if we want to consider also movie plots, the similarity computation becomes more complex. Our approach is based on the Vector Space Model (VSM) [5], this model creates a space in which both documents and queries are represented by vectors. The VSM behaviour has also been studied applied on recommendation systems [6].

Our system takes advantage of this model to represent the different movie plots: each plot (or document from now on) is represented as a vector of keywords with associated weights. These weights depend on the distribution of the keywords in the given training set of plots that are stored in the database. Vectors representing plots are then joined in a matrix representation where each row corresponds to a plot and each column corresponds to a keyword extracted from the training set plots (i.e. the *document by keyword matrix*). Thus, each cell of the matrix represents the weight of a specific keyword according to a specific plot.

The matrix computation goes through four main steps:

1. *Plot Vectorization* - relevant keywords are extracted and then stop words removal and lemmatization techniques are applied;
2. *Weights Computation* - weights are defined as the occurrences of keywords in the plots; the initial weights are then modified by using the tf-idf technique [5] (but other suitable weighting techniques could be used as well), thus building the *document by keyword matrix*;
3. *Matrix Reduction by using Topic Models* - the *document by keyword matrix* is reduced to a lower dimensional space by using the Topic Models LDA and LSA, thus it is transformed into a *document by topic matrix*.
4. *Movie Similarity Computation* - starting from the *document by topic matrix*, the similarity between two plots is computed by considering their topics as features instead of words.

3.1 Plot Vectorization

If two plots are to be compared, they will need to be converted into vectors of keywords. As preliminary operations, keyword extraction and filtering activity are performed. Keywords correspond to terms within the document that are representative of the document itself and that, at the same time, are discriminating. Less discriminative words, the so called *stop words*, are discarded, while the other terms are preprocessed and substituted in the vector by their lemmas (*lemmatization*). Lemmatization and keyword extraction are performed by using *TreeTagger*[6], developed at the Institute for Computational Linguistics of the University of Stuttgart. This tool can annotate documents with part-of-speech and lemma information in both English and German language. Keywords extracted from plots as well as their local frequencies (occurrences in the description of the plot) are stored as features of the media item in the local database

---

[6] http://www.cis.uni-muenchen.de/~schmid/tools/TreeTagger/.

MongoDB. This choice has been made for two main reasons. First, the keyword extraction process is relatively slow[7] compared to the access to database values. Since the weighting techniques are based on the global distribution of the keywords over the whole corpus of plots, it is necessary to generate all the vectors before applying the weighting technique. Second, while weights change when new multimedia plots are added into the system, the local keyword occurrences do not.

3.2 Weights Computation

Weighting techniques are used for computing keyword weights. A weight is a value in the range $[0, 1]$ that represents the relevance of a specific keyword according to a specific document. A weight is calculated on the basis of the local distribution of the keyword within the document as well as on the global distribution of the keyword in the whole corpus of plots. Keywords with a document frequency equal to 1 are discarded. Since, our previous work [4] has compared *tf-idf* and *log* weighting techniques revealing that the results are very similar, in this paper we employ only the tf-idf technique for computing the weights.

3.3 Matrix Reduction by Using Topic Model

The Vector Space Model treats keywords as independent entities. To find documents on specific concepts, we must provide the correct key terms. This representation leads to several issues: (1) there can be an high number of keywords when we have to deal with a huge amount of documents; (2) if any keyword changed, the document would not convey the same concept.

These problems can be faced by a representation into a Topic Model [7]. The Topic Model explores the idea that the concept held by a set of terms can be represented as a weighted distribution over a set of topics. Each topic is a linear combination of terms, where to each term a weight reflecting the relevance of the term for that topic is associated. For example, high weights for *family* and *house* would suggest that a topic refers to a social unit living together, whereas high weights for *users* and *communication* would suggest that a topic refers to social networking.

Topics can be found by clustering the set of keywords. The use of topics drastically reduces the dimension of the keyword Matrix obtained by Vector Space Model. Moreover, if a keyword changes, the document conveys the same idea as long as the new keyword is taken from the same topic pool.

Topic vectors may be useful in the context of movie recommendation systems for three main reasons: (1) the number of topics that is equal to the number of non-zero eigenvectors is usually significantly lower than the number of keywords, the topic representation of the plots is more compact[8]; (2) the topic representation of the keywords makes possible to add movies that have been released after

---

[7] One database access, using MongoDB, takes about 0.3 ms while the extraction of keywords from a plot takes more than one second.

[8] Thus, we store the matrix of document-topic vectors to represent the training set.

LSA

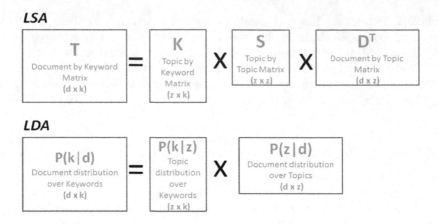

Fig. 2. Matrix decomposition for LSA and LDA.

the definition of the matrix without recomputing it; (3) to find similar movies starting from a given one, we just need to compute the topic vectors for the plot of the movie and then compare these vectors with the ones we have stored in the matrix finding the top relevant.

In the following, we describe the LSA and LDA models and how they can be applied to our movie recommendation system.

Latent Semantic Analysis (LSA). LSA is a model for extracting and representing the contextual-usage meaning of words by statistical computations applied to a large corpus of documents. The LSA consists of a *Singular Value Decomposition* (SVD) of the matrix T (Training set matrix) followed by a *Rank lowering* [8]. The SVD consists of representing the matrix T as the product of three matrices (see also the top of Fig. 2):

$$T = KSD^T$$

Where K and D are orthogonal matrices and S is a diagonal matrix. The original matrix T is the *document by keyword matrix* as it represents the relationships between keywords and plots. Matrix K, *the topic by keyword matrix*, represents the relationships between keywords and topics. Matrix S is a diagonal matrix. Its values represent the square roots of the so called eigenvalues of the matrix TT^T. Matrix D^T, *document by topic matrix*, represents the relationships between plots and topics.

The SVD of the matrix is consequently followed by a *Rank lowering* by which the transformation of the matrix S into a matrix S' is performed which set the lowest values of S to zero. The purpose of dimensionality reduction is to reduce *noise* in the latent space, resulting in a richer word relationship structure that reveals latent semantics present in the collection. The T, S and D matrices are truncated to z dimensions (i.e. topics). The transformed *document by keyword matrix T'* is then obtained by the following product:

$$T' = KS'D^T$$

Each row and column of the matrix T' can be represented as a vector combination of the eigenvectors of the matrix $T'T'^T$

$$v = \sum_i c_i \cdot vector_i$$

Where the coefficients c_i of the above formula represent how strong the relationship between a keyword (or a description) and a topic $eigenvector_i$ is. The eigenvectors define the so-called *topic space*, thus, the coefficients related to a vector v represent a *topic vector*.

Queries are represented in the reduced space by $T_z^T q$, where T_z^T is the transpose of the term by topics matrix, after truncation to z topics. Queries are compared to the reduced document vectors, scaled by the singular values $(S_z D_z)$ by computing the cosine similarity. The optimal z is determined empirically for each collection. In general, smaller z values are preferred when using LSA, due to the computational cost associated with the SVD algorithm, as well as the cost of storing and comparing large dimension vectors[9].

Latent Dirichlet Allocation (LDA). LSA provides a simple and efficient procedure for extracting a topic representation of the associations between terms from a term-document co-occurrence matrix. However, as shown in [9], this representation makes it difficult for LSA do deal with the polysemous terms. The key issue is that its representation does not explicitly identify the different senses of a term. To address this problem we investigated the use of the LDA Topic Model. LDA is a generative model for document collections that has been already successfully applied in several areas: document modeling and classification, Word Sense Disambiguation, Information Retrieval etc. [9–11].

Unlike LSA, LDA is a probabilistic Topic Model, where the goal is to decompose a conditional *term by the document probability distribution* $p(t|d)$ into two different distributions, *the term by topic distribution* $p(t|z)$, and *the topic by document distribution* $p(z|d)$ as follow (see also the bottom of Fig. 2):

$$p(k|d) = \sum_z p(k|z)p(z|d)$$

this allows each semantic topic z to be represented as a multinominal distribution of terms $p(k|z)$, and each document d to be represented as a multinominal distribution of semantic topics $p(z|d)$. The model introduces a conditional independence assumption that document d and keyword k are independent conditioned on the hidden variable, topic z.

In [9] it has been shown that LDA outperforms LSA, in the representation of ambiguous words and in a variety of other linguistic processing and memory tasks.

---

[9] In [4] work we determined 500 as a good number of topic. This value allows to have reasonable computational costs, and to maintain an appropriate level of accuracy.

LDA can be interpreted as matrix factorization where document over keyword probability distribution $p(k|d)$ can be split into two different distributions: the topic over keyword distribution $p(k|z)$, and the document over topic distribution $p(z|d)$. Thus, it appears clear, that we can easily make a direct correspondence between the document by topic matrix D^T obtained from LSA and the document over topic distribution $p(z|d)$ obtained by using LDA.

Both LDA and LSA permit to find a low dimensional representation for a set of documents w.r.t. the simple term by document matrix. This dimensionality in both cases has to be decided a priori. By adopting LSA, we were able to represent each plot of the IMDb database with 500 topics, instead of 220000 keywords[10]. For LDA (which has been demonstrated working well for a number of topics over 50 [10]), after a few experimental evaluations, we decided to use 50 topics.

3.4   Movie Similarity Computation

As previously described by using LSA or LDA the *document by keyword matrix* is decomposed into several matrices. The *document by topic matrix* (D^T or $P(z|d)$) is the one that is used to represent the movie of our database in a lower dimensional space, i.e. the matrix that is used to compute the similarity score between two plots.

The cosine similarity is used as a distance metric to calculate the similarity score between two documents. It is used to either compare plots within the training set or plots that are not included in the training set.

Definition - cosine similarity: *Given two vectors v_i, and v_j, that represent two different plots, the cosine angle between them can be calculated as follows:*

$$cosin(v_i, v_j) = \frac{\sum_k \left(v_i[k] \cdot v_j[k] \right)}{\sqrt{\sum_k v_i[k]^2} \cdot \sqrt{\sum_k v_j[k]^2}}$$

The value of the cosine angle is a real number in the range $[-1, 1]$. If the cosine is equal to 1 the two vectors are equivalent, whereas if it is -1 the two vectors are opposite.

The similarity of plots can also be combined with the similarity of other features such as directors, genre, producers, release year, cast etc. as proposed in [4].

4   Experiments

We performed several tests in order to evaluate our system, the goal was to compare the effectiveness of LDA and LSA techniques and to evaluate the performance of the system on real users.

In [4] we have demonstrated that:

---

[10] Several experiments where conducted on a subset of the test set.

- There is not a big difference in the results obtained by applying log or tf-idf weighting techniques. Thus, we can use one of them.
- The use of the LSA model shows a noticeable quality improvement compared to the use of the SVD model. LSA allows to select plots that are better related to the target's plot themes.

Starting from these results, we conducted new tests and evaluations of the system. First of all, we loaded data from IMDb into the local database MongoDB and evaluated the computational costs of building the LSA and LDA matrices. Then, we compared the two Topic Models manually, by analyzing their behaviours in some special cases. Finally, we conducted off-line tests. We built two surveys asking real users to judge the similarity of each film in a list with regard to a target movie. The first test compared the performance of LDA and LSA. The second test compared the performance of LSA and a commercial system, IMDb. A third test evaluates the precision of the three recommendation systems.

4.1   Evaluation of the Computational Costs

The SVM of the plot-keyword matrix have a complexity of $O(d \times k)$ where d is the number of multimedia (rows of the matrix) and k is the number of keywords and $d \geq k$. There are about 1,861,736 multimedia in the IMDb database, but only for 200,000 there is a plot available. These plots contain almost 220,000 different keywords. Thus, the time cost for the decomposition of the matrix is $O = 3 \cdot 10^{15}$. Furthermore, the decomposition requires random access to the matrix, which implies an intensive usage of the central memory.

Both LSA and LDA decrease this cost by using a reduced matrix. The Document by Topic Matrix used by LSA has a dimension of $d \times z$ where z is the number of topic (columns). The Document Distribution over Topic Matrix used by LDA has a dimension of $d \times z$. Usually LSA requires more topics then LDA. Thus, the cost for the computation of the LDA matrix is further decreased. In order to avoid the central memory saturation, we employ the framework Gensim[11]. It offers functions to process plain document including algorithms performing both LSA and LDA which are independent from the training corpus size.

Table 1 shows the computational costs to create the LSA and LDA models[12].

Table 2 summarizes the configuration adopted for LSA and LDA and the time performance of the topic models when, starting from a given plot, they rank all the other plots in the database. Since the LDA model requires less topics (50 instead of the 500 required by LSA), it has a computation cost and a similarity time cost lower than the ones for LSA.

---

[11] http://radimrehurek.com/gensim/.

[12] The cost refers to a virtual machine set up with VMWare Workstation 9.0.1, installed on a server that has the following features: OS: Ubuntu 12.04 LTS 64-bit; RAM: 8 GB; 20 GB dedicated to the virtual hard disk; 4 cores. The DataBase Management System used is MongoDB 2.4.1, and it was installed on a machine with the following characteristics: OS: Windows Server 2008 R2 64-bit; CPU: Intel (R) Xeon E5620 Ghz 2:40; RAM: 12 GB.

Table 1. Computational costs.

Operation	Time (minutes)	CPU avg use	Memory avg use
Plot vect	5	75 %	11 %
Tf-idf weights	1	97 %	10 %
LSA weights	120	97 %	42 %
LDA weights	60	95 %	40 %

Table 2. LSA and LDA topic model comparison.

Configuration	LSA	LDA
min. document freq	10	10
min. vector length	20	20
min. tf-idf weight	0.09	0.09
min. lsa/lda weight	0.001	0.001
n. of topics	**500**	**50**
matrix size	204285 × 500	204285 × 50
Similarity time cost	**12 s**	**6 s**

4.2   Manual Comparison of Topic Models

We performed several manual evaluations in order to understand the behaviour
of both the Topic Models. In Table 3 we report the top 5 recommendations
calculated by using LDA and LSA models on two kind of movies: a movie of a
saga and a movie that is not part of a sequel. For "The Matrix" (see the right part
of the table), LSA selected movies referring to the topics of computer, network,
programmer, hacker, while the outcome of the LDA technique showed two movies
of the trilogy and other movies containing terms and names that appear also
in the target plot, but that do not refer to similar topics. The quality of the
outcome decreases with movies that do not have a sequel, like "Braveheart" (see
the left part of the table). For this kind of movies, it is difficult to evaluate the
recommended movie list. For this reason, we built a survey of popular movies
that do not have a sequel and asked to real users to judge the similarity of the
recommended movies (as presented in Sect. 4.3).

4.3   Testing the Recommendation System with Real Users

In order to evaluate the performance of our recommendation system, we identified two crucial steps: first it is necessary to understand which of the two Topic
Models is more appropriate in the movie domain, then, we need to estimate its
behaviour next to a commercial recommendation system, as IMDb. We defined
three off-line tests: the first collecting the recommendations of LDA and LSA
for 18 popular movies (excluding sagas), the second comparing the recommendations of the best Topic Model with respect to the recommended movie list of

Table 3. A comparison between LSA and LDA techniques.

	"Braveheart (1995)"		"The Matrix (1999)"	
	LSA	LDA	LSA	LDA
1	Braveheart (1995)	Braveheart (1995)	The Matrix (1999)	The Matrix (1999)
2	The Enemy Within (2010)	Windwalker (1981)	Computer Warriors (1990)	The Matrix Reloaded (2003)
3	Journey of a Story (2011)	Lipgloss Explosion (2001)	Electric Dreams (1984)	Simulacrum (2009)
4	Audition (2007)	Race for Glory (1989)	Willkommen in Babylon (1995)	Virus X (2010)
5	The Process (2011)	Voyager from the Unknown (1982)	TRON 2.0 (2003)	Fallen Moon (2011)
6	Comedy Central Roast of William Shatner (2006)	Elmo Saves Christmas (1996)	Hackers (1995)	The Matrix Revolutions (2003)

IMDb, the third analyzing in more detail the preferences expressed by 5 users on the three recommendation systems. We asked users to fill out the survey by selecting the films that looked similar to the film in question. These evaluations have enabled us to draw some conclusions on the performance of the implemented Topic Models and on our system in general.

LDA Versus LSA. The first off-line experiment involved 18 movies; for each of these movies, we selected the top 6 movies in the recommendation lists of both LSA and LDA. In order to propose results that can be easily judged by users, we discarded from the recommended movie lists: tv series, documentaries, short films, entries whose released year is before 1960, entries whose title is reported only in the original language, entries whose plot contains less than 200 characters.

We presented this list to users in a random order and asked them to judge for each movie in the list if it is similar to the target one, users can reply by choosing among "similar", "not similar" and "I do not know". Figure 4 reports the percentage of users' judgements received (here we do not consider the movies for which users have not expressed a judgement). We collected 594 evaluations from 20 users in total. We also evaluated the behavior of the Topic Models on each film: on the 18 movies, we found that in 15 cases LSA selected the best recommendations and in 3 cases LDA selected the best recommendations (see left part of Fig. 3). As expected from the previous comparison of the two models (reported in Table 3), LSA supplied better recommendations than LDA.

LSA Versus IMDb. In order to compare our system with respect to IMDb, we built another survey collecting recommendations for 18 popular movies (different with respect to the ones used in the LDA comparison): we selected them from

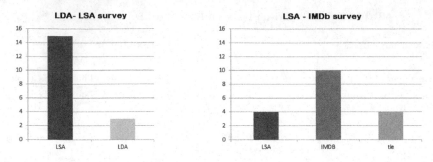

Fig. 3. Performance of the topic models and IMDb on the two surveys.

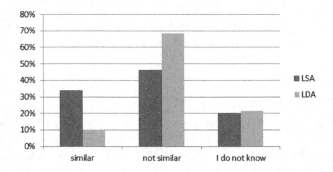

Fig. 4. Percentage of users' judgements on LSA-LDA survey.

the top 250 movies of IMDb[13]). Also in this case, we extracted only the top 6 movies in the recommendation lists of both LSA and IMDb.

In the previous survey, we obtained many void answers (i.e. on several recommended movies users do not expressed any opinion), moreover, some users highlighted that filling out the entire survey was very time consuming. Therefore, we decided to limit the options only to "similar".

We presented this list to users in a random order and asked users to judge for each movie in the list if it is similar to the target one. The experiment has been conducted on 30 test participants.

We collected 146 evaluations from 30 users in total. On the 18 movies, we found that in 4 cases LSA selected the best recommendations, in 10 cases IMDb selected the best recommendations and in 4 cases both systems showed the same performances (see right part of Fig. 3).

User Preference Evaluation. We added an in-deep evaluation of the users preferences for the 18 popular movies used in Sect. 4.3. This evaluation has been based on the precision measure computes by using the classification of recommendation results introduced in [12] as

---

[13] http://www.imdb.com/chart/top.

$$Precision = \frac{\#tp}{\#tp + \#fp}$$

On the 18 movies, we examine punctual preferences expressed by 5 expert users on the top 6 items of the recommendation list, for this evaluation we consider the "similar" and "not similar" judgement expressed by the users. Thus for each recommendation list we calculate the precision of the system based on the user judgement.

We computed the average precision among users (AVG_P@6) and the standard deviation among the movies (DEV_M_P@6) and the users (DEV_U_P@6) (see Table 4). AVG_P@6 reflects the average ratio of the number of relevant movies over the top-6 recommended movies for all users.

We found that the precision of LDA is quite low (about half as much as the LSA precision), while both LSA and IMDb reach a good precision. From this preliminary evaluation (that is quite limited since it is performed only on 5 users), it seems that the average precision on the entire set of movies of LSA is quite the same as the precision of IMDb. As it can be noticed, there is however a strong deviation of the precision value among different movies.

4.4   Results and Discussion

Based on the results of the above-mentioned experiments, we can draw some conclusions:

- LDA does not have good performance on movie recommendations as demonstrated by the user evaluation;
- LSA achieves good performance on movie recommendations;
- both LDA and LSA suggest erroneous entries for movies that have a short plot;
- our system did not outperform the IMDb performance; however, an in-deep evaluation of users preferences has shown that the average precision gained by LSA is very close to the precision of IMDb.

5   Related Work

Recommendation algorithms are usually classified in content-based and collaborative filtering [13]. Collaborative filtering systems are widely industrially utilized, for example by Amazon, MovieLens and Netflix, and recommendation is

Table 4. Precision of the systems based on a punctual user preference evaluation.

	AVG_P@6	DEV_M_P@6	DEV_U_P@6
LDA	0.215	0.163	0.133
LSA	0.468	0.258	0.056
IMDb	0.416	0.281	0.064

computed by analysing user profiles and user ratings of the items. When user preferences are not available, as in the start-up phase, or not accessible, due to privacy issues, it might be necessary to develop a content-based recommendation algorithm, or combined different approaches as in hybrid systems.

Among recommendation systems [14], content-based recommendation systems rely on item descriptions that usually consist of punctual data. Jinni[14] is a movie recommendation system that analyses as well movie plots, but, differently from our approach, relies on user ratings, manual annotations and machine learning techniques.

LSA was shown to perform better than the simpler word and n-gram feature vectors in an interesting study [15] where several types of vector similarity metrics (e.g., binary vs. count vectors, Jaccard vs. cosine vs. overlap distance measure, etc.) have been evaluated and compared. Due to the high computational cost of LSA there have been many work around in the area of approximate matrix factorization; these algorithms maintain the spirit of SVD but are much easier to compute [16]. For example, in [17] an effective distributed factorization algorithm based on stochastic gradient descent is shown. We opted for a scalable implementation of the process that does not require the term-document matrix to be stored in memory and is therefore independent of the corpus size [18].

Also the LDA Topic Model has been already applied in recommendation systems to analyze textual information. In particular in [19] a Web recommendation system to help users in locating information on the Web is proposed. In this system LDA is used as technique for discovering hidden semantic relationships among Web items by analyzing their content information. Another interesting application is described in [20] where the authors propose a tag recommendation system where LDA is exploited to suggest tags for new resources.

In the specific domain of movie recommendation systems, we found only few frameworks that make use of plots. In particular in [21] a Context-Aware Recommendation algorithm is introduced, the framework combines the similarity based on plot keywords with a mood-specific movie similarity for providing recommendations. Also in [22] authors attempts to solve the cold start problem (where there is no past rating for an item) for collaborative filtering recommendation systems. The paper describes a framework, based on an extended version of LDA, able to take into account item-related emotions, extracted from the movie plots, and semantic data, inferred from movie features.

6   Conclusions and Future Work

The paper presented a plot-based recommendation system. The system classifies two videos as being similar if their plots are alike. Two Topic Models, LDA and LSA, have been implemented and integrated within the recommendation system. The techniques have been compared and tested over a large collection of movies. The local movie database MongoDB has been created to store a large amount

---

[14] http://www.jinni.com/.

of metadata related to multimedia content coming from different sources with heterogeneous schemata.

Experimental evaluation of both LDA and LSA has been conducted to provide answers in term of efficiency and effectiveness. LSA turns out to be superior to LDA. The performance of both the techniques have been compared to user evaluation, and commercial approaches. LSA has been revealed to be better then LDA in supporting the suggestion of similar plots, but it does not outperform the commercial approach (IMDb). However, we can not ignore that IMDb is strongly affected by user experiences: it uses features such as user votes, genre, title, keywords, and, most importantly, user recommendations themselves to generate an automatic response. On the contrary, our content-based recommendations system is user independent and can be also used to make recommendations when knowledge of user preferences is not available.

The results shown in this paper highlight some limitations and stimulate some future directions for our research: (1) *Combination with other techniques,* (2) *Making Use of Lexical Resources* and (3) *Exploring new application scenarios.*

(1) The plot-based recommendation techniques assume that the main feature a user likes in a movie is the plot, i.e. the content of the movie, if this is not the case, the system will fail in suggesting similar movies. An improvement might be to couple our recommendation system with other techniques that do not totally rely on the plot.

(2) While LDA deals with the polysemy issue, LSA does not. This problem can be faced by making use of a lexical database as WordNet[15]. Each keyword might be replaced by its meaning (synset), before the application of the weight techniques. To understand which of the synsets better express the meaning of a keyword in a plot we might adopt Word Sense Disambiguation techniques [23]. The semantic relationships between synsets can be used for enhancing the keyword meaning by adding all its hypernyms and hyponyms [24–26].

(3) Our system does not rely on human effort and can be ported to any domain where natural language descriptions exist (like news, book plots, book reviews etc.). For example, the system might be able to find movies that contain a story similar to the one told in a book, e.g. a movie or a television series that used it as a script, or dramatic movies based on true events similar to a news. The database could be expanded with other contents to suggest further items similar to the selected movie (e.g. if I liked a movie about the war in Cambodia I should be interested in newspaper articles, essays, or books about that topic).

Acknowledgements. The system has been developed in collaboration between the database group of the University of Modena and Reggio Emilia and vfree.tv (http://vfree.tv), a young and innovative German company focused on creating new ways of distributing television content and generating an unprecedented watching experience for the user.

We also want to express our gratitude to Tania Farinella, Matteo Abbruzzo and Olga Kryukova, master students in Computer Engineering and Science at the

---

[15] http://wordnet.princeton.edu/.

Department of Engineering "Enzo Ferrari" at University of Modena and Reggio Emilia for their contribution in term of implementation of the first and second version of the system (without and with LDA) and for their support during the evaluation of the system. Particular appreciation goes to Serena Sorrentino that helps us to integrate the LDA models in our system.

References

1. Resnick, P., Varian, H.R.: Recommender systems. Commun. ACM **40**, 56–58 (1997)
2. Rashid, A.M., Karypis, G., Riedl, J.: Learning preferences of new users in recommender systems: an information theoretic approach. SIGKDD Explor. Newsl. **10**, 90–100 (2008)
3. Bergamaschi, S., Po, L., Sorrentino, S.: Comparing topic models for a movie recommendation system. In: Proceedings of 10th International Conference on Web Information Systems and Technologies (WEBIST 2014), Barcelona, Spain, Number 2, SCITEPRESS, pp. 172-183 (2014). ISBN 978-989-758-024-6
4. Farinella, T., Bergamaschi, S., Po, L.: A non-intrusive movie recommendation system. In: Meersman, R., et al. (eds.) OTM 2012, Part II. LNCS, vol. 7566, pp. 736–751. Springer, Heidelberg (2012)
5. Salton, G., Wong, A., Yang, C.S.: A vector space model for automatic indexing. Commun. ACM **18**, 613–620 (1975)
6. Musto, C.: Enhanced vector space models for content-based recommender systems. In: Proceedings of the Fourth ACM Conference on Recommender Systems. RecSys 2010, pp. 361–364. ACM, New York (2010)
7. Park, L.A.F., Ramamohanarao, K.: An analysis of latent semantic term self-correlation. ACM Trans. Inf. Syst. **27**, 8:1–8:35 (2009)
8. Deerwester, S., Dumais, S.T., Furnas, G.W., Landauer, T.K., Harshman, R.: Indexing by latent semantic analysis. J. Am. Soc. Inf. Sci. **41**, 391–407 (1990)
9. Griffiths, T., Steyvers, M., Tenenbaum, J.: Topics in semantic representation. Psychol. Rev. **114**, 211–244 (2007)
10. Blei, D.M., Ng, A.Y., Jordan, M.I.: Latent dirichlet allocation. J. Mach. Learn. Res. **3**, 993–1022 (2003)
11. Sorrentino, S., Bergamaschi, S., Parmiggiani, E.: A supervised method for lexical annotation of schema labels based on wikipedia. In: Atzeni, P., Cheung, D., Ram, S. (eds.) ER 2012 Main Conference 2012. LNCS, vol. 7532, pp. 359–368. Springer, Heidelberg (2012)
12. Gunawardana, A., Shani, G.: A survey of accuracy evaluation metrics of recommendation tasks. J. Mach. Learn. Res. **10**, 2935–2962 (2009)
13. Ekstrand, M.D., Riedl, J.T., Konstan, J.A.: Collaborative filtering recommender systems. Found. Trends Hum.-Comput. Interact. **4**, 81–173 (2011)
14. Adomavicius, G., Tuzhilin, A.: Toward the next generation of recommender systems: a survey of the state-of-the-art and possible extensions. IEEE Trans. Knowl. Data Eng. **17**, 734–749 (2005)
15. Lee, M. D., Welsh, M.: An empirical evaluation of models of text document similarity. In: Proceedings of the 27th Annual Conference of the Cognitive Science Society. CogSci2005, Erlbaum (2005) 1254–1259
16. Koren, Y., Bell, R., Volinsky, C.: Matrix factorization techniques for recommender systems. Computer **42**, 30–37 (2009)

17. Gemulla, R., Nijkamp, E., Haas, P.J., Sismanis, Y.: Large-scale matrix factorization with distributed stochastic gradient descent. In: Proceedings of the 17th ACM SIGKDD International Conference on Knowledge Discovery and Data Mining, KDD 2011, pp. 69–77. ACM, New York (2011)
18. Rehurek, R., Sojka, P.: Software framework for topic modelling with large corpora. In: Proceedings of the LREC 2010 Workshop on New Challenges for NLP Frameworks, Valletta, Malta, ELRA, pp. 45–50 (2010)
19. Jin, X., Mobasher, B., Zhou, Y.: A web recommendation system based on maximum entropy. In: ITCC, pp. 213–218. IEEE Computer Society (2005)
20. Krestel, R., Fankhauser, P., Nejdl, W.: Latent dirichlet allocation for tag recommendation. In: Bergman, L.D., Tuzhilin, A., Burke, R.D., Felfernig, A., Schmidt-Thieme, L. (eds.) RecSys, pp. 61–68. ACM (2009)
21. Shi, Y., Larson, M., Hanjalic, A.: Mining contextual movie similarity with matrix factorization for context-aware recommendation. ACM Trans. Intell. Syst. Technol. 4, 16:1–16:19 (2013)
22. Moshfeghi, Y., Piwowarski, B., Jose, J. M.: Handling data sparsity in collaborative filtering using emotion and semantic based features. In: Proceedings of the 34th International ACM SIGIR Conference on Research and Development in Information Retrieval. SIGIR 2011, pp. 625–634. ACM, New York (2011)
23. Navigli, R.: Word sense disambiguation: a survey. ACM Comput. Surv. 41, 1–69 (2009)
24. Po, L., Sorrentino, S.: Automatic generation of probabilistic relationships for improving schema matching. Inf. Syst. 36, 192–208 (2011)
25. Sorrentino, S., Bergamaschi, S., Gawinecki, M., Po, L.: Schema label normalization for improving schema matching. Data Knowl. Eng. 69, 1254–1273 (2010)
26. Bergamaschi, S., Bouquet, P., Giacomuzzi, D., Guerra, F., Po, L., Vincini, M.: An incremental method for the lexical annotation of domain ontologies. Int. J. Semantic Web Inf. Syst. 3, 57–80 (2007)

Generating Product Feature Hierarchy
from Product Reviews

Nan Tian[1]([✉]), Yue Xu[1], Yuefeng Li[1], Ahmad Abdel-Hafez[1],
and Audun Josang[2]

[1] Faculty of Science and Engineering, Queensland University of Technology,
Brisbane, Australia
{n.tian,yue.xu,y2.li,a.abdelhafez}@qut.edu.au
[2] Department of Informatics, University of Oslo, Oslo, Norway
josang@mn.uio.no

Abstract. User generated information such as product reviews have been booming due to the advent of web 2.0. In particular, rich information associated with reviewed products has been buried in such big data. In order to facilitate identifying useful information from product (e.g., cameras) reviews, opinion mining has been proposed and widely used in recent years. In detail, as the most critical step of opinion mining, feature extraction aims to extract significant product features from review texts. However, most existing approaches only find individual features rather than identifying the hierarchical relationships between the product features. In this paper, we propose an approach which finds both features and feature relationships, structured as a feature hierarchy which is referred to as feature taxonomy in the remainder of the paper. Specifically, by making use of frequent patterns and association rules, we construct the feature taxonomy to profile the product at multiple levels instead of single level, which provides more detailed information about the product. The experiment which has been conducted based upon some real world review datasets shows that our proposed method is capable of identifying product features and relations effectively.

Keywords: Feature extraction · Opinion mining · Association rules · Feature taxonomy · User reviews

1 Introduction

In recent years, the user generated online content exploded due to the advent of Web 2.0. For instance, online users write reviews to how they enjoy or dislike a product they purchased. This helps to identify features or characteristics of the product from users' point of view, which is an important addition to the product specification. However, to identify the relevant features from users' subjective review data is extremely challenging.

Feature-based opinion mining has attracted big attention recently. A significant amount of research has been proposed to improve the accuracy of feature

© Springer International Publishing Switzerland 2015
V. Monfort and K.-H. Krempels (Eds.): WEBIST 2014, LNBIP 226, pp. 264–278, 2015.
DOI: 10.1007/978-3-319-27030-2_17

generation for products [2,4,5,8,11,16]. However, most techniques only extract features; the structural relationship between product features has been omitted. For example, *"picture resolution"* is a common feature of digital camera in which *"resolution"* expresses the specific feature concept to describe the general feature *"picture"*. Yet, existing approaches treat *"resolution"* and *"picture"* as two individual features instead of finding the relationship between them. Thus, the information derived by existing feature extraction approaches is not sufficient for generating a precise product model since all features are allocated in the same level and independent from each other.

Association rule mining is a well explored method in data mining [7]. Based on association rules generated from a collection of item transactions, we can discover the relations between items. However, the amount of generated association rules is usually huge and selecting the most useful rules is challenging [10]. In our research, we propose to identify a group of frequent patterns as potential features to assist selecting useful association rules. The selected rules are used to identify relationships between features. Furthermore, in order to ensure that the most useful rules are to be selected, we also propose to apply statistical topic modelling technique [13] to the selection of association rules.

Our approach takes advantages of existing feature extraction approaches and makes two contributions. Firstly, we present a method to make use of association rules to find related features. Secondly, we create a product model called feature taxonomy which represents the product more accurately by explicitly representing the concrete relationships between general features and specific features.

2 Related Work

Our research aims to extract useful product information based on user generated information to create a product model. This work is closely related to feature-based opinion mining which has drawn many researchers' attention in recent years. In detail, identifying features that have been mentioned by users is considered the most significant step in opinion mining [17]. Hu and Liu (2004) first proposed a feature-based opinion mining method to extract features and sentiments from customer reviews. They use pattern mining to find frequent itemsets (nouns). These itemsets are pruned and considered frequent product features. A list of sentiment words (adjectives) that are nearby frequent features in reviews can be extracted and used to identify those product features that cannot be identified by pattern mining. Scaffidi et al. (2007) improved the performance of feature extraction in their proposed system called Red Opal. Specifically, they made use of a language model to find features by comparing the frequency of nouns in the review and in common use of English. Those frequent nouns in both reviews and in common use are considered invalid features. Hu et al. (2010) make use of SentiWordNet to identify all sentences that may contain users' sentiment polarity. Then, the pattern mining is applied to generate explicit features based on these opinionated sentences. In addition, a mapping database has been constructed to find those implicit features represented by sentiment words(e.g., *expensive* indicates *price*). To enhance the accuracy of finding correct features from free text review, Hai et al. (2013) proposed a novel method which evaluates the domain relevance of a feature by exploiting features' distribution disparities across different corpora (domain-dependent review corpus such as cellphone reviews and domain-irrelevant corpus such as culture article collection). In detail, the *intrinsic-domain relevance* (IDR) and *extrinsic-domain relevance* (EDR) have been proposed to benchmark if a examined feature is related to a certain domain. The candidate feature with low IDR and high EDR scores will be pruned.

Lau et al. (2009) presented an ontology-based approach to profile the product. In detail, a number of ontology levels, such as feature level that contains identified features for a certain product and sentiment level in which sentiment words that describe a certain feature are stored, have been constructed [6]. This method provides a simple product profile rather than extracting product features only.

The statistical topic modeling technique has been used in various fields such as text mining [13, 14] in recent years. Latent Semantic Analysis (LSA) is first proposed to capture the most significant features of a document collection based upon semantic structure of relevant documents [12]. Then, Probabilistic LSA (pLSA) [14] and Latent Dirichlet Allocation (LDA) [13] are proposed to improve the interpretation of results from LSA. These techniques have been proven more effective on document modeling and topic extraction, which are represented by topic-document and word-topic distribution, respectively. Particularly, multinomial distribution over words which is derived based upon word frequency can be generated to represent topics in a given text collection.

None of aforementioned feature identification approaches is able to identify the relationships between the extracted product features. The structural relationships that exist between features can be used to describe the reviewed product in more depth. However, how to evaluate and determine the relations between features is still challenging.

The remainder of the paper is organized as follows. The next section illustrates the construction process of our proposed feature taxonomy. Then, the evaluation of our approach is reported afterwards. Finally, we conclude and describe future direction of our research work.

3   The Proposed Approach

Our proposed approach consists of two main steps: product taxonomy construction using association rules and taxonomy expansion based on reference features. The input of our system is a collection of user reviews for a certain product. The output is a product feature taxonomy which contains not only all generated features but also the relationships between them.

3.1   Pre-processing and Transaction File Generation

First of all, we construct a single document called an *aggregated review document* which combines all the reviews in a collection of reviews, keeping each sentence in the original reviews as one sentence in the constructed *aggregated review document*. Three steps are undertaken to process the review text in order to extract useful information. Firstly, we generate the part-of-speech (POS) tag for each word in the *aggregated review document* to indicate whether the word is a *noun, adjective* or *adverb* etc. For instance, after the POS tagging, *"The flash is very weak."* would be transformed to *"The/DT flash/NN is/VBZ very/RB weak/JJ ./."*, where *DT, NN, VBZ, RB*, and *JJ* represent Determiner, Noun, Verb, Adverb and Adjective, respectively. Secondly, according to the thumb rule that most product features are nouns or noun phrases [3], we process each sentence in the *aggregated review document* to only keep words that are nouns. All the remaining nouns are also pre-processed by stemming and spelling correction. Each sentence in the *aggregated review document* consists of all identified nouns of a sentence in the original reviews. Finally, a transactional dataset is generated from the *aggregated review document*. Each sentence which consists of a sequence of nouns in the *aggregated review document* is treated as a transaction in the transactional dataset.

3.2   Potential Features Generation

Our first task is to generate potential product features that are expressed by those identified nouns or noun phrases. According to [4], significant product features are discussed extensively by users in reviews (e.g., *"battery"* for cameras). Upon this, most existing feature extraction approaches make use of pattern mining techniques to find potential features. Specifically, an itemset is a set of items (i.e., words in review text in this paper) that appear together in one or multiple transactions in a transactional dataset. Given a set of items, $I = \{i_1, i_2, ..., i_n\}$, an itemset is defined as $X \subseteq I$. The support of an itemset X, denoted as $Supp(X)$, is the percentage of transactions in the dataset that contain X. All frequent itemsets from a set of transactions that satisfy a user-specified minimum support will be extracted as the potential features. However, not all frequent itemsets are genuine since some of them may be just frequent but meaningless. We use compactness pruning method proposed by [4] to filter frequent itemsets. After the pruning, we can get a list of frequent itemsets that are considered potential features, denoted as FP.

3.3   Product Feature Taxonomy Construction

In this step, we propose to utilize association rules generated from the discovered potential product features to identify relations in order to construct a feature taxonomy.

Association rule mining can be described as follows: Let $I = \{i_1, i_2, ..., i_n\}$, be a set of items, and the dataset consists of a set of transactions $D = \{t_1, t_2, ..., t_m\}$. Each transaction t contains a subset of items from I. Therefore, an association rule r represents an implication relationship between two itemsets which can be defined as the form $X \rightarrow Y$, where $X, Y \subseteq I$ and $X \cap Y = \emptyset$. The itemsets X and Y are called antecedent and consequent of the rule, respectively. To assist selecting useful rules, the support $Supp(X \cup Y)$ and the confidence $Conf(X \rightarrow Y)$ of the rule can be used [10].

For easily describing our approach, we define some useful and important concepts as follows:

Definition 1 (Feature Taxonomy). A feature taxonomy consists of a set of features and their relationships, denoted as $FH = \{F, L\}$, F is a set of features where $F = \{f_1, f_2, ..., f_n\}$ and L is a set of relations. The feature taxonomy has the following constraints:

(1) The relationship between a pair of features is the sub-feature relationship. For $f_i, f_j \in F$, if f_j is a sub feature of f_i, then (f_i, f_j) is a link in the taxonomy and $(f_i, f_j) \in L$, which indicates that f_j is more specific than f_i. f_i is called the parent feature of f_j and denoted as $P(f_j)$.
(2) Except for the root, each feature has only one parent feature. This means that the taxonomy is structured as a tree.
(3) The root of the taxonomy represents the product itself.

Definition 2 (Feature Existence). For a given feature taxonomy $FH = \{F, L\}$, let $W(g)$ represent a set of words that appear in a potential feature g, let $ES(g) = \{a_i | a_i \in 2^{w(g)}, a_i \in F\}$ contain all subsets of g which exist in the feature taxonomy, $ES(g)$ is called the existing subsets of g, if $\bigcup_{a_i \in ES(g)} W(a_i) = W(g)$, then g is considered exist in FH, denoted as $exist(g)$, otherwise $\neg exist(g)$.

Opinion mining is also referred as sentiment analysis [1,9,18]. Adjectives or adverbs that appear together with product features are considered as the sentiment words in opinion mining. The following definition defines the sentiment words that are related to a product feature.

Definition 3 (Related Sentiments). For a feature $f \in F$, let $RS(f)$ denote a set of sentiment words which appear in the same sentences as f in user reviews, $RS(f)$ is defined as the related sentiments of f.

Definition 4 (Sentiment Sharing). For features $f_1, f_2 \in F$, the sentiment sharing between f_1 and f_2 is defined as $SS(f_1, f_2) = |RS(f_1) \cap RS(f_2)|$.

For deriving sub features using association rules, we need to select a set of useful rules rather than using all the rules. In the next two subsections, we will first propose two methods to select rules, one method is to select rules based on the sentiment sharing among features and the other method is to select rules by using the word relatedness derived from the results generated by using the typical topic model technique method LDA [13]; then introduce some strategies to update the feature taxonomy by adding sub features using the selected rules.

In order to explain the topic modelling based method, we first define some related concepts. Let $RE = \{r_1, r_2, ..., r_M\}$ be a collection of reviews, each review consists of nouns only, $W = \{w_1, w_2, ..., w_n\}$ be a set of words appearing in RE, and $Z = \{Z_1, ..., Z_v\}$ be a set of pre-specified hidden topics. LDA can be used to generate topic models for representing the collection as a whole and also for each review in the collection. At the collection level, the topic model represents the collection RE using a set of topics each of which is represented by a probability distribution over words (i.e., nouns in the context of this paper) for topic. In this paper, we will use the collection level representation to find the relatedness between words.

At collection level, each topic Z_j is represented by a probability distribution over words, $\phi_j = \{p(w_1|Z_j), p(w_2|Z_j), ..., p(w_n|Z_j)\}$, $\sum_{k=1}^{n} \varphi_{j,k} = 1$, $p(w_k|Z_j)$ is the probability of word w_k being used to represent the topic Z_j. Based on the probability $p(w_k|Z_j)$, we can choose the top words to represent the topic Z_j.

Definition 5 (Topic Words). Let $\phi_j = \{p(w_1|Z_j), p(w_2|Z_j), ..., p(w_n|Z_j)\}$ be the topic representation for topic Z_j produced by LDA and $0 \leq \delta \leq 1$ be a threshold, a set of the topic words for Z_j, denoted as $TW(Z_j)$, is defined as $TW(Z_j) = \{w|w \in W, p(w|Z_j) > \delta\}$.

Definition 6 (Word Relatedness). We use word relatedness to indicate how likely that two words have been used to represent a topic together. Let $w_i, w_j \in W$ be two words, the word relatedness between two words with respect to topic z is defined below:

$$WR_z(w_i, w_j) = \begin{cases} 1 - |p(w_i|z) - p(w_j|z)| & w_i \in TW(z) \ and \ w_j \in TW(z) \\ 0 & otherwise \end{cases} \quad (1)$$

Definition 7 (Feature Topic Representation). For feature $f \in F$, let $WD(f)$ be a set of words appearing in f and $TW(z)$ be the topic words of topic z. If $WD(f) \subset TW(z)$, the feature topic representation of feature f for topic z is defined as $FTP(f, z) = \{(w, p(w|z)) | w \in WD(f)\}$.

Definition 8 (Feature Relatedness). For features $f_i, f_j \in F$, if both features appear in a certain topic z, then the feature relatedness between f_i and f_j with respect to z is defined as:

$$FR_z(f_i, f_j) = min_{\substack{w_i \in WD(f_i) \\ w_j \in WD(f_j)}} \{WR_z(w_i, w_j)\} \quad (2)$$

Rule Selection. Let $R = \{r_1, r_2, ..., r_n\}$ be a set of association rules generated from the frequent itemsets FP, each rule r in R has the form $X_r \rightarrow Y_r$, X_r and Y_r are the antecedent and consequent of r, respectively.

Assuming that f_e is a feature which has already been in the current feature taxonomy FH, to generate the sub features for f_e, we first select a set of candidate rules, denoted as $R_{f_e}^c$, which could be used to generate the sub features:

$$R_{f_e}^c = \{X \rightarrow Y | X \rightarrow Y \in R, X = f_e, Supp(X) > (Y)\} \quad (3)$$

As defined in Eq. (3), the rules in $R_{f_e}^c$ should satisfy two constraints. The first constraint, $X = f_e$, specifies that the antecedent of a selected rule must be the same as the feature f_e. Sub features represent specific cases of a feature, they are more specific compared to the feature. The second constraint is based on the assumption that more frequent itemsets usually represent more general concepts, and less frequent itemsets usually represent more specific concepts. For instance, according to our observation toward features, a general feature (e.g., *"picture"*, its frequency is 62) appears more frequently than a specific feature (e.g., *"resolution"*, its frequency is 9) in reviews for the camera 2 in the dataset published by Liu [2]. Therefore, only the rules which can derive more specific features will be selected.

However, not all selected rules represent correct sub-feature relationship. For instance, *mode* → *auto* is more appropriate for describing a sub-feature relationship rather than *camera* → *auto*. Therefore, the rule *camera* → *auto* should not be considered when we generate the sub features for *"camera"*. Upon this, we aim to prune the unnecessary rules before generating sub features for each taxonomy feature. Firstly, a feature and its sub features should share similar sentiment words since they describe the same aspect of a product at different abstract levels (e.g., *vivid* can be use to describe both *picture* and *color*). Therefore, we should select rules whose antecedent (representing the feature) and consequent (representing a possible sub feature) share as many sentiment words as possible because the more sentiment words they share, the more possible they are about the same aspect of the product. Secondly, based on topic models generated from LDA, the more a feature and its potential sub feature appear in the same topics, the more likely they are related to each other.

Let f_X, f_Y be two features and $Z_{(f_X, f_Y)}$ be a set of topics that contains both features, the feature relatedness between f_X, f_Y with respect to all topics, denoted as $FR_{avg}(f_X, f_Y)$, is defined as the average feature relatedness between the two features over $Z_{(f_X, f_Y)}$:

$$FR_{avg}(f_X, f_Y) = \frac{\sum_{z \in Z_{(f_X, f_Y)}} FR_z(f_X, f_Y)}{|Z_{(f_X, f_Y)}|} \tag{4}$$

Based on this view, we propose the following equation to calculate a score for each candidate rule $X \to Y$ in $R_{f_e}^c$:

$$Weigh(X \to Y) = \alpha(Supp(Y) \times Conf(X \to Y))$$
$$+ \beta \frac{SS(X, Y)}{|RS(X) \cup RS(Y)|} + \gamma FR_{avg}(X, Y) \tag{5}$$

$0 < \alpha, \beta, \gamma < 1$. The value of α, β, and γ is set to 0.8, 0.1, and 0.1, respectively in our experiment described in Sect. 4. There are three parts in Eq. (5). The first part is used to measure the belief to the consequent Y by using this rule since $Conf(X \to Y)$ measures the confidence to the association between X and Y and $Supp(Y)$ measures the popularity of Y. The second part is the percentage of the shared sentiment words given by $SS(X, Y)$ over all the sentiment words used for either X or Y. Yet, the third part in the equation is the average feature relatedness between X and Y. Given a threshold σ, we propose to use the following equation to select the rules from the candidate rules in $R_{f_e}^c$. The rules in R_{f_e} will be used to derive sub features for the features in FP. R_{f_e} is called the rule set of f_e.

$$R_{f_e} = \{X \rightarrow Y | X \rightarrow Y \in R^c_{f_e}, Weigh(X \rightarrow Y) > \sigma\} \qquad (6)$$

Feature Taxonomy Construction. Let $FH = \{F, L\}$ be a feature taxonomy which could be an empty tree, FP be a set of frequent itemsets generated from user reviews which are potential features, and R be a set of rules generated from user reviews. This task is to construct a feature taxonomy if F is empty or update the feature taxonomy if F is not empty by using the rules in R. Let UF be a set of features on the tree which need to be processed in order to construct or update the tree. If F is empty, the itemset in FP which has the highest support will be chosen as the root of FH, it will be the only item in UF at the beginning. If F is not empty, UF will be F, i.e., $UF = F$.

Without losing generality, assuming that F is not empty and the set of features currently on the tree, UF is the set of features which need to be processed to update or construct the tree. For each feature in UF, let f_e be a feature in UF, i.e., $f_e \in UF$ and $X \rightarrow Y \in R_{f_e}$ be a rule with $X = f_e$, the next step is to decide whether or not Y should be added to the feature taxonomy as a sub feature of f_e. There are two possible situations: Y does not exist in the feature taxonomy, i.e., $\neg exist(Y)$ and Y does exist in the taxonomy, i.e., $exist(Y)$. In the first situation, the feature taxonomy will be updated by adding Y as a sub feature of f_e, i.e., $F = F \cup \{Y\}$, $L = L \cup (f_e, Y)$, and Y should be added to UF for further checking.

In the second situation, i.e., Y already exists in the taxonomy, i.e., according to Definition 2, there are two cases, $Y \notin ES(Y)$ (i.e., Y is not in the tree) or $Y \in ES(Y)$ (i.e., Y is in the tree). In the first case, Y is not considered a sub feature of f_e and consequently, no change is required to the tree. In the second case, $\exists f_y \in F$, f_y is the parent feature of Y, i.e., $P(Y) = f_y$ and $(f_y, Y) \in L$. Now, we need to determine whether to keep f_y as the parent feature of Y or change the parent feature of Y to f_e. That is, we need to examine f_y and f_e to see which of them is more suitable to be the parent feature of Y. The basic strategy is to compare f_y and f_e to see which of them has more sentiment sharing and feature relatedness with Y. Let f_P, f_C be a potential parent feature and sub feature, respectively. We propose a ranking equation to indicate how likely f_C is related to f_P: $Q(f_P, f_C) = \frac{SS(f_P, f_C)}{RS(f_C)} + FR_{avg}(f_P, f_C)$. Thus, if $Q(f_y, Y) < Q(f_e, Y)$, the link (f_y, Y) will be removed from the taxonomy tree, (f_e, Y) will be added to the tree, otherwise, no change to the tree and f_y is still the parent feature of Y.

Algorithms. The construction of the feature taxonomy is to generate a feature tree by finding all sub features for each feature. In this section, we will describe the algorithms to construct the feature taxonomy. As mentioned above, if the tree is empty, the feature with the highest support will be chosen as the root. So, at the very beginning, F and UF contain at least one item which is the root. Algorithm 1 describes the method to construct or update a feature taxonomy.

After the taxonomy construction, some potential features may be left over in RF and have not been added to the taxonomy. The main reason is because

---

Algorithm 1. Feature Taxonomy Construction.

Input:
    R, $FH = \{F, L\}$, FP.

Output:
    FH, RF //RF is the remaining features which are not added to FH after the construction

1: if $F = \emptyset$, then $root := argmax_{f \in FP}\{supp(f)\}$, $F := UF := \{root\}$;
2: else $UF := F$;
3: for each feature $f_e \in UF$
4:     if $R_{f_e} \neq \emptyset$ //the rule set of f_e is not empty
5:       for each rule $X \rightarrow Y \in R_{f_e}$
6:         if $\neg exist(Y)$ //Y does not exist on the tree
7:           $F := F \cup \{Y\}$, $L := L \cup (f_e, Y)$,
             $UF := UF \cup \{Y\}$, $FP := FP - \{Y\}$;
8:         else //Y exists on the tree
9:           if $Y \in ES(Y)$ and $Q(f_y, Y) < Q(f_e, Y)$
             //f_y is $Y's$ parent feature
10:             $L := L \cup (f_e, Y)$, $L := L - (f_y, Y)$;
             //add (f_e, Y) and remove (f_y, Y)
11:           else //$Y \notin ES(Y)$, Y is not on the tree
12:             $FP := FP - \{Y\}$;
13:       endfor
14:     endif
15:     $UF := UF - \{f_e\}$; //remove f_e from UF
16: endfor
17: $RF := FP$

---

these itemsets may not frequently occur in the reviews together with the features that have been added in the taxonomy. In order to prevent valid features from being missed out, we check those remaining itemsets in RF by examining the shared sentiment words and feature relatedness between the remaining itemsets and the features in the taxonomy. Let $FH = \{F, L\}$ be the constructed feature taxonomy, RF be the set of remaining potential features, for a potential feature g in RF, the basic strategy to determine whether g is a feature or not is to examine the Q ranking between g and the features in the taxonomy. Let $F_g = \{f | f \in F, Q(f, g) > 0\}$ be a set of features which are related to g, if $F_g \neq \emptyset$, g is considered a feature. The most related feature is defined as $f_m = argmax_{f \in F_g}\{Q(f, g)\}$. g will be added to the taxonomy with f_m as its parent feature. If there are multiple such features f_m which have the highest ranking score with g, the one with the highest support will be chosen as the parent feature of g.

Algorithm 2 formally describes the method mentioned above to expand the taxonomy by adding the remaining features.

After the expansion, the features left over in RF are not considered as features for this product.

Algorithm 2. Feature Taxonomy Expansion.

Input:
  $FH = \{F, L\}$, RF.
Output:
  FH

1: for each feature $g \in RF$
2:   if $(F_g := \{f | f \in F, Q(f, g) > 0\}) \neq \emptyset$
3:     $M := \{a | a \in F_g$ and $Q(a, g) = max_{f \in F_g}\{Q(f, g)\}\}$
4:     $f_m := argmax_{f \in M}\{supp(f)\}$
5:     $F := F \cup \{g\}$, $L := L \cup (f_m, g)$
6:     $RF := RF - \{g\}$

4   Experiment and Evaluation

We use three datasets in the experiments. Each dataset contains user reviews for a certain type of digital cameras. One dataset is used in [4], while the other two are used in [2]. Each review in the datasets has been manually annotated. In detail, a human examiner read a review sentence by sentence. If a sentence is considered indicating the user's opinions, such as positive and negative, all possible features in the sentence that are modified by sentiment words are tagged. We take these annotated features as the correct features to evaluate the performance of our proposed method in feature extraction. The number of reviews and number of annotated features are 51 and 98 for camera 1, 34 and 75 for camera 2, and 45 and 105 for camera 3.

Our proposed feature taxonomy captures both product features and relations between features. Therefore, the evaluations are twofold: feature extraction evaluation and structural relations evaluation.

4.1   Feature Extraction Evaluation

First of all, we evaluate the performance of our approach by examining the number of accurate features in user reviews that have been extracted. We use the feature extraction method (FBS) proposed in [4] as the baseline for comparison. In addition, in order to examine the effectiveness of using the sentiment sharing measure, the feature relatedness measure, and the combination of the two, we conduct our experiment in four runs:

(1) *Rule:* construct the feature taxonomy by only utilizing the information of association rules (i.e., support and confidence value only) without using the sentiment sharing and the feature relatedness measures;
(2) *SS:* construct the feature taxonomy by taking the information of association rules and the sentiment sharing measure without using the feature relatedness measure;
(3) *FR:* construct the feature taxonomy by taking the information of association rules and the feature relatedness measure without using the sentiment sharing measure;

Table 1. Recall comparison.

	Camera 1	Camera 2	Camera 3	Average
FBS	0.57	0.63	0.57	0.59
Rule	0.38	0.52	0.45	0.45
SS	0.56	0.65	0.58	0.60
FR	0.56	0.67	0.58	0.60
Hybrid	0.56	0.68	0.58	0.61

Table 2. Precision comparison.

	Camera 1	Camera 2	Camera 3	Average
FBS	0.45	0.42	0.51	0.46
Rule	0.55	0.57	0.74	0.62
SS	0.62	0.57	0.63	0.61
FR	0.60	0.56	0.63	0.60
Hybrid	0.62	0.59	0.68	0.63

Table 3. F1 Score comparison.

	Camera 1	Camera 2	Camera 3	Average
FBS	0.50	0.50	0.54	0.51
Rule	0.45	0.54	0.56	0.52
SS	0.59	0.61	0.60	0.60
FR	0.58	0.61	0.60	0.60
Hybrid	0.59	0.63	0.63	0.62

(4) *Hybrid:* the sentiment sharing and the feature relatedness are combined together with the information of association rules to construct the feature taxonomy.

Tables 1, 2 and 3 illustrate the recall, precision, and F1 score results produced in the four runs, respectively. From the results, we can see that using both the sentiment sharing and feature relatedness can obtain better feature extraction performance than the use of association rule's information only. In particular, the hybrid method, which uses both sentiment sharing and feature relatedness, achieves the best results in most cases. However, the size of the review dataset and the number of annotated features can affect the precision and recall, which makes the values of the precision and recall vary in different range for different datasets. For instance, camera 3 has higher precision values than camera 2 due to more reviews in camera 3 dataset than that in camera 2 dataset, but camera 3 has lower recall values than camera 2 due to more manually annotated features in camera 3 dataset.

4.2   Structural Relation Evaluation

The evaluation of the relations requires the standard taxonomy or knowledge from experts [15]. Since there is no existing standard taxonomy available for comparison, we manually created taxonomy for the three cameras according to the product technical specifications provided online by manufacture organizations[1,2,3]. From the product specifications on these websites, each camera has a number of attributes such as *lens system* and *shooting modes*. In addition, each attribute may also have several sub attributes. For instance, the *shooting modes* of the camera contains more specific attributes (e.g., *intelligent auto* and *custom*). Based upon such information, we create the product feature taxonomy for three digital cameras and use the taxonomy as the testing taxonomy, called Manual Feature Taxonomy (MFT), to evaluate the relations within our proposed feature taxonomy.

Due to the difference between the technical specifications from domain experts and the subjective reviews from online users, the words used to represent a feature in user reviews are very often different from the words for the same feature specified by domain experts in the product specification. For example, the feature *lens system* in the testing taxonomy and the feature *lens* in our generated taxonomy should be the same according to common knowledge even though they are not exactly matched with each other. Because of this fact, we will determine the match between two features based on overlapping of the two features rather than exact matching.

Let $MFT = \{F_{MFT}, L_{MFT}\}$ be the testing taxonomy with F_{MFT} being a set of standard features given by domain experts and L_{MFT} being a set of links in the testing taxonomy. For a given link $(f_{Fp}, f_{Fc}) \in L$ in the constructed product feature taxonomy and two features $f_{Mp}, f_{Mc} \in F_{MFT}$ in the testing taxonomy, the link (f_{Fp}, f_{Fc}) is considered matched with (f_{Mp}, f_{Mc}) and therefore represent a correct feature relation if the following conditions are satisfied:

1. $W(f_{Mp}) \cap W(f_{Fp}) \neq \emptyset$ and $W(f_{Mc}) \cap W(f_{Fc}) \neq \emptyset$
2. There exists a path in MFT, $\langle f_{Mp}, f_1, f_2, ..., f_n, f_{Mc} \rangle$, (f_{Mp}, f_1), (f_i, f_{i+1}), $(f_n, f_{Mc}) \in L_{MFT}$, $i = 1, ..., n - 1$

We examine the testing taxonomy and the constructed taxonomy to identify all matched links in the constructed taxonomy. The traditional measures precision and recall are used to evaluate the correctness of the feature relations in the constructed feature taxonomy. Let $ML(FH)$ denote the matched links in the constructed taxonomy, the precision and recall are defined as: Precision $= ML(FH)/|L|$ and Recall $= ML(FH)/|L_{MFT}|$.

---

[1] http://www.canon.com.au/Personal/Products/Camerasand-Accessories/ Digital-Cameras/PowerShot-S100.

[2] http://www.nikonusa.com/en/Nikon-Products/Product/ Compact-Digital-Cameras/26332/COOLPIX-S4300.html.

[3] http://www.usa.canon.com/cusa/support/consumer/digital_cameras/ powershot_g_series/powershot_g3#Specifications.

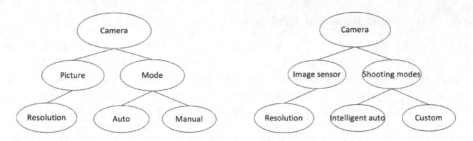

Fig. 1. Constructed feature taxonomy.   **Fig. 2.** Testing feature taxonomy.

Table 4. Recall and precision of relation evaluation.

	Relations in MFT	Relations in FH	Recall	Precision
Camera 1	75	97	0.40	0.46
Camera 2	63	97	0.57	0.65
Camera 3	71	102	0.51	0.57

Table 4 illustrates the evaluation results including the number of relations within the testing taxonomy, the number of relations within our generated taxonomy, recall and precision for the three different cameras, respectively. From the results, we can see that our generated feature taxonomy correctly capture around 50 % of the relationships. Figures 1 and 2 show a part of the feature taxonomy generated from our proposed approach and the testing taxonomy generated based on the product specification available online given by domain experts, respectively. From the comparison, our generated feature taxonomy identifies the relation between *picture* and *resolution*. Although the testing taxonomy uses more technical terms, which are *image sensor* instead of *picture*; in fact, they refer to the same attribute of the camera according to common knowledge. Similarly, the (*mode,auto*) and (*shooting modes,intelligent auto*) indicate the same relationship between two features.

As aforementioned, the online users and manufacture experts may describe the same feature by using totally different terms or words. This does affect the performance (both recall and precision) of our proposed approach in feature relationship identification negatively. For instance, the user may prefer using *"manual"* to depict a specific camera mode option. By contrast, the manufacture experts usually pick the term *"custom"* to describe this sub feature which belongs to *"shooting modes"*. In such a case, the two relations: (*mode, manual*) and (*shooting modes, custom*) cannot match.

5   Conclusions and Future Work

In this paper, we introduced a product feature taxonomy learning approach based on frequent patterns and association rules. The objective is to not only extract product features mentioned in user reviews but also identify the relationship between the generated features. The results of our experiment indicate that our proposed approach is effective in both identifying correct features and structural relationship between them. Particularly, the feature relationships captured in the feature taxonomy provide more detailed information about products. This leads us to represent products profiles as multi-levels of feature, rather than a single level as most other methods do.

In the future, we plan to improve and evaluate our proposed product model by utilizing semantic similarity tools. For instance, the vocabulary mismatch can be handled by examining the semantic similarity when we undertake the structural relation evaluation. In addition, we are to develop a review recommender system that makes use of the proposed product model in order to identify high quality reviews. The structural relations of the product model are able to assist identifying some characteristics of reviews, such as how a certain feature and its sub features have been discussed and how many different features have been covered. Our system will therefore aim at recommending reviews based upon such criteria to help users make purchasing decisions.

References

1. Abbasi, A., Chen, H., Salem, A.: Sentiment analysis in multiple languages: feature selection for opinion classification in Web forums. ACM Trans. Inf. Syst. **26**(3), 12–34 (2008)
2. Ding, X., Liu, B., Yu, P. S.: A holistic Lexicon-based approach to opinion mining. In: International Conference on Web Search and Web Data Mining, pp. 231–240 (2008)
3. Hu, M., Liu, B.: Mining opinion features in customer reviews. In: 19th National Conference on Artifical Intelligence, pp. 755–760 (2004)
4. Hu, M., Liu, B.: Mining and summarizing customer reviews. In: 10th ACM SIGKDD International Conference on Knowledge Discovery and Data Mining, pp. 168–177. ACM, New York (2004)
5. Hu, W., Gong, Z., Guo, J.: Mining product features from online reviews. In: IEEE 7th International Conference on E-Business Engineering, pp. 24–29 (2010)
6. Lau, R. Y. K., Lai, C. C. L., Ma, J., Li, Y.: Automatic domain ontology extraction for context-sensitive opinion mining. In: Thirtieth International Conference on Information Systems (2009)
7. Pasquier, N., Bastide, Y., Taouil, R., Lakhal, L.: Efficient mining of association rules using closed itemset lattices. Inf. Syst. **24**(1), 25–46 (1999)
8. Scaffidi, C., Bierhoff, K., Chang, E., Felker, M., Ng, H., Jin, C.: Red Opal: product-feature scoring from reviews. In: 8th ACM Conference on Electronic Commerce, pp. 182–191. ACM, New York (2007)
9. Subrahmanian, V., Reforgiato, D.: AVA: adjective-verb-adverb combinations for sentiment analysis. IEEE Intell. Syst. **23**, 43–50 (2008)
10. Xu, Y., Li, Y., Shaw, G.: Reliable representations for association rules. Data Knowl. Eng. **70**(6), 237–256 (2011)
11. Popescu, A.-M., Etzioni, O.: Extracting product features and opinions from reviews. In: Proceedings of the Conference on Human Language Technology and Empirical Methods in Natural Language Processing, pp. 339–346 (2005)

12. Lewis, D.D.: An evaluation of phrasal and clustered representations on a text categorization task. In: SIGIR 1992, 15th ACM International Conference on Research and Development in Information Retrieval, pp. 37–50 (1992)
13. Blei, D.M., Ng, A.Y., Jordan, M.I.: Latent dirichlet allocation. J. Mach. Learn. Res. **3**, 993–1022 (2003)
14. Hofmann, T.: Unsupervised learning by probabilistic latent semantic analysis. Mach. Learn. **42**(1), 177–196 (2001)
15. Tang, J., Leung, H.-F., Luo, Q., Chen, D., Gong, J.: Towards ontology learning from folksonomies. In: Proceedings of the 21st International Jont Conference on Artifical Intelligence (2009)
16. Zhang, Y., Zhu, W.: Extracting implicit features in online customer reviews for opinion mining. In: Proceedings of the 22nd International Conference on World Wide Web Companion, pp. 103–104 (2013)
17. Hai, Z., Chang, K., Kim, J., Yang, C.: Identifying features in opinion mining via intrinsic and extrinsic domain relevance. IEEE Trans. Knowl. Data Eng. **26**, 623–634 (2013)
18. Wright, A.: Our sentiments, exactly. Commun. ACM **52**(4), 14–15 (2009)

Automatic Web Page Classification Using Visual Content for Subjective and Functional Variables

Nuno Goncalves[✉] and Antonio Videira

Institute of Systems and Robotics, University of Coimbra, Coimbra, Portugal
{nunogon,avideira}@isr.uc.pt

Abstract. Automatic classification of webpages has several applications in industry: digital marketing, search engines, content filtering and many more. Traditionally this classification has been done using only the textual information of webpages, which includes the html code, tags, title and more lately also the url. The aim of this paper is to prove that for some subjective variables, although very important to the applications mentioned, the visual information of webpages as they are rendered by the browser has extremely rich content for the classification task. The variables studied are the aesthetic value (whether pages are beautiful or ugly) and the design recency of them (whether pages are old fashioned or look modern). We then proved that automatic classifications that rely only on the visual *look and feel* can achieve very high accuracies. As we used several low-level and mid-level features and studied several criteria for selection and classification, our classifiers were able to improve one step further the stat of the art. Finally, we applied this framework to classify webpages in their topic (content aware) and also to classify whether pages are a blog or not (functional aware).

Keywords: Web page classification · Feature extraction · Feature selection · Machine learning · Blog classification · Aesthetic value · Design recency

1 Introduction

The automatic classification of documents, namely web pages, has been studied in the last years. The advantages of having a robot that is able to classify web pages in the most diverse variables, from those totally technical and objective, to those that are subjective, personal or even fuzzy, are significant and extremely current. This is the main task of web crawlers that browse all internet pages to classify them. Web page classification hence helps in focused crawling, assists in the development and expanding of web directories, helps in the analysis of specific web link topic, in the analysis of the content structure of the web, improves the quality of web search (e.g., categories view, ranking view), web content filtering, assisted web browsing and much more.

Most of the classification methods, however, rely only on the textual information of the web page. This methodology is highly convenient since it is fast

© Springer International Publishing Switzerland 2015
V. Monfort and K.-H. Krempels (Eds.): WEBIST 2014, LNBIP 226, pp. 279–294, 2015.
DOI: 10.1007/978-3-319-27030-2_18

and relatively content-rich for variables like topic or for segmenting their users for market purposes. Yet, textual information is very poor for some subjective variables usually connected to the so-called *look and feel* of a given web page. In fact, text and tags of web pages do not contain information about the aesthetic value of that page, neither about the recency of its design. There is, however, a rich content about these variables encoded in the visual information of pages, especially since nowadays the use of images and banners with embedded text is increasing and non-textual items are becoming unavoidable.

Furthermore, besides the usual classification of the topic of web pages, there is a less usual, but not less important, functional classification. For instance, since blogs are a significant channel for digital advertising, and since their content is changing in a daily base frequency, much higher than the crawler frequency of classification, it is important to build alternatives to classify these web pages in terms of functionality, more specifically whether they are blogs or not.

In this paper we are interested in the web page classification (WPC) in subjective variables, such as aesthetic value and design recency, relying only on visual features. We prove that the look and feel contain rich information for this classification and that it can be used to improve that classification task. We also prove that the visual features can be used to classify the page topic and is much effective for classifying blog functionality. This paper is an extended version of our work published at the 10th International Conference on Web Information Systems and Technologies (WEBIST-2014) [1].

2   Related Work

The text content that is directly located on the page is the most used feature. A WPC method presented by Selamat and Omatu [2] used a neural network with inputs based on the Principal Component Analysis and class profile-based features. By selecting the most regular words in each class and weighted them, and with several methods of classification, they were able to demonstrate an acceptable accuracy. Chen and Hsieh [3] proposed a WPC method using a SVM based on a weighted voting scheme. This method uses Latent semantic analysis to find relations between keywords and documents, and text features extracted from the web page content. Those two features are then sent to the SVM model for training and testing respectively. Then, based on the SVM output, a voting scheme is used to determine the category of the web page.

There are few studies of WPC using the visual content, because tradition-ally only text information is used, achieving reasonable accuracy. It has been, however, noticed [4] that the visual content can help in disambiguating the clas-sification based only on this text content. Additionally, another factor in favor of using the visual content is the fact that subjective variables as design recency and aesthetic value cannot be studied using text content contained in the html code. These variables are increasing in importance due to web marketing strategies.

A WPC approach based on the visual information was implemented by Asirvatham et al. [5], where a number of visual features, as well as text features, were used. They proposed a method for automatic categorization of web pages into a few broad categories based on the structure of the web documents and the images presented on it. Another approach was proposed by Kovacevic et al. [6], where a page is represented as a hierarchical structure - Visual Adjacency Multigraph, in which, nodes represent simple HTML objects, texts and images, while directed edges reflect spatial relations on the browser screen.

As mentioned previously, Boer et al. [4] has successfully classified web pages using only visual features. They classified pages in two binary variables: aesthetic value and design recency, achieving good accuracy. The authors also applied the same classification algorithm and methods to a multi-class categorization of the website topic and although the results obtained are reasonable, it was concluded that this classification is more difficult to perform.

3   Classification Process

In Fig. 1 it is possible to see the necessary steps to predict the class of new web pages. The algorithms were developed in C/C++ using the OpenCV library.

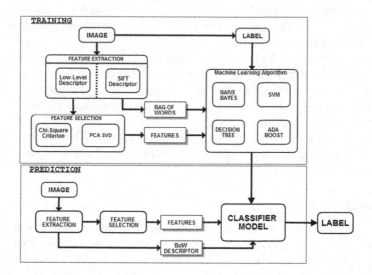

Fig. 1. Classification Process diagram.

3.1   Visual Feature Extraction

The concept of feature in computer vision and image processing refers to a piece of information which is relevant and distinctive. For each web page, different feature descriptors (feature vector) are computed. More details are presented in [1].

Low Level Descriptor. Visual descriptors are descriptions of visual features of the content of an image. These descriptors describe elementary characteristics such as shape, color, texture, motion, among others. To built this descriptor, with 166 feature-components, the following features were extracted from each image: color histogram, edge histogram, tamura features [7,8] and gabor features [9]. See more details in [1].

SIFT Descriptor Using Bag of Words Model. Keypoints are salient image patches that contain rich local information. The Scale Invariant Feature Transform was developed in 1999 by David Lowe. The SIFT features are one of the most popular local image features for general images, and was later refined by [10]. This approach transforms image data into scale-invariant coordinates of local features.

On the other hand, the bag-of-words (BoW) model [11] is a feature summarization technique that can be defined as follows. Given a training dataset D, that contains n images, where $D = \{d_1, d_2, ..., d_n\}$, where d are the extracted features, a specific algorithm is used to group D based on a fixed number of visual words W represented by $W = \{w_1, w_2, ..., w_v\}$, where v is the number of clusters. Then, it is possible to summarize the data in a $n \times v$ co-occurrence table of counts $N_{ij} = N(w_i, d_j)$, where $N(w_i, d_j)$ denotes how often the word w_i occurred in an image d_j.

To extract the BoW feature from images the following steps are required: (i) detect the SIFT keypoints, (ii) compute the local descriptors over those keypoints, (iii) quantize the descriptors into words to form the visual vocabulary, and (iv) to retrieve the BoW feature, find the occurrences in the image of each specific word in the vocabulary.

We use the SIFT and BoW implementations of OpenCV which outputs a 128-dimensional vector, training the classifier with different dictionary sizes: 100, 200 and 500 words.

3.2   Feature Selection

An important component of both supervised and unsupervised classification problems is feature selection - a technique that selects a subset of the original attributes by selecting the most relevant features. Two algorithms for applying feature selection are built. One is based on the Chi-Square Criterion, the other uses the Principal Components Analysis. In both methods a different percentage of the most relevant features is selected. To this work we used 1 %, 2 %, 5 %, 10 %, 20 % and 50 % of the total features.

As for the classifiers used, we opted for a wide variety of the most representative ones, by using their implementation of OpenCV. The classifiers used were then the Naïve Bayes, SVM, Decision Trees and AdaBoost.

4   Web Pages Database

In this work, different web page classification experiments are evaluated. There are three binary classifications and one multi-category classification. The three

Fig. 2. An example of the web pages retrieved for the Aesthetic classification. In the left, there are 6 beautiful web pages, and in the right 6 ugly web pages.

binary classifications are: the aesthetic value of a web page, i.e., if a web page is beautiful or ugly (a measure that depends on the notion of aesthetic of each person), the design recency of a web page, i.e., trying to distinguish between old fashioned and new fashioned web pages and the blog functionality, i.e., whether a web page is a blog or not. The multi category classification involves classification on the web page topic.

Using the Fireshot plugin[1] for the Firefox web browser, allows to retrieve a screen shot of a web page and save it as a. PNG file. Different training sets of 30, 60 and 90 pages are built for each class of the classification experiment. For the blog classification we built a database with 800 blogs and 800 non blog pages. For each site we only retrieved the landing page which is generally the index page.

4.1   Aesthetic

The notion of aesthetic differs from person to person, because what can be beautiful for someone, can be ugly for another. That is why this classification depends of each classifier and it is a subjective classification. Nevertheless, there is a generic notion of the beautiful and of the ugly that is common to the individuals of a certain culture. We emphasize that this underlying notion of the aesthetic value is of extremely importance to marketing and psychological explorations.

In this classification experiment two classes are then defined: ugly and beautiful web pages. Notice that in Aesthetic, the important aspect is the visual design ("Look and Feel") of a web page, and not the quality of information or popularity of the page.

The ugly pages were downloaded from two articles [12,13] and their corresponding comment section, and also from the website World Worst Websites of the Year 2012 – 2005 [14]. The beautiful pages were retrieved, consulting a

---

[1] https://addons.mozilla.org/pt-pt/firefox/addon/fireshot/.

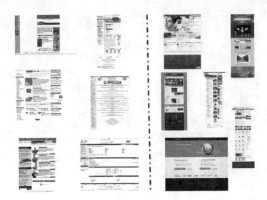

Fig. 3. An example of the web pages retrieved for the Recency classification. In the left, there are 6 old fashioned web pages from 1999, and in the right 6 new fashioned web pages from 2012.

design web log, listing the author's selection of the most beautiful web pages of 2008, 2009, 2010, 2011 and 2012 [15].

After analyzing the web pages retrieved (Fig. 2), it was possible to notice that, in general, an ugly web page don't transmit a clear message, uses too much powerful colors, lacks clarity and a consistent navigation. While, on the opposite side, a beautiful web page usually has an engaging picture, an easy navigation, the colors compliment each other and it is easy to find the information needed. Obviously these are some directives observed from the database and do not correspond to strict conclusions.

4.2   Design Recency

The objective of this classification is to be able to distinguish between old fashioned and new fashioned pages. The principal differences between these pages (Fig. 3) is that nowadays the web design of a page has firmly established itself as an irreplaceable component of every good marketing strategy. Recent pages usually have large background images, blended typography, colorful and flat graphics, that is, every design element brings relevant content to the user. In the past the use of GIFs, very large comprised text and blinding background were common in most sites.

The old web pages were retrieved consulting the article [16], that shows the most popular pages in 1999, and using the Internet Archive web site[2] allowed to retrieve the versions of those websites in that year. To retrieve the new pages, the Alexa[3] web page popularity rankings was used, selecting then the 2012 most popular pages.

---

[2] http://archive.org/web/web.php.

[3] http://www.alexa.com.

Fig. 4. Examples of web pages extracted for four web site topic classes.

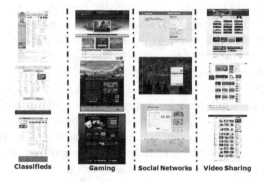

Fig. 5. Examples of web pages extracted for the other four web site topic classes.

4.3   Web Page Topic

In this classification eight classes are defined: newspapers, hotels, celebrities, conferences, classified advertisements, social networks, gaming and video-sharing.

For the newspaper and celebrity classes, the http://Alexa.com was consulted, retrieving the most well-known and popular newspapers and celebrity sites. The celebrity sites also include popular fan sites. The conferences class consist in the homepages of the highest ranked Computer Science Conferences. And for the hotel class, different sites from bed-and-breakfast businesses are retrieved. The classes include different pages from different countries. The classified advertisements sites were extracted using also the http://Alexa.com, retrieving the most visited sites of classifieds of all world (sections devoted to jobs, housing, personals, for sale, items wanted, services, community, gigs and discussion forums). The video-sharing class and the gaming class (company gaming websites and popular gaming online websites), were extracted consulting the google search engine for the most popular sites in this type of websites. Social networks class consist in the major social networking websites homepages (e.g., websites that allow people to share interests, activities, backgrounds or real-life connections).

Fig. 6. An example of the blog pages retrieved.

A topic of a web site is a relevant area in the classification of web pages. Each topic has a relevant visual characteristic that distinguishes them, being possible to classify the web pages despite of their language or country. Looking at the pages retrieved (Figs. 4 and 5), it is possible to perceive a distinct visual characteristic in each class. The newspaper sites have a lot of text followed with images, while celebrity sites have more distinct colors and embedded videos. The conferences sites usually consist in a banner in the top of the page, and text information about the conference. Hotel sites have a more distinct background, with more photographs. Classifieds sites consist almost in blue hyperlinks with images or text, with a soft color background and banner. The body content of a video-sharing site consist in video thumbnails. The gaming sites have a distinct banner (an image or huge letters), with a color background and embedded videos. The social networks homepages, have a color pattern that is persistent.

4.4   Blog Classification

Classify a web page as being a blog or not can also be important for marketing and crawling reasons. This is why we added to this extended version of the paper [1] this study.

We thus built a database with 800 blogs and 800 non-blog pages. The blog pages were retrieved by random search in Google blogspot (http://blogspot.com). We retrieved 400 blogs written in Portuguese and 400 blogs written in English. For the non-blog pages we used random pages retrieved from the web index http://Alexa.com. See Fig. 6.

5   Results and Discussion

For the experiments, each classifier was evaluated with the low feature descriptor (containing 166 features), just the Color Histogram, Edge Histogram, Tamura Features, Gabor Features, and the descriptor containing the most relevant features selected by the methods of feature selection. Additionally the same data sets were used to train the classifiers with the SIFT descriptor using the bag of words model. The results for each classification task are shown in the next sections, as well as a comparison with the results of [4].

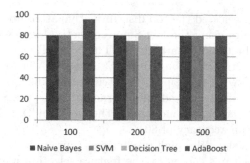

Fig. 7. SIFT Descriptor using BoW Model prediction results with different dictionary sizes (100, 200 and 500) for the Aesthetic Value.

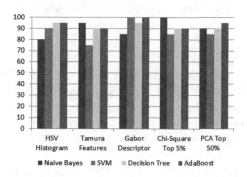

Fig. 8. Best prediction results for the Recency value for four different classifiers, using the low-level descriptor.

To test all methods after the training phase, new web pages were used to the prediction phase. Our results are based on the accuracy achieved by this prediction phase.

5.1 Aesthetic Value Results

In their experiments with the 166 features, [4] achieved an accuracy using the Naïve Bayes and a Decision Tree of 68 % and 80 % respectively. Using just the Simple Color Histogram and Edge Histogram they correctly classified 68 % and 70 % respectively for the Naïve Bayes, and 66 % and 53 % for the Decision Tree classifier.

For this experiment, Fig. 7 show the best rate prediction for our classifiers, when used the SIFT descriptor. Using different sizes for the dictionary, we obtained good result for each classifier. The best results for the Naïve Bayes, SVM and the Decision Tree was of 80 %, and for the AdaBoost we achieved a prediction accuracy of 85 %.

When trained the model using just the Color Histogram attributes, the results show an accuracy of 65 % for Naïve Bayes, 85 % in SVM, 70 % for the Decision Tree and 85 % using the AdaBoost when trained with 90 images for each class. When we selected the top discriminative attributes to train the classifiers, the best results using the Chi-Squared method was when the classifiers were trained with the top 50 % attributes. The Naïve Bayes and SVM achieved an accuracy of 65 %, the Decision Tree 80 % and the AdaBoost an accuracy of 75 %. When trained with the top 20 % attributes by using the PCA method, the Naïve Bayes classifier achieved an accuracy of 75 %, the SVM classifier predicted 65 % of corrected pages, and finally, the Decision Tree and the AdaBoost classifiers both had an accuracy of 80 %.

All the classifiers showed a high prediction accuracy, with different features. Since most of the features chosen by the feature selection method are from the Color Histogram, it is possible to achieve a good prediction rate just by passing this simple descriptor. The SIFT descriptor give the best results, proving that the images from this two classes have distinctive keypoints.

5.2   Design Recency Results

In this experiment, [4] achieved an accuracy using the Naïve Bayes and a Decision Tree of 82 % and 85 % respectively. Using just the Simple Color Histogram the Naïve Bayes performed slightly worse than the baseline and the Decision Tree classifier sightly better. Using only the edge information, both models correctly classified 72 % and 78 % respectively for the Naïve Bayes and Decision Tree classifier.

Our best results for this experiment, using the low-level descriptor, are shown in Fig. 8. The Naïve Bayes, SVM and AdaBoost achieved an accuracy of 100 %, when the top 5 % attributes were selected using the Chi-Square method for the first one and the Gabor descriptor for the other two. The Decision Tree best accuracy (95 %), was when the PCA method selected the top 5 % attributes.

Relatively to the SIFT descriptor, all the classifiers obtained good accuracy. Notice that all the classifiers obtained an accuracy of 90 % when they used a dictionary size of 500. The best accuracy result achieved was for the Naïve Bayes with a 95 % rate of success, with a dictionary size of 200 words.

These results prove that the classifiers can learn just by using simple visual features. All the classifiers obtained good accuracy around 85 %, using the top 1 % attributes selected by both methods. Instead of using a more complex method like BoW, the use of simple visual features allows to decrease the computational cost for larger databases.

5.3   Web Page Topic Results

Experiment 1 - Four Classes. [4] define the following four classes for the topic: newspapers, hotel, celebrities and conference sites. The classification results obtained were the following: when all features are used, an accuracy of 54 % and 56 % for the Naïve Bayes and the Decision Tree respectively. Using the Color Histogram subset results in a much worse accuracy. Using only the Edge Histogram attributes, the Naïve Bayes predict with an accuracy of 58 %, whereas

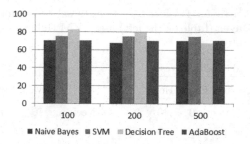

Fig. 9. SIFT Descriptor using BoW Model. Best prediction results with different dictionary sizes (100, 200 and 500). Experiments with 4 classes.

the Decision Tree predicts with an accuracy of 43 %. When they performed feature selection they show that the best predicting attributes are all from the Tamura and Gabor feature vectors. Using the top 10 attributes a prediction accuracy of 43 % for both classifiers was obtained.

Using the same low-level descriptor that they used, all our classifiers obtained better results. The Naïve Bayes achieved an accuracy of 62,5 % using the Tamura Features. The SVM and Decision Tree achieved an accuracy rate of 72,5 %, when used the selected top 20 % attributes using the PCA method and using the whole descriptor, respectively. While the AdaBoost classifier achieved an accuracy of 70 % using the PCA method selecting the top 50 % attributes.

Furthermore, the results showed in Fig. 9 are an improvement of the accuracy of approximately 22 % using the BoW model. Every classifier have an acceptable accuracy, where the best accuracy result is as high as 82,5 % for the Decision Tree using just 100 words to construct the dictionary. In fact, all the classifiers have accuracy higher than or equal to 70 % when used just 100 words in the dictionary.

Examining the results of the confusion matrices (Tables 1 and 2 corresponding to the best predictions of each classifier using the SIFT with BoW model (Fig. 9), it was verified, when analyzing the accuracy by class, that the Naïve Bayes, Decision Tree and AdaBoost perform much worse for the Hotel class. The Naïve Bayes and AdaBoost classifiers reports false positives for the Hotel class as Conference or Celebrity pages. While the Decision Tree returns false positives for Celebrities web pages as Hotel web pages, and vice versa. By his hand, the SVM classifiers perform much worse for the Celebrity web pages where most of the instances are erroneously classified as Hotel pages. Since the Newspapers and Conference classes have simpler designs, when compared with the other classes, they are easier to distinguish. On the other hand, it is harder to distinguish between more complex and sophisticated classes like Hotel and Celebrity.

Although the results obtained for this multi-class categorization are worse than those obtained for aesthetic value and design recency, generally good accuracy was obtained with best values usually near or above 80 %. Additionally, our results are better than those obtained by Boer et al. [4], mainly if SIFT with BoW is used.

Table 1. Confusion Matrix for 4 classes each with 10 web pages, for the best prediction result of the **Naïve Bayes** (table on the left) and **SVM** (table on the right) classifiers, using the SIFT descriptor.

| | Actual - **Naïve Bayes** | | | | | Actual - **SVM** | | | |
	Newsp.	Conf.	Celeb.	Hotel		Newsp.	Conf.	Celeb.	Hotel
Newsp.	7	0	0	0	Newsp.	10	1	1	0
Conf.	2	7	2	2	Conf.	0	8	1	0
Celeb.	0	0	8	2	Celeb.	0	0	4	2
Hotel	1	3	0	6	Hotel	0	1	4	8

Table 2. Confusion Matrix for 4 classes each with 10 web pages, for the best prediction result of the **Decision Tree** (table on the left) and **AdaBoost** (table on the right) classifiers, using the SIFT descriptor.

| | Actual - **Naïve Bayes** | | | | | Actual - **SVM** | | | |
	Newsp.	Conf.	Celeb.	Hotel		Newsp.	Conf.	Celeb.	Hotel
Newsp.	10	0	1	0	Newsp.	10	0	1	0
Conf.	0	9	0	1	Conf.	0	6	1	3
Celeb.	0	1	7	2	Celeb.	0	1	8	3
Hotel	0	0	2	7	Hotel	0	2	0	4

Experiment 2 - Eight Classes. Along with the four classes defined in the experiment 1, four additional classes were added to this classification: classified advertisements sites, gaming sites, social networks sites and video-sharing sites.

Using the low-level descriptor the Naïve Bayes had the best accuracy with 47,5 %, while the SVM achieved an accuracy of 41,25 % using the Tamura descriptor. The Decision Tree and AdaBoost classifiers had a poor performance, where the best accuracy was 37,5 % and 33,75 %, respectively. When we used the Chi-Square and PCA method to select the top attributes the classifiers performance didn't improve. We conclude that for this type of classification more complex features or a bigger database are necessary.

When we used the SIFT descriptor (Fig. 10) all the classifiers had a better accuracy relatively to the results obtained using the low-level descriptor. The SVM achieved an accuracy of 58,75 %, and the Naïve Bayes 63,75 %. The Decision Tree best accuracy was 48,75 %, while the AdaBoost only predict the correct class in 38,75 % of the predictions.

When examining the confusion matrices (Tables 3 and 4) of Naïve Bayes and SVM classifiers (which achieved accuracy over 50 % when using the SIFT descriptor), it is possible to verify that both classifiers have problems distinguishing celebrities web pages. The Naïve Bayes also struggles in identify Video-Sharing

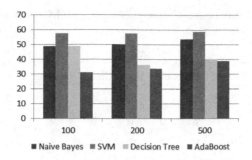

Fig. 10. SIFT Descriptor using BoW Model in experiment 2. Best prediction results with different dictionary sizes (100, 200 and 500).

Table 3. Confusion Matrix for 8 classes, by the **Naïve Bayes** classifier, using the SIFT descriptor.

		Actual							
		Newsp.	Conf.	Celeb.	Hotel	Classif.	Gaming	Social N.	Video
	Newsp.	9	0	1	1	3	1	0	4
	Conf.	1	5	0	0	1	0	0	0
Predicted	Celeb.	0	0	3	2	0	2	2	1
	Hotel	0	1	0	5	0	1	1	0
	Classif.	0	1	1	1	6	0	0	1
	Gaming	0	0	5	0	0	6	0	0
	Social N.	0	1	0	1	0	0	6	1
	Video	0	0	0	0	0	0	1	3

pages (only 3 correct predictions), while the SVM have troubles in identifying Social Networks web pages (only 2 correct predictions). The body of video-sharing web pages that consist mostly in video thumbnails are easily mistaken as newspapers web page (mostly images followed by text). In both methods some classifieds advertisements web pages are also predicted as newspapers (most classifieds advertisement websites use a simple color background with a lot of images). To overcome this drawbacks a bigger database is necessary.

5.4 Blog Classification Results

The results obtained for this binary classification are described by the confusion matrix Table 5. The results presented correspond to the best global accuracy, obtained using the Decision Tree classifier, achieving a global accuracy of 85 %. As can be observed the classification is much effective as expected, using only visual content.

Table 4. Confusion Matrix for 8 classes, by the **SVM** classifier, using the SIFT descriptor.

	Actual							
	Newsp.	Conf.	Celeb.	Hotel	Classif.	Gaming	Social N.	Video
Newsp.	9	1	1	1	4	0	1	2
Conf.	1	8	0	0	0	0	0	0
Celeb.	0	0	4	2	0	3	2	1
Hotel	0	0	0	7	0	1	1	1
Classif.	0	0	1	0	6	1	0	0
Gaming	0	0	4	0	0	5	2	0
Social N.	0	1	0	0	0	0	2	0
Video	0	0	0	0	0	0	2	6

(Predicted, left margin label)

Table 5. Confusion Matrix for Blog classification test (40 web pages per class), by the **Decision Tree** classifier, using the Low Level features (table on the left) and the SIFT feature descriptor (table on the right). Both descriptors achieved a global accuracy of 85 %.

	Actual - Low Level				Actual - SIFT	
	Blog	Non Blog			Blog	Non Blog
Blog	34	6		Blog	34	6
Non Blog	6	34		Non Blog	6	34

(Predicted, left margin label)

Furthermore, we emphasize that some Non-blog web pages that were classified as Blog pages are, actually, very close to the usual or typical blog. Figure 11 shows two examples of web pages classified as blogs that were in the non-blog database (false positives).

5.5 Discussion

The results show that based on aesthetic value and design recency, simple features such as color histogram and edges provide quite good results, where in some cases an accuracy of 100 % is achieved (average best accuracy of 85 %). It is also concluded that SIFT+BoW can also improve the accuracy at a considerably computational cost. For the topic classification, the use of a SIFT with BoW provide much better results too.

As expected when more website topics are added, the classification gets harder and the classifiers accuracy decreases to an average around 60 %. This indicates that even if the pages have visual characteristics that distinguishes

Fig. 11. False positives (non-blog pages classified as blog) that are, actually, very close to the typical blog.

them, they also have some attributes or characteristics in common. To overcome this setbacks a bigger database is necessary. Nevertheless, the aim of this work was to demonstrate that it is possible to classify web pages in different topics with reasonable accuracy and to prove that this visual content is very rich and can be successfully used to complement, not to substitute, the current classification by text crawlers. Notice too, that in the design of web pages, there is a growing tendency to include content in the images used, preventing text-based crawlers to get to this rich content (mainly in titles, separators and banners).

6   Conclusions

In this work we described an approach for the automatic web page classification by exploring the visual content "Look and feel" of web pages. The results obtained are quite encouraging, proving that the visual content of a web page should not be ignored, when performing classification.

In the future, in order to improve the classification accuracy we can also follow some additional paths. The integration of these visual features with other features of web pages can thus boost the accuracy in the classifiers. The analysis of the visual appearance of a web page can be combined with the well-established analysis based on text content, URL, the underlying HTML, or others. In this case, associate this visual features with the text content may give rise to a powerful classification system. Additionally, we also intend to mix the classification using visual features with a semantic analysis of them. We expect to improve the results by integrating the semantic content of a webpage image not only in the classification of the aesthetic or recency value but also for the classification of the topic. Another approach is the extraction of more sophisticated features that can analyze their dynamic elements (animated gifs, flash, advertisement content, and so on).

As for the applications of the visual classification of web pages, the methods studied may be applied to an advice system able to assist the design and rating of web sites to be applied to content filtering. In a research perspective, the fact that the aesthetic and design recency value are such a subjective measures, also make of great interest studies of the consumer profile for the field of digital marketing.

References

1. Videira, A., Goncalves, N.: Automatic web page classification using visual content. In: 10th International Conference on Web Information Systems and Technologies (WEBIST 2014) (2014)
2. Selamat, A., Omatu, S.: Web page feature selection and classification using neural networks. Inf. Sci. Inf. Comput. Sci. **158**, 69–88 (2004)
3. Chen, R.C., Hsieh, C.H.: Web page classification based on a support vector machine using a weighted vote schema. Expert. Syst. Appl. **2**(31), 427–435 (2006)
4. de Boer, V., van Someren, M., Lupascu, T.: Classifying web pages with visual features. In: 6th International Conference on Web Information Systems and Technologies (WEBIST 2010), pp. 245–252 (2010)
5. Asirvatham, A.P., Ravi, K.K.: Web page classification based on document structure. In: IEEE National Convention (2001)
6. Kovacevic, M., Diligenti, M., Gori, M., Milutinovic, V.: Visual adjacency multigraphs, a novel approach for a web page classification. In: Workshop on Statistical Approaches to Web Mining (SAWM), pp. 38–49 (2004)
7. Tamura, H., Mori, S., Yamawaki, T.: Textural features corresponding to visual perception. IEEE Trans. Syst. Man Cybern. **8**, 460–472 (1978)
8. Deselaers, T.: Features for Image Retrieval (thesis). RWTH Aachen University (2003)
9. Zhang, D., Wong, A., Indrawan, M., Lu, G.: Content-based image retrieval using Gabor texture features. In: IEEE Pacific-Rim Conference on Multimedia, University of Sydney, Australia (2000)
10. Lowe, D.: Distinctive image features from scale-invariant keypoints. Int. J. Comput. Vision **2**(60), 91–110 (2004)
11. Liu, J.: Image Retrieval based on Bag-of-Words model (2013). arXiv preprint arXiv:1304.5168
12. Andrade, L.: The worlds ugliest websites!!! (2009). http://www.nikibrown.com/designoblog/2009/03/03/theworlds-ugliest-websites. Acessed October 2009
13. Shuey, M.: 10-worst-websites-for-2013 (2013). http://www.globalwebfx.com/10-worst-websites-for-2013/
14. Flanders, V.: Worst Websites of the Year 2012–2005 (2012).http://www.webpagesthatsuck.com/worst-websites-of-the-year.html
15. Crazyleafdesign.com: Most beautiful and inspirational website designs (2013). http://www.crazyleafdesign.com/blog/
16. waxy.org: Den.net and the top 100 websites of 1999 (2010). http://waxy.org/2010/02/dennet_and_the_top_100_web-sites_of_1999/

Rocchio Algorithm to Enhance Semantically Collaborative Filtering

Sonia Ben Ticha[1,2]([✉]), Azim Roussanaly[1], Anne Boyer[1], and Khaled Bsaïes[2]

[1] LORIA-KIWI Team, Lorraine University, Nancy, France
{sonia.benticha,azim.roussanaly,anne.boyer}@loria.fr
[2] LIPA Lab, Tunis El Manar University, Tunis, Tunisia
khaled.bsaies@fst.rnu.tn

Abstract. Recommender system provides relevant items to users from huge catalogue. Collaborative filtering and content-based filtering are the most widely used techniques in personalized recommender systems. Collaborative filtering uses only the user-ratings data to make predictions, while content-based filtering relies on semantic information of items for recommendation. Hybrid recommendation system combines the two techniques. In this paper, we present another hybridization approach: User Semantic Collaborative Filtering. The aim of our approach is to predict users preferences for items based on their inferred preferences for semantic information of items. In this aim, we design a new user semantic model to describe the user preferences by using Rocchio algorithm. Due to the high dimension of item content, we apply a latent semantic analysis to reduce the dimension of data. User semantic model is then used in a user-based collaborative filtering to compute prediction ratings and to provide recommendations. Applying our approach to real data set, the MoviesLens 1M data set, significant improvement can be noticed compared to usage only approach, content based only approach.

Keywords: Hybrid recommender system · Latent semantic analysis · Rocchio algorithm

1 Introduction

Thanks to computers and computer networks, our society is undergoing rapid transformation in almost all aspects. We buy online, read news online, listen music online, gather information by search engines and live a significant part of our social life on the Internet. However, the ongoing rapid expansion of the Internet, requires to help user to access to items that may interest her or him. Recommender Systems (RS) provide relevant items to users from a large number of choices. Several recommendations techniques exist in the literature. Among these techniques, there are those that provide personalized recommendations by defining a profile for each user. In this work, we are interested in personalized recommender systems where the user model is based on an analysis of usage.

© Springer International Publishing Switzerland 2015
V. Monfort and K.-H. Krempels (Eds.): WEBIST 2014, LNBIP 226, pp. 295–311, 2015.
DOI: 10.1007/978-3-319-27030-2_19

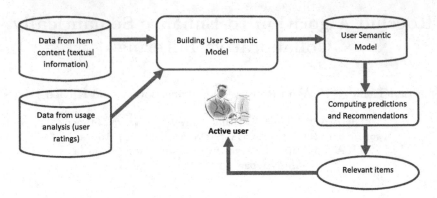

Fig. 1. User Semantic Collaborative Filtering (USCF) architecture.

This model is usually described by a user-item ratings matrix, which is extremely sparse ($\geq 90\%$ of missing data).

Collaborative Filtering (CF) and Content-Based (CB) filtering are the most widely used techniques in RS. In CF, user will be recommended items that people with similar tastes and preferences liked in the past [1]. CB filtering assumes that each user operates independently and user will be recommended items similar to the ones he preferred in the past [2]. The major difference between CF and CB recommender systems is that CF relies only on the user-item ratings data to make predictions and recommendations, while CB relies on item content (semantic information) for recommendations. Hybrid approach [3] is another important technique, which combine collaborative and content-based methods to provide recommendations.

In this paper, we present a new approach: *User Semantic Collaborative Filtering (USCF)*, that takes into account the semantic information of items to enhance collaborative recommendations. User Semantic Collaborative Filtering (USCF) consists of two components as shown in Fig. 1: the first builds a new user model, the *User Semantic Model*, by inferring user preferences for item content; the second computes predictions and provides recommendations by using the User Semantic Model in a user-based collaborative filtering algorithm [4] to calculate the similarity between users. The originality of this work is in the building of the User Semantic Model. Indeed, assuming that items are represented by structured data in which each item is described by a same set of attributes, we build a *User Semantic Attribute Model* for each relevant attribute. With this aim, we define two classes of attributes: *dependent* and *non dependent* and we propose a suited algorithm for each class. User Semantic Model is then deducted from the horizontal concatenation of all User Semantic Attribute Model. In previous works [5,6] we have presented solutions based on machine learning algorithm to build a User Semantic Attribute Model for non dependent attribute.

In this work, we present a new approach for building a user semantic attribute model for dependent attribute by using Rocchio algorithm [7]. Due to the high number of attribute values, and to reduce the expensiveness of user similarity computing, we apply a Latent Semantic Analysis (LSA) [8] to reduce the size of the user semantic attribute model. We compare our results to the standards user-based CF, item-based CF and Content Based algorithms. Our approach results in an overall improvement in prediction accuracy.

The rest of this paper is organized as follows: Section 2 summarizes the related work. Section 3 presents the Latent Semantic Analysis (LSA) algorithm. The algorithm of building the User Semantic Model is described in Sect. 4. Section 5 describes our approach to build User Semantic Attribute Model for non dependent attribute. Section 6 describes the recommendation component of our system. Experimental results are presented and discussed in Sect. 7. Finally, we conclude with a summary of our findings and some directions for future work.

2   Related Work

Recommender Systems (RS) [9] have become an independent research area since the appearance of the first papers on collaborative filtering in the mid-1990s [4,10,11]. Collaborative Filtering (CF) [12] is the most widespread used technique in RS. The fundamental assumption of CF is that if users X and Y rate n items similarly and hence will rate or act on other items similarly [13]. In CF, the user model is usually described by a user-item rating matrix (users in lines and items in columns). Each value in the matrix is either a rating assigned by the user to the corresponding item, or a missing value if no information is available about the corresponding couple (user, item). Thus, CF systems try to predict ratings of items for the active user based only on the items previously rated by other users. BREESE et al. [14] have identified two classes of CF algorithms: *Memory-based* and *Model-based* algorithms. Memory-based algorithms use heuristic functions and the entire of the user-item ratings matrix to generate predictions. This allows them to be very reactive by integrating immediately modifications of users profiles into the system. User-based CF, introduced by Resnick et al. [4], and Item-based CF, introduced by SARWAR et al. [15], are the most prevalent memory-based algorithms. They are both based on the k-Nearest-Neighbors algorithm. The first computes similarities between users and the second computes similarities between items. However, even if these methods work well with small-sized database, BREESE et al. [14] think that their scalability is problematic for big databases with great number of items and/or users. The model-based algorithms [16–18] constitute an alternative to this problem. These algorithms build descriptive models via a learning process. Thus, predictions are inferred from these models.

Content Based filtering (CB) [19] is another important technique used in RS. Unlike CF recommendation methods, CB recommender systems rely on the content of items to provide personalized recommendations to active user. CB assumes that each user operates independently and recommends items similar to the ones he or she preferred in the past. Content-based systems focus on recommending items containing textual information, such as documents, web page, news or item attributes. That is why, Content-based filtering has its roots in information retrieval [20, 21] and information filtering [22] research. Furthermore, in content based filtering, item profile is usually represented by a Vector Space Model (VSM). Like collaborative filtering, there are two classes of CB algorithms: *Memory-based* and *Model-based* algorithms [23]. In memory-based algorithms [24], various candidate items are compared with items previously rated by the active user and the best matching item(s) are recommended. The similarities between items are computed using heuristic formula like cosine measure. In model base techniques [2, 25], predictions are provided based on a model learned from the underlying data using statistical learning and machine learning techniques.

However, CF and CB filtering must face many challenges [23], like the *data sparsity* problem due to missing data in user-item matrix; the *scalability problem* for large datasets with the increasing numbers of users and items; the *cold start problem* when new user logs in, the system ignores his or her preferences. Furthermore, each technique introduced its own shortcomings. In CF technique, if new item appears in the database, there is no way to be recommended before it is rated, this problem is known also as *Cold-start problem*. *Neighbor transitivity* refers to a problem with sparse data, in which users with similar tastes may not be identified as such if they have any items rated in common. CB filtering suffers a problem of over-specialization where a user is restricted to seeing items similar to those already rated.

To overcome the disadvantages of both techniques and benefit from their strengths, several recommender systems use a hybrid approach by combining CF and CB techniques. The Fab System [26] counts among the first hybrid RS. Many systems have been developed since [3]. Moreover, because of the huge number of items and users, calculating the similarity between users in CF algorithm becomes very expensive in time computing. Dimension reduction of data is one of the solution to alleviate the expensiveness of users similarity computing [27]. Mobasher et al. [28] combine values of all attributes and then apply a Latent Semantic Analysis (LSA) to reduce dimension of data. Sen et al. [29] are inferring user preferences for only one attribute, the item' tags, without reducing dimension. Manzato [30] computes a user semantic model for only the movie genre attribute and applies a Singular Value Decomposition (SVD) to reduce the dimension of data.

3   Latent Semantic Analysis (LSA)

Latent Semantic Analysis (LSA) [8] is a dimensionality reduction technique which is widely used in information retrieval [20] and information filtering [22] research. Given a term-document frequency matrix $M_{d,l}$ (d documents and l terms), in witch each document is described by a Vector Space Model (VSM), LSA is used to decompose it into two matrices of reduced dimensions and a diagonal matrix of singular values. Each dimension in the reduced space is a latent factor representing groups of highly correlated index terms.

Singular Value Decomposition (SVD) is a well known technique used in LSA to perform matrix decomposition. SVD decomposes the term-document frequency matrix M into three matrices D, Σ and T:

$$M = D_{d,r} * \Sigma_{r,r} * T_{r,l}^t \tag{1}$$

where D and T are two orthogonal matrices; $r = min(d, l)$ is the rank of matrix M. Σ is a diagonal matrix, where its diagonal entries contain all singular values of matrix M stored in decreasing order. D and T matrices are the left and right singular vectors. LSA uses a truncated SVD, keeping only the k largest singular values and their associated vectors, so

$$M \approx M' = D_{d,k} * \Sigma_{k,k} * T_{k,l}^t \tag{2}$$

M' is the rank-k approximation of M. M' is what LSA uses for its semantic space. The rows in $D_{d,k}$ are the document vectors in LSA space and the rows in $T_{l,k}$ are the term vectors in LSA space. Each document in $D_{d,k}$ is represented by a set of k latent variables, instead of the original terms. Each term in $T_{l,k}$ is represented by a set of k latent variables instead of the original document. This, results in a much less sparse matrix. Furthermore, the generated latent variables represent groups of highly correlated terms in the original data, thus potentially reducing the amount of noise associated with the semantic information.

4   User Semantic Model

In this paper, we are interested only to items described by structured data. According to the definition of Pazzani et al. [2], in structured representation, item can be represented by a small number of attributes, and there is a known set of values that each attribute may have. For instance, the attributes of a movie can be *title*, *genre*, *actor* and *director*. In the following, we will use the term *feature* to refer to an attribute value. For instance, *Documentary*, *Musical* and *Thriller* are features of *movie genre* attribute.

4.1   Dependent and Non Dependent Attribute

In structured representation, each attribute has a set of restricted features. However, the number of features can be related or not to the number of items. That is why we have defined two classes of attributes:

- **Dependent Attribute:** attribute, which having very variable number of features. This number is closely related to the number of items. So, when the number of items is increasing, the number of features is increasing also. For example: *directors* and *actors of movies, keywords*.
- **Non Dependent Attribute:** attribute, which having a very few variable number of features, and this number is not related to the number of items. Thus, the increasing number of items has no effect on the number of features. For example: *movie genre*, *movie origin* and *cuisine of restaurants*.

In addition, all attributes do not have the same degrees of importance to users. There are attributes more relevant than others. For instance, the *movie genre* can be more significant, in the evaluation criteria of user, than the *origin*. Experiments that we have conducted (see Sect. 7.4) confirmed this hypothesis. In this paper, we assume that relevant attributes will be provided by a human expert. Therefore, for each relevant attribute A, we build a *user semantic attribute model* that predicts the users preferences for its features (or group of features). This model is described by a matrix Q_A (users in lines and features (or group of features) of A in columns). In our approach, we design a suited algorithm for building the *user semantic attribute model* for each class of attribute.

For non dependent attribute, due to the low number of features, we have used a clustering algorithm. Section 4.2 briefly described the operating principle of our solutions that have been addressed in previous works [5,6].

For dependent attribute, we have explored techniques issues from information retrieval (IR) research. In [31] we have presented an approach based on user rating frequency. In this paper we present an other approach based on Rocchio algorithm [7].

The user semantic model for all relevant attributes, described by the matrix Q, is the result of the horizontal concatenation of all user semantic attribute models Q_A as shown in Algorithm 1.

Algorithm 1. Building User Semantic Model.

Require: *L: List of relevant attributes, users ratings, items content*
Ensure: Q *the User Semantic Matrix*
 1: **for** A *in* L {This loop is fully parallelizable} **do**
 2:     *build* Q_A *the User Semantic Attribute Model of* A
 3: **end for**
 4: **for** A *in* L **do**
 5:     $Q \leftarrow$ *horizontal concatenation of* $(Q$ *and* $Q_A)$
 6: **end for**

4.2 User Semantic Model for Non Dependent Attribute

Let us denote by S the set of items, U the set of users, s a given item $\in S$, u a given user $\in U$ and a rating value $r \in \{1, 2, ..., 5\} \equiv R$. U_s the set of users that rating the item s, then we define the rating function for item s by $\delta_s : u \in U_s \longmapsto \delta_s(u) \in R$. We denote also by F_A the set of features of attribute A, f a given feature $\in F_A$ and S_f the set of items associated to feature f. For instance if we consider the *movie genre* attribute, S_{action} is the set of all action movies.

An item s is represented by its usage profile vector $s_{up} = (\delta_s(u) - \overline{\delta_u})_{(u=1..|U|)}$, where $\overline{\delta_u}$ is the average rating of all rated items by user u. The idea is to partition all items described by their usage profile in K clusters, each cluster is labeled by a feature $f \in F_A$ (or a set of features).

The number K of clusters and the initial center of each cluster is computed by the initialization step of the clustering algorithm. In initial step, each cluster C_k consists of items in $\bigcup_{f \ labeling \ C_k} S_f$ and labeled by the set of corresponding features; so its center is the mean of its items described by their usage profile vector s_{up}. Moreover, an attribute can be mono valued or multivalued depending on the number of features that can be associated to a given item s. For example, the attribute *movie genre* is multivalued because a movie can have several genres while *movie origin* is a mono valued attribute because a movie has only one origin. Thus, if an attribute is multivalued, s can belong to several clusters C_k, while for mono valued attribute, an item should belong only to one cluster. Therefore, for multivalued attribute, the clustering algorithm should provide non disjointed clusters (a fuzzy clustering), whereas, for mono valued attribute, the clustering algorithm should provide disjointed clusters.

After running the clustering algorithm, we obtain K cluster centers; each center k is described by a vector $c_k = (q_{k,u})_{(u=1..|U|)}$. The K centers is modeling k latent variables issued from the features of the attribute A. Thus, the user semantic attribute model is described by the matrix $Q_A = (q_{u,k})_{(u=1..|U|, k=1..K)}$.

With non dependent attribute, the number of associated features is low, this is why the clustering is suitable. Moreover, the user semantic attribute model allows an important reduction of dimension and so reduce the expensiveness of user similarity computing. In [6], we have used the Fuzzy CMean Algorithm on the movie *genre* attribute, we have obtained good performance because the user semantic attribute model has no missing values and all similarities between users were able to be computed. In [5], we have used the KMean clustering algorithm on the movie *origin* attribute. Because of the missing values in the user item rating matrix, we have proposed an algorithm for the initialization step of the KMean clustering using a movie origin ontology. We obtained good results compared to user-based CF but not as good as results for the *genre* attribute.

5   User Semantic Model for Dependents Attributes

For a dependent attribute A, the set F_A of its features can be important and it augments with the increasing of the set of items S. In this paper, we present our solution to compute a user semantic attribute model for dependent attribute.

In addition to the formalism used in Sect. 4.2, we denote by F_{A_s} the set of features $f \in F_A$ associated to item s and by S_u the set of items $s \in S$ rated by user u. We define also, the rating function of user u as $\delta_u : s \in S_u \mapsto \delta_u(s) \in R$; and the Item Frequency Function of item s as $freq_s$ described in formula 3.

$$\forall s \in S, f \in F_A, freq_s(f) = \begin{cases} 1 & \text{if } f \in F_{A_s}. \\ 0 & \text{otherwise.} \end{cases} \tag{3}$$

The Frequency Item Matrix $F = (freq_s(f))_{s \in S \text{ and } f \in F_A}$ is provided by computing $freq_s(f)$ for all items and all features. Table 1 provides an example of Frequency Item matrix for $S = \{i_1, i_2, i_3\}$ and $F_A = \{f_1, f_2, f_3, f_5\}$.

The building of user semantic attribute model consists of three steps:

1. Computing the TF-IDF measure on the Frequency Item Matrix F.
2. Reducing the dimension of feature space by applying a LAS.
3. Computing the user semantic attribute model on items in LSA space by using the Rocchio algorithm.

Table 1. Example of Item Frequency Matrix.

	f_1	f_2	f_3	f_4
i_1	0	1	0	1
i_2	0	0	1	1
i_3	1	1	0	1

5.1 Computing the TF-IDF Measure on the Frequency Item Matrix F

One of the best-known measures for specifying keyword weights in Information Retrieval is the TF-IDF (Term Frequency/Inverse Document Frequency) [20]. It is a numerical statistic, which reflects how important a word is to a document in a corpus. In our case, we replace document by item and term by feature and compute TF-IDF on the Frequency Item Matrix F.

$$TF(f,s) = \frac{freq_s(f)}{max_j freq_s(j)} \tag{4}$$

where the maximum is computed over the $freq_s(j)$ of all features in F_{A_s} of item s.

The measure of Inverse Document Frequency (IDF) is usually defined as:

$$IDF(f) = \log \frac{|S|}{|S_f|} \tag{5}$$

where $|S_f|$ is the number of items assigned to feature f (i.e. $freq_s(f) \neq 0$). Thus, the TF-IDF of feature f for item s is defined as:

$$TFIDF(s,f) = TF(f,s) \times IDF(f) \tag{6}$$

In the flowing, we will denote by F_{TFIDF} the TF-IDF frequency matrix provided by computing TF-IDF measure on the item frequency matrix F, so $F_{TFIDF} = TFIDF(s,f)_{s \in S \text{ and } f \in F_A}$.

5.2 Reducing Dimension of the TF-IDF Frequency Matrix

For dependent attribute, the number of feature is correlated to the number of items. So it can be very elevated and even higher than the number of items. Thus, the semantic user attribute model can have dimension greater than the user rating matrix thereby aggravating the scalability problem. Therefore, in order to reduce the dimension of features space, we apply a LSA with rank k (see Sect. 3) to the F_{TFIDF} matrix. The rank k is well below the number of features of attribute A ($k << |F_A|$). As shown in Sect. 3, LSA uses a truncated SVD (see formula 2) keeping only the k largest singular values and their associated vectors. So, the rank-k approximation matrix of the F_{TFIDF} matrix is provided by formula 7.

$$F_{TFIDF} \approx I_{|S|,k} * \Sigma_{k,k} * V_{k,|F_A|}^t \tag{7}$$

The rows in I_k are the item vectors in LSA space and the rows in V are the feature vectors in LSA space. Thus, each item is represented in the LSA space by a set of k latent variables instead of the features of F_A. This, results in a much less sparse matrix and a reduced dimension of feature space.

5.3   Computing the User Semantic Attribute Model

Rocchio algorithm [7] is a relevance feedback procedure, which is used in information retrieval. It designed to produce improved query formulations following an initial retrieval operation. In a vector processing environment, both the stored information document D and the requests for information B can be represented as t-dimensional vectors $D = (d_1, d_2, ..., d_t)$ and $B = (b_1, b_2, ..., b_t)$. In each case, d_i and b_i represent the weight of term i in D and B respectively. A typical query-document similarity measure can then be computed as the inner product between corresponding vectors.

Rocchio showed in [7], that in a retrieval environment that uses inner product computations to assess the similarity between query and document vectors, the best query leading to the retrieval of many relevant items from a collection of documents is:

$$B_{opt} = \frac{1}{|R|} \sum_R \frac{D_i}{|D_i|} - \frac{1}{|NR|} \sum_{NR} \frac{D_i}{|D_i|} \tag{8}$$

where D_i represent document vectors, and $|D_i|$ is the corresponding Euclidean vector length; R is the set of relevant documents and NR is the set of non relevant documents.

We have applied the Rocchio formula (8) for computing the user semantic attribute profile of user u. We replace documents by items in S described in LSA space. Thus, the user semantic attribute model $Q_A(u)$ for user u and attribute A is given by formula 9.

$$Q_A(u) = \frac{1}{|R_u|} \sum_R \frac{s_i}{|s_i|} - \frac{1}{|NR_u|} \sum_{NR} \frac{s_i}{|s_i|} \tag{9}$$

where R_u is the set of relevant items of u. It is composed of all items in S_u having rating greater than the rating average of u ($\delta_u(s) \geq \overline{\delta_u}$). NR_u is the set of non relevant items of u. It is composed of all items in $S_u \setminus R_u$ ($(\delta_u(s) < \overline{\delta_u})$).

6   Recommendation

To provide recommendations for the active user u_a, we use the user-based CF algorithm [4]. User-Based CF predicts the rating value of active user u_a on non rated item $s \in S$ based on his or her nearest neighbors. The principle of the user-based CF consists of the following steps:

Similarity: compute the similarities between u_a and all others users. The similarity between two users u and v is equal to the cosine of the angle between u and v (see Eq. 10). The set of the nearest neighbors of u_a is equal to the B users with the highest similarity values. In the standard user-based CF algorithm, the users-items rating matrix $(\delta_u(s)_{(u \in U, \, s \in S)})$ is used to compute users' similarities. In our algorithm, the user semantic matrix Q is used instead for computing the similarities between users. As we have already mentioned, the matrix Q is the horizontal concatenation of user semantic attribute model Q_A for each relevant attribute A.

$$sim(u, v) = \cos(\boldsymbol{u}, \boldsymbol{v}) = \frac{\boldsymbol{u} \bullet \boldsymbol{v}}{\|\boldsymbol{u}\| \, \|\boldsymbol{v}\|} \tag{10}$$

Prediction: compute the prediction value $p(u_a, s) =$ of rating of user u_a on non rated item s. Prediction value is equal to a weighted aggregate of the b nearest neighbor ratings of user u_a (see Eq. 11).

$$p(u_a, s) = \overline{\delta_{u_a}} + \frac{\sum_{v \in V} sim(u_a, v)(\delta_v(s) - \overline{\delta_v})}{\sum_{v \in V} |sim(u_a, v)|} \tag{11}$$

where V is the set of the B nearest neighbors (most similar users) to u_a that have rated item s. B can range anywhere from 1 to the number of all users.

Recommendation: recommend to the active user u_a a list $L(u)$ of the Top-N relevant items. Relevant items are those having predicted ratings greater than or equal a given threshold.

Although we apply a user-based CF for recommendation, our approach is also a model-based method because it is based on a new user model to provide ratings of active user on non rated items. Our approach resolves the scalability problem for several reasons. First, the building process of user semantic model is fully parallelizable (because the computing of user semantic attribute model is done in independent way for each other) and can be done off line. Second, this model allows a dimension reduction since the number of columns in the user semantic model is much lower than those of user item rating matrix, so, the computing of similarities between users is less expensive than in the standard user-based CF. In addition, our approach allows inferring similarity between two users even when they have any co-rated items because the users-semantic matrix has less missing values than user item ratings matrix. Thus, our approach provides solution to the neighbor transitivity problem emanates from the sparse nature of the underlying data sets. In this problem, users with similar preferences may not be identified as such if they haven't any items rated in common.

7   Performance Study

In this section, we study the performance of our algorithm, User Semantic Collaborative Filtering (*USCF* in plots), against the standards CF algorithms: User-Based CF (*UBCF* in the plot) [4], and Item-Based CF (*IBCF* in the plot) [17]; standard CB algorithm (*CB* in the plot) [19].

It should be noted that the building of User Semantic Attribute Model for the non dependent attributes *genre* and *origin* have been addressed respectively in previous works [5,6]. Therefore, we will not detail the experiments conducted for these attributes in this paper.

7.1   Data Set

We have experimented our approach on real data from the MovieLens1M data set [32] of the MovieLens recommender system [33]. The MovieLens1M provides the usage data set and contains 1,000,209 explicit ratings of approximately 3,900 movies made by 6,040 users. The ratings are user-provided star ratings, from 1 to 5 stars. For the semantic information of items, we use the HetRec 2011 data set [34] that links the movies of MovieLens data set with their corresponding web pages at Internet Movie Database (IMDb) and Rotten Tomatoes movie review systems. We use *movie genre* and *movie origin* as non dependent attributes, *movie director*, *movie actor* and *movie keyword* as dependent attributes.

We have filtered the data by maintaining only users with at least 20 ratings and available features for all movies. After the filtering process, we obtain a data set with 6020 users, 3552 movies, 19 genres, 43 origins, 1825 directors, 4237 actors and 12367 keywords . The usage data set has been sorted by the timestamps, in ascending order, and has been divided into a training set (including the first 80 % of all ratings) and a test set (the last 20 % of all ratings). Thus, ratings of each user in test set have been assigned after those of training set.

7.2   Evaluation Metrics

Several metrics have been used to evaluate the prediction accuracy of recommendation algorithms [35,36]. There are mainly two classes of metrics. The first measure the ratings prediction accuracy and are used to evaluate the accuracy of algorithms predicting the rating values. The second measure the accuracy of recommendation and are used to evaluate algorithms that provide a Top-N list of relevant items. In this paper, we have used the widely accepted metrics for each class. Thus, for measuring the accuracy of rating prediction we have used the Root Mean Squared Error (RMSE)(see Eq. 12). RMSE computes the square root of the average of the absolute difference between the predictions and true ratings in the test data set. RMSE disproportionally penalizes large errors. Lower the RMSE is, better is the prediction accuracy.

$$RMSE = \sqrt{\frac{\sum_{u,s}(p(u,s) - \delta_u(s))^2}{d}} \qquad (12)$$

where d is the total number of ratings over all users, $p(u, s)$ is the predicted rating for user u on item s, and $\delta_u(s)$ is the actual rating for user u on item s in test data set.

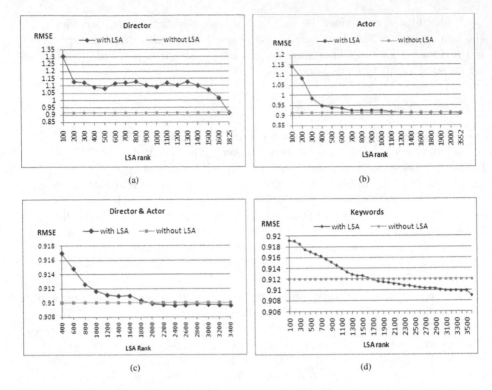

Fig. 2. Impact of LSA on prediction accuracy of Rocchio algorithm.

For Top-N recommendation list, we have used the Precision metric. We have computed a Precision for each test user u in the test set by using formula 13. Then, the Precision for all users is equal to the average.

$$Precision(u) = \frac{|L(u) \cap R_{test}(u)|}{|L(u)|} \qquad (13)$$

where $L(u)$ is the list of N items recommended to user u. $R_{test}(u)$ is the set of relevant items for u in the test data set. In all our experiments, an item is relevant if its rating is greater than or equal to 4. The Precision measure describes the proportion of the recommendations were actually suitable for the user. Higher the Precision is, better is the recommendation accuracy.

7.3   Impact of LSA on Prediction Accuracy of Rocchio Algorithm

In Fig. 2, the RMSE has been plotted with respect to the LSA rank. It compares the Rocchio approach *with* and *without* applying LSA (dimension reduction) on *director* attribute (Fig. 2(a)), *actor* attribute (Fig. 2(b)), combined attribute *director_actor* (Fig. 2(c)) and *Keyword* attribute (Fig. 2(d)). For attributes *director* and *actor*, the plots (Fig. 2(a) and (b)) have the same look, the RMSE of Rocchio with LSA decreases until it reaches the RMSE value of Rocchio without

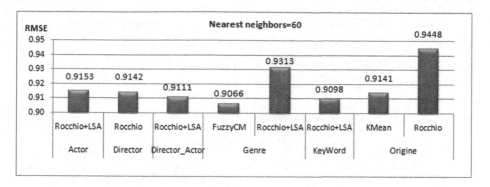

Fig. 3. Impact of user semantic attribute algorithm on prediction accuracy.

LSA. So, LSA dimension reduction has no effect on improving the accuracy of Rocchio approach on *director* and *actor* attributes. The poor performance of these two attributes may be explained by the fact that their features are not highly correlated. Indeed, for the *director* attribute, for instance, the RMSE without reduction (1825 features) is equal to 0.9142 while the best value with LSA is equal to 1.017. For *actor* attribute, the best accuracy (RMSE = 0.9153) of Rocchio with LSA is reached for LSA rank = 1100, it is equal to the performance of Rocchio without LSA, with a dimension reduction about 75 %.

However, for combined attributes *director_actor* (Fig. 2(a)) and *Keyword* (Fig. 2(d)) the LSA dimension reduction improves the accuracy of Rocchio approach. Because of features in *keyword* attribute are more correlated than in *actor* or *director* attribute, using LSA can potentially reduces the amount of noise associated with the semantic information. For *keyword* attribute, the best accuracy (RMSE = 0.909) is reached for LSA rank = 3552 a reduction of about 71 %. For rank equal to 1000, RMSE = 0.9145, so a dimension reduction about 91 % for a loss of accuracy about 0.60 % against the best accuracy of Keyword attribute.

Although the LSA doesn't improve the accuracy, dimension reduction is significant. Thus, it allows to reduce the cost of users similarity computing, specially when the number of features is very high, as is the case of combined attributes *director_actor*.

7.4 Impact of Attribute Class on Prediction Accuracy

Figure 3 compares algorithms for building user semantic attribute model in term of RMSE. *Fuzzy C Mean* algorithm (FuzzyCM in plot) is a fuzzy clustering used for non dependent and multivalued attribute (here *genre*) and *KMean* algorithm (KMean in plot) is used on non dependent and mono valued attribute (here *origin*). Moreover, Rocchio algorithm (Rocchio in plot) is applied here for all attributes dependent and non dependent. For *origin* and *director* attributes, Rocchio without LSA provides best results than with dimension reduction. For *actor* attribute, LSA with rank equal to 1100 is performed, for *genre* attribute a factorization (LSA with rank equal to 18) is applied, for *keyword* attribute

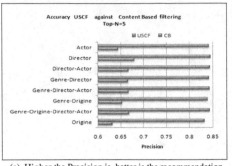 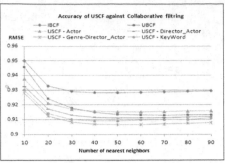

(a) Higher the Precision is, better is the recommendation   (b) Lower the RMSE is, better is the prediction

Fig. 4. Evaluation of USCF against CB in terms of Precision (a) against standards CF in terms of RMSE (b).

LSA with rank equal to 3400 is applied. Rocchio+LSA in plot means the Rocchio approach is performed with LSA. When analyzing this figure we note that, if we performed the *Rocchio* algorithm to non dependent attribute the performance compares unfavorably against the dependent attribute. Indeed, the best performance is achieved by *FuzzyCM* algorithm on *genre* attribute and the difference with Rocchio approach, even with factorization, is important (0.9066 for FuzzyCM and 0.9314 for Rocchio with LSA (rank = 18)). This allows us to deduce that, using a suited algorithm for each attribute class provides best performance than applying the same algorithm for all attributes. Second, the *origin* attribute has the worst performance compared to the other three attributes and this for all algorithms. This is confirm our hypothesis that all attributes don't have the same relevance to users. The attribute *origin* can be less significant in the choice of users than the *genre*, *actor* or *director*, which is intuitively understandable.

7.5   Comparative Results of USCF Against CF and CB Recommender System

Figure 4 depicts the recommendation accuracy of USCF in contrast to those produced by pure CB (CB in plots) recommender system (Fig. 4(a)) using Precision metric to measure the recommendation accuracy; and standard Item-Based CF (IBCF) and User-Based CF (UBCF) (Fig. 4(b)). USCF-<*Attributes*> in plot means the list of relevant attributes involved in building the user semantic model Q. For each relevant attribute, the suited algorithm is applied. So, Fuzzy CMean for *genre*, KMean for *origin*, Rocchio with LSA (rank = 1200) for combined attribute *director_actor* and Rocchio with LSA (rank = 3400) for Keyword attribute. Pure CB algorithm exploits only item-content for recommendations. Thus, we have built an item-item similarity matrix based on Cosinus. Item is described by a Vector Space Model (VSM) composed by features of selected attributes as shown in Fig. 4(a). In Fig. 4(a), recommendations are computed for 60 nearest neighbors. We note that our algorithm USCF results in an overall improvement in accuracy against CB for all combinations of attributes. In Fig. 4(b), RMSE has been plotted with respect to the number of neighbors (similar users) for computing rating prediction (see Sect. 6). In all cases, the RMSE converges between 50 and 60 neighbors, however, USCF results in an overall improvement in accuracy. In addition, the best performance is achieved by the combination *genre-director_actor*. This improvement can be explained by many reasons. First, taking into account the semantic profile of items in a CF recommendation process. Second, for non dependent attribute, User Semantic Attribute Model is built according to a collaborative principle; ratings of all users are used to compute the semantic profile of each user. Third, the choice of the attribute can have significant influence on improving the accuracy. Lastly, Users Semantic Model has few missing values, so, it allows inferring similarity between two given users even when they have any items rated in common.

8   Conclusions and Future Work

The approach presented in this paper is a component of a global work, which the aim, is to semantically enhance collaborative Filtering recommendation and to resolve the scalability problem by reducing the dimension. For this purpose, we have designed a new hybridization technique, which predicts users' preferences for items based on their inferred preferences for semantic information. We have defined two classes of attributes: *dependent* and *non dependent* attribute, and presented a suited algorithm for each class for building user semantic attribute model. The aim of this paper is to present our approach for building user semantic attribute model for dependent attribute. We have defined an algorithm based on Rocchio algorithm and have applied Latent Semantic Analysis (LSA) for dimension reduction. Our approach provides solutions to the scalability problem, and alleviates the data sparsity problem by reducing the dimensionality of data. The experimental results show that USCF algorithm improves the prediction accuracy compared to usage only approach (UBCF and IBCF) and Content based only approach. In addition, we have shown that applying Rocchio formula on non dependent attribute, decreases significantly the prediction accuracy compared to results obtained with machine learning algorithms. Furthermore, we have experimentally shown that all attributes don't have the same importance to users. Finally, experiments have shown that the combination of relevant attributes enhances the recommendations.

An interesting area of future work is to use machine learning techniques to infer relevant attributes. We will also study the extension of the user semantic model to non structured data in witch items are described by free text. Lastly, study how our approach can provide solution to the cold start problem in which new user has few ratings. Indeed, CF cannot provide recommendation because similarities with others users cannot be computed.

References

1. Schafer, J.B., Frankowski, D., Herlocker, J., Sen, S.: Collaborative filtering recommender systems. In: Brusilovsky, P., Kobsa, A., Nejdl, W. (eds.) Adaptive Web 2007. LNCS, vol. 4321, pp. 291–324. Springer, Heidelberg (2007)

2. Pazzani, M.J., Billsus, D.: Content-based recommendation systems. In: Brusilovsky, P., Kobsa, A., Nejdl, W. (eds.) Adaptive Web 2007. LNCS, vol. 4321, pp. 325–341. Springer, Heidelberg (2007)

3. Burke, R.: Hybrid web recommender systems. In: Brusilovsky, P., Kobsa, A., Nejdl, W. (eds.) Adaptive Web 2007. LNCS, vol. 4321, pp. 377–408. Springer, Heidelberg (2007)

4. Resnick, P., Iacovou, N., Suchak, M., Bergstrom, P., Riedl, J.: GroupLens: an open architecture for collaborative filtering of netnews. In: 1994 ACM Conference on Computer supported Cooperative Work, pp. 175–186 (1994)

5. Ben Ticha, S., Roussanaly, A., Boyer, A., Bsaies, K.: User semantic preferences for collaborative recommendations. In: Huemer, C., Lops, P. (eds.) EC-Web 2012. LNBIP, vol. 123, pp. 203–211. Springer, Heidelberg (2012)

6. Ben Ticha, S., Roussanaly, A., Boyer, A.: User semantic model for hybrid recommender systems. In: The 1st International Conference on Social Eco-Informatics - SOTICS, pp. 95–101. IARIA, Barcelona, Espagne (2011)

7. Rocchio, J.: Relevance feedback in information retrieval. In: Salton, G. (ed.) The Smart Retrieval System - Experiments in Automatic Document Processing, pp. 313–323. Prentice-Hall Inc, Englewood Cliffs (1971)

8. Dumais, S.T.: Latent semantic analysis. Ann. Rev. Inf. Sci. Technol. **38**, 188–230 (2004)

9. Goldberg, D., Nichols, D., Oki, B.M., Terry, D.: Using collaborative filtering to weave an information tapestry. Commun. ACM **35**, 61–70 (1992)

10. Shardanand, U., Maes, P.: Social information filtering: Algorithms for automating "word of mouth". In: Proceedings of the SIGCHI Conference on Human Factors in Computing Systems. CHI 1995, pp. 210–217. ACM Press/Addison-Wesley Publishing Co., New York, USA (1995)

11. Hill, W., Stead, L., Rosenstein, M., Furnas, G.: Recommending and evaluating choices in a virtual community of use. In: Proceedings of the SIGCHI Conference on Human Factors in Computing Systems. CHI 1995, pp. 194–201. ACM Press/Addison-Wesley Publishing Co., New York, USA (1995)

12. Ekstrand, M.D., Riedl, J.T., Konstan, J.A.: Collaborative filtering recommender systems. Found. Trends Hum. Comput. Interact. **4**, 81–173 (2011)

13. Su, X., Khoshgoftaar, T. M.: A survey of collaborative filtering techniques. Adv. in Artif. Intell. **2009**, Article No. 4 (2009)

14. Breese, J., Heckerman, D., Kadie, C.: Empirical analysis of predictive algorithms for collaborative filtering. In: Proceeding of the Fourteenth Conference on Uncertainty in Artificial Intelligence (UAI), pp. 43–52. Morgan Kaufmann, San Francisco, Madison, Wisconsin (1998)

15. Sarwar, B., Karypis, G., Konstan, J., Riedl, J.: Item-based collaborative filtering recommendation algorithms. In: Proceedings of the 10th International Conference on World Wide Web WWW 2001, pp. 285–295. ACM, New York, USA (2001)

16. Miyahara, K., Pazzani, M.J.: Collaborative filtering with the simple bayesian classifier. In: Mizoguchi, R., Slaney, J.K. (eds.) PRICAI 2000. LNCS, vol. 1886, pp. 679–689. Springer, Heidelberg (2000)

17. Sarwar, B., Karypis, G., Konstan, J., Riedl, J.: Recommender systems for large-scale e-commerce: scalable neighborhood formation using clustering. In: Proceedings of the Fifth International Conference on Computer and Information Technology (ICCIT 2002) (2002)

18. Xue, G. R., Lin, C., Yang, Q., Xi, W., Zeng, H. J., Yu, Y., Chen, Z.: Scalable collaborative filtering using cluster-based smoothing. In: Proceedings of the 28th Annual International ACM SIGIR Conference on Research and Development in Information Retrieval SIGIR 2005, pp. 114–121. ACM, New York, USA (2005)
19. Lops, P., de Gemmis, M., Semeraro, G.: Content-based recommender systems: state of the art and trends. In: Ricci, F., Rokach, L., Shapira, B., Kantor, P.B. (eds.) Recommender Systems Handbook, pp. 73–105. Springer, New York (2011)
20. Salton, G.: Automatic Text Processing. Addison-Wesley, Boston (1989)
21. Baeza-Yates, R., Ribeiro-Neto, B.: Modern Information Retrieval. Addison-Wesley, Boston (1999)
22. Belkin, N.J., Croft, W.B.: Information filtering and information retrieval: two sides of the same coin? Commun. ACM 35, 29–38 (1992)
23. Adomavicius, G., Tuzhilin, A.: Toward the next generation of recommender systems: a survey of the state-of-the-art and possible extensions. IEEE Trans. Knowl. Data Eng. 17, 734–749 (2005)
24. Pazzani, M., Billsus, D.: Learning and revising user profiles: the identification of interesting web sites. Mach. Learn. 27, 313–331 (1997)
25. Mooney, R. J., Roy, L.: Content-based book recommending using learning for text categorization. In: Proceedings of the Fifth ACM Conference on Digital Libraries DL 2000, pp. 195–204. ACM, New York, USA (2000)
26. Balabanović, M., Shoham, Y.: Fab: Content-based, collaborative recommendation. Commun. ACM 40, 66–72 (1997)
27. Sarwar, B., Karypis, G., Konstan, J., Riedl, J.: Application of dimensionality reduction in recommender system-a case study. In: Proceedings of the ACM WebKDD 2000 Web Mining for E-Commerce Workshop (2000)
28. Mobasher, B., Jin, X., Zhou, Y.: Semantically enhanced collaborative filtering on the web. In: Berendt, B., Hotho, A., Mladenič, D., van Someren, M., Spiliopoulou, M., Stumme, G. (eds.) EWMF 2003. LNCS (LNAI), vol. 3209, pp. 57–76. Springer, New York (2004)
29. Sen, S., Vig, J., Riedl, J.: Tagommenders: Connecting users to items through tags. In: Proceedings of the 18th International Conference on World Wide Web WWW 2009, pp. 671–680. ACM, New York, USA (2009)
30. Manzato, M.G.: Discovering latent factors from movies genres for enhanced recommendation. In: Proceedings of the Sixth ACM Conference on Recommender Systems RecSys 2012, pp. 249–252. ACM, New York, USA (2012)
31. Ben Ticha, S., Roussanaly, A., Boyer, A., Bsaïes, K.: Feature frequency inverse user frequency for dependant attribute to enhance recommendations. In: The Third International Conference on Social Eco-Informatics - SOTICS, Lisbon, Portugal, IARIA (2013)
32. data set, M July 2014: http://grouplens.org/datasets/movielens/
33. MovieLens July 2014. www.movielens.org
34. HetRec2011. In: 2nd International Workshop on Information Heterogeneity and Fusion in Recommender Systems, The 5th ACM Conference on Recommender Systems (2011)
35. Herlocker, J.L., Konstan, J.A., Terveen, L.G., Riedl, J.T.: Evaluating collaborative filtering recommender systems. ACM Trans. Inf. Syst. 22, 5–53 (2004)
36. Shani, G., Gunawardana, A.: Evaluating recommendation systems. In: Ricci, F., Rokach, L., Shapira, B., Kantor, P.B. (eds.) Recommender Systems Handbook, pp. 257–297. Springer, Heidelberg (2011)

Mobile Information Systems

Cascading Information for Ubiqitous Mobility Assistance

Christian Samsel[1][✉], Shirley Beul-Leusmann[2], Maximilian Wiederhold[1],
Karl-Heinz Krempels[1], Martina Ziefle[2], and Eva-Maria Jakobs[2]

[1] Information Systems, RWTH Aachen University, Aachen, Germany
{samsel,wiederhold,krempels}@dbis.rwth-aachen.de
[2] Human-Computer Interaction Center, RWTH Aachen University,
Aachen, Germany
{beul-leusmann,ziefle}@comm.rwth-aachen.de,
e.m.jakobs@tk.rwth-aachen.de

Abstract. Over the last years, personal mobility has become both more prominent and more diverse. Because of the complex structure of today's transport networks, an electronic guidance is effectively required. Usually different transport modalities and service providers offer their own mobile application to which the traveler has to adapt after changing between services. Additionally a current trend in mobile applications is the customization of GUI elements which leads to appealing looks but usually also to cluttered presentation of information. Both these problems cause a high cognitive stress on the traveler using the mobile application, especially while conducting other activities at the same time. Our approach to mitigate these issues is to create a mobile application applying the principle *Cascading Information Theory* to simplify the usage. A prototype of the application was evaluated in an user test for comparing our approach to the most popular mobile travel application in Germany.

Keywords: Context-awareness · Gamification · Travel information · Mobile applications · Usability

1 Introduction

Global trends like urbanization, climate change, and peak oil enforce and accelerate the change of people's mobility; the focus shifts back from individual transport to public transport. Traditional public transport networks, like subways and bus networks, have grown in size and new forms of transport systems like carsharing have been introduced. Consequently, the number of potential itineraries from one point to another raises, each with specific features, e.g., different prices and comfort levels. To use public transport efficiently, meaning to decide on the most suitable itinerary and to follow it closely, the traveler requires effective electronic assistance. To do so a large number of more or less appropriate travel information systems have been established. Such travel information vary from traditional web platforms used for plane or train ticket booking to modern mobile applications for sharing rides.

V. Monfort and K.-H. Krempels (Eds.): WEBIST 2014, LNBIP 226, pp. 315–330, 2015.
DOI: 10.1007/978-3-319-27030-2_20

1.1   Motivation

From our continuous work on travel information, indoor navigation, diversity, and mobile applications we recognized that most current mobile applications for public transport are flawed in terms of usability under cognitive stress. Current applications (see Sect. 2.1) shine with a fancy Graphical User Interface (GUI), many configuration options and a high amount of information. Such applications perform well in situations where the traveler can direct all of her cognitive capacity to the application, but fall back in terms of usability in stressful situations. Stress can be introduced by noise, time pressure, unknown surroundings, or required multitasking (e.g., walking and using a device at the same time).

To improve the usability under stress we wanted to create a concept and a prototype which simplifies mobile travel assistance compared to already existing applications. While creating a concept based on our experience in indoor navigation [1] we realized that the initial GUI layout and interaction pattern is strongly related to archetypical Massively Multiplayer Online Role-Playing Game (MMORPGs) like World of Warcraft [2]. World of Warcraft, for example, uses non-intrusive, still useful indicators/descriptions for the next waypoint in a quest. The user has access to exactly the required information she needs to fulfill the given task (e.g. travel to a specific location) at one glance. This principle of providing exactly the required information in the current context is called Cascading Information Theory. We wanted to transfer this principle to a real world application.

1.2   Cascading Information Theory

In his 2010 blog entry[1], Erick Schonfeld issued his company's "playdeck" of game dynamics terms which included most if not all of the currently employed elements of gamification. Gamification is a term which was coined by Nick Pelling in the early 2000s. Recently, there have been efforts by several researchers to reach a mutually agreed on definition. One of the more elaborate and most cited versions originates with [3]. They define gamification as: "The use of game design elements characteristic for games in non-game contexts." Elements of games are components or interaction patterns that, in combination, create the game experience. By abstracting these elements from their game implementation and employing them in another context (e.g. business software etc.) the developer makes use of people's play instinct. If a user is familiar with the ported game element there is a high probability that she will associate it with its original purpose and therefore be able to correctly utilize it.

Along with well known Gamification components like achievements, Schonfeld lists the principle of *Cascading Information Theory*. Cascading Information Theory suggests to unveil information about the game in as small amounts as possible to ensure the user's focus exactly on the desired objective. Thereby, confusion and misdirection of players by providing excess information is prevented and each iteration of new data can be applied directly.

---

[1] http://techcrunch.com/2010/08/25/scvngr-game-mechanics/.

2   Related Work

This section lists popular related applications and recent research.

2.1   Public Transport Applications

The following part exhibits commonly used and high rated mobile applications for public transportation in Germany, not only explaining the benefits but also elaborating on flaws and drawbacks of the individual application, in order to convey the motivation for a new interface design. We considered only European applications because travel information applications are only meaningful applicable in the area for which they are created.

DB Navigator. Figure 1(a) shows a screenshot of the most popular [4] application for public transport in Germany, the DB Navigator. The DB Navigator is developed by HaCon AG on behalf of Deutsche Bahn. Therefore the assumption that its prevalence is due to the fact that its publisher is the main German provider of inter-regional public transportation suggests itself. The application also features fully compatible intermodal trip planning and supports real-time information about delays and arrival times. In addition to these functions there is also support for rudimentary walking directions and direct online purchase of tickets.

Despite its vast amount of features, the decent appearance, and the possibility of providing the company's own data the application has a few drawbacks. The trip view shows the complete trip information in one tabular environment which requires the traveler to scroll vertically if the trip involves more than one change. To get walking directions the traveler has to press the button which resembles a map. The high number of GUI elements, the inconsistent coloring and required interaction complicate the interpretation and filtering of the needed information for the traveler and might delay the usage especially in a high stress situation.

Citymapper. The Citymapper application (London version tested) is well-known in England. The application includes a broad range of features such as generating intermodal trip plans using real-time information. Having selected the departure and destination locations the application suggests a variety of different possibilities to reach the desired spot. In addition to the intermodal route suggestions the user is presented with variations like routes only involving buses or rain safe ones and information about the current context such as the weather at the destination. The route detail view consists of a large map view displaying the selected trip itinerary and a table below it listing the individual parts of the journey (see Fig. 1(b)).

The Citymapper application addresses many of the crucial, common issues of public transportation and is appealing. However, it is specifically designed to match the London network transportation. This is a major drawback, adapting to a different application based on the whereabouts requires cognitive resources.

(a) The DB Navigator application includes all trip data plus various buttons in one view.

(b) The London Citymapper is specifically adjusted to the needs of the London inhabitants.

Fig. 1. Public Transport Applications.

This issue is exacerbated by the quantity of features which might be difficult to comprehend in a short amount of time.

2.2   Existing Research Work

This section presents recent work in the area of public transportation and mobile navigation systems and aims to give a short insight into the current state of research.

An attempt to create a multimodal routing service with directions for pedestrians is made in [5]. In addition to evaluating travel modes by the criteria of distance, time, fare, and transfer, they use dynamic information about real-time and historic traffic data to enable accurate estimations. The computation of transit routes is aided by a high priority mode expansion strategy which incrementally generates parts of the most suited path. Similarly, the sophisticated algorithm developed by [6] allows for accurate generic and personalized recommendations solely based on the analysis of user GPS traces. By correlating the travel behavior of users with their locations they are able to estimate user interests.

[7] introduce their concept of a pedestrian navigation system with a hybrid solution titled Project REAL. Already accurately predicting the evolution of personal navigation systems ("Personal navigation systems that extend beyond today's use in cars will play a major role in the future.") they present their approach featuring a combination of indoor and outdoor navigation. The system is capable of automatically adapting to location changes and presenting directions to the traveler on a variety of different devices.

Since the primary instruments for outdoor navigation are geolocation services, accomplishing indoor navigation is an incomparably more difficult task because exact positions are hard to determine. Nevertheless, considering the topic is crucial for any attempt at implementing a complete navigation system. In [8] a solution for the guidance of pedestrians inside transport interchange buildings is proposed which relies on generating a hierarchical model of the complex and providing instructions augmented with map views. [1,9] present a turn-by-turn approach to manage navigation inside large, complicated buildings using landmark representations for orientation rather than street names. The work is based on the idea that pedestrians mostly rely on landmarks as navigation cue [10].

The TransitGenie project [11] aims at implementing a public transportation navigator with a transit tracking service which consists of an activity classification algorithm to determine user context as well as trajectory matching to enhance vehicle tracking.

The UbiBus project started an attempt to create an ubiquitous system for public transport assistance using context information [12]. The authors incorporated access to an intelligent transportation system application in buses as well as web services and smart phone apps, so that passengers are enabled to receive information about the progress of their bus. In [13] the authors proposed a framework which is capable of extracting high-level information about user context. Initially the system recognizes and collects very basic data to create a foundation. Complex user activities are then broken down into smaller parts and connected via conditional relationships which are afterwards matched with the previously recorded basic contexts. If a complex context is identified this way, an application is capable of requesting detailed activity recommendations from a central server using a four-part scoring model. In [14] the authors proposed an integrated context-detection service architecture which combines information from different approaches.

In [15] the authors observed that creating an ideal representation of public transit trip information on a mobile device is a difficult task. Using paper prototypes, the authors compare different approaches to display intermodal travel chains.

3   Approach

While working on public transportation information systems we identified parallels between real world navigation and navigation in, e.g., MMORPGs. Navigation elements in games are usually lean and unobtrusive as to not distract the player from her main task, but still are easy to comprehend. In a real world environment full of distractions, noise, and confusion the traveler's concentration can rarely be focused entirely on operating her mobile device. When traveling on a bus, entering a rail station, or even just walking towards a bus stop the traveler needs to be capable of checking her itinerary as quickly as possible. Therefore, an assistant application is required to be uncomplicated and easy to

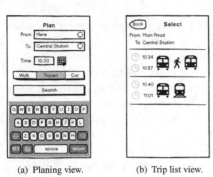

(a) Planing view.   (b) Trip list view.   (c) Bus view.   (d) Walking view.

Fig. 2. Early development sketches.

use. In order to minimize the amount of cognitive resources needed by the navigator, the user interface needs to be plain and responsive, similar to navigation elements in MMORPGs.

Following the general principle of Cascading Information we divided and analyzed information presented by mobile travel information applications regarding necessity. We only considered essential information for inclusion in our GUI concept. For every piece of essential information we assigned a time span at which it is required, and an order of priority (results in Sect. 3.3). Information will be presented if and only if it is required at this particular point in time and is shown in descending order of priority.

This is achieved by creating a turn-by-turn-like interaction. Travelers continuously progress through the trip by steering from intermediate target to target and ultimately arrive at the destination. Only information required to reach the next intermediate target is conveyed to the user. The design of the GUI is intended to noticeably enhance users' public transport navigation experience in comparison with existing applications. It is supposed to aid the traveler's navigation and make processing routing information as easy as possible. Device-independent mockups presented in Fig. 2(c) and (d) show an early stage of design.

3.1 Planning the Trip

A trip is the journey from a specified starting point (usually in the vicinity of the traveler's current location) to a destination point in a previously set time frame, using one or several different modes of travel. Although it is possible to add numerous other parameters to the plan, they are not included in the application for the sake of simplicity. Conceivable additional options for planning the trip, although increasing complexity, include specifying the desired date/time of arrival instead of departure, preference of direct connections or favored traveler profiles. Users of public transport navigation aids often are in need of public transit information regarding their current location, such as to quickly return home from a friend's house or when to take the train to get to university. Therefore incorporating the latest position update as a location parameter for the trip request is deemed appropriate.

Figure 2(a) shows the first depiction of the initial planning view to input the desired trip parameters. The time of departure is shown in a textual representation and changeable by using a mechanism or by input via a (virtual) keyboard. Finally, the modes of travel are to be chosen using a multiple-selection segmented control which lists all possibilities and indicates their selection state. The bottom-most button labeled "Search" will then issue the request and fetch one or more trip plans. One reasonable improvement to the interface might be the use of meaningful icons instead of the textual description of the travel modes in the segmented control. This is due to the fact that reading a piece of plain text usually takes longer than recognizing a commonly used icon.

3.2   Selecting a Trip

After submitting the trip inquiry, the traveler has to be presented with the trips suggested. The mockup in Fig. 2(b) depicts an early version of a table view whose rows each contain one of the provided itineraries. The times of beginning and arrival of the journey are mandatory attributes for people to judge the expediency of a proposed trip plan. Especially if there are multiple possibilities for the modal composition of a route, displaying the different transport modes during the selection progress distinguishes any unique features of the trip. Displaying icons unambiguously depicting the travel modes not only saves screen space but also makes it easier to comprehend the complete routing process at a glance. In addition the starting and destination locations which the traveler had previously specified are presented on top of the table.

3.3   Assisting the Trip

The trip view shown in Fig. 2(c) and (d) represents the most significant component of the interface and is also where the traveler is likely to spend the highest amount of time while actually using the application. Being the main source of detailed information about the journey, the trip view needs to fulfill certain requirements. Most importantly, all required information needs to be quickly accessible and easily comprehensible. A traveler should be able to capture the information which is necessary for her navigation at one glance without any interaction. Following the principle of *Cascading Information* introduced in Sect. 1.2, it is assumed that the traveler does not require the complete trip information during her navigation process. Therefore, the whole trip plan can be subdivided into small entities containing only the features of a single step along the route. Using this distinction allows displaying these entities individually. A type of view is needed which enables comfortable progression through the route and is easy-to-use. Consequently, the interface will not feature a vertical scrolling view. Instead, it is intended all the data necessary for the corresponding stage of the trip are visible at once, eliminating any need to perform time-consuming repositioning of screen elements or going through all the information to find the respective piece of information.

Using Context Awareness. To present exactly the required information for the current situation, respectively the current step, knowledge about the current situation is required. The multitude of sensors included in current mobile devices allows for precise determination of user contexts and their surroundings, and therefore the situation of the traveler. By using the context data, e.g., time and date, the location and the type of transportation vehicle the application is enabled to ascertain whether a user has entered the vehicle she was headed for on her itinerary. Using this information we can automatically deduct which step of the planned route should be presented.

Since one step in the plan has a variety of attributes, which are potentially subject to change, the possibilities of how to visualize them are manifold. In general one can distinguish between purely textual and graphical representations of data. As depicted in Fig. 2(d), the mockup GUI contains a combination of both methods in order to take into account different user habits. Independent of the type of transport the general interface layout stays the same. The information is always displayed at the same area to enable the traveler to recognize relevant information at a glance.

Textual Elements. There are a few characteristics which are essential to the navigation procedure and therefore any major change to them is improbable. If the step required public transportation, the required characteristics, in descending order of priority, are (also shown in Fig. 2(c)):

Departure and Arrival Stations. Naturally, the traveler needs to know the stations of the transit vehicle she intends to travel by. The description of the stop should not only include its name, but also some kind of information about which platform to enter. This holds especially true for large buildings like central stations or coach terminals.

Vehicle Information. Public transport vehicles are usually identified by a line number and direction headsign. Both are displayed to enable the traveler to find the vehicle easily.

Departure and Arrival Times. Knowing the respective departure and arrival times is a crucial factor for the traveler to catch the vehicle and leave it at the right time.

When providing on-foot navigation important characteristics include (shown in Fig. 2(d)):

Direction. Walking navigation thrives on supplying the traveler with the direction she is supposed to walk in. While people usually tend to use relative directions like "left" or "slightly right" absolute directions based on points of the compass are a possible alternative.

Distance. Information about how long the current step will take is generally of great interest to a traveler. Since the individual walking speed may differ significantly between people, the better alternative is displaying the distance that has to be traveled.

Street Names. The traveler requires identifiers to exactly recognize the planned walking route she is supposed to follow. This is most easily accomplished by providing either the name of the street or an identifier of a nearby junction or a well-known public place.

Also, the final destination of the journey should always be visible so that the traveler is reassured she is traveling in the right direction. The top area provides sufficient space to display a text which slightly resembles the head sign of a bus or tram and therefore seem familiar to the traveler.

Graphical Elements. The graphical representation of trip data is primarily performed by a map view which displays the surroundings of the traveler and her route using an online map service as data source. All of the steps which are transmitted in the planned route are marked on the map and a path overlay approximately indicates the track that will be traversed during the journey. The traveler's progress on the route is shown by highlighting the map marker which corresponds to the current step. A compass is shown on the map to add an additional easy to follow navigation cue. For the traveler to always be aware of her advancement we added a progress bar at the bottom of the display. To prevent distraction, all graphical elements should be kept simple and lean.

4   Implementation

This section describes the actual implementation based on our previously introduced approach. We begin with the process of drafting and assembling the prototype, including detailed explanations of the GUI followed by a brief description of the used back-end.

In the following we address the realization of the views of the prototype GUI. Since there was relatively little time between the creation of the mockups and the implementation of the application, and also because of the sophistication of modern mockup tools, the differences are not always apparent. Because of its popularity, stability, and the great amount of well-written documentation, Apple iOS 6 became the platform of choice for the development of the application prototype. In order to fully ensure compatibility with a real device, the application was also regularly tested on an iPhone 4.

4.1   The Planning View

The trip planning view presented in Fig. 3(a) consists of *from* and *to* text fields, a date selector, and a *Plan!* button. Upon beginning text input a virtual keyboard is displayed alongside several possible text buttons. These buttons include a green position marker which resembles the traveler's position. By tapping it, the traveler starts a positioning process which uses the current geolocation, coordinates supplied by the device sensors to look up the current address using reserve geocoding. This trip planning may be used in two different scenarios: Either a traveler wants to make a request for an entirely new route, or she issued the command to reschedule an active trip. In the first case, the next step in the navigation chain is displaying the list of feasible itineraries provided by the backend server. If, on the other hand, a reschedule is supposed to happen, the application skips displaying the trip list and selects the first itinerary, optimistically assuming that it embodies the temporally closest possibility.

4.2   The Selection View

After receiving a response from the back-end server the trip information needs to be conveyed to travelers using the selection view in Fig. 3(b). The shown table contains a variety of information; on the top of the list, the full description of both the origin as well as the destination location is presented. Each following row sums up the trip, containing on the left hand side the time of departure and arrival. Furthermore the full duration of the trip is written below. Next to the times the utilized modes of transportation are listed in an array of icons. Below the icons the line identifier (e.g., line number) is shown. To maintain consistency the icons from the planning view are reused throughout the application. By reducing the icon size after reaching a certain threshold an overflow is prevented.

4.3   The Assistance View

Presenting the stages of the trip to the traveler was one of the main challenges in designing and implementing the prototype GUI. Therefore drafting it included devising the functions which had to be employed in order to satisfy user needs while keeping a plain profile. The view grew in functionality and its features matured during the process of implementation.

Since the trip is split into several parts, a similar graphical representation is an obvious consequence. The trip plan is segmented into a number of steps which have to be subsequently completed in order to arrive at the destination. These steps are visualized on the map view by adding a position marker to the map layer at the geographical coordinates of the starting point of each step.

In addition to showing the route path and progress on the map, a *compass* was incorporated into the view. Using a rotatable image of a green arrow in the upper left corner, the traveler ought to always be aware of the direction in which her destination lies. This is achieved by computing the angle (i.e., the bearing) between the traveler's location and her destination. Utilizing iOS ability to not only monitor the position but also the heading, the application uses the bearing and the travelers heading to create and apply an affine transformation to the arrow image, thus rotating it. As a result, travelers are able to discern the correct direction of their destination at any given moment which is especially beneficial for walking directions. The concept of this orientation aid is derived from games, which often provide navigation instructions by displaying a compass. As the compass is only relevant for walking directions, it is disabled for other modes of transportation.

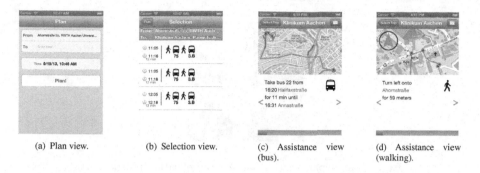

(a) Plan view.   (b) Selection view.   (c) Assistance view   (d) Assistance view
                                                   (bus).   (walking).

Fig. 3. Screenshots showing the prototype implementation (Color figure online).

The part of the GUI displaying the textual representation presents either a step of the walking directions or a transit stage of the trip and contains a number of labels and one image view for depicting the current mode of the step, again reusing the mode icons from the planning view. If the step is part of the turn-by-turn walking directions it includes information about the absolute and relative direction, the street the traveler is supposed to follow, and the distance that will be traversed during this part of the journey (shown in Fig. 3(d)). If, on the other hand, the view shows a transit stage, it contains details regarding the type of vehicle, the transit route, departure times and station as well as arrival time and name of the destination (Fig. 3(c)).

At the bottom of the view, a progression indicator is placed which uses a bar style and is filled according to the progression in the trip. However, merely iterating over the steps does not accurately resemble the progression through the trip plan, because the route is generally not of a linear nature. Instead, the various parts of the journey each consume different amounts of time and therefore the advancement of the progress view was adjusted to precisely mirror the traveler's progress.

5   Evaluation

For evaluating the prototype a user-oriented evaluation was applied.

5.1   Methodology and Test Participants

The prototype application and the DB Navigator were evaluated in a lab user test (see Fig. 4) in order to identify usability problems and have an insight in prospective users' assessment. The test encompassed a leading scenario and three tasks which had to be solved by interacting with the applications. The purpose of the leading scenario was to give the test tasks a contextual framing for supporting test participants in understanding the whole point of the test. Scenario:

> You are a student in Aachen and you have a student ticket, which allows
> you to use all public transportation in your state. For this reason, you are

Fig. 4. Participant interacting with application prototype.

a frequent user of Aachen's public transportation. You own an iPhone and use trip assistant apps to inform yourself about departure times.

After reading this, test participants were given the task instructions which focused to test the app's main functionality routing. To reduce the cognitive load and concentrate on the task processing, instructions for the next task were handed out after finishing the current one. Task 1 was about routing from the actual location to a bus stop:

It is 09:18 a.m. at the 3rd of August 2013. You are running through an unknown street. You have to go to the Audimax, a university building, to write an exam. The exam will start at 10:00 a.m. Use your app to find information about a bus ride to your exam. Use the integrated functionality to find your actual location.

Task 2 was about routing from a bus stop to an address and Task 3 was about routing from one address to another. The experimental design was varied for controlling position effects: Half of the test participants carried out the test tasks first with the prototype and then again with DB Navigator, the other half of test participants vice versa. During the test the test participants were instructed to apply the thinking aloud method which means to comment on their interaction with the apps. Verbal comments were recorded via audio and video. In addition, the interaction with the apps was recorded by a screen record software. The feedback of participants was collected with a questionnaire consisting of six sections: Demographic data, mobility profile, technology use, assessment of the prototype and final rating.

Ten test participants took part in the user test. Five were male, five female. Their age was $M = 23.9$ years, $SD = 3.03$ years. All of them were students. About their daily mobility profile they stated to go by foot (10), to ride the bus (5), to cycle (2), and to use the train (1). They were all using a smartphone (six iOS, one Android, one unknown, two others). Concerning mobility apps, nine used the DB Navigator, eight Google Maps, and three Navigon. Participants' experience with the DB Navigator was assessed as problematic because it impacts results of performance tests. However, this experience with several mobility apps could also be helpful for assessing the prototype's quality and utter specific optimization proposals.

Table 1. Mean of required time for solving tasks.

Application	Task 1	Task 2	Task 3
DB Navigator	1:13	2:44	4:22
Prototype	2:26	3:24	5:55

5.2   Evaluation Results

The expenditure of time for solving tasks varied (see Table 1). According to the measured data, the processing of the tasks with the application prototype took longer than with DB Navigator. As mentioned before, nine of ten participants know and use DB Navigator and have learned to use the application to a certain extent. Therefore the result of the final rating for one app was predictable: seven participants preferred DB Navigator, two the prototype application, one neither of both apps.

5.3   Participant Feedback

Participants gave very detailed feedback about the prototype visualization and features. They assessed positively that prototype was clearly and simply designed. For them it seemed to be easy to manage. No unnecessary gimmicks or icons were integrated. Furthermore, they appreciated the presentation of the map and the step-by-step support during the whole trip. The choice of means of transportation by marking icons was also a pro argument for the protoype application. Negative comments were predominantly related to missing features or information. For instance, participants missed the feature for defining the time of arrival/departure, choosing a bus stop from a selection, and a default setting of the territory, which should be considered (e.g. data for town, not for whole country). Moreover, information such as details of vehicles (e.g. bus number) was absent.

Technical problems were mentioned in connection with the GPS-based definition of the actual location. The range of participants' assessments concerning the size of the map was from "too small" to "ok". Also zooming was a little challenging for test participants. In general, the quality of icons rated as comprehensive. Two icons, bus and train, were named as too similar. The visualization of process progress within the app was also questioned. Three participants opted for page control dots, seven for a progress bar, two for displaying the percentage (multiple answers possible). Two participants stated that it was not clear, which kind of progress was visualized in the prototype – distance, time, or steps within the step-by-step assistance.

5.4   Discussion

Based on the presented results our prototype application can be considered slightly inferior to the reference application DB Navigator. This outcome was expected; the majority of the test subjects had previous experience with the DB Navigator application. While this allows for potentially increased competence in operating the applications, it may have caused a biased outcome of the evaluation. The feedback highlighted the core usability issues of the interface, which severely influence the performance and satisfaction of users. While any problems identified by users during the tests are unfortunate, designing a flawless user interface right from the start is close to impossible. Last but not least, the employed lab test enviroment misses congnitive stress, which we believe will change the outcome.

6   Conclusions and Future Work

This section discusses options of extending the prototype and the research topic in general and afterwards draws the conclusion of this paper.

6.1   Future Work

The presented mobile application is the foundation for a possibly holistic mobile application. However, the developed application is merely a prototype and therefore does not aspire to be complete or even a valid competitor on the market. During the process of implementation and beyond, many opportunities for extending and improving the design as well as the application itself were discovered or proposed by others. This section presents promising ideas which are currently been worked on.

Social Networking and Gamification. Social networking is an aspect which increasingly finds its way into many everyday activities and often manages to make ordinary tasks more appealing. We added social components like interaction with friends by e.g., sharing and commenting itineraries to enhance the user experience. We also added the Gamification element *Badges* to the mobile application and are currently evaluating the use of it to incentivize the usage of ecofriendly means of transportation.

Wearables. We are currently developing a SmartWatch application presenting the respective information described in Sect. 3.3. By enabling the traveler to check his itinary on his wrist, we hope to simplify the mobility assistance even more. Other wearable devices, e.g., SmartGlasses, seem also be promising and are subjected to later research.

6.2   Conclusions

This paper presented the attempt to design a novel Graphical User Interface for planning and routing through multimodal transit trips. The interface prototype was designed to alleviate the issues of travelers and guide them while they embark on their journey. The first draft of the GUI was produced employing the principle of cascading information and classic user interface design methods, determining the scope of this work.

Based on the derived concepts and drafts, a prototype mobile application was developed for Apple iOS. The trip planning was based on a backend server running OpenTripPlanner. The developed application was finally evaluated in a laboratory test user study in order to obtain information about usability, design issues and the comparability of the prototype with established applications for public transport navigation. The results of this study revealed the crucial usability problems and provided detailed feedback about the aspects of the GUI. While the prototype lacks the developmental stage of a commercial application and offers room for improvement, the positive user feedback showed that presented approach is reasonable and worth further attention.

Acknowledgements. The authors would like to thank Teresa Schmidt and Christian Paul for conducting the user study and their former colleague Paul Heiniz for productive discussions and his work on indoor navigation. The authors would also like to thank ASEAG AG and IVU Traffic Technologies AG for supplying the required timetable data. This work was supported by the German Federal Ministry of Economics and Technology for Project econnect Germany (01ME12052).

References

1. Heiniz, P., Krempels, K. H., Terwelp, C., Wüller, S.: Landmark-based navigation in complex buildings. In: Proceedings of the International Conference on Indoor Positioning and Indoor Navigation (IPIN), pp. 1–9 (2012)
2. Corneliussen, H., Rettberg, J.: Digital Culture, Play, and Identity: A World of Warcraft Reader. MIT Press, Cambridge (2008)
3. Deterding, S., Sicart, M., Nacke, L.: Gamification. using game-design elements in non-gaming contexts. In: Extended Abstracts on Human Factors in Computing Systems, pp. 4–7 (2011)
4. Statista GmbH: App Monitor Deutschland. Technical report, Hamburg, Germany November 2012
5. Yu, H., Lu, F.: Advanced multi-modal routing approach for pedestrians. In: Proceedings of the 2nd International Conference on Consumer Electronics, Communications and Networks (CECNet), pp. 2349–2352 (2012)
6. Zheng, Y., Xie, X.: Learning travel recommendations from user-generated GPS traces. ACM Trans. Intell. Syst. Technol. **2**, 2:1–2:29 (2011)
7. Baus, J., Krüger, A., Wahlster, W.: A resource-adaptive mobile navigation system. In: Proceedings of the 7th International Conference on Intelligent User Interfaces (IUI), pp. 15–22. ACM (2002)
8. Rehrl, K., Leitinger, S., Bruntsch, S., Mentz, H. J.: Assisting orientation and guidance for multimodal travelers in situations of modal change. In: Proceedings of the 8th International IEEE Conference on Intelligent Transportations Systems (ITSC), pp. 407–412 (2005)
9. Chowaw-Liebman, O., Christoph, U., Krempels, K.H., Terwelp, C.: Indoor navigation approach based on approximate positions. In: Proceedings of the International Conference on Indoor Positioning and Indoor Navigation (IPIN), pp. 15–17 (2010)

10. May, A.J., Ross, T., Bayer, S.H., Tarkiainen, M.J.: Pedestrian navigation aids: information requirements and design implications. Pers. Ubiquit. Comput. **7**, 331–338 (2003)
11. Biagioni, J., Agresta, A., Gerlich, T., Eriksson, J.: TransitGenie: a context-aware, real-time transit navigator. In: Proceedings of the 7th ACM Conference on Embedded Networked Sensor Systems (SenSys), pp. 329–330. ACM (2009)
12. Vieira, V., Caldas, L. R., Salgado, A. C.: Towards an ubiquitous and context sensitive public transportation system. In: Proceedings of the 4th International Conference on Ubi-Media Computing (U-Media), pp. 174–179 (2011)
13. Pessemier, T., Dooms, S., Martens, L.: Context-aware recommendations through context and activity recognition in a mobile environment. Multimedia Tools Appl. **72**, 2925–2948 (2013)
14. Christoph, U., Krempels, K. H., von Stülpnagel, J., Terwelp, C.: Automatic context detection of a mobile user. In: Proceedings of the International Conference on Wireless Information Networks and Systems (WINSYS), pp. 1–6 (2010)
15. Keller, C., Korzetz, M., Kühn, R., Schlegel, T.: Nutzerorientierte Visualisierung von Fahrplaninformationen auf mobilen Gerten im öffentlichen Verkehr [User-oriented Visualization of Train Schedule Information on Mobile Devices for Public Transportation]. In: Mensch & Computer 2011. Oldenbourg Wissenschaftsverlag GmbH, pp. 59–68 (2011)

Measuring Energy Consumption of Cross-Platform Frameworks for Mobile Applications

Matteo Ciman[✉] and Ombretta Gaggi

Department of Mathematics, University of Padua, Via Trieste 63,
35121 Padua, Italy
{mciman,gaggi}@math.unipd.it

Abstract. In this paper we analyze frameworks for mobile cross-platform development according to their influence on energy consumed by the developed applications. We consider the use of different smartphones sensors, e.g., GPS, accelerometer, etc., and features, e.g., acquiring video or audio from the environment. In particular, we have studied how the amount of required energy for the same operation changes according to the used framework. We use an hardware and software tool to measure energy consumed by the applications developed natively, as a web application or using two frameworks, Titanium and PhoneGap. Our experiments have shown that frameworks have a significant impact on energy consumption which greatly increases compared to an equal native application. Moreover, the amount of consumed energy is not the same for all frameworks.

Keywords: Mobile applications development · Cross-platform frameworks · Energy consumption

1 Introduction

Modern mobile devices are equipped with an ample set of sensors, like GPS, accelerometer, light sensor, etc., which are able to "sense" the real world, thus allowing the implementation of more attractive applications. As an example, applications can use GPS to provide information about interesting places near the user, the accelerometer to understand the current user activity (e.g., if he/she is walking, riding a bike or using a car), and the light sensor to adapt the screen brightness.

Acquiring data from all these sensors have a cost in terms of energy and power is a vital resource, so the software implementing the data acquisition from sensors must conserve battery power to allow for smartphones to operate for days without being recharged.

Battery life is a critical performance and user experience metric on mobile devices. Even the best ever app can be deleted by the user if it wastes all smartphone power within few hours. Unfortunately, it is difficult for developers to

© Springer International Publishing Switzerland 2015
V. Monfort and K.-H. Krempels (Eds.): WEBIST 2014, LNBIP 226, pp. 331–346, 2015.
DOI: 10.1007/978-3-319-27030-2_21

measure the energy used by their apps both before and after its implementation. As stated by Bloom et al. [1], battery life is one of the most important aspects considered by users when dealing with mobile devices, and most of the time users request a longer battery life. For this reason, energy consumption is an extremely important factor to consider when developing applications for smartphones.

In this paper, we analyze the impact of frameworks for cross-platform development on energy consumption of mobile applications which acquire data using different smartphones sensors, e.g., GPS, accelerometer, etc., and features, e.g., acquiring video or audio from the environment. We compare the request in terms of power consumption of different sensors, using different frameworks and with different samples frequency. We use the Monsoon Power Monitor [2] during our experiments to reduce the impact of external events. We must note here that this tool requires to have direct access to the battery, therefore cannot be used with iOS devices without opening them.

We studied both native applications and applications developed with Phone-Gap and Titanium to verify whether these frameworks influence the amount of required energy for the same operation. Moreover we analyze power consumption for HTML5 applications accessed using different browsers.

Our experiments have shown that the frameworks have a significant impact on the total amount of consumed energy, since an application developed using a cross-platform framework for mobile development can consume up to 50 % more energy than an equal native application, which means, a strong reduction in terms of battery life. Moreover, the amount of consumed energy is not the same for all frameworks. This means that power consumption can be one of the factors to be considered in the choice between native implementation and using a framework, or in the choice between two different frameworks.

The paper is organized as follows: related works are discussed in Sect. 2. Section 3 describes the frameworks for cross-platform mobile development already present in literature. The experiments made are presented in Sect. 4. We conclude in Sect. 5.

2   Related Works

Other works in literature analyze power consumption of mobile applications but they usually do not cover all sensors/features available on smartphones, and do not consider the use of cross-platform framework for development of mobile applications.

Balasubramanian et al. [3] measure energy consumption of mobile networking technologies, in particular 3G, GSM and WiFi. They find out that 3G and GSM incur in tail energy overhead since they remain in high power states also when the transfer is complete. They developed a model for energy consumed by networking activity and an efficient protocol that reduces energy consumption of common mobile applications.

A model-driven methodology to emulate the power consumption of smartphone application architectures is proposed by Thompson et al. [4]. They develop

SPOT, *Power Optimization Tool*, a tool that automates code generation for power consumption emulation and simplifies analysis. The tool is very useful since it allows to estimate energy consumption of potential mobile architecture, therefore *before* its implementation. This is very important since changes after the development can be very expensive. Moreover the tool is able to identify which hardware components draw significantly more power than others (e.g., GPS).

Mittal et al. [5] propose an energy emulation tool that allows to estimate the energy use for mobile applications without deploying the application on a smartphone. The tool considers the network characteristics and the processing speed. They define a power model describing different hardware components and evaluate the tool through comparison with real device energy measurements.

PowerScope [6,7] is a tool to measure energy consumption of mobile applications. The tool calculates energy consumption for each programming structure. The approach combines hardware instrumentation to measure current level with software to calculate statistical sampling of system activities. The authors show how applications can modify their behavior to preserve energy: when energy is plenty, the application allows a good user experience, otherwise it is biased toward energy conservation.

AppScope [8] is an Android-based energy metering system which estimates, in real-time, the usage of hardware components at a microscopic level. AppScope is implemented as a kernel module and provides an high accuracy, generating a low overhead. For this reason, the authors also define a power model and measure energy consumption with external tools to estimate the introduced error, which is, in the worst case of about 5.9 %.

Eprof [9], is a fine-grained energy profiler for mobile apps, which accurately captures complicated power behavior of smartphone components in a system-call-driven Finite State Machine (FSM). *Eprof* tries to map the power drawn and energy consumption back to program entities. The authors analyzed the energy consumption of 21 apps from Android Market including AngryBirds, Android Browser, and Facebook, and they found that third party advertisement modules in free apps could consume up to 65–75 % of the total app energy, and tracking user data (e.g., location, phone stats) consumes up to 20–30 % of the total energy. Moreover, smartphone apps spend a major portion of energy in I/O components such as 3G, WiFi, and GPS.

Pathak et al. [10] study the problem of no-sleep energy bugs, i.e., errors in energy management resulting in the smartphone components staying on for an unnecessarily long period of time. They develop a static analysis tool to detect, at compile-time no-sleep bug in Android apps.

In other papers, the authors compare different framework for cross-platform mobile development according to a set of features. [11] compare jQuery Mobile [12], Sencha Touch [13], The-M-Project [14] and Google Web Toolkit combined with mgwt [15] according to a particular set of criteria, which includes license and costs, documentation and support, learning success, user interface elements, etc. They conclude that jQuery Mobile is a good solution for simple applications or as first attempt in developing mobile apps, while Sencha Touch is suited for more complex applications.

Palmieri et al. [16] evaluate Rhodes [17], PhoneGap [18], dragonRAD [19] and MoSync [20] with particular attention to the programming environment and the APIs they provide. The authors provide an analysis of the architecture of each framework and they conclude highlighting Rhodes over other frameworks, since this is the only one which supports both MVC framework and web-based services.

Phonegap, Titanium, jQuery Mobile and MoSync, are evaluated in [21] focusing on applications with animations, i.e. games. Besides the standard evaluation parameters like IDE, debug tools, programming complexity, etc., they evaluate more mobile and games-related aspects like APIs for animations, mobile devices supported, support for native user interface, performances etc. They conclude that, according to the actual state of art of the frameworks, Titanium is the best framework, since it supports animations and transitions, and its performances are good even in case of complex applications.

Issues about performances are discussed in [22]. They stated frameworks based on web technologies experience a decrease in performances when the applications implement transition effects, effects during scrolling, animations, etc., but this problem affects essentially games, while the loss in performances are unnoticeable in business application, i.e., applications which support business tasks.

All the addressed works make a critical analysis of the chosen frameworks according to criteria which never include power consumption. In some case they include performances which are considered in terms of user experience. In this paper we want to study how the use of a cross-platform framework for mobile device may affect the energy consumption of the final application with respect to native development.

3   Frameworks for Cross-Platform Mobile Development

According to Raj and Tolety [23], frameworks for cross-platform development can be divided into four approaches: *web, hybrid, interpreted* and *cross compiled*. They highlight strength and weakness of each approach, concluding that a preferred solution for each kind of application does not exist, but the decision about which framework to use should be made considering the features of the application to be developed. To help the developers in this decision, they provide a matrix which shows which are the best choices to develop a specific feature. This classification can help to correctly interpret the results of our tests.

The *Web Approach (WA)* allows programmers to develop a web application using HTML, CSS and Javascript. Given the new emerging features of HTML5 and CSS3, these technologies allow the creation of rich and complex applications, therefore their use cannot be considered a limitation. The application can be accessed through a mobile device using only its integrated browser, connecting to the right public internet address. Figure 1 shows this approach. Thanks to

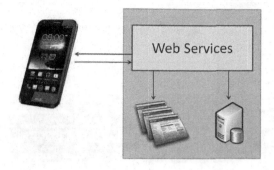

Fig. 1. Architecture of an application using the WA.

the new features introduced by HTML5 for mobile devices, web applications can now access device sensors, i.e. accelerometer, gyroscope etc., or user and device specific information, i.e. contacts. Device support for this features depends on the browser maturity used by the user, meaning that the adoption of recent features could reduce the number of final possible users. Since between different browsers the implementation of the W3C Recommendations could be different, i.e. accelerometer frequency update, the developer has to take into account these differences when developing web applications. *jQuery Mobile* [24] and *Sencha Touch* [13] are examples of this framework.

The *Hybrid Approach (HA)* is a middle way between *Native* and *Web Approach*. In this case, the application operates in two different ways. It uses the webkit rendering engine to display controls, buttons and animations. The webkit engine is therefore responsible to draw and manage user interface objects. On the other side, the framework and its APIs provide access to device features and use them to increase the user experience. In this case, the application will be distributed and installed and appears on the user device as native mobile applications, but the performances are often lower than native applications because its execution requires to run the browser rendering engine. An example of this

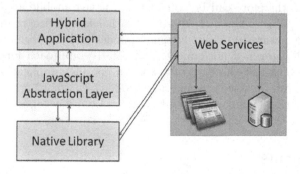

Fig. 2. *Hybrid approach* application architecture.

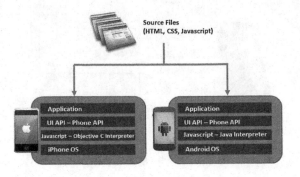

Fig. 3. *Interpreted Approach* architecture.

kind of frameworks is PhoneGap, also known as Apache Cordova [18], and the architecture of the final application is shown in Fig. 2.

With the *Interpreted Approach (InA)*, the developer has the possibility to write the code of the application using a language which is different from languages natively supported by the different platforms. An example can be Javascript: developers who already knows this language are simply required to learn how to use the APIs provided by the framework. When the application is installed on the device, the final code contains also a dedicated interpreter which is used to execute the non-native code. Even in this case, the developer has access to device features (how many and which features depend on the chosen framework) through an abstraction layer. This approach allows the developer to design a final user interface that is identical to the native user interface without any additional line of code. This approach can reach an high level of reusable code, but can reduce a little the performances due to the interpretation step. Titanium [25] is an example of this kind of framework and Fig. 3 shows the architecture of the framework.

The last approach, the *Cross Compiled Approach (CCA)*, lets the developer write only one application using a common programming language, e.g. C#. Frameworks which follow this approach generate, after compilation, different native applications for different mobile platforms. The final application uses native language, therefore can be considered a native mobile application to all intents and purposes. Therefore, this approach lets the programmer have full access to all the features provided by smartphones and the performances can be considered similar (even if not equal) to the native approach for simple application. In fact some tests have shown that for complex applications the native solution remains better since the generated code gives worst performances of the resulting application, compared to code written by a developer. An example of this framework is Mono [26].

4 Experiments

Our goal is to provide objective information about the amount of consumed energy by the most common sensors available on the smartphones. To perform

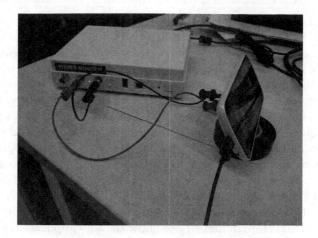

Fig. 4. Hardware setup of the system.

the best measure of energy consumption, it is important to avoid influences from external factors. A simple possibility is to run a background application that measures battery power at fixed intervals of time. This solution is adopted by some of the related works discussed in Sect. 2, but clearly introduces an overhead and must consider the possibility that other external events like call, messages, network problems and connectivity may influence energy consumption. Moreover these external events are almost unpredictable and unlikely reproducible, thus leading to unequal test sets.

4.1 Study Setup

For the reason mentioned before, during our experiments we use the Monsoon Power Monitor [2]. This hardware device comes with a software tool, the Power Tool, which gives the possibility to analyze data about energy consumption of any device that uses a single lithium battery. The information retrieved are energy consumption, average power and current, expected battery life, etc. These data are extremely important because can help the developer to understand which tasks use most of the energy of the battery, for how much time, etc. Moreover, it helps to analyze and improve the application code according to its power consumption. Using data acquired by Power Monitor, it is possible to understand if and where some energy can be saved, thus increasing battery life, an extremely important aspect when working with mobile devices. Figure 4 shows the hardware setup of the system.

Our goal is to compare energy consumption of applications developed in a native way or using a cross-platform framework, and to compare performances, in terms of energy consumption, among different frameworks. For each sensor that we want to analyze, we develop a basic application that simply retrieves and show data. Each application can be considered a sort of lower bound for applications behavior in terms of energy consumption, because usually applications that collect data from sensors perform several computation before updating the user interface.

As explained before, to use the Power Monitor tool it is necessary to have direct access to the battery of the smartphone, in order to be able to connect the entire system and to measure the consumed energy. For this reason, we made our comparison using an Android device with removable battery, because the iOS devices do not allow to have direct access to the battery in a safe way.

For our experiments we compared three different approaches: *Web*, *Hybrid* and *Interpreted*. To test the *Web Approach*, we developed web applications and used the most common mobile browsers available for Android: Google Chrome, Mozilla Firefox and Opera. Each web application was tested offline, with the smartphone in "flight" mode, using the new HTML5 offline feature, that lets the developer specify, through a *cache manifest* file, a list of file that the browser has to download and store in memory to show the web application even without internet connectivity. In this way we avoid interference due to the operating system which can connect to the Internet to answer to request from other apps, or to search for new updates.

For the other two approach, we select Titanium and PhoneGap. As already explained in Sect. 3, these two frameworks belong to two different categories. Titanium belongs to the *Interpreted* frameworks, while PhoneGap follows an *Hybrid* approach.

Our test smartphone is a Samsung Galaxy i9250. The (theoretical) capacity of the battery is 1750 mAh. Even if this smartphone is not an up-to-date device, what is important for us is if the usage of a cross-platform framework has negative effects on energy consumption, and in which measure, for applications that use smartphone's sensors. With this question in mind, is easy to see that what we want to retrieve from the experiments is how much (in percentage) the energy consumption increases. Even if characteristics and performances of sensors may vary between different smartphones, our tests are performed on the same device and comparisons are made on the percentage increase of energy consumption, to limit the influence of the chosen device on our final results. We must note here, that many devices, although different in terms of brand and model, share the same hardware components for sensors.

To make our tests, we developed one application for each sensor for each framework: a native mobile application, a web application, an application built with PhoneGap and another one used to test the Titanium framework. We developed from scratch the native, the web and the Phonegap application. These applications let the user chooses, when possible, the sampling frequency. Instead, we tested the Titanium framework using the Kitchen Sink app provided by Appcelerator [27], a sample application built to show the different APIs and features provided by the framework.

All the applications retrieve data from the accelerometer and the compass, and display this information simply as a numerical value with a label. To test the microphone API, we record audio from the microphone and save it on the device as a 3GPP file. To test energy consumption due to the usage of the camera, all the developed applications show the image captured from the camera for a predefined time interval, and take a picture at its end. Since satellite signal is not available inside buildings, to test the GPS sensor we simply start a location update without showing anything.

Each test lasted two minutes. Previous experiments show that, after an initial interval, the duration of a test does not influence the final results in terms of differences of energy consumption, and we chose this amount of time to get a stable final value from the system. For our tests we used: Android API v4.2.2, PhoneGap v3.5.0, Titanium SDK v3.2., Mozilla Firefox v30.0, Google Chrome v35.0 and Opera 22.0.

4.2 Results

In this section we report the final results of our analysis. We analyze the most common sensors which can be used through the APIs provided by at least one the two analyzed frameworks. For each sensor, our application (either native or developed using a cross-platform framework) starts to acquire data coming from the selected sensor and display them on the user screen.

We made our experiments keeping the screen on, since this situation is much more adherent to reality where it's very difficult that an user interact with an application keeping the screen off: consider, as an example, Google Maps, which uses the GPS sensor to capture the position of the user and to give the correct directions.

Measures are repeated three times, in order to get a mean final value of each test. The main value we are interested in is the consumed energy, which shows how much energy is used by that particular task during the two minutes test. The smartphone was in "flight" mode (thus unable to receive any phone call or message that could arbitrarily increase energy consumption) and WiFi and Bluetooth connectivity are turned off.

To get an idea about energy consumption of an application, we need a base value to compare with. For our purpose, we decided to measure the consumed energy when the smartphone is turned on, with the screen on and without any running applications. This is the base value for our analysis. Clearly, it is quite impossible to measure the same value from another smartphone, but, since our discussion does not deal with absolute values of energy consumption, but with the increment in energy consumption in term of percentage, this initial value is important for our computation. Using our test smartphone, the consumed energy in two minutes is 5126 μAh. Moreover, the analysis of the increment in energy consumption reported in percentage helps to give results which are not tightly related to the chosen hardware.

Tables 1 and 2 show the results of our experiments, i.e., they compare how the consumed energy increases when the smartphone uses its sensors with a native application, with a web application accessed using the different browsers and with applications developed using the other two frameworks, PhoneGap and Titanium. We must note here that native development provides full access to all the available sensors of the device, while the number and type of supported

Table 1. Energy consumption comparison between native applications and apps developed using the Interpreted or Hybrid Approach.

Sensor	Native Consumed Energy (μAh)	Δ (%)	PhoneGap Consumed Energy (μAh)	Δ (%)	Titanium Consumed Energy (μAh)	Δ (%)
Only App	5129	+0.06 %	5281	+3.03 %	5180	+1.06 %
Accelerometer	7001	+36.58 %	8971	+75.01 %	9191	+79.29 %
Compass	6708	+30.87 %	7572	+47.72 %	-	-
Microphone (Rec)	6180	+20.56 %	6241	+21.76 %	-	-
GPS	7320	+42.80 %	7338	+43.15 %	7355	+43.48 %
Camera	17653	+244.37 %	18062	+252.36 %	17950	+250.17 %

Table 2. Energy consumption using the Web Approach. Note that data marked with (*) use a faster updating frequency.

Sensor	Firefox Consumed Energy (μAh)	Δ (%)	Chrome Consumed Energy (μAh)	Δ (%)	Opera Consumed Energy (μAh)	Δ (%)
Only App	5255	+2.51 %	5315	+3.69 %	5318	+3.74 %
Accelerometer	13738*	+168.01 % *	11040*	+115.38 % *	11469*	+123.74 %*
Compass	-	-	-	-	-	-
Microphone (Rec)	7862	+53.57 %	7636	+48.97 %	7649	+49.22 %
GPS	7488	+46.07 %	8329	+62.49 %	8209	+60.15 %
Camera	15801	+208.26 %	15386	+200.15 %	18354	+258.06 %

sensors may vary between different cross-platform frameworks, depending on the state of the art of the frameworks themselves. For example, Titanium provides access to the microphone and record audio data only for iOS devices and not for Android devices, while PhoneGap supports this features for iOS, Android and Windows Phone.

The columns denoted with Δ in Tables 1 and 2 show how the consumed energy increases compared to the consumed energy of our base value, i.e. the smartphone with the screen on, without running applications. This value gives an idea of how much more expensive is to perform a particular task among our initial idle state. Table 3 presents a resume of the increments in energy consumption reporting all the Δ columns.

As it is easy to see, the differences between power consumed by the native app and the solutions developed with a framework for cross-platform development is very high.

Let us begin the analysis with the comparison between applications which do not capture any data from sensors. The purpose of this test is essentially to investigate if the adoption of a cross-platform framework instead of a native development requires more energy consumption simply to "show" the application

Table 3. Resume table with all the tested framework. Data marked with (*) uses an higher update frequency.

	Native Δ (%)	Firefox Δ (%)	Chrome Δ (%)	Opera Δ (%)	PhoneGap Δ (%)	Titanium Δ (%)
Only App	+0.06 %	+2.51 %	+3.69 %	+3.74 %	+3.03 %	+1.06 %
Accelerometer	+36.58 %	+168.01 %*	+115.38 %*	+123.74 %*	+75.01 %	+79.29 %
Compass	+30.87 %	-	-	-	+47.42 %	-
Microphone (Rec)	+20.56 %	+53.57 %	+48.97 %	+49.22 %	+21.76 %	-
GPS	+42.80 %	+46.07 %	+62.49 %	+60.15 %	+43.15 %	+43.48 %
Camera	+244.37 %	+326.25 %	+200.15 %	+258.06 %	+252.36 %	+250.17 %

without any computation behind. The results are shown in the first row of Table 1 (and Table 2) denoted with the label "Only App". As we can see, the energy consumption increases from at least 1.06 % (Titanium) to at most 3.74 % for Opera, i.e. the adoption of a cross-platform framework produces, basically, a little more expensive applications in terms of power consumption, and this increment is not equal for all frameworks.

Considering applications that use smartphones sensors to retrieve data, we can measure differences only for sensors that are supported at least from one of the two frameworks. The measurements made show that the usage of the accelerometer requires about 39 % more energy using the PhoneGap application instead of the native one. This is an extremely high value, which means that the usage of this sensor in a cross-platform application is really a battery consuming task that can decrease user experience. This value is even bigger for browsers (and a bit more for Titanium), as we will discuss later. Therefore, if the application needs to retrieve data from the accelerometer it is necessary to consider if it would be better to develop different, more performing, native applications for each platform. Even with the *Interpreted Approach*, the energy consumption is much more higher (about 43 %). Moreover, we can compare PhoneGap with Titanium, showing how the latter is more expensive than the first one.

The results reported for the *Web Approach* require particular attention. Web Applications do not let the developer specify the preferred update frequency of a particular sensor. This means that new data is available at not controllable intervals by the developer. For example, with Web Applications the update frequency is in general 20 Hz (1 sample every 50 ms), while with Mozilla Firefox it is even faster (25 Hz).

Analyzing the *Web Approach*, it is clear that to read data and update the user interface faster leads to an higher energy consumption with respect to the PhoneGap framework. However, the difference between PhoneGap and *Web Approach* in terms of update frequency (15 Hz against 20 Hz or 25 Hz) does not justify an increase of about 40 % (PhoneGap vs Chrome) to 90 % (PhoneGap vs Firefox) of energy consumption, meaning that this approach is much more expensive[1].

---

[1] Since PhoneGap does not allow to have data faster than 20 Hz, it was not possible to have an objective comparison of this data.

PhoneGap performs worst even for data acquisition from compass, since it requires 17 % more battery than the native solution (Titanium and web browsers do not support this feature at the time of writing).

The only two sensors where the difference between the native solution and the cross-platform framework is lower are the GPS and the microphone. Despite the *Web Approach*, where there could be several performances problems due to a not complete optimization of the sensor (Chrome and Opera with the GPS), the energy consumption of the frameworks is quite the same of the native solution, as we can see in Table 2. This behavior can be explained because in this case the cross-platform application makes only one call to the system API, and waits from the system the result (an image or location coordinates) and so the difference between the native and the cross-platform solution is really low.

Considering the energy consumption for the camera using web browsers, Mozilla Firefox and Google Chrome seem to be better that the native solution. This strange data is explained from the fact that, differently from the native solution, images coming from the camera do not cover the entire window, but only a small portion of it. This makes the application much less expensive since it collects less data. Opera, differently from the other two browsers, shows the images from the camera in the entire window, and, as we can see from Table 2, its consumption is higher that the native solution.

Comparing together all the frameworks, it is clear that the nature of the framework influences energy consumption. In particular, Web Applications are the most expensive applications, both for a not complete optimization of the API for sensor data acquisition, and because user interface updates for a browser is an expensive task. Comparing together PhoneGap and Titanium, the overhead of energy consumed introduced by the two frameworks is different when the user interface has to be updated frequently. This difference comes from the nature of the two frameworks. As already mentioned in Sect. 3, PhoneGap belongs to the *hybrid* family, while Titanium to the *interpreted* frameworks. This means that if we compare the two different platforms in terms of performances and energy consumption, the *hybrid* application is better, since the consumed energy by this application is lower, meaning that the overhead introduced is lower.

Another possibility to compare different development frameworks, and in particular how sensors usage affects application performances and energy consumption, would be to test these applications without updating the values of the retrieved information on the screen or turning off the screen while performing operations. In this case, the differences between the native solution and the cross-platform solutions when acquiring data from accelerometer or compass are much more lower, about 5 % (at most 20 % for Web Approach). Unfortunately, this is only a theoretical result. In fact, every application that retrieves data from sensors does not use this raw data immediately, but it usually elaborates the data and updates the user interface accordingly. Therefore, to use this theoretical results to promote the use of cross-platform framework would not adhere to the reality because we would not consider two extremely important parts of the applications, i.e., data elaboration and user interface management.

Table 4. Consumed energy using different sampling frequencies to capture data with PhoneGap.

Sensor	Consumed Energy increase (%)			
	60 ms	150 ms	300 ms	600 ms
Accelerometer	+75.01 %	+38.60 %	+24.09 %	+15.55 %
Compass	+47.72 %	+41.02 %	+29.36 %	+19.33 %

If we compare together the same cross-platform application, what we can note is that the difference in terms of consumed energy to show or not to show data from sensors is about 70 % (PhoneGap and Titanium) to 30 % (Web Approach). This means that, without concern on the chosen cross-platform framework, the most expensive task is to update the user interface.

Unlike Titanium, PhoneGap allows the developer to decide the frequency to retrieve data from sensors. This is an extremely important option, because lets the developer to define the right update frequency depending on the target application and the needs of data. This possibility is available for both the accelerometer and the compass sensor. In this cases, we made several test at predefined update frequencies (60 ms, 150 ms, 300 ms, 600 ms) to see how, and in which measure, changing the update frequency affects energy consumption. The results are shown in Table 4. As it is easy to see, if the update frequency decreases, the consumed energy decreases, with a difference that can reach 60 % between 60 ms and 600 ms update frequency. This means that the developer has to pay extremely attention when developing a cross-platform application, because if the user experience do not requires an extremely fast update, it is useful to reduce the update frequency of sensor data in order to save energy, and so battery life.

5 Conclusions

Due to the diffusion of different smartphones and tablet devices from different vendors, the cross-platform development approach, i.e., to develop only one single application and distribute it to different devices and mobile platforms, is growing and becoming extremely important. This cross-platform development incorporates several approaches, i.e., *web, hybrid, interpreted* or *cross compiled*. All these approaches have several positive and negative aspects, either from a developer or a user point of view.

Many papers address the problem of how to choose the best framework for the development of a particular application, but, to the best of our knowledge, no one considers the power consumption as one of the key issue to make a correct choice.

In this paper we analyze the influence of the different approaches on energy consumption of mobile devices, in particular for the *Web* (Google Chrome,

Mozilla Firefox and Opera), *Hybrid* (PhoneGap) and the *Interpreted* (Titanium) approach. We compared the performances of a simple application, built with a particular framework, that retrieves data from sensors and updates the user interface, to a native application with the same behavior, to measure differences in terms of power consumption. Despite other previous analysis, we do not use a software to measure energy consumption since it introduces a not valuable overhead; for this reason we used the Monsoon Power Tool which allows to measure, through hardware links, consumed energy and to understand how this consumption increases with the two frameworks.

Our comparison shows that, visualization of data (business applications) perform better on the *interpreted* approach (Titanium), that can be a good solution for simple applications that do not retrieve data from sensors, e.g., on-line shopping, home banking, games which do not use accelerometer, etc.

A particular sensor needs specific discussion. Even if Titanium seems to be the right choice if energy consumption is a key issue, our experiments have shown that it fails in case of retrieval of data from accelerometer for two reasons: the available API does not allow to impose an update frequency, and compared to other framework with the same update frequency it consumes about 5 % more energy than PhoneGap. This result derives from the *Interpreted approach*: the necessary interpretation step can be extremely expensive and lead to more energy consumption. We must note here that this sensor consume a lot of energy, therefore if the application make a strong use of the accelerometer, the developer has to consider also the native solution.

The results we got show that a cross-platform approach involves an increase in terms of energy consumption that is extremely high, in particular in presence of an high usage of sensors data and user interface updates. This increase can vary even in order of about 40 %, meaning that it is important to choose the right framework to preserve the battery duration and to avoid negatively affecting user experience with usage of a cross-platform framework during development. In fact, several research studies have shown that energy consumption and battery life are the most important aspects considered by mobile devices users.

Talking about the *Web Approach*, it is clear that at the moment this kind of approach is not ready for a wide adoption, since the energy required to perform the same task of a native application is extremely higher, reducing battery life and stressing of the user.

The results provided are clearly related to the state of art of the frameworks and browsers under examination at the time of writing. This means that, they can change in the future according to the improvements of the frameworks and browsers.

As future works, we plan to increase the total number of analyzed frameworks considering event the *Cross-compiled Approach*, trying to cover all the different approaches. Moreover, we will try to follow the development of the different frameworks in order to reach a complete analysis of the different sensors provided by the smartphones and their consumption in user applications.

References

1. Bloom, L., Eardley, R., Geelhoed, E., Manahan, M., Ranganathan, P.: Investigating the relationship between battery life and user acceptance of dynamic, energy-aware interfaces on handhelds. In: Proceedings of the International Conference Human Computer Interaction with Mobile Devices and Services, pp. 13–24 (2004)
2. Monsoon Solutions Inc. (2013). http://www.msoon.com/LabEquipment/PowerMonitor/
3. Balasubramanian, N., Balasubramanian, A., Venkataramani, A.: Energy consumption in mobile phones: a measurement study and implications for network applications. In: Proceedings of the 9th ACM SIGCOMM Conference on Internet Measurement Conference, IMC 2009, pp. 280–293 (2009)
4. Thompson, C., Schmidt, D.C., Turner, H.A., White, J.: Analyzing mobile application software power consumption via model-driven engineering. In: Benavente-Peces, C., Filipe, J. (eds.) PECCS, pp. 101–113. SciTePress, Portugal (2011)
5. Mittal, R., Kansal, A., Chandra, R.: Empowering developers to estimate app energy consumption. In: Proceedings of the 18th Annual International Conference on Mobile Computing and Networking, MobiCom 2012, pp. 317–328 (2012)
6. Flinn, J., Satyanarayanan, M.: Energy-aware adaptation for mobile applications. In: Proceedings of the Seventeenth ACM Symposium on Operating Systems Principles, SOSP 1999, pp. 48–63 (1999)
7. Flinn, J., Satyanarayanan, M.: Powerscope: a tool for profiling the energy usage of mobile applications. In: Proceedings of the Second IEEE Workshop on Mobile Computer Systems and Applications, WMCSA 1999. IEEE Computer Society, Washington, DC, USA (1999)
8. Yoon, C., Kim, D., Jung, W., Kang, C., Cha, H.: Appscope: application energy metering framework for android smartphones using kernel activity monitoring. In: Proceedings of the 2012 USENIX Conference on Annual Technical Conference, USENIX ATC 2012, pp. 36–36. USENIX Association, Berkeley, CA, USA (2012)
9. Pathak, A., Hu, Y.C., Zhang, M.: Where is the energy spent inside my app?: fine grained energy accounting on smartphones with eprof. In: Proceedings of the 7th ACM European Conference on Computer Systems, EuroSys 2012, pp. 29–42 (2012)
10. Pathak, A., Jindal, A., Hu, Y.C., Midkiff, S.P.: What is keeping my phone awake?: Characterizing and detecting no-sleep energy bugs in smartphone apps. In: Proceedings of the 10th International Conference on Mobile Systems, Applications, and Services. MobiSys 2012, pp. 267–280 (2012)
11. Heitkötter, H., Hanschke, S., Majchrzak, T.A.: Evaluating cross-platform development approaches for mobile applications. In: Cordeiro, J., Krempels, K.-H. (eds.) WEBIST 2012. LNBIP, vol. 140, pp. 120–138. Springer, Heidelberg (2013)
12. Firtman, M.: jQuery Mobile: Up and Running - Using HTML5 to Design Web Apps for Tablets and Smartphones. O'Reilly Media, Sebastopol (2012)
13. Sencha Inc.: Sencha touch (2013). http://www.sencha.com/products/touch
14. Panacoda GmbH.: The-m-project (2013). http://www.the-m-project.org/
15. Kurka, D.: mgwt - making gwt work with mobile (2013). http://www.m-gwt.com/
16. Palmieri, M., Singh, I., Cicchetti, A.: Comparison of cross-platform mobile development tools. In: 16th International Conference on Intelligence in Next Generation Networks. ICIN 2012, pp. 179–186 (2012)
17. Motorola Solutions Inc: Rhodes (2013). http://www.motorolasolutions.com/us-en/rhomobile+suite/rhodes

18. Apache Software Foundation: Phonegap (2013). http://phonegap.com/
19. Seregon Solutions Inc.: dragonrad (2013). http://dragonrad.com/
20. MoSync Inc.: MoSync (2013). http://www.mosync.com
21. Ciman, M., Gaggi, O., Gonzo, N.: Cross-platform mobile development: a study on apps with animations. In: Proceedings of the 29th Annual ACM Symposium on Applied Computing, SAC 2014 (2014)
22. Charland, A., Leroux, B.: Mobile application development: web vs. native. Commun. ACM **54**, 49–53 (2011)
23. Raj, R., Tolety, S.: A study on approaches to build cross-platform mobile applications and criteria to select appropriate approach. In: Annual IEEE India Conference, INDICON 2012, pp. 625–629 (2012)
24. Firtman, M.: jquery mobile (2013). http://jquerymobile.com/
25. Appcelerator Inc.: Titanium (2013). http://www.appcelerator.com/platform/titanium-platform/
26. Monologue Inc.: Mono framework (2013). http://www.mono-project.com/
27. Appcelerator Inc.: Titanium Mobile Kitchen Sink Demo (2013). https://github.com/appcelerator/KitchenSink

Process-Driven Data Collection with Smart Mobile Devices

Johannes Schobel[✉], Marc Schickler, Rüdiger Pryss, and Manfred Reichert

Institute of Databases and Information Systems, Ulm University, Ulm, Germany
{johannes.schobel,marc.schickler,ruediger.pryss,
manfred.reichert}@uni-ulm.de

Abstract. Paper-based questionnaires are often used for collecting data in application domains like healthcare, psychology or education. Such paper-based approach, however, results in a massive workload for processing and analyzing the collected data. In order to relieve domain experts from these manual tasks, we propose a process-driven approach for implementing as well as running respective mobile business applications. In particular, the logic of a questionnaire is described in terms of an explicit process model. Based on this process model, in turn, multiple questionnaire instances may be created and enacted by a process engine. For this purpose, we present a generic architecture and demonstrate the development of electronic questionnaires in the context of scientific studies. Further, we discuss the major challenges and lessons learned. In this context the presented process-driven approach offers promising perspectives in respect to the development of mobile data collection applications.

Keywords: Process-aware information system · Electronic questionnaire · Mobile business application

1 Introduction

During the last years smart mobile applications have been increasingly used in business environment. Examples include applications for task management and location-based services. In particular, smart mobile devices offer promising perspectives in respect to mobile data collection as well [1]. For example, data could be collected with sensors (e.g., pulse sensor), communicating with the smart mobile device [2] or with form-based end-user applications [3]. Such a mobile data collection becomes necessary, for example, in the context of clinical trials, psychological studies, and quality management surveys.

In order to enable mobile data collection, specific knowledge on how to implement such smart mobile applications is required on one hand. On the other, domain-specific knowledge is needed, which is usually not available to application developers. Consequently, costly interactions between domain experts and IT experts are required. To reduce overall efforts, a framework for rapidly developing and evolving mobile data collection applications shall be developed. In

© Springer International Publishing Switzerland 2015
V. Monfort and K.-H. Krempels (Eds.): WEBIST 2014, LNBIP 226, pp. 347–362, 2015.
DOI: 10.1007/978-3-319-27030-2_22

particular, respective business applications shall be easy to maintain for non-computer experts as well. Our overall vision is to enable domain experts to develop mobile data collection applications themselves at a high level of abstraction. Specifically, this paper focuses on the process-driven design, implementation and enactment of mobile questionnaires that support end users with their daily data collection tasks.

As application domain for demonstrating the benefits of our approach we choose psychological studies. Here, domain experts mostly use paper-based questionnaires for collecting required data from subjects. However, such a paper-based data collection shows several drawbacks, e.g., regarding the structuring and layout of a questionnaire (e.g., questions may still be answered even if they are no longer relevant) as well as the later analysis of answers (e.g., errors might occur when transferring the paper-based collected data to electronic worksheets).

To cope with these issues and to understand the differences between paper-based and electronic questionnaires in a mobile context, first of all, we implemented selected questionnaire applications for smart mobile devices and applied them in real world application settings [4–6]. In particular, we were able to demonstrate that mobile electronic questionnaires relieve end users from costly manual tasks, like the transfer, transformation and analysis of the collected data. As a major drawback, however, all these applications were hard-coded and their implementation required considerable interactions with end users. As a consequence, the respective applications were neither easy to maintain nor extensible. In order to overcome the gap between the domain-specific design of a questionnaire and its technical implementation enacted on smart mobile devices, therefore, an easy to handle, flexible and generic *questionnaire system* is required.

From the insights we gained during the practical use of the aforementioned mobile applications as well as from lessons learned in related implemented projects [7], we elicited the requirements for electronic questionnaire applications that allow for a flexible mobile data collection. In order to evaluate whether the use of process management technology contributes to the satisfaction of these requirements, we mapped the logic of a complex questionnaire from psychology to a process model, which was then deployed to a process engine. In particular, the process model served as basis for driving the execution of questionnaire instances at runtime. Note that this mapping allows overcoming many of the problems known from paper-based questionnaires. In turn, the use of a process modeling component and a process execution engine in the given context raised additional challenges. Especially, the implemented questionnaire runs on a mobile device and communicates with a remote process engine to enact psychological questionnaires. As a major lesson, we learned that process management technology may not only be applied in the context of business process automation, but also provides a promising approach for generating mobile data collection applications. In particular, a process-driven approach enables end users (i.e., non-computer experts) to develop mobile electronic questionnaires as well as to deploy them on smart mobile devices.

The contributions of this paper are as follows:

- We discuss fundamental problems of paper-based questionnaires and present requirements regarding their transfer to smart mobile devices.
- We provide a mental model for mapping the logic of questionnaires to process models and illustrate this mental model through a real-world application scenario from psychology.
- We present a generic architecture for data collection applications on smart mobile devices. This architecture can be applied to model, visualize and enact electronic questionnaires. In particular, it uses process models to define and control the flow logic of a questionnaire.
- We share fundamental insights we gathered during the process of implementing and evaluating mobile data collection applications.

The remainder of this paper is organized as follows: Sect. 2 discusses issues related to paper-based questionnaires. Further, it elicitates the requirements that emerge when transferring a paper-based questionnaire to an electronic version running on smart mobile devices. Section 3 describes the mental model we suggest for meeting these requirements. In Sect. 4, we present the basic architecture of an approach for developing mobile data collection applications. Section 5 provides a detailed discussion, while Sect. 6 presents related work. Finally, Sect. 7 concludes the paper with a summary and outlook.

2   Case Study

In a case study involving 10 domain experts, we analyzed more than 15 paper-based questionnaires from different domains, including questionnaires used in the context of psychological studies. Our goal was to understand issues that emerge when transferring paper-based questionnaires to smart mobile applications. Section 2.1 discusses basic issues related to *paper & pencil* questionnaires, while Sect. 2.2 elicitates fundamental requirements for their electronic mobile support.

2.1   Paper-Based Questionnaires

We analyzed 15 paper-based questionnaires from psychology and medicine. In this context, a variety of issues emerged. First, in the considered domains, a questionnaire must be *valid*. This means that it should have already been applied in several studies, and statistical evaluations have proven that the results obtained from the collected data are representative. In addition, the questions are usually presented in a neutral way in order to not affect or influence the subject (e.g., patient). Creating a valid instrument is one of the main goals when setting up a psychological questionnaire. In particular, reproducible and conclusive results must be guaranteed. Furthermore, a questionnaire may be used in two different modes. In the *interview mode*, the subject is interviewed by a supervisor who also fills in the questionnaire; i.e., the supervisor controls which questions he is going to ask or skip. This mode usually requires a lot of experience since the interviewer must also deal with questions that might be critical for the subject. The other mode we consider is *self-rating*. In this mode, the questionnaire is handed out to the subject who then answers the respective questions herself; i.e., no supervision is provided in this mode.

Another challenging issue of paper-based questionnaires concerns the *analysis* of the data collected. Gathered answers need to be transfered to electronic worksheets, which constitutes a time-consuming and error-prone task. For example, when filling in a questionnaire, typographical errors or wrong interpretations of given answers might occur. In general, both sources of error (i.e., errors occurring during the interviews or transcription) decrease the quality of the data collected, which further underlines the need of an electronic support for data collection.

In numerous interviews we conducted with 10 domain experts from psychology, additional issues have emerged. Psychological studies are often performed in developing countries, e.g., surveying of child soldiers in rural areas in Africa [4]. *Political restrictions* regarding data collection further require attention and influence the way in which interviews and assessments may be performed by domain experts (i.e., psychologists). Since in many geographic regions the available infrastructure is not well developed, the data collected is usually digitalized in the home country of the scientists responsible for the study. Taking these issues into account, it is not surprising that psychological studies last from *several weeks up to several months*. From a practical point of view, this raises the problem of allocating enough space in luggage to transfer the paper-based questionnaires safely to the home country of the respective researcher.

Apart from these *logistic problems*, we revealed issues related to the interview procedure itself. In particular, it has turned out that questionnaires often need to be *adapted by authorized domain experts to a particular application context* (e.g., changing the language of a questionnaire or adding/deleting selected questions). In turn, these adaptations must be propagated to all other interviewers and smart mobile devices respectively to keep the results valid and comparable.

Considering these issues, we had additional discussions with domain experts, which revealed several requirements as discussed in the next section.

2.2   Requirements

In the following, we discuss basic requirements for the mobile support of electronic questionnaires. We derived these requirements in the context of case studies, literature analyses, expert interviews, and hands-on experiences regarding the implementation of mobile data collection applications [5,6]. Especially, when interviewing domain experts, fundamental requirements could be elicitated. The same applies to the paper & pencil questionnaires we analyzed.

Basic requirements derived from the interviews are listed below:

R1 (Mobility). The process of collecting data should be flexible and usually requires extensive interactions. Data may have to be collected even though no computer is available at the place the questionnaire should be filled in.

For example, consider data collection at the bedside of a patient in a hospital or interviews conducted by psychologists in a meeting room. Computers are often disturbing in such situations, particularly if the interviewer is "hiding" himself behind a screen. To enable flexible data collection, the device needs to be portable instead. Further, it should not distract the participating actors in communicating and interacting with each other.

R2 (Multi-user Support). Since different users may interact with a mobile questionnaire, multi-user support is crucial. Furthermore, it must be possible to distinguish between different user roles (e.g., interviewers and subjects) involved in the processing of an electronic questionnaire. Note, that a user may possess different roles. For example, he could be interviewer in the context of a specific questionnaire, but subject in the context of another one.

R3 (Support of Different Questionnaire Modes). Generally, a questionnaire may be used in two different modes: interview and self-rating mode (cf. Sect. 2.1). These two modes of questioning diverge in the way the questions are posed, the possible answers that may be given, the order in which the questions are answered, and the additional features provided (e.g., freetext notes). In general, mobile electronic questionnaire applications should allow for both modes. Note, that this requirement is correlated with R2 as the considered roles determine the modes available for a questionnaire.

R4 (Multi-language Support). The contents of a questionnaire (e.g., questions and field labels) may have to be displayed in different languages (e.g., when conducting a psychological study globally). The actor accessing the questionnaire should be allowed to choose the preferred language.

R5 (Maintainability). Questionnaires evolve over time and hence may have to be changed occasionally. Therefore, it should be possible to quickly and easily change the structure and content of an electronic questionnaire; e.g., to add a question, to edit the text of a question, to delete a question, or to change the order of questions. In particular, no programming skills should be required in this context; i.e., domain experts (e.g., psychologists) should be able to introduce respective changes at a high level of abstraction.

Due to the lack of space, not all requirements are listed here. More requirements with respect to the user interface and native application design are summarized in [8]. Especially, requirement R5 constitutes a major challenge. It necessitates a high level of abstraction when defining and changing electronic questionnaires, which may then be enacted on various smart mobile devices. To cope with this challenge, we designed a specific mental model for electronic questionnaires, which will be presented in Sect. 3.

3   Mental Model

To transfer paper-based questionnaires into electronic ones and to meet the requirements discussed, we designed a mental model for the support of mobile

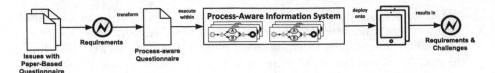

Fig. 1. Mental model.

electronic questionnaires (cf. Fig. 1). According to this model, the logic of a paper-based questionnaire is described in terms of a process model, which is then deployed to a process management system. The latter allows creating and executing process (i.e., questionnaire) instances.

Generally, a process model serves as template for specifying, enacting and evolving structured processes based on process management systems. In addition, *adaptive* process management systems allow for dynamic changes of process instances in order to cope with unpredictable situations [9]. In the following, we show that process models and process management technology are not only useful in the context of business process automation, but may be applied for mobile data collection as well. However, this raises additional challenges (cf. Sect. 5). This paper will show how to realize a process-aware questionnaire system whose models guide the users in filling in electronic questionnaires.

3.1   Process Model and Process Instances

As opposed to traditional information systems, *process-aware information systems* (PAIS) separate process logic from application code. This is accomplished based on process models, which provide the schemes for executing the respective processes [10]. In addition, a process model allows for a visual (i.e., graph-based) representation of the respective process, comprising the process steps (i.e., activities) as well as the relations (i.e., control and data flow) between them. For control flow modeling, both control edges and gateways (e.g., ANDsplit, XORsplit) are provided.

A process model P is represented as a directed, structured graph, which consists of a set of nodes N (of different types NT) and directed edges E (of different types ET) between them. We assume that a process model has exactly one start node ($NT = StartFlow$) and one end node ($NT = EndFlow$). Further, a process model must be connected; i.e., each node n can be reached from the start node. In turn, from any node n of a process model, the end node can be reached. In this paper, we solely consider block-structured process models. Each branching (e.g. parallel or alternative branching) has exactly one entry and one exit node. Furthermore, such blocks may be nested, but are not allowed to overlap [11]. In turn, data elements D correspond to global variables, which are connected with activities through data flow edges ($ET\_DataFlow$). These data elements can either be read ($ReadAccess$) or written ($WriteAccess$) by activities of the process model [12]. Figure 3 shows an example of a process model.

In turn, a process instance I represents a concrete case that is executed according to a process model P. In general, for a given process model multiple

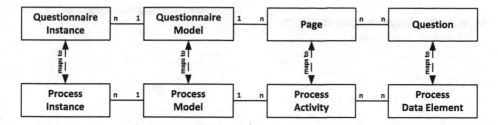

Fig. 2. Mapping a questionnaire model to a process model.

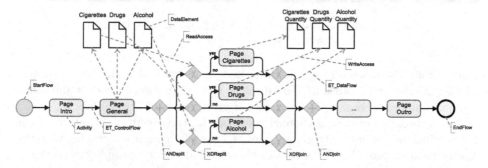

Fig. 3. Application scenario: an abbreviated questionnaire with annotations.

instances may be created and concurrently executed. Thereby, the state of a particular instance is defined by the markings (i.e., states) of its nodes and edges as well as the values of its data elements. Altogether, respective information corresponds to the execution history of an instance. Usually, a process engine relies on a set of execution rules describing the constraints for which a particular activity may be activated [12]. If the end node of the process model is reached, the respective process instance terminates.

3.2   Mapping a Questionnaire to a Process Model

Our mental model for enabling a process-driven enactment of questionnaires is as follows: We capture both the logic and the content of a questionnaire in a corresponding process model. Accordingly, pages of the questionnaire logically correspond to process activities, whereas the flow between these activities specifies the control flow logic of the questionnaire. The questions themselves are mapped to process data elements, which are connected with the respective activity. There are separate elements containing the text of a question, which can be read by the activity. Moreover, there are data elements that can be written by the activity. The latter are used to store the given answers for a specific question. Figure 2 presents an overview of the mapping of the elements of a questionnaire to the ones of a process model.

To illustrate the process-driven modeling of electronic questionnaires, we present a scenario from psychology. Consider the process-centric questionnaire

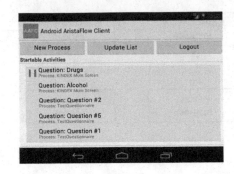

Fig. 4. Activity "Page Cigarettes".   **Fig. 5.** Startable activities for an actor.

model from Fig. 3 whose logic is described in terms of BPMN 2.0 (Business Process Model and Notation). To establish the link between process and questionnaire model, we annotate the depicted graph with additional labels.

The processing of the questionnaire starts with the execution of activity *Page Intro*, which presents an introductory text to the participant interacting with the electronic questionnaire. This introduction includes, for example, instructions on how to fill in the questionnaire or interact with the smart mobile device. After completing this first step in the processing of the questionnaire, activity *Page General* becomes enabled. In this form-based activity, data elements *Cigarettes*, *Drugs* and *Alcohol* are written. More precisely, the values of these data elements correspond to the answers given for the questions displayed on the respective page of the questionnaire. For example, the question corresponding to data element *Cigarettes* is as follows: *"Do you smoke?"* (with the possible answers *"yes/no"*). After completing activity *Page General*, an *AND gateway* (ANDsplit) becomes enabled. In turn, all outgoing paths of this ANDsplit (i.e., parallel split node) become enabled and are then executed concurrently. In the given application scenario, each of these paths contains an *XOR gateway* (XOR-split), which reads one of the aforementioned data elements to make a choice among its outgoing paths. For example, assume that in *Page General* the participant has answered question *"Do you smoke?"* with *"yes"*. Then, in the respective XORsplit, the upper path (labeled with *"yes"*) will be chosen, which consists of exactly one activity, i.e., *Page Cigarettes*. In the context of this activity, additional questions regarding the consumption of cigarettes will be displayed to the actor. This activity and page, respectively, is exemplarily displayed in Fig. 4. Assume further that question *"Do you take drugs? (yes / no)"* has been answered with *"no"* in *Page General*. Then, activity *Page Drugs* will be skipped as the lower path (labeled with *"no"*) of the respective XOR split is chosen. As soon as all three branches are completed, the *ANDjoin* will become enabled and the succeeding activity be displayed. We omit descriptions of the other activities of the questionnaire model due to lack of space. The processing of a questionnaire ends with activity *Page Outro*. Note that, in general, an arbitrary number of questionnaire instances processed by different participants may be created.

Figure 4 gives an impression of the *Page Cigarettes* activity. It displays additional questions regarding the consumption of cigarettes. This page is layouted automatically by the electronic questionnaire application based on the specified process model, which includes the pages to be displayed (cf. Fig. 3). Note that the user interface is created based on the data elements which contain the text of the questions as well as the possible answers to be displayed (i.e., the answers among which the user may choose).

3.3 Requirements for Process-Based Questionnaires

When using process management technology to coordinate the collection of data with smart mobile devices, additional challenges emerge. In particular, these are related to the modeling of a questionnaire as well as the process-driven execution of questionnaire instances on smart mobile devices.

Since questionnaire-based interviews are often interactive, the participating roles (e.g., interviewer and interviewed subject) should be properly assisted when interacting with the smart mobile device. For example, it should be possible for them to start or abort questionnaire instances. In the context of long-running questionnaire instances, in addition, it might be required to interrupt an interview and continue it later. For this purpose, it must be possible to suspend the execution of a questionnaire instance and to resume it at a later point in time (with access to all data and answers collected so far). In the context of long-running interviews, one must be able to display an entire questionnaire and process model respectively. Therefore, already answered questions should be displayed differently (e.g., different color) compared to upcoming questions. Note that this is crucial for providing a quick overview about the current progress.

Since domain experts might not be familiar with existing process modeling notations like BPMN 2.0, an easy-to-understand, self-explaining and domain-specific process notation is needed. In addition, the roles participating in a questionnaire should be provided with specific views on the process model (i.e., questionnaire), e.g., hiding information not required for this role [13]. For example, a subject might not be allowed to view subsequent questions in order to ensure credibility of the given answers.

Regarding the execution of the activities of a questionnaire (i.e., pages) additional challenges emerge.

The questions of a (psychological) questionnaire might have to be answered by different actors each of them possessing a specific role. For example, follow-up questions related to the subject involved in a psychological questionnaire have to be answered by a psychologist and not by the subject itself. In order to avoid bad quality of the data collected, actors should be further assisted when interacting with the smart mobile device; e.g., through error messages, help texts, or on-the-fly validations of entered data. Consequently, the electronic questionnaire application must ensure that only those questions are displayed to an actor that are actually intended her. Figure 5 shows the startable activities, currently available for a specific actor using the smart mobile device.

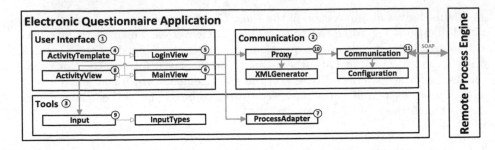

Fig. 6. Architecture of the electronic questionnaire application.

To foster the subsequent analysis of the data collected, the latter needs to be archived in a central repository. Furthermore, additional information (e.g., the time it took the subject to answer a particular question) should be recorded in order to increase the expressiveness of the data collected. Finally, anonymization of the data might have to be ensured as questionnaires often collect personal data and privacy constitutes a crucial issue. In certain cases, it might also become necessary to dismiss the results of an already answered question.

Taking these general requirements into account, we designed an architecture for an electronic questionnaire application.

4   Architecture and Implementation

This section introduces the architecture we developed for realizing electronic questionnaires. In particular, the latter run on smart mobile devices and interact with a remote process engine. This architecture is presented in Sect. 4.1. Since this paper focuses on the requirements, challenges and lessons learned when applying state-of-the-art process management technology to realize electronic questionnaires, we will not describe the architecture of the remote process management system in detail (see [14, 15] for respective work). The general architecture of our electronic questionnaire application is depicted in Fig. 6.

4.1   Electronic Questionnaire Application

The electronic questionnaire application is divided into three main packages, which are related to the *user interface* ①, the *communication* ② with the external process engine, and useful *tools* for interacting with the client ③.

The user interface representing a particular page of the questionnaire is represented by an *ActivityTemplate* ④, which provides basic methods for the questionnaire (e.g., to start or stop an activity). In turn, the *LoginView* ⑤ is used to query the user credential and to select an available role for this actor (e.g., *name = JohnDoe, role = Interviewer*). Furthermore, the *Main-View* ⑥ provides a list (e.g., worklist) with the pages currently available for the user interacting with the questionnaire. The list items are represented using the *ProcessAdapter* ⑦. Since the user interface of a questionnaire is generated dynamically depending on the underlying process model that has been deployed on the process engine, a user interface generator is needed. This service is provided by the *ActivityView* ⑧. To interact with the device, different classes of the *Input* ⑨ elements used within a questionnaire are provided. These classes provide the necessary logic to interact with the input elements as well as the corresponding graphical representation of this element. As certain input elements are platform-specific (e.g., there is no spinning wheel for standard desktop applications), missing input elements might be rendered differently, depending on the underlying platform (e.g., the spinning wheel on iOS could be rendered as a dropdown element on a normal computer).

The entire communication with the external process engine should be handled by a *Proxy* ⑩ service. The latter is capable of generating the necessary request messages, which are then converted to SOAP request messages by the *Communication* ⑪ service and sent to the process engine. The response messages (e.g., the next page to display) sent by the process engine are then received by the *Communication* and decomposed by the *Proxy*. Afterwards, the data within this message is visualized in the *ActivityView*, which includes the already mentioned user interface generator as well.

4.2 Proof-of-Concept Prototype

To validate the feasibility of the described architecture as well as to apply it in a real setting, we implemented a proof-of-concept prototype for Android. The prototype application was then used to verify the prescribed mental model, and to detail the requirements regarding the execution of process-aware questionnaires. Furthermore, additional insights into the practical use of this application by domain experts in the context of their studies could be gathered. We were able to meet the requirements presented in Sect. 2.2 when implementing the questionnaire client application, even though certain drawbacks still exist. In order to enable domain experts, who usually have no programming skills, to create a mobile electronic questionnaire, we implemented a fully automated user interface generator for the mobile application itself. In addition, we were able to provide common types for questions used within a questionnaire (e.g., likert-scale, free-text or yes-no-switches). These types are automatically mapped to appropriate input elements visualized within the application.

5 Discussion

This section discusses our approach and reflects on the experiences we gained when applying state-of-the-art process management technology to support mobile data collection with electronic questionnaires. Since we applied an implemented questionnaire in a psychological study, we were also able to gain insights into practical issues as well.

The presented approach has focused on the development of mobile business applications enabling flexible data collection rather than on the design of a development framework. Therefore, we have used an existing process modeling editor for defining the logic of electronic questionnaires. However, since the domain experts who have been using our questionnaire application have been unfamiliar with the BPMN 2.0 modeling notation, a number of training sessions were required. Afterwards, they were able to create their own questionnaires.

In particular, the abstraction introduced by the use of process models for specifying questionnaire logic was well understood by domain experts. However, the training sessions have shown that there is a need for a more user-friendly, domain-specific modeling notation, enabling domain experts to define questionnaires on their own. In particular, such a domain-specific modeling language needs to be self-explaining and easy to use. Further, it should hide modeling elements not required in the given use case. Note that BPMN 2.0 provides many elements not needed for defining the logic of electronic questionnaires. Consider, for example, the AND gateways, which allow modeling parallel execution paths. Regarding the use case of mobile data collection, it does not matter which path is going to be evaluated first. In addition, the elements for modeling a questionnaire should have a clear semantics and be expressive enough. Therefore, an activity should be represented as page-symbol to add context-aware information to the questionnaire model.

As we further learned in our case study, the creation and maintenance of a questionnaire constitutes a highly interactive, flexible and iterative task. In general, the editing of already existing, but not yet published questionnaires, should be self-explaining. Basic patterns dealing with the adaptation of the logic of a questionnaire (e.g., moving a question to another position or adding a new question) should be integrated in a modeling editor to provide tool support for creating and managing questionnaires.

As discussed in Sect. 3.3, we use process management technology for both modeling and enacting electronic questionnaires. Accordingly, the created questionnaire model needs to be deployed on a process engine. Regarding the described client server architecture (cf. Sect. 4.1), all process (i.e., questionnaire) models are stored and executed on the server running the process engine. Keeping in mind that mobile questionnaires might be also used in areas without stable Internet connection, any approach requiring a permanent internet connection between the mobile client and the process engine running on an external server will not be accepted. In order to cope with this issue, a light-weight process engine is required, which can run on the smart mobile device. We have started working in this direction as well (e.g., see [16,17]).

Since the user interface of the electronic questionnaire is automatically generated based on the provided process model, the possibilities to customize the layout of a questionnaire are rather limited. From the feedback we had obtained from domain experts, however, it became clear that an expressive layout component is needed that allows controlling the visual appearance of a questionnaire running on smart mobile devices. Among others, different text styles (e.g., bold), spacing between input elements (e.g., bottom spacing), and absolute positioning of elements should be considered. In addition, the need for integrating images has been expressed several times.

Since we use process-driven electronic questionnaires for collecting data with smart mobile devices, the answers provided by the actors filling in the questionnaire could be directly transferred to the server. This will relieve the actors from time-consuming manual tasks. Furthermore, as there exists a process model describing the flow logic of the questionnaire as well as comprehensive instance data (e.g., instance execution history), process mining techniques for analyzing questionnaire instances might be applied [18]. In addition, Business Intelligence Systems [19] could reveal further interesting aspects with respect to the data collected in order to increase the expressiveness of the analysis. Such systems would allow for a faster evaluation and relieve domain experts from manual tasks such as transferring the collected data into electronic worksheets.

Finally, we have experienced a strong acceptance among all participating actors (e.g., interviewers, domain experts, and subjects) regarding the practical benefits of electronic questionnaire applications on smart mobile devices. Amongst others this was reflected by a much higher willingness to fill out an electronic questionnaire compared to the respective paper-based version [5,6]. Furthermore, a higher motivation to complete the questionnaire truthfully could be observed. Of course, this acceptance partly results from the modern and intuitive way to interact with smart mobile devices.

6   Related Work

There exists a variety of questionnaire systems available on the market. In general, these systems can be classified into two groups: *online services* [20] and *standalone applications* [21]. Due to the fact that a questionnaire might contain sensitive information (e.g., the mental status of a subject or personal details), online surveys are often not appropriate for this type of data collection applications. As another limitation of online systems, local authorities do often not allow third-party software systems to store the information of a subject. However, these applications also must deal with privacy issues. Standalone applications usually offer possibilities to create a questionnaire, but do not deal with the requirements discussed in this paper. Furthermore, they lack a flexible and mobile data collection. Usually, respective questionnaires are displayed as web applications, which cannot be used when no Internet connection is available.

To the best of our knowledge, the process-aware enactment of questionnaires on smart mobile devices has not been considered comprehensively by other groups so far. In previous studies, we identified crucial issues regarding the implementation of psychological questionnaires on smart mobile devices [4–6]. In these studies, we aimed at preserving the validity of psychological instruments, which is a crucial point when replacing paper-based questionnaires with electronic ones. Although the implemented applications have already shown several advantages in respect to data collection and analysis, they have not been fully suitable for realizing psychological questionnaires in the large scale yet. In particular, maintenance efforts for domain experts and other actors were considerably high. More precisely, changes of an implemented questionnaire (or its structure) still had to be accomplished by computer experts, due to its implementation. Therefore, we aim to integrate a process-aware information system to overcome this limitation.

Focusing on the complete lifecycle of paper-based questionnaires and supporting every phase with mobile technology has actually not been considered by other groups so far. However, there exists related work regarding mobile data collection. In particular, mobile process management systems, as described in [1, 22], could be used to realize electronic questionnaires. However, this use case has not been considered by existing mobile process engines so far.

The QuON platform [23] is a web-based survey system, which provides a variety of different input types for the questions of a questionnaire. As opposed to our approach, QuON does not apply a model-based representation for specifying a questionnaire. Another limitation of QuON is its restriction to web-based questionnaires. Especially, in psychological field studies, the latter will result in problems as the QuON platform does not use responsive webdesign.

Movilitas applies SAP Sybase Unwired Platform to enable a mobile data collection for business scenarios [24]. In turn, the Sybase Unwired Platform constitutes a highly adaptive implementation framework for mobile applications, which interacts with a backend, that provides all relevant business data. Further research is required to show whether this approach can be applied to realize mobile electronic questionnaires in domains like psychology or healthcare as well.

Finally, [25] presents a set of patterns for expressing user interface logic based on the same notation as used for process modeling. In particular, a transformation method applies these patterns to automatically derive user interfaces based on a bidirectional mapping between process model and user interface.

7   Summary and Outlook

In this paper, limitations of paper-based questionnaires for data collection were discussed. To deal with these limitations, we derived characteristic requirements for electronic questionnaire applications. In order to meet these requirements, we suggested the use of process management technology. According to the mental model introduced, a questionnaire and its logic can be described in terms of a process model at a higher level of abstraction. To evaluate our approach, a sophisticated application scenario from the psychological domain was considered. We have shown how a questionnaire can be mapped to a process model.

In the interviews we conducted with domain experts as well as from other mobile business applications we implemented, general requirements for flexible mobile data collection on smart mobile devices were elaborated. These cover major aspects like a secure and encrypted communication. Note that the latter is crucial, especially in domains like medicine and psychology, which both deal with sensitive information of the subjects involved. We further presented an architecture enabling mobile data collection applications based on a smart mobile device and a process engine. As another contribution, we demonstrated the feasibility of our proof-of-concept application. Several features as well as problems regarding the implementation and communication with the server component, hosting the process engine, have been highlighted. Finally, we discussed the benefits of using process-driven questionnaires for mobile data collection.

In future work, we plan to extend our approach with additional features. Currently, we are working on a mobile process engine running on the smart mobile device. In turn, this will enable a process-driven enactment of questionnaire instances, even if no Internet connection is available. We consider this as a fundamental feature for enabling flexible data collection applications on smart mobile devices. A first prototype is already implemented and integrated into the presented electronic questionnaire application. However, this will cause new problems, as the questionnaire models must be properly synchronized among multiple devices (e.g., if changes were made to the questionnaire model). In addition, we are working on a questionnaire modeling notation. This is crucial to allow domain experts, who are unfamiliar with standard process modeling notations. This domain-specific questionnaire modeling notation shall be easy to understand, but still precise enough for defining process-aware questionnaires. The notation will be part of a *generic questionnaire system* supporting the complete lifecycle of a questionnaire. Furthermore, we started to integrate sensors measuring vital signs in order to gather other information about subjects during interviews [2]. As a major benefit of the framework, we expect higher data quality, shorter evaluation cycles and a significant decrease of workloads.

References

1. Pryss, R., Musiol, S., Reichert, M.: Collaboration support through mobile processes and entailment constraints. In: 9th IEEE International Conference on Collaborative Computing: Networking, Applications and Worksharing. IEEE Computer Society Press (2013)
2. Schobel, J., Schickler, M., Pryss, R., Nienhaus, H., Reichert, M.: Using vital sensors in mobile healthcare business applications: challenges, examples, lessons learned. In: 9th International Conference on Web Information Systems and Technologies (WEBIST 2013), pp. 509–518 (2013)
3. Pryss, R., Langer, D., Reichert, M., Hallerbach, A.: Mobile task management for medical ward rounds – the MEDo approach. In: Rosa, M., Soffer, P. (eds.) BPM Workshops 2012. LNBIP, vol. 132, pp. 43–54. Springer, Heidelberg (2013)
4. Crombach, A., Nandi, C., Bambonye, M., Liebrecht, M., Pryss, R., Reichert, M., Elbert, T., Weierstall, R.: Screening for mental disorders in post-conflict regions using computer apps - a feasibility study from burundi. In: XIII Congress of European Society of Traumatic Stress Studies (ESTSS) (2013)
5. Ruf-Leuschner, M., Pryss, R., Liebrecht, M., Schobel, J., Spyridou, A., Reichert, M., Schauer, M.: Preventing further trauma: KINDEX mum screen - assessing and reacting towards psychosocial risk factors in pregnant women with the help of smartphone technologies. In: XIII Congress of European Society of Traumatic Stress Studies (ESTSS) Conference (2013)
6. Isele, D., Ruf-Leuschner, M., Pryss, R., Schauer, M., Reichert, M., Schobel, J., Schindler, A., Elbert, T.: Detecting adverse childhood experiences with a little help from tablet computers. In: XIII Congress of European Society of Traumatic Stress Studies (ESTSS) Conference (2013)
7. Robecke, A., Pryss, R., Reichert, M.: DBIScholar: an iPhone application for performing citation analyses. In: CAiSE Forum-2011, vol-73 of Proceedings CAiSE 2011 Forum, CEUR Workshop Proceedings (2011)

8. Schobel, J., Schickler, M., Pryss, R., Maier, F., Reichert, M.: Towards process-driven mobile data collection applications: requirements, challenges, lessons learned. In: 10th International Conference on Web Information Systems and Technology (WEBIST 2014), pp. 371–382 (2014)
9. Reichert, M., Weber, B.: Enabling Flexibility in Process-Aware Information Systems: Challenges, Methods, Technologies. Springer, Berlin (2012)
10. Weber, B., Reichert, M., Mendling, J., Reijers, H.: Refactoring large process model repositories. Comput. Ind. **62**, 467–486 (2011)
11. Reichert, M., Dadam, P.: Enabling adaptive process-aware information systems with ADEPT2. In: Handbook of Research on Business Process Modeling, pp. 173–203 (2009)
12. Reichert, M., Dadam, P.: ADEPTflex-supporting dynamic changes of workflows without losing control. J. Intell. Inf. Syst. Spec. Issue Workflow Manag. Syst. **10**, 93–129 (1998)
13. Kolb, J., Reichert, M.: A flexible approach for abstracting and personalizing large business process models. Appl. Comput. Rev. **13**, 6–17 (2013)
14. Dadam, P., Reichert, M.: The ADEPT project: a decade of research and development for robust and flexible process support - challenges and achievements. Comput. Sci. Res. Dev. **23**, 81–97 (2009)
15. Reichert, M., Dadam, P., Rinderle-Ma, S., Jurisch, M., Kreher, U., Goeser, K.: Architectural principles and components of adaptive process management technology. In: Process Innovation for Enterprise Software. LNI, vol. 151, pp. 81–97. IEEE Computer Society Press, GI, Koellen-Verlag (2009)
16. Pryss, R., Tiedeken, J., Kreher, U., Reichert, M.: Towards flexible process support on mobile devices. In: Soffer, P., Proper, E. (eds.) CAiSE Forum 2010. LNBIP, vol. 72, pp. 150–165. Springer, Heidelberg (2011)
17. Pryss, R., Tiedeken, J., Reichert, M.: Managing processes on mobile devices: the MARPLE approach. In: CAiSE 2010 Demos (2010)
18. van der Aalst, W.M., Reijers, H.A., Weijters, A.J., van Dongen, B.F., Alves de Medeiros, A., Song, M., Verbeek, H.: Business process mining: an industrial application. Inf. Syst. **32**, 713–732 (2007)
19. Anandarajan, M., Anandarajan, A., Srinivasan, C.A.: Business Intelligence Techniques: a Perspective from Accounting and Finance. Springer, Berlin (2003)
20. SurveyMonkey: SurveyMonkey: free online survey software and questionnaire tool (2013). http://www.surveymonkey.com/. Accessed 6 July 2014
21. Electric Paper Evaluationssysteme: EvaSys (2013). http://www.evasys.de/. Accessed 6 July 2014
22. Kunze, C.P., Zaplata, S., Lamersdorf, W.: Mobile processes: enhancing cooperation in distributed mobile environments. J. Comput. **2**, 1–11 (2007)
23. Paul, D., Wallis, M., Henskens, F., Nolan, K.: QuON: a generic platform for the collation and sharing of web survey data. In: International Conference on Web Information Systems and Technologies (2013)
24. Movilitas: Movilitas Consulting AG (2013). http://www.movilitas.com/. Accessed 6 July 2014
25. Kolb, J., Hübner, P., Reichert, M.: Automatically generating and updating user interface components in process-aware information systems. In: Meersman, R., Panetto, H., Dillon, T., Rinderle-Ma, S., Dadam, P., Zhou, X., Pearson, S., Ferscha, A., Bergamaschi, S., Cruz, I.F. (eds.) OTM 2012, Part I. LNCS, vol. 7565, pp. 444–454. Springer, Heidelberg (2012)

An Engine Enabling Location-Based Mobile Augmented Reality Applications

Marc Schickler[✉], Rüdiger Pryss, Johannes Schobel,
and Manfred Reichert

Institute of Databases and Information Systems, Ulm University, Ulm, Germany
{marc.schickler,ruediger.pryss,johannes.schobel,
manfred.reichert}@uni-ulm.de

Abstract. Contemporary smart mobile devices are already capable of running advanced mobile applications with demanding resource requirements. However, utilizing the technical capabilities of such devices constitutes a challenging task (e.g., when querying their sensors at run time). This paper deals with the design and implementation of an advanced mobile application, which enables location-based mobile augmented reality on different mobile operating systems (i.e., iOS and Android). In particular, this kind of application is characterized by high resource demands. For example, at run time various calculations become neccessary in order to correctly position and draw virtual objects on the screen of the smart mobile device. Hence, we focus on the lessons learned when implementing a robust and efficient, location-based mobile augmented reality engine as well as efficient mobile business applications based on it.

Keywords: Smart mobile applications · Location-based mobile augmented reality

1   Introduction

Daily business routines increasingly require mobile access to information systems, while providing a desktop-like feeling of mobile applications to the users. However, the design and implementation of mobile applications constitutes a challenging task [1,2]. Amongst others, developers must cope with limited physical resources of smart mobile devices (e.g., limited battery capacity or limited screen size) as well as non-predictable user behaviour (e.g., mindless instant shutdowns). Moreover, mobile devices provide advanced technical capabilities the mobile applications may use, including motion sensors, a GPS sensor, and a powerful camera system. On the one hand, these capabilities allow for new kinds of business applications. On the other, the design and implementation of such mobile applications is challenging. In particular, integrating sensors and utilizing the data recorded by them constitute a non-trivial task when taking requirements like robustness into and scalability into account as well.

© Springer International Publishing Switzerland 2015
V. Monfort and K.-H. Krempels (Eds.): WEBIST 2014, LNBIP 226, pp. 363–378, 2015.
DOI: 10.1007/978-3-319-27030-2_23

Furthermore, mobile business applications need to be developed for various mobile operating systems (e.g., iOS and Android) in order to allow for their widespread use. Hence, developers of mobile business applications must not only cope with the above mentioned challenges, but also with the heterogeneity of existing mobile operating systems, while at the same time fully utilizing their technical capabilities. In particular, if the same functions shall be provided on different mobile operating systems, additional challenges emerge due to scalability and robustness demands.

This paper deals with the development of a generic mobile engine, that enables location-based mobile augmented reality for a variety of advanced business applications. We discuss the core challenges emerging in this context and report on the lessons learned when applying the developed engine to implement mobile business applications. Finally, existing approaches deal with location-based mobile augmented reality as well [3–6]. To the best of our knowledge, however, they do not focus on aspects regarding the efficient integration of location-based mobile augmented reality with mobile business applications.

1.1   Problem Statement

The overall purpose of this paper is to give insights into the development of the core of a *location-based mobile augmented reality engine* for the mobile operating systems *iOS 5.1 (or higher)* and *Android 4.0 (or higher)*. We denote this engine as *AREA*[1]. As a particular challenge, the augmented reality engine shall be able to display *points of interest (POIs)* from the surrounding of a user on the video camera screen of his smart mobile device. The development of such an engine constitutes a non-trivial task, raising the following challenges:

- In order to enrich the image captured by the camera of the smart mobile device with virtual information about POIs in the surrounding, basic concepts enabling location-based calculations need to be developed.
- An efficient and reliable technique for calculating the distance between two positions is required (e.g., based on data of the GPS sensor in the context of location-based outdoor scenarios).
- Various sensors of the smart mobile device must be queried correctly in order to determine the attitude and position of the smart mobile device.
- The angle of view of the smart mobile device's camera lens must be calculated to display the virtual objects on the respective position of the camera view.

Furthermore, a location-based mobile augmented reality engine should be made available on all established mobile operating systems. Realizing the required robustness and ease-of-use for heterogenous mobile operating systems, however, constitutes a non-trivial task.

---

[1] AREA stands for *Augmented Reality Engine Application*. A video demonstrating AREA can be viewed at: http://vimeo.com/channels/434999/63655894. Further information can be found at: http://www.area-project.info.

1.2   Contribution

In the context of AREA, we developed various concepts for coping with the limited resources of a smart mobile device, while realizing advanced features with respect to mobile augmented reality at the same time. In this paper, we present a sophisticated application architecture, which allows integrating augmented reality with a wide range of applications. However, this architecture must not neglect the characteristics of the respective mobile operating system. While for many scenarios, the differences between mobile operating systems are rather uncritical in respect to mobile application development, for the mobile application considered in this paper this does not apply. Note that there already exist augmented reality frameworks and applications for mobile operating systems like Android or iOS. These include proprietary and commercial engines[2] as well as open source frameworks and applications [7]. To the best of our knowledge, however, these proposals neither provide insights into the functionality of such an engine nor its customization to a specific purpose. Furthermore, insights regarding the development of engines running on more than one mobile operating systems are usually not provided. To remedy this drawback, we report on the lessons learned when developing AREA and integrating mobile business applications with it.

The remainder of this paper is organized as follows: Sect. 2 introduces the core concepts and architecture of AREA. In Sect. 3, we discuss the lessons learned when implementating AREA on the mobile operating systems iOS and Android. In particular, this section discusses differences we experienced in this context. Section 4 gives detailed insights into the use of AREA for implementing real-world business applications. In Sect. 5 related work is discussed. Section 6 concludes the paper with a summary and outlook.

2   AREA Approach

The basic concept realized in AREA is the *location View*. The points of interest inside the camera's field of view are displayed on it, having a size of $\sqrt{width^2 + height^2}$ pixels. The *location View* is placed centrally on the screen of the mobile device.

2.1   The LocationView

Choosing the particular approach provided by AREA's *location View* has specific reasons, which will be discussed in the following.

First, AREA shall display *points of interest* (POIs) correctly, even if the device is hold obliquely. Depending on the device's attitude, the POIs have to be rotated with a certain angle and moved relatively to the rotation. Instead of rotating and moving every POI separately, however, it is possible to only rotate the *location View* to the desired angle, whereas the POIs it contains are rotated automatically; i.e., the resources needed for complex calculations can be significantly reduced.

---

[2] Wikitude (http://www.wikitude.com).

Fig. 1. LocationView examples depicting its characteristics.

Second, a complex recalculation of the camera's field of view is not required if the device is in an oblique position. The vertical and horizontal dimensions of the field of view are scaled proportionally to the diagonal of the screen, such that a new maximum field of view results with $\sqrt{width^2 + height^2}$ pixels. Since the *locationView* is placed centrally on the screen, the camera's actual field of view is not distorted. Further, it can be customized by rotating it contrary to the rotation of the device. The calculated maximal field of view is needed to efficiently draw POIs visible in portrait mode, landscape mode, or any oblique position inbetween.

Figure 1 presents an example illustrating the concept of the *locationView*. Each sub-figure represents one *locationView*. As can be seen, a *locationView* is larger than the display of the respective mobile device. Therefore, the camera's field of view must be increased by a certain factor such that all POIs, which are either visible in portrait mode (cf. Fig. 1c), landscape mode (cf. Fig. 1a), or any rotation inbetween (cf. Fig. 1b), are drawn on the *locationView*. For example, Fig. 1a shows a POI (on the top) drawn on the *locationView*, but not yet visible on the screen of the device in landscape mode. Note that this POI is not visible for the user until he rotates his device to the position depicted in Fig. 1b. Furthermore, when rotating the device from the position depicted in Fig. 1b to portrait mode (cf. Fig. 1c), the POI on the left disappears again from the field of view, but still remains on the *locationView*.

The *third* reason for using the presented *locationView* concept concerns performance. When the display shall be redrawn, the POIs already drawn on the *locationView* can be easily queried and reused. Instead of first clearing the entire screen and afterwards re-initializing and redrawing already visible POIs, POIs that shall remain visible need not to be redrawn. Finally, POIs located outside the field of view after a rotation are deleted from it, whereas POIs that emerge inside the field of view are initialized.

Figure 2 sketches the basic algorithm used for realizing this *locationView*[3].

---

[3] More technical details can be found in a technical report [8].

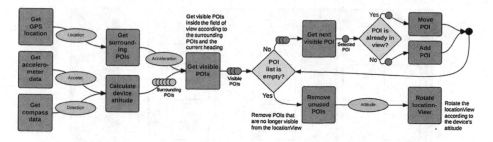

Fig. 2. Algorithm realizing the locationView.

2.2   Architecture

The AREA architecture has been designed with the goal to easily exchange and extend its components. The design comprises four main modules organized in a multi-tier architecture and complying with the *Model View Controller* pattern (cf. Fig. 3). Lower tiers offer their services and functions through interfaces to upper tiers. In particular, the tier ② (cf. Fig. 3) will be described in detail in Sect. 3 when discussing the differences regarding the development of AREA on iOS and Android respectively. Based on this architectural design, modularity can be ensured; i.e., both data management and other elements (e.g., POIs) can be customized and easily extended on demand. Furthermore, the compact design of AREA enables us to build new mobile business applications based on it as well as to easily integrate it with existing applications.

The tier ③, the *Model*, provides modules and functions to exchange POIs. In this context, we use both an *XML*- and a *JSON*-based interface to collect and parse POIs. In turn, these POIs are stored in a global database. Note that we do not rely on the *ARML* schema [9], but use a proprietary XML schema instead. In particular, we will be able to extend our *XML*-based format in the context of future research on AREA. Finally, the JSON interface uses a light-weight, easy to understand and extendable format developers are familiar with.

The next tier ②, the *Controller*, consists of two main modules. The *Sensor Controller* is responsible for culling the sensors needed to determine the device's location and orientation. The sensors to be culled include the *GPS sensor*, *accelerometer*, and *compass sensor*. The GPS sensor is used to determine the position of the device. Since we currently focus on location-based outdoor scenarios, GPS coordinates are predominantly used. In future work, we will consider indoor scenarios as well. Note that AREA's architecture has been designed to easily change the way coordinates will be obtained. Using the GPS coordinates and its corresponding altitude, we can calculate the distance between mobile device and POI, the horizontal bearing, and the vertical bearing. The latter is used to display a POI higher or lower on the screen, depending on its own altitude. In turn, the accelerometer provides data for determining the current rotation of the device, i.e., the orientation of the device (landscape, portrait, or any orientation inbetween) (cf. Fig. 1). Since the accelerometer is used to determine

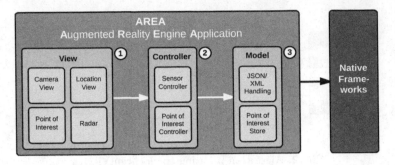

Fig. 3. Multi-tier architecture of AREA.

the vertical viewing direction, we need the compass data of the mobile device to determine the horizontal viewing direction of the user as well. Based on the vertical and horizontal viewing directions, we are able to calculate the direction of the field of view as well as its boundaries according to the camera angle of view of the device. The *Point of Interest Controller* (cf. Fig. 3) uses data of the *Sensor Controller* in order to determine whether a POI lies inside the vertical and horizontal field of view. Furthermore, for each POI it calculates its position on the screen taking the current field of view and the camera angle of view into account.

The tier ①, the *View*, consists of various user interface elements, e.g., the *locationView*, the *Camera View*, and the specific view of a POI (i.e., the *Point of Interest View*). Thereby, the *Camera View* displays the data captured by the device's camera. Right on top of the *Camera View*, the *locationView* is placed. It displays POIs located inside the current field of view at their specific positions as calculated by the *Point of Interest Controller*. To rotate the *locationView*, the interface of the *Sensor Controller* is used. The latter allows determining the orientation of the device. Furthermore, a radar can be used to indicate the direction in which invisible POIs are located (Fig. 5 shows an example of the radar). Finally, AREA uses libraries of the mobile development frameworks, which provide access to core functionality of the underlying operating system, e.g., sensors and screen drawing functions (cf. *Native Frameworks* in Fig. 3).

3 Implementing AREA on Existing Mobile Operating Systems

The kind of business application we consider utilizes the various sensors of smart mobile devices and hence provides new kinds of features compared to traditional business applications. However, this significantly increases complexity for application developers. In turn, this complexity further increases in case the mobile application shall be provided for various mobile operating systems as well.

Picking up the scenario of mobile augmented reality, this section gives insights into ways for efficiently handling the POIs relevant for realizing the *locationView* of our mobile augmented reality engine. In this context, the implementation of the *Sensor Controller* and the *Point of Interest Controller* are most interesting when studying the subtle differences one must consider in the context of the development of such an engine on different mobile operating systems.

In order to reach a high efficiency when displaying or redrawing POIs on the screen, we choose a native implementation of AREA on the iOS and Android mobile operating systems. Thus, we can make use of built-in APIs of these operating systems, and can call native functions without any translation as required in frameworks like *Phonegap*[4]. Note that efficiency is crucial for mobile business applications since smart mobile devices rely on battery power [10]. To avoid high battery usage by expensive framework translations, therefore, only a native implementation is appropriate in our context. Apart from this, most cross-platform development frameworks do not provide a proper set of functions to work with sensors [11]. In the following, we present the implementation of AREA on both the iOS and the Android mobile operating systems.

3.1 Implementing AREA on iOS

The iOS version of AREA has been implemented using the programming language Objective-C and iOS Version 7.0 on Apple iPhone 4S. Furthermore, for developing AREA, the Xcode environment (Version 5) has been used.

Sensor Controller. The *Sensor Controller* is responsible for culling the needed sensors in order to correctly position the POIs on the screen of the smart mobile device. To achieve this, iOS provides the *CoreMotion* and *CoreLocation* frameworks. We use the latter framework to get notified about changes of the location as well as compass heading. Since we want to be informed about every change of the compass heading, we adjusted the heading filter of the *CoreLocation* framework accordingly. When the framework sends us new heading data, its data structure contains a real heading as well as a magnetic one as floats. The real heading complies to the geographic north pole, whereas the magnetic heading refers to the magnetic north pole. Since our coordinates correspond to GPS coordinates, we use the real heading data structure. Note that the values of the heading will become (very) inaccurate and oscillate when the device is moved. To cope with this, we apply a *lowpass* filter to the heading in order to obtain smooth and accurate values, which can then be used to position the POIs on the screen [12]. Similar to the heading, we can adjust how often we want to be informed about location changes. On one hand, we want to get notified about all relevant location changes; on the other, every change requires a recalculation of the surrounding POIs. Thus, we deciced to get notified only if a difference of at least 10 meters occurs between the old and the new location. Note that this is generally acceptable for the kind of applications we consider (cf. Sect. 4). Finally, the data structure representing a location contains GPS coordinates of

---

[4] Phonegap (http://phonegap.com).

the device in degrees north and degrees east as decimal values, the altitude in meters, and a time stamp.

In turn, the *CoreMotion* framework provides interfaces to cull the accelero-meter. The latter is used to determine the current rotation of the device as well as the direction it is pointing to (e.g., upwards or downwards). As opposed to location and heading data, accelerometer data is not automatically pushed to the application by the *CoreMotion* framework of iOS. Therefore, we had to define an application loop polling this data every $\frac{1}{90}$ s. On one hand, this rate is fast enough to obtain smooth values; on the other, it is low enough to save battery power.

Basically, the data delivered by the accelerometer consists of three values; i.e., the accelerations in x-, y-, and z-direction. In general, gravity is required for calculating the direction a device is pointing to. However, we cannot obtain the gravity directly from the acceleration data, but must additionally apply a *lowpass* filter to the x-, y-, and z-direction values; i.e., the three values are averaged and filtered. In order to obtain the vertical heading as well as the rotation of the device, we then apply the following steps: First, by calculating $\arcsin(z)$ we obtain a value between $\pm 90°$ describing the vertical heading. Second, by calculating $\arctan 2(-y, x)$, we obtain a value between $0°$ and $359°$, describing the device's degree of the rotation.

Since we need to consider all possible orientations of the smart mobile device, we must adjust the compass data accordingly. For example, assume that we hold the device in portrait mode in front of us towards North. Then, the compass data we obtain indicate that we are viewing in Northern direction. As soon as we rotate the device, however, compass data will change although our view still goes to Northern direction. Reason for this is that the reference point of the compass corresponds to the upper end of the device. To cope with this issue, we must adjust compass data using the rotation calculation presented above. When subtracting the rotation value (i.e., $0°$ and $359°$) from compass data, we obtain the desired compass value, while still viewing in Northern direction after rotating the device.

Point of Interest Controller. As soon as the *Sensor Controller* has collected the required data, it notifies the *Point of Interest Controller* at two points in time: (1) when detecting a new location and (2) after gathering new heading and accelerometer data. When a new location is detected, the POIs in the sur-rounding of the user must be determined. For this purpose, we use an adjustable radius (see Fig. 5 for an example of such an adjustable radius). Using the latter, a user can determine the maximum distance she shall have to the POIs to be displayed. By calculating the distance between the device and the POIs based on their GPS coordinates, we can determine the POIs located inside the chosen radius and hence the POIs to be displayed on the screen. Since only POIs inside the field of view (i.e., POIs actually visible for the user) shall be displayed on the screen, we must further calculate the vertical and horizontal bearing of the POIs inside the radius. Due to space limitations, we do not describe these calculations in detail, but refer interested readers to a technical report [8].

As explained in [8], the vertical bearing can be calculated based on the altitudes of both the POIs and the smart mobile device (the latter can be determined from the current GPS coordinates). The horizontal bearing, in turn, can be computed with the *Haversine* formula by applying it to the GPS coordinates of the POI and the smart mobile device. In order to avoid costly recalculations of these surrounding POIs in case the GPS coordinates do not change (i.e., movings are within 10 m), we buffer POI data inside the controller implementation.

The heading and accelerometer data need to be processed when a notification from the *Sensor Controller* is obtained (Sect. 3.1). Then it needs to be determined which POIs are located inside the vertical and horizontal field of view, and at which positions they shall be displayed on the *locationView*. Recall that the *locationView* extends the actual field of view to a larger, orientation-independent field of view (cf. Fig. 4a). First, the boundaries of the *locationView* need to be determined based on the available sensor data. In this context, the heading data provides the information required to determine the direction the device is pointing. The left boundary of the *locationView* can be calculated by determining the horizontal heading and decreasing it by the half of the maximal angle of view (cf. Fig. 4a). In turn, the right boundary is calculated by adding half of the maximal angle of view to the current heading. Since POIs also have a vertical heading, a vertical field of view must be calculated as well. This can be accomplished analogously to the calculation of the horizontal field of view, except that the data of the vertical heading is required instead. Finally, we obtain a directed, orientation-independent field of view bounded by left, right, top, and bottom values. Then we use the vertical and horizontal bearings of a POI to determine whether it lies inside the *locationView* (i.e., inside the field of view). Since we use the *locationView* concept, we do not have to deal with the rotation of the device, i.e., we can normalize calculations to portrait mode since the rotation itself is handled by the *locationView*.

The camera view can be created and displayed by applying the native *AVFoundation* framework. Using the screen size of the device, which can be determined at run time, the *locationView* can be initialized and placed centrally on top of the camera view. As soon as the *Point of Interest Controller* has finished its calculations (i.e., it has determined the positions of the POIs), it notifies the *View Controller* that organizes the view components. The *View Controller* then receives the POIs and places them on the *locationView*. Recall that in case of a device rotation, only the *locationView* must be rotated. As a consequence, the actual visible field of view changes accordingly. Therefore, the *Point of Interest Controller* sends the rotation of the device calculated by the *Sensor Controller* to the *View Controller*, together with the POIs. Thus, we can adjust the field of view by simply counterrotating the *locationView* using the given angle. The user will only see those POIs on his screen, which are inside the actual field of view; then other POIs will be hidden after the rotation, i.e., they will be moved out of the screen (cf. Fig. 1). Related implementation issues are discussed in [8].

(a) Illustration of the new maximal angle view   (b) Rotation of a POI and field of view.
and the real one.

Fig. 4. Usage of *locationView*.

3.2   Android Mobile Operating System

We also developed AREA for the Android mobile operating system. This section gives insights into the respective implementation and compares it with the iOS one. Although AREA's basic architecture is the same for both mobile operating systems, there are subtle differences regarding its implementation.

Sensor Controller. For implementing the *Sensor Controller*, the packages *android.location* and *android.hardware* can be used. The *location package* provides functions to retrieve the current GPS coordinate and altitude of the respective device; hence, it is similar to the corresponding iOS package. Additionally, the Android location package allows retrieving an approximate position of the device based on network triangulation. Particularly, if no GPS signal is available, the latter approach can be applied. As a drawback, however, no information about the current altitude of the device can be determined in this case. In turn, the *hardware package* provides functions to get notified about the current magnetic field and accelerometer. The latter corresponds to the one of iOS. It is used to calculate the rotation of the device. However, the heading is calculated in a different way compared to iOS. Instead of obtaining it with the location service, it must be determined manually. Generally, the heading depends on the rotation of the device and the magnetic field. Therefore, we create a rotation matrix using the data of the magnetic field (i.e., a vector with three dimensions) and the rotation based on the accelerometer data. Since the heading data depends on the accelerometer as well as the magnetic field, it is rather inaccurate. More precisely, the calculated heading is strongly oscillating. Hence, we apply a lowpass filter to mitigate this oscillation. Note that this lowpass filter differs from the one used in Sect. 3.1 when calculating the gravity.

As soon as other magnetic devices are located nearby the actual mobile device, the heading is distorted. To notify the user about the presence of such

Fig. 5. AREA's user interface for iOS and Android.

a disturbed magnetic field, which leads to false heading values, we apply functions of the hardware package. Another difference between iOS and Android concerns the way the required data can be obtained. Regarding iOS, location-based data is pushed, whereas sensor data must be polled. As opposed to iOS, on Android all data is pushed by the framework, i.e., application programmers rely on Android internal loops and trust the up-to-dateness of the data provided. Note that such subtle differences between mobile operating systems and their development frameworks should be well understood by the developers of advanced mobile business applications.

Point of Interest Controller. Regarding Android, the *Point of Interest Controller* works the same way as the one of iOS. However, when developing AREA we had to deal with one particular issue. The *locationView* manages the visible POIs as described above. Therefore, it must be able to add child views (e.g., every POI generating one child view). As described in Sect. 3.1, on iOS we simply rotate the *locationView* to actually rotate the POIs and the field of view. In turn, on Android, a layout containing child views cannot be rotated the same way. Thus, when the *Point of Interest Controller* receives sensor data from the *Sensor Controller*, the x- and y-coordinates of the POIs must be determined in a different way. Instead of placing the POIs independently of the device's current rotation, we utilize the degree of rotation provided by the *Sensor Controller*. Following this, the POIs are rotated around the centre of the *locationView* and they are also rotated about their centres (cf. Fig. 4b). Using this approach, we can still add all POIs to the field of view of the *locationView*. Finally, when rotating the POIs, they will automatically leave the device's actual field of view.

3.3   Comparing the iOS and Android Implementaion

This section compares the two implementations of AREA on iOS and Android. First of all, it is noteworthy that both implementations support the same features and functions. Moreover, the user interfaces realized for AREA on iOS and Android, respectively, are the same (see Fig. 5).

Realizing the locationView. The developed *locationView* and its specific features differ between the Android and iOS implementations of AREA. Regarding the iOS implementation, we are able to realize the *locationView* concept as described in Sect. 2.1. On the Android operating system, however, not all features of this concept have worked properly. More precisely, extending the device's current field of view to the bigger size of the *locationView* worked well. Furthermore, determining whether a POI lies inside the field of view, independent of the current rotation of the device, worked well. By contrast, rotating the *locationView* with its POIs to adjust the visible field of view as well as moving invisible POIs out of the screen has not worked on Android as expected. As a particular challenge we faced in this context, a simple view on Android must not contain any child views. Therefore, on Android we had to use the *layout* concept for realizing the described *locationView*. However, simply rotating a layout does not work on all Android devices. For example, on a Nexus 4 device this worked well by implementing the algorithm in exactly the same way as on iOS. In turn, on a Nexus 5 device this led to failures regarding the redraw process. When rotating the layout on Nexus 5, the *locationView* is clipped by the camera surface view, which is located behind our *locationView*. As a consequence, to ensure that AREA is compatible with a wider set of Android devices, running Android 4.0 (or higher version), we applied the adjustments described in Sect. 4.

Accessing Sensors. The use of sensors on the two mobile operating systems differs. This concerns the access to the sensors as well as their preciseness and reliability. Regarding iOS, the location sensor provides both GPS coordinates and compass heading. This data is pushed to the application by an underlying iOS service. In turn, on Android, the location sensor solely provides data of the current location. Furthermore, this data must be polled by the application. Heading data, in turn, is calculated through the fusion of several motion sensors, including the accelerometer and magnetometer.

The accelerometer is used on both platforms to determine the current orientation of the device. However, the preciseness of the provided data differs significantly. Compiling and running AREA on iOS 6 results in very reliable compass data with an interval of one degree. Compiling and running AREA on iOS 7, leads to different results compared to iOS 6. One one hand, iOS 7 allows for a higher resolution of the data intervals provided by the framework due to the use of floating point data instead of integers. On the other, delivered compass data is partially unreliable. Furthermore, in the context of iOS 7 compass data tend to oscillate within a certain interval when moving the device. Therefore, we need to apply a stronger lowpass filter in order to compensate this oscillating data. Furthermore, on Android the internal magnetometer, which is required for calculating the heading, is vulnerable to noisy sources (e.g., other devices, magnets, or computers). Consequently, delivered data might be unreliable and thus the application must wait until more reliable sensor data becomes available.

For each sensor, the respective documentation should be studied to use it in a proper and efficient manner. In particular, the large number of devices running Android constitutes a challenge with respect to the deployment of AREA on these devices. Finally, Android devices are often affected by distortions of other electronic hardware and, therefore, delivered data might be unreliable.

Altogether, these subtle differences indicate that the development of mobile business applications, which make use of the technical capabilities of modern smart mobile devices, is far from being trivial for application developers.

4 Validation

This section gives insights into the development of business applications based on AREA and the lessons we learned from this. AREA has been integrated with several business applications. For example, the [13] application, which has been realized based on AREA, can be used to provide residents and tourists of a city with the opportunity to explore their surrounding by displaying points of interests (e.g., public buildings, parks, and event locations). When implementing respective business applications based on AREA, one can take benefit from the modular design of AREA as well as its extensibility.

For developing *LiveGuide*, the following two steps were sufficient: first, the appearance of the POIs was adapted to meet UI requirements of the customers. Second, the AREA data model need to be adapted to an existing one. When developing applications like *LiveGuide*, we gained profound practical insights regarding the use of AREA.

Release Updates of Mobile Operating Systems. Both the iOS and Android mobile operating systems are frequently updated. In turn, respective updates must be carefully considered when developing and deploying an advanced mobile business application like AREA. Since the latter depends on the availability of accurate sensor data, fundamental changes of the respective native libraries might affect the proper execution of AREA. For example, consider the following scenarios we needed to cope with in the context of an Android operating system update (from Android 4.2 to 4.3). In Android 4.2, the sensor framework notifies AREA when measured data becomes unreliable. By contrast, with Android 4.3, certain constants (e.g., *SENSOR_STATUS_UNRELIABLE*) we had used before were no longer known on the respective devices. To deal with such an issue, the respective constant had to be replaced by a listener (*onAccuracyChanged*).

As another example consider the release of iOS 7, that led to a significant change of the look and feel of the entire user interface. In particular, some of the user interface elements we customized in the deployed version of the *LiveGuide* applications got hidden from one moment to the other or did not react to an user interaction anymore. Altogether, adjusting mobile applications in the context of operating system updates might cause considerable efforts.

Overlapping POIs. In the context of the *LiveGuide* business application we also explored scenarios for which certain POIs located in the same direction

(a) Overlapping POIs.   (b) Alternative visualization.

Fig. 6. Concept for handling overlapping POIs.

overlap with each other, making it difficult for users to precisely touch them. To cope with this issue, we have designed specific concepts for detecting clusters of POIs and offering a way for users to interact with these clusters. Figure 6 illustrates one of the realized concepts. Again, the modular design of AREA enabled us to implement these extensions efficiently.

5 Related Work

Previous research related to the development of a location-based augmented reality application, which is based on GPS coordinates and sensors running on *head-mounted* displays, is described in [14,15]. In turn, [16] applies a smart mobile device, extended with additional sensors, to develop an augmented reality system. Another application using augmented reality is described in [7]. Its purpose is to share media data and other information in a real-world environment and to allow users to interact with this data through augmented reality. However, none of these approaches addresses location-based augmented reality on smart mobile devices as AREA. In particular, no insights into the development of such mobile business applications are provided.

The growing market of smart mobile devices as well as their increasing technical maturity has also motivated software vendors to realize *augmented reality software development kits* (SDKs) [17–19]. In addition to these SDKs, there exist applications like *Yelp*[5] that use additional features of augmented reality to assist users when interacting with their surrounding.

Only little work can be found dealing with the engineering of augmented reality systems itself. As an exception, [20] validates existing augmented reality browsers. However, neither software vendors nor academic approaches related to augmented reality provide insights into the way a location-based mobile augmented reality engine can be developed.

6 Summary

This paper gives insights into the development of the core framework of an augmented reality engine for smart mobile devices. We further show how business

---

[5] Yelp (http://www.yelp.com).

applications can be implemented based on the functions provided by this mobile augmented reality engine. As discussed along selected implementation issues, such an engine development is challenging.

First, a basic knowledge about mathematical calculations is required, e.g., formulas to calculate the distance and heading of points of interest on a sphere in the context of outdoor scenarios. Furthermore, profound knowledge about the various sensors of smart mobile devices is required from application developers.

Second, resource and energy consumption must be addressed. Since smart mobile devices have limited resources and performance capabilities, the points of interest should be displayed in an efficient way and without delay. Hence, the calculations required to handle sensor data and screen drawing must be implemented efficiently. The latter is accomplished through the concept of *location View*, that allows increasing the field of view by reusing already drawn points of interest. In particular, the increased size allows the AREA engine to easily determine whether a point of interest is inside the *location View* without need to consider the current rotation of the smart mobile device. In addition, all displayed points of interest can be easily rotated.

Third, we argue that an augmented reality engine like AREA must provide a sufficient degree of modularity to allow for a full and easy integration with existing applications as well as to implement new applications on top of it.

Fourth, we have demonstrated how to integrate AREA in a real-world business application (i.e., *LiveGuide*) and utilize its functions in this context. The respective application has been made available in the Apple App and Android Google Play Stores showing a high robustness. Finally, we have given insights into the differences between Apple's and Google's mobile operating systems when developing AREA.

Currently, AREA can only be applied in outdoor scenarios due to its dependency on GPS. In future research AREA shall be extended to cover indoor scenarios as well. In this context, we will consider Wi-Fi triangulation as well as Bluetooth 4.0 beacons to be able to determine the indoor position of the device.

References

1. Geiger, P., Schickler, M., Pryss, R., Schobel, J., Reichert, M.: Location-based mobile augmented reality applications: challenges, examples, lessons learned. In: 10th International Conference on Web Information Systems and Technologies (WEBIST 2014), pp. 383–394 (2014)
2. Pryss, R., Mundbrod, N., Langer, D., Reichert, M.: Supporting medical ward rounds through mobile task and process management. Inf. Syst. e-Business Manage. **13**(1), 1–40 (2014)
3. Fröhlich, P., Simon, R., Baillie, L., Anegg, H.: Comparing conceptual designs for mobile access to geo-spatial information. In: Proceedings of the 8th Conference on Human-computer Interaction with Mobile Devices and Services, pp. 109–112 (2006)
4. Carmigniani, J., Furht, B., Anisetti, M., Ceravolo, P., Damiani, E., Ivkovic, M.: Augmented reality technologies, systems and applications. Multimedia Tools Appl. **51**, 341–377 (2011)

5. Paucher, R., Turk, M.: Location-based augmented reality on mobile phones. In: IEEE Conference on Computer Vision and Pattern Recognition Workshops, pp. 9–16 (2010)
6. Reitmayr, G., Schmalstieg, D.: Location based applications for mobile augmented reality. In: Proceedings of the 4th Australasian Conference on User Interfaces, pp. 65–73 (2003)
7. Lee, R., Kitayama, D., Kwon, Y., Sumiya, K.: Interoperable augmented web browsing for exploring virtual media in real space. In: Proceedings of the 2nd International Workshop on Location and the Web (2009)
8. Geiger, P., Pryss, R., Schickler, M., Reichert, M.: Engineering an advanced location-based augmented reality engine for smart mobile devices. Technical report UIB-2013-09, University of Ulm, Germany (2013)
9. ARML: Augmented reality markup language. http://openarml.org/wikitude4.html. Accessed 07 May 2014
10. Corral, L., Sillitti, A., Succi, G.: Mobile multiplatform development: an experiment for performance analysis. Procedia Comput. Sci. **10**, 736–743 (2012)
11. Schobel, J., Schickler, M., Pryss, R., Nienhaus, H., Reichert, M.: Using vital sensors in mobile healthcare business applications: challenges, examples, lessons learned. In: International Conference on Web Information Systems and Technologies, pp. 509–518 (2013)
12. Kamenetsky, M.: Filtered audio demo. http://www.stanford.edu/boyd/ee102/conv_demo.pdf. Accessed 07 May 2014
13. CMCityMedia: City liveguide. http://liveguide.de. Accessed 07 May 2014
14. Feiner, S., MacIntyre, B., Höllerer, T., Webster, A.: A touring machine: prototyping 3d mobile augmented reality systems for exploring the urban environment. Pers. Technol. **1**, 208–217 (1997)
15. Kooper, R., MacIntyre, B.: Browsing the real-world wide web: maintaining awareness of virtual information in an AR information space. Int. J. Hum. Comp. Interaction. **16**, 425–446 (2003)
16. Kähäri, M., Murphy, D.: Mara: Sensor based augmented reality system for mobile imaging device. In: 5th IEEE and ACM International Symposium on Mixed and Augmented Reality (2006)
17. Wikitude: Wikitude. http://www.wikitude.com. Accessed 07 May 2014
18. Layar: Layar. http://www.layar.com/. Accessed 07 May 2014
19. Junaio: Junaio. http://www.junaio.com/. Accessed 07 May 2014
20. Grubert, J., Langlotz, T., Grasset, R.: Augmented reality browser survey. Technical report, University of Technology, Graz, Austria (2011)

Author Index

Printed in the United States
by Bookmasters

Printed in the United States
By Bookmasters